EASTERN EUROPEAN PHRASEBOOK

Thomas Cook

12 LANGUAGES

BULGARIAN CROATIAN CZECH
ESTONIAN HUNGARIAN LATVIAN
LITHUANIAN POLISH ROMANIAN
RUSSIAN SLOVENIAN UKRAINIAN

Published by Thomas Cook Publishing
A division of Thomas Cook Tour Operations Limited
PO Box 227
Units 15/16, Coningsby Road
Peterborough PE3 8SB
United Kingdom

E-mail: books@thomascook.com
www.thomascookpublishing.com

ISBN: 1-841575-01-1

Head of Thomas Cook Publishing: Chris Young
Project Editor: Michelle Warrington
DTP: Steven Collins
Original translation by Tongue-Tied, Sussex/Hertfordshire, UK,
UPS Translations, London, and Transtec, Stamford, Lincs
Original Editor: Wendy M Wood
New translations for this edition by Atlas Translations, London
Text design and layout, editorial and project management by
183 Books, Peterborough
Cover design: Liz Lyons Design, Oxford
Cover picture: Medioimages/Alamy
Printed and bound in Spain by: Grafo Industrias Graficas, Basauri

Bulgarian

Croatian

Czech

CONTENTS

Lithuanian

Polish

Romanian

CONTENTS

This newly updated phrasebook from Thomas Cook Publishing contains a selection of essential and helpful vocabulary in twelve of the languages most commonly spoken in Eastern Europe. In general the English phrase is shown first, followed by the foreign-language translation and then a simple phonetic transcription, which will prove the most useful guide when trying to speak words and phrases if you are not familiar with the language. In cases where the phrase is most likely to be seen on a notice or sign, or spoken by a native language speaker to you, the foreign-language version is shown first, followed by its phonetic transcription and then the English meaning.

Where there is both a formal and informal way of speech, the formal one will be indicated so that no offence could inadvertently be caused.

Each chapter has been divided into themed sections with subheadings for quick reference. You will find shaded boxes which explain essential words that will help you at the station or airport, and while dining out, shopping and driving. Chapters begin with an introduction to the language and some practical details about the language's mother country or countries, and sometimes a few technical pointers on grammar and pronunciation.

Any attempt to speak a few words in the native tongue of these countries is always greatly appreciated by locals, and this phrasebook aims to enrich your travelling experience as well as help with day-to-day essentials.

Good luck!

Czech — Language found in this book.

Hungarian — Most useful second language.

FINLAND

ESTONIA
Estonian

LATVIA
Latvian

RUSSIA
Russian

LITHUANIA
Lithuanian

RUSSIA
Russian

BELARUS
Russian

GERMANY

POLAND
Polish

CZECH REP
Czech

UKRAINE
Ukrainian *Russian*

SLOVAKIA
Czech

AUSTRIA

HUNGARY
Hungarian

SLOVENIA
Slovenian

ROMANIA
Romanian,
Hungarian

MOLDOVA

CROATIA
Croatian

**BOSNIA-
HERZEGOVINA**

**SERBIA-
MONTENEGRO**

BULGARIA
Bulgarian,
Russian

ITALY

ALBANIA

**F.Y.R.O
MACEDONIA**

GREECE

TURKEY

BULGARIAN

B U L G A R I A N

INTRODUCTION

Bulgarian is a Slavic language and like Russian, to which it is distantly related, it uses Cyrillic script, which is a development of the Greek alphabet. Russian itself is widely understood in Bulgaria; English and German may also be spoken to a degree in larger cities.

As with Greek, body language can be confusing if you are unaware that Bulgarians traditionally nod their heads up and down to signify no and shake them from side to side to mean yes. However, Bulgarians who are familiar with Western influences – younger people and those working in the main tourist resorts – often do the opposite, so be careful that you have understood correctly.

Addresses for Travel and Tourist Information

Australia: *Consulate-General,* 14 Carlotta Road, Double Bay, Sydney NSW 2028; tel: (02) 327 7592; fax: (02) 327 8067.

Canada: *Embassy,* 325 Steward Street, Ottawa, Ontario N1K 6K5; tel: (613) 789 3215; fax: (613) 789 3524.

South Africa: *Embassy,* Techno Plaza E., 305 Brooks St, Melo Park, Pretoria 0102; tel: (12) 342 3720; fax: (12) 324 3721.

UK: *Bulgarian Tourism Office,* 186–188 Queen's Gate, London SW7 5HL; tel: (020) 7589 8402; fax: (020) 7589 4875.

USA: *Bulgarian Tourist Information Center,* 41 E. 42nd St #508, New York, NY 10017; tel: (212) 573 5530.

Official tourism website: www.bulgariatravel.org.

Bulgaria Facts

CAPITAL: Sofia

CURRENCY: Leva (Lv.); 1 Lev = 100 stotinki, obtainable only in Bulgaria.

OPENING HOURS: Banks: Mon–Fri 0900–1600. Some exchange offices open weekends. Shops: Mon–Fri 0900–1900, Sat 0900–1300, closed 1200–1400 outside major towns. Museums: vary widely, but often 1000–1730, closed 1 hour lunchtimes and sometimes one whole weekday.

TELEPHONES: To dial in, + 359. Outgoing, 00 and the country code. Police, 166. Fire, 160. Ambulance, 150.

PUBLIC HOLIDAYS: 1 Jan; 3 Mar; Orthodox Good Friday and Easter Sunday; 6, 24 May; 6, 22 Sept; 1 Nov; 25 Dec.

Technical Language Hints

- Adjectives always agree in gender and number with the noun. For example: "this beautiful house" – 'тази красива къща'

- There is no word for the indefinite article "a"; instead, you use "the" and add a special ending to the noun itself to indicate either one of the three genders (masculine, feminine or neuter) or plural. These are the endings you would apply:

- if the noun is masculine and singular: ending would be either '-а', '-ът' or '-ят', e.g. 'влакът' – 'the train'

- if the noun is feminine and singular, the ending would be '-та', e.g. 'къщата' – 'the house'

- if the noun is neuter and singular, the ending would be '-то', e.g. 'морето' – 'the sea'

- and if it is plural, the ending becomes either '-ите' or '-ете', for feminine and masculine, e.g. 'къщите', or '-ата' for neuter, e.g. 'моретата' – 'the seas'

ESSENTIALS

B U L G A R I A N

Alphabet and Pronunciation

	Name	Pronounced
А а	ah	long a as in father
Б б	bah	like English b
В в	vah	like English v
Г г	gah	like English g
Д д	dah	like English d
Е е	eh	short e as in bet
Ж ж	zhe	zh sound as in measure
З з	ze	like English z
И и	ee	short i as in bit
Й й	iy	y as in yet
К к	kah	like English k
Л л	lah	like English l
М м	meh	like English m
Н н	neh	like English n
О о	o	short o as in lock
П п	pe	like English p
Р р	re	like English r
С с	ce	hard s as in sit
Т т	te	like English t
У у	ou	u as in put
Ф ф	fa	like English f
Х х	ha	h as in hot
Ц ц	tsa	ts as in cats
Ч ч	ch	ch as in chair
Ш ш	sh	sh as in shoe
Щ щ	sht	sht as in ashtray
Ъ ъ	eu	er sound as in fur
Ь ь	y	y as in mayor
Ю ю	yu	yu sound as in tune
Я я	ya	ya sound as in yard

Basic Words and Phrases

Yes	**No**
Да	Не
Dah	*Neh*

Please	**Thank you**
Моля	Благодаря
Molya	*Blagodarya*

Hello	**Goodbye**
Здравейте	Довиждане
Zdraveiteh	*Dovizhdaneh*

Excuse me	**Sorry**
Извинете	Съжалявам
Izvinyavaite	*Sazhalyavam*

How	**When**
Как	Кога
Kak	*Kogah*

Why	**What**
Защо	Какво
Zashto	*Kakvo*

Who	
Кой	
Koy	

That's O.K.	**Perhaps**
Няма проблеми	Може би
Nyama problemi	*Mozhe bi*

To	**From**
До	От
Doh	*Ot*

Here	**There**
Тук	Там
Tuk	*Tam*

I don't understand
Не разбирам
Neh razbiram

I don't speak Bulgarian
Не говоря български
Ne govoryah bulgarski

Do you speak English?
Говорите ли английски?
Govoriteh li angleeski?

Can you please write it down?
Може ли да го напишете?
Mozhe li da go napisheteh?

Please can you speak more slowly?
Моля, може ли да говорите по-бавно?
Molya, mozhe li dah govoriteh po-bavno?

Greetings

**Good Morning/
Good Afternoon/
Good Evening/Good Night**
Добро утро/Добър ден/
Добър вечер/Лека нощ/
Лека нощ
Dobro utro/Dobar den/Dobar vecher/Lekah nosht/Lekah nosht

Pleased to meet you
Приятно ми е да се запознаем
Priatno mi eh da se zapoznaem

How are you?
Как сте?
Kak steh?

I am well, thank you. And you?
Аз съм добре, благодаря. А Вие?
Az sam dobreh, blagodarya. A Vieh?

My name is …
Казвам се …
Kazvam se …

This is my friend/boyfriend/girlfriend/husband/wife/brother/sister.
Това е моят приятел/моят приятел/моята приятелка/моят съпруг/моята съпруга моят брат/моята сестра
Tova e moyat priyatel/moyat priyatel/moyata priyatelka/moyat saprug/moyata sapruga/moya brat/moyata sestra

Where are you travelling to?
За къде пътувате?
Za kadeh patuvateh?

I am/we are going to…
Аз отивам/ние отиваме в …
Az otivam/nieh otivameh v …

How long are you travelling for?
Колко дълго ще пътувате?
Kolko dalgo shteh patuvateh?

Where do you come from?
Откъде сте?
Otkadeh ste?

**I am/we are from …
Australia/Britain/Canada/America**
Аз съм/ние сме от …
Австралия/Великобритания/
Канада/САЩ

B
U
L
G
A
R
I
A
N

*Az sam/nieh smeh ot … Avstralia/
Velikobritania/Kanada/Se-Ah-Sht*

We are on holiday
Ние сме на почивка
Nieh smeh na pochivka

This is our first visit here
Тук сме за първи път
Tuk smeh za parvi pat

How old are you?
На колко години сте?
Na kolko godini steh?

I am … years old
Аз съм на … години
Az sam nah … godini

**I am a business person/
doctor/journalist/manual
worker/administrator/
scientist/student/teacher**
Аз съм бизнесмен/лекар/
журналист/работник/служител
/учен/студент/учител
*Az sam biznesmen/lekar/
zhurnalist/rabotnik/sluzhitel/uchen/
student/uchitel*

**I am waiting for my husband/
wife/boyfriend/girlfriend**
Чакам съпруга си/
съпругата си/приятеля
си/приятелката си
*Chakam sapruga si/saprugata
si/priyatelya si/priyatelkata si*

**Would you like/may I have
a cigarette?**
Искате ли/имате ли цигара?
Iskateh li/imateh li tsigara?

Do you mind if I smoke?
Имате ли нещо против ако
пуша?

Imateh li neshto protiv ako pusha?

Do you have a light?
Имате ли огънче?
Imateh li ogancheh?

Days

Monday	**Tuesday**
Понеделник	Вторник
Ponedelnik	*Vtornik*
Wednesday	**Thursday**
Сряда	Четвъртък
Sryada	*Chetvartak*
Friday	**Saturday**
Петък	Събота
Petak	*Sabotah*
Sunday	**Morning**
Неделя	Сутрин
Nedelya	*Sutrin*

Afternoon/Evening/Night
Следобед/Вечер/Нощ
Sledobed/Vecher/Nosht

Yesterday/Today/Tomorrow
Вчера/Днес/Утре
Vchera/Dnes/Utreh

Numbers

Zero	**One**
Нула	Едно
Nula	*Edno*
Two	**Three**
Две	Три
Dveh	*Trih*

Four
Четири
Chetiri

Five
Пет
Pet

Six
Шест
Shess

Seven
Седем
Sedem

Eight
Осем
Osem

Nine
Девет
Devet

Ten
Десет
Desset

Eleven
Единайсет
Edinaiset

Twelve
Дванайсет
Dvanaiset

Thirteen
Тринайсет
Trinaiset

Fourteen
Четиринайсет
Chetirinaiset

Fifteen
Петнайсет
Petnaiset

Sixteen
Шестнайсет
Shesnaiset

Seventeen
Седемнайсет
Sedemnaiset

Eighteen
Осемнайсет
Osemnaiset

Nineteen
Деветнайсет
Devetnaiset

Twenty
Двайсет
Dvaiset

Twenty-one
Двайсет и
едно
Dvaiset ih edno

Twenty-Two
Двайсет и две
Dvaiset ih dveh

Thirty
Трийсет
Treeset

Forty
Четиридесет
Chetiridesset

Fifty
Петдесет
Petdesset

Sixty
Шейсет
Sheyset

Seventy
Седемдесет
Sedemdesset

Eighty
Осемдесет
Osemdesset

Ninety
Деветдесет
Devetdesset

One hundred
Сто
Stoh

Five hundred
Петстотин
Petstotin

One thousand
Хиляда
Hillyada

One million
Един милион
Edin million

Time

What time is it?
Колко е часът?
Kolko eh chasat?

It is .....
Часът е ...
Chasat eh ...

9.00
Девет
Devet

9.05
Девет и пет
Devet i pet

9.15
Девет и петнайсет
Devet I petnaiset

9.20
Девет и двайсет
Devet i dvaiset

9.30
Девет и половина
Devet i polovina

B
U
L
G
A
R
I
A
N

B U L G A R I A N

9.35
Десет без двайсет и пет
Desset bez dvaiset i pet

9.40
Десет без двайсет
Desset bez dvaiset

9.45
Десет без петнайсет
Desset bez petnaiset

9.50
Десет без десет
Desset bez desset

9.55
Десет без пет
Desset bez pet

12.00/Midday/Midnight
Дванайсет/Обед/Полунощ
Dvanaiset/Obed/Polunosht

Money

I would like to change these traveller's cheques/this currency
Искам да обменя тези пътнически чекове/тази валута
Iskam da obmenya tezi patnicheski checkoveh/tazi valuta

How much commission do you charge? (What is the service charge?)
Колко ви е комисионната?
Kolko vi eh komisionnata?

Can I obtain money with my Mastercard?
Мога ли да изтегля пари с моята карта Mastercard?

Moga li da izteglya pari s moyata karta Mastercard?

Where is the nearest ATM?
Къде се намира най-близкият банкомат?
Kudeh se namira nay blizkiyat bankomat?

My name is ... Some money has been wired to here for me to collect
Казвам се ... Изпратили са ми пари, които трябва да получа тук
Kazvam se ... Ispratili sa mi parih, koito tryabva da polucha tuk

ARRIVING AND DEPARTING

Airport

Excuse me, where is the check-in desk for ... airline?
Извинявайте, къде е чекин за авиолиния ...?
Izvinyavaite, kadeh eh checkin za aviolinia ...?

What is the boarding gate for my flight?
Кой е изходът за моя полет?
Koy eh iz-hodat za moya polet?

What is the time for my flight?
В колко часа е моят полет?
V kolko chasa e moyat polet?

How long is the delay likely to be?
Колко ще е закъснението?
Kolko shte e zakasnenieto?

Where is the duty-free shop?
Къде е безмитният магазин?
Kadeh eh bezmitniyat magazin?

Which way is the luggage reclaim?
Откъде се взима багажът?
Otkadeh seh vzima bagazha?

I have lost my luggage. Please can you help?
Загубил съм си багажа. Можете ли да ми помогнете?
Zagubil sam si bagazha. Mozhete li da mi pomogneteh?

I am flying to …
Пътувам за …
Patuvam za …

Where is the bus for the city centre?
Къде е автобусът за центъра на града?
Kadeh eh avtobussa za tsentara na grada?

Trains and Boats

Where is the ticket office/information desk?
Къде е гишето за билети/бюрото за информация?
Kadeh eh gisheto za bileti/byuroto za informatsiya?

Which platform does the train/speedboat/ferry to … depart from?
От коя платформа тръгва влакът/корабът/фериботът до …?
Ot koya platforma tragva vlaka/koraba/ferribota do …?

Where is platform …?
Къде е перон …?
Kadeh eh peron …?

When is the next train/boat to …?
Кога е следващият влак/кораб до …?
Koga eh sledvashtiya vlak/korab do …?

Is there a later train/boat to …?
Нма ли по-късен влак/кораб до …?
Ima li po-kasen vlak/korab do …?

Notices and Signs

Вагон-ресторант
Vagon-restorant
Buffet (dining) Car

Автобус
Avtobus
Bus

Питейна/непитейна вода
Piteyna/nepiteyna voda
Drinking/Non-drinking water

Вход
Vhod
Entrance

Изход
Iz-hod
Exit

Болница
Bolnitsa
Hospital

BULGARIAN

**B
U
L
G
A
R
I
A
N**

Информация
Informatsya
Information

Загубен багаж
Zaguben bagazh
**Left Luggage
(Baggage Claim)**

Гардероб за багаж
Garderob za bagazh
Luggage Lockers

Поща
Poshta
Post Office

Перон
Peron
Platform

Ж. П. Гара
Zh. P. Gara
Railway (Railroad) Station

Летище/Аерогара
Letishteh/Aerogara
Airport

Полиция
Politsiya
Police Station

Пристанище
Pristanishteh
Port

Ресторант
Restaurant
Restaurant

Пушенето забранено/
Пушенето позволено
*Pusheneto zabraneno/
Pusheneto pozvoleno*
Smoking/Non Smoking

Телефон
Telefon
Telephone

Билети
Bileti
Ticket Office

Чекин
Checkin
Check-in desk

Разписание
Razpisanieh
Timetable (Schedule)

Тоалетни
Toaletni
Toilets (Restroom)

Жени/Мъже
Zheni/Muzheh
Ladies/Gentlemen

Метро
Metro
Underground (Subway)

Чакалня
Chakalnya
Waiting Room

Buying a Ticket

**I would like a first-class/
second-class/third-class single
(one-way)/return (round-trip)
ticket to …**
Бих искал първокласен/
второкласен/третокласен
единичен билет/билет за
отиване и връщане до …
*Bih iskal parvoklassen/vtoroklassen/
tretoklassen edinichen bilet/bilet za
otivane i vrashtane do …*

**Is it an express (fast)
train/bus?**
Този влак/автобус експресен
ли е?
Tozi vlak/avtobus expressen li eh?

**Is my rail pass valid on this
train/ferry/bus?**
Валиден ли е моят
билет/пропуск за този влак/
ферибот/автобус?
*Validen li eh moyat bilet/propusk
za tozi vlak/ferribot/avtobus?*

**I would like an aisle/window
seat**
Бих желал място до
пътеката/до прозореца
*Bih zhelal myasto do puhtekata/do
prozoretsa*

No smoking/smoking please
За непушачи/За пушачи, моля
Za nepushachi/Za pushachi, molya

We would like to sit together
Искаме съседни места
Iskame sasedni mesta

**I would like to make a seat
reservation**
Искам да запазя място

Iskam da zapazya myasto

**I would like to reserve a
couchette/sleeper for one
person/two people/my
family**
Искам да запазя място в
спален вагон за едно лице/
две лица/моето семейство
*Iskam da zapazya myasto v spalen
vagon za ednolitseh/dveh
litsa/moeto semeistvo*

**I would like to reserve a
cabin**
Искам да запазя каюта
Iskam da zapazya kayuta

Timetables (Schedules)

Пристига
Pristiga
Arrive

Спира в …
Spira v …
Calls (Stops) at

С вагон-бюфет
S vagon byufet
Catering service

Смяна в …
Smyana v …
Change at

Връзка/през
Vrazka/prez
Connection/via

Ежедневно
Ezhednevno
Daily

B
U
L
G
A
R
I
A
N

19

B U L G A R I A N

На всеки 40 минути
Na vseki 40 minuti
Every 40 minutes

Първа класа
Parva klasa
First Class

На всеки час
Na vseki chas
Hourly

Препоръчва се местата да
се резервират
*Preporachva se mestata da se
rezervirat*
**Seat reservations are
recommended**

Втора класа
Vtora klasa
Second Class

Допълнително заплащане
Dopalnitelno zaplashtaneh
Supplement payable

Luggage

**How much will it cost to
send (ship) my luggage in
advance?**
Колко ще струва да изпратя
багажа си предварително?
*Kolko shte struva da izpratya
bagazha si predvaritelno?*

**Where is the left luggage
(baggage claim) office?**
Къде е службата за загубен
багаж?
*Kadeh eh sluzhbata za zaguben
bagazh?*

**What time do you
open/close?**
В колко часа
отваряте/затваряте?
*V kolko chasa otvaryateh/
zatvaryateh?*

**Where are the luggage
trolleys (carts)?**
Къде са количките за баяаж?
Kadeh sa kolichkiteh za bagazh?

Where are the lockers?
Къде е гардеробната?
Kadeh eh garderobnata?

I have lost my locker key
Изгубих си ключа за
гардероба
Izgubih si klyucha za garderoba

On Board

Is this seat free?
Свободно ли е това място?
Svobodno li eh tova myasto?

**Excuse me, you are sitting in
my reserved seat**
Извинете, вие седите на
моето запазено място
*Izvinete, vie sediteh na moeto
zapazeno myasto*

Which station is this?
Коя е тази гара?
Koya e tazi gara?

**What time is this train/bus/
ferry/flight due to arrive/
depart?**
В колко часа трябва да
тръгне/пристигне този
влак/автобус/ферибот/полет?
V kolko chasa tryabva da

*tragne/pristigne tozi vlak/avtobus/
ferribot/polet?*

Travelling with Children

**Do you have a high chair/
baby-sitting service/cot?**
Имате ли висок стол/служба
за гледане на деца/креватче?
*Imateh li vissok stol/sluzhba za
gledane na detsa/krevatcheh?*

**Where is the nursery/
playroom?**
Къде е стаята за деца?
Kadeh e stayata za detsa?

**Where can I warm the
baby's bottle?**
Къде мога да стопля шишето
на бебето?
*Kadeh moga da stoplya shisheto na
bebeto?*

Customs and Passports

Паспорти, моля!
Passporti, molya!
Passports please!

**I have nothing/wine/spirits
(alcohol)/tobacco to declare**
Нямам нищо за деклариране
/имам да декларирам вино/
спиртни напитки/тютюнени
изделия
*Nyamam nishto za deklarirane/
imam da deklarim vino/spirtni
napitki/tyutyuneni izdeliya*

**I will be staying for ... days/
weeks/months**
Ще остана ... дни/седмици/
месеца

*Shte ostana ... dni/sedmitsi/
messetsa*

Asking the Way

**Excuse me, do you speak
English?**
Извинете, говорите ли
английски?
Izvinete, govorite li angleeski?

**Excuse me, can you help me
please?**
Извинете, може ли да ми
помогнете?
*Izvinete, mozhe li da mi
pomognete?*

**Where is the Tourist
Information Office?**
Къде се намира бюрото за
туристическа информация?
*Kadeh seh namira byuroto za turis-
ticheska informatsiya?*

**Excuse me, is this the right
way to...?**
Извинете, това ли е пътят за
...?
Izvinete, tova li eh puhtyat za ...?

**... the cathedral/the tourist
office/the castle/the old town**
... катедралата/
туристическото
бюро/замъка/стария град
*... katedralata/turisticheskoto
byuro/zamuhka/stariya grad*

Can you tell me the way to the railway station/ bus station/taxi rank/ city centre/beach?
Може ли да ми кажете как да стигна до ж.п. гарата/ автогарата/стоянката за таксита/центъра на града/ плажа?
Mozhe li da mi kazhete kak da stigna do zh.p. garata/avtogarata/ stoyankata za taksita/tsentara na grada/plazha?

Първата/втората наляво/надясно/направо
Parvata/vtorata nalyavo/nadyasno/ napravo
First/second/left/right/ straight ahead

На ъгъла/на светофара
Na ugala/na svetofara
At the corner/at the traffic lights

Where is the nearest police station/post office?
Къде е най-близкият/ близката полицейски участък/поща?
Kade e nai-blizkiyat/blizkata politseiski uchastak/poshta?

Is it near/far?
Близо/далече ли е?
Blizo/daleche li eh?

Do I need to take a taxi/catch a bus?
Трябва ли да взема такси/ автобус?
Tryabva li da vzema taxi/avtobus?

Do you have a map?
Имате ли карта?
Imate li karta?

Can you point to it on my map?
Може ли да ми покажете на моята карта?
Mozhe li da mi pokazhete na moyata karta?

Thank you for your help
Благодаря Ви за помощта Ви
Blagodarya Vi za pomoshta Vi

How do I reach the motorway/main road?
Как се стига до магистралата/главния път?
Kak se stiga do magistralata/glavniya pat?

I think I have taken the wrong turning
Мисля, че съм завил по погрешен път
Mislya, che sam zavil po poreshen pat

I am looking for this address
Търся този адрес
Tarsya tozi adress

I am looking for the... hotel
Търся хотел ...
Tarsya hotel ...

How far is it to... from here?
Колко е далече оттук до ...?
Kolko e daleche ottuk do ...?

Продължете направо ... километра
Prodalzhete napravo... kilometra
Carry straight on for... kilometres

На следващата пресечка
завийте надясно/наляво
*Na sledvashtata presechka
zaveeteh nadyasno/nalyavo*
**Take the next turning on the
right/left**

На следващата пресечка/
светофар завийте надясно/
наляво
*Na sledvashtata presechka/
svetofar zaveeteh nadyasno/nalyavo*
**Turn right/left at the next
crossroads/traffic lights**

Вие отивате в погрешна
посока
Vieh otivateh v pogreshna posoka
**You are going in the wrong
direction**

**Where is the cathedral/
church/museum/bank/
pharmacy?**
Къде се намира
катедралата/църквата/музея/
банката/аптеката?
*Kade seh namira katedralata/
tsarkvata/muzeya/bankata/
aptekata?*

**How much is the admission/
entrance charge?**
Колко струва входът?
Kolko struva vhoda?

**Is there a discount for
children/students/senior
citizens?**
Има ли намаление за деца/
студенти/възрастни хора?
*Ima li namalenie za
detsa/studenti/vazrastni hora?*

**What time does the next
guided tour (in English)
start?**
В колко часа започва
следващата обиколка
с превод (на английски)?
*V kolko chasa zapochva
sledvashtata obikolka s prevod
(na angleeski)?*

**One/two adults/children
please**
Един/два за възрастни/деца,
моля
Edin/dvama za vazrastni/detsa, molya

May I take photographs here?
Мога ли да снимам тук?
Moga li da snimam tuk?

At the Tourist Office

**Do you have a map of the
town/area?**
Имате ли карта на града/
района?
Imate li karta na grada/raiona?

**Do you have a list of
accommodation?**
Имате ли списък на Местата
за Ношуване?
*Imate li spisak na Mestata za
Nozhuvane?*

**Can I reserve
accommodation?**
Мога ли да запазя
квартира/хотел?
Moga li da zapazya kvartira/hotel?

23

B U L G A R I A N

Hotels

I have a reservation in the name of ...
Имам резервация на името на ...
Imam rezervatsiya na imeto na ...

I wrote to/faxed/telephoned you last month/last week
Писах ви/пуснах ви факс/
телефонирах ви миналия
месец/миналата седмица
Pisah vi/pusnah vi fax/telefonirah vi minalia mesets/minalata sedmitsa

Do you have any rooms free?
Имате ли свободни стаи?
Imate li svobodni stai?

I would like to reserve a single/double room with/ without bath/shower
Искам да запазя
единична/двойна стая с/без
баня/душ
Iskam da zapazya edinichna/dvoina stay s/bez banya/dush

I would like bed/breakfast/ (room and) full board
Бих искал легло/закуска/
(стая и) пълен пансион
Bih iskal leglo/zakuska/(staya i) palen pansion

How much is it per night?
Колко струва на вечер?
Kolko struva na vecher?

Is breakfast included?
Закуската включва ли се?
Zakuskata vklyuchva li seh?

Do you have any cheaper rooms?
Имате ли по-евтини стаи?
Imate li po-evtini stai?

I would like to see/take the room
Искам да видя/взема стаята
Iskam da vidya/vzema stayata

I would like to stay for ... nights
Искам да остана за ... нощи
Iskam da ostana za ... noshti

The shower/light/tap/hot water doesn't work
Душът/лампата/мивката/
топлата вода не работи
Dushat/lampata/mivkata/toplata voda neh raboti

At what time/where is breakfast served?
В колко часа/къде се сервира
закуската?
V kolko chasa/kadeh se servira zakuskata?

What time do I have to check out?
В колко часа трябва да
напусна?
V kolko chasa tryabva da napusna?

Can I have the key to room number ...?
Може ли да дадете ключа
за стая номер ...?
Mozhe li da mi dedete klyucha za staya nomer ...?

My room number is ...
Номерът на стаята ми е ...
Nomerat na stayata mi eh ...

24

My room is not satisfactory/not clean enough/too noisy. Please can I change rooms?
Стаята не ми харесва/не е достатъчно чиста/е твърде шумна. Мога ли да взема друга стая, моля?
Stayata ne mi haresva/neh eh dostatchno chista/eh tvrdeh shumna. Moga li da vzema druga staya, molya?

Where is the bathroom?
Къде е банята?
Kadeh e banyata?

Do you have a safe for valuables?
Имате ли сейф за ценни вещи?
Imateh li seif za tsenni veshti?

Is there a laundry/do you wash clothes?
Имате ли пералня/перете ли дрехи?
Imate li peralnya/pereteh li drehi?

I would like an air - conditioned room
Искам стая с климатична инсталация
Iskam staya s klimatichna instalatsia

Do you accept traveller's cheques/credit cards?
Приемате ли пътнически чекове/кредитни карти?
Priemate li patnicheski checkove/ kreditni karti?

May I have the bill please?
Сметката, моля?
Smetkata, molya?

Excuse me, I think there may be a mistake in this bill
Извинете, мисля че в тази сметка има грешка
Izvinete, mislya, che v tazi smetka ima greshka

Youth Hostels

How much is a dormitory bed per night?
Колко струва едно легло на нощ?
Kolko struva edno leglo na nosht?

I am/am not an HI member
Аз не съм член на HI
Az ne sam chlen na HI

May I use my own sleeping bag?
Мога ли да използвам собствен спален чувал?
Moga li da izpolzvam sobstven spalen chuval?

What time do you lock the doors at night?
В колко часа заключвате вратите нощем?
V kolko chasa zaklyuchvate vratite noshtem?

Camping

May I camp for the night/two nights?
Мога ли да престоя една нощ/две нощи?
Moga li da prestoya edna nosht/dve noshti?

B
U
L
G
A
R
I
A
N

Where can I pitch my tent?
Къде мога да си опъна
палатката?
*Kadeh moga da si opuhna
palatkata?*

**How much does it cost for
one night/week?**
Колко струва за една
нощ/седмица?
*Kolko struva za edna nosht/
sedmitsi?*

**Where are the washing
facilities?**
Къде са умивалните/
душовете?
Kadeh sa umivalnite/dushovete?

**Is there a restaurant/
supermarket/swimming pool
on site/nearby?**
Има ли ресторант/
супермаркет/плувен басейн
в къмпинга/наблизо?
*Ima li restaurant/supermarket/
pluven basein v kampinga/nablizo?*

**Do you have a safety deposit
box?**
Имате ли сейф за ценни вещи?
Imate li seif za tsenni veshti?

EATING AND DRINKING

Cafés and Bars

**I would like a cup of/two cups
of/another coffee/tea**
Искам чаша/две чаши/още
една чаша кафе/чай
*Iskam chasha/dve chashi/oshteh
edna chasha kafeh/chai*

With/without milk/sugar

С/без мляко/захар
S/bez mlyako/zahar

**I would like a bottle/glass/two
glasses of mineral water/red
wine/white wine, please**
Бих искал бутилка/чаша/две
чаши минерална вода/
червено/бяло вино, моля
*Bih iskal butilka/chasha/dve chashi
mineralna voda/cherveno/byalo vino,
molya*

**I would like a beer/two beers,
please**
Бих искал една бира/две
бири, моля
Bih iskal edna bira/dve biri, molya

Please may I have some ice?
Извинете, може ли да ми
донесете малко лед?
*Izvinete, mozhe li da mi donesete
malko led?*

**Do you have any matches/
cigarettes/cigars?**
Имате ли кибрит/цигари/
пури?
Imate li kibrit/tsigari/puri?

Restaurants

**Can you recommend a good/
cheap restaurant in this area?**
Може ли да препоръчате
добър/евтин ресторант
наоколо?
*Mozhe li da preporachateh
dobar/evtin restaurant naokolo?*

**I would like a table for ...
people**
Бих искал маса за ... души
Bih iskal masa za ... dushi

Do you have a non-smoking area?
Имате ли маси за непушачи?
Imate li masi za nepushachi?

Waiter/waitress!
Келнер!
Kelner!

Excuse me, please may we order?
Извинете, може ли да поръчаме?
Izvinete, mozhe li da porachame?

Do you have a set menu/ children's menu/wine list …/ in English?
Имате ли фиксирано меню/детско меню/списък на вината …
на английски?
Imate li fixirano menyu/detsko menyu/spisak na vinata … na angleeski?

Do you have any vegetarian dishes?
Имате ли нещо вегетарианско?
Imate li neshto vegetaryansko?

Do you have any local specialities?
Имате ли местни специалитети?
Imateh li mestni spetsialiteti?

Are vegetables included?
Включени ли са зеленчуци?
Vklyucheni li sah zelenchutsi?

Could I have it well-cooked/ medium rare please?
Може ли да го приготвите добре опечено/средно
опечено, моля?
Mozhe li da go prigotvite dobre opecheno/sredno opecheno, molya?

What does this dish consist of?
От какво се състои това ястие?
Ot kakvo se sastoi tova yastieh?

I am a vegetarian. Does this contain meat?
Аз съм вегетарианец.
Има ли месо тук?
Az sm vegetarianets. Ima li mesoh tuk?

I do not eat nuts/dairy products/meat/fish.
Аз не ям ядки/млечни продукти/месо/риба
Az ne yam yadki/mlechni produkti/meso/riba

Not (very) spicy please
Без (много) подправки, моля
Bez (mnogo) podpravki, molya

I would like the set menu please
Искам да видя фиксираното меню, моля
Iskam da vidia fixiranoto menu, molya

We have not been served yet
Още не са ни сервирали
Oshte ne sa ni servirali

Please bring a plate/knife/ fork
Моля, донесете чиния/нож/ вилица
Molya, donesete chiniya/nozh/vilitsa

27

B U L G A R I A N

Excuse me, this is not what I ordered
Извинете, но аз не съм поръчвал това
Izvinete, no az ne sam porachval tova

May I have some/more bread/water/coffee/tea?
Може ли да ми донесете малко/още хляб/вода/кафе/чай?
Mozhe li da mi doneseteh malko/oshteh hlyab/voda/kafeh, chai?

May I have the bill please?
Сметката, моля?
Smetkata, molya?

Does this bill include service?
Сметката включва ли обслужване?
Smetkata vklyuchva li obsluzhvane?

Do you accept traveller's cheques/Mastercard/ US dollars?
Приемате ли пътнически чекове/Mastercard/щатски долари?
Priemate li patnecheski checkoveh/Mastercard/shtatski dollari?

Can I have a receipt please?
Може ли касовата бележка, моля?
Mozhe li kasovata belezhka, molya?

Where is the toilet (restroom) please?
Къде е тоалетната, моля?
Kadeh eh toaletnata, molya?

On the Menu	
Закуска/Обяд/Вечеря *Zakuska/Obyad/Vecherya* **Breakfast/Lunch/Dinner**	
Ордьоври *Ordeuvri* **First Courses**	Супи *Supi* **Soups**
Предястия *Predyastia* **Main Courses**	Рибни ястия *Ribni yastia* **Fish Dishes**
Месни ястия *Mesni yastia* **Meat Dishes**	Говеждо месо *Govezhdo mesoh* **Beef**
Пържола *Parzhola* **Steak**	Свинско месо *Svinsko mesoh* **Pork**
Телешко месо *Teleshko mesoh* **Veal**	Пилешко месо *Pileshko mesoh* **Chicken**
Агнешко месо *Agneshko mesoh* **Lamb**	Шунка *Shunka* **Ham**
Вегетариански ястия *Vegetarianski yastia* **Vegetarian Dishes**	
Зеленчуци *Zelenchutsi* **Vegetables**	
Пържени картофи *Purzheni kartofi* **Chips (french fries)**	

Варени картофи/задушени картофи (соте)/картофено пюре
Vareni kartofi/zadusheni kartofi (sote)/kartofeno pyure
Boiled/sauté/mashed potatoes

Ориз
Oriz
Rice

Сирене
Sireheh
Cheese

Десерти
Desserti
Desserts

Сладолед
Sladoled
Ice cream

Торти
Torti
Cakes

Сладкиши
Sladkishi
Pastries

Плодове
Plodovi
Fruit

Хляб
Hlyab
Bread

Кифли
Kifli
Rolls

Препечени филийки
Prepechenih filiyki
Toast

Масло
Maslo
Butter

Сол/пипер
Sol/piper
Salt/pepper

Захар
Zahar
Sugar

Специалитети
Spetsialiteti
Specialities

Местни специалитети
Mestni spetsialiteti
Local specialities

Фиксирано меню
Fiksirano menyu
Set Menu

Винена листа
Vinena lista
Wine list

Червени вина
Cherveni vina
Red wines

Бели вина
Beli vina
White wines

Розови вина (розе)
Rozovi vina (roze)
Rosé wines

Шампанско (шумящи вина)
Shampansko (shumyashti vina)
Sparkling wines

Бира
Bira
Beer

Бутилирана бира/Наливна бира
Butilirana bira/nalivna bira
Bottled beer/ Draught (draft) beer

Безалкохолни напитки
Bezalkoholni napitki
Non-alcoholic drinks

Минерална вода
Mineralna voda
Mineral water

Плодови сокове
Plodovi sokoveh
Fruit juices

Портокалов сок
Portokalov sok
Orange juice

**B
U
L
G
A
R
I
A
N**

B
U
L
G
A
R
I
A
N

Лимонада Лед
Limonada *Led*
Lemonade **Ice**

Кафе с мляко/черно
кафе/еспресо
*Kafeh s mlyako/cherno
kafeh/espreso*
**White coffee/black
coffee/espresso coffee**

Чай с мляко/с лимон
Chai s mlyako/s limon
Tea with milk/with lemon

Шоколад (питие)
Shokolad (pitiye)
Chocolate (drink)

Мляко Закуски/леки ястия
Mlyako *Zakuski/Leki yastiya*
Milk **Snacks/Light meals**

Салати Сандвичи
Salati *Sandvichi*
Salads **Sandwiches**

Яйца Наденица, салам
Yayitsa *Nadenitsa, salam*
Eggs **Sausage**

Варени/пържени/бъркани
яйца
Vareni/purzheni/burkani yayitsa
Boiled/fried/scrambled eggs

Typical Local Dishes

Таратор
Tarator
**Cold yoghurt and cucumber
soup**

Сарми
Sarmi
Stuffed vine leaves

Баница Кюфтета
Banitsa *Kyufteta*
Pie **Meatballs**

Мешана скара
Meshana skara
Mixed grill

GETTING AROUND

Public Transport

**Where is the bus stop/coach
stop/nearest metro (subway)
station?**
Къде е най-близката
автобусна спирка/станция на
метрото?
*Kadeh e nai-blizkata avtobusna
spirka/stantsia na metroto?*

**When is the next/last bus
to ...?**
Кога е следващият/
последният автобус до ...?
*Koga e sledvashtia/poslednia
avtobus do ...?*

**How much is the fare to the
city centre (downtown)/
railway (railroad) station/
airport?**
Колко струва билетът до
центъра на града/ж.п.
гарата/летището?
*Kolko struva bileta do tsentara na
grada/zh.p. garata/letishteto?*

Will you tell me when to get off?

Може ли да кажете кога трябва да сляза?

Mozhe li da mi kazhete koga tryabva da slyaza?

Does this bus go to ...?

Този автобус отива ли до ...?

Tozi avtobus otiva li do ...?

Which number bus goes to ...?

Кой номер автобус отива до ...?

Koi nomer avtobus otiva do ...?

May I have a single (one way)/return (round trip)/day ticket/book of tickets?

Бих искал единичен билет/ билет за отиване и връщане/дневна карта/талон?

Bih iskal edinichen bilet/bilet za otivane i vrashtane/dnevna karta/talon?

Taxis (Таксита)

I would like to go to ... How much will it cost?

Бих искал да отида до...
Колко ще струва?

*Bih iskal da otida do ...
Kolko shteh struva?*

Please may I stop here?

Може ли да спрете тук?

Mozhe li da sprete tuk?

I would like to order a taxi today/tomorrow at 2pm to go from ... to ...

Бих искал да поръчам такси за днес/утре за 2 ч., тръгване от ... за ...

Bih iskal da poracham taxi za dnes/utre za 2 chasa, tragvanreh ot ... za ...

Entertainment

Can you recommend a good bar/nightclub?

Може ли да препоръчате добър бар/нощен клуб?

Mozhe li da preporachate dobar bar/noshten klub?

Do you know what is on at the cinema (playing at the movies)/theatre at the moment?

Знаете ли кои филми прожектират в киното/какви пиеси играят в театъра в момента?

Znaete li koi filmi prozhektirat v kinoto/kakvi piesi igrayat v teatara v momenta?

I would like to book (purchase) ... tickets for the matinee/evening performance on Monday

Бих искал да резервирам (купя) ... билета за сутрешното/вечерното представление в понеделник

Bih iskal da rezerviram (kupia) ... bileta za sutreshnoto/bechernoto predstavlenie v ponedelnik

What time does the film/ performance start?

В колко часа започва филмът/представлението?

V kolko chasa zapochva filma/ predstavlenieto?

B
U
L
G
A
R
I
A
N

B
U
L
G
A
R
I
A
N

Post

How much will it cost to send a letter/postcard/this package to Britain/Ireland/America/Canada/Australia/New Zealand?
Колко струва да изпратя писмо/картичка/този пакет до Великобритания/Ирландия/САЩ/Канада/Австралия/Нова Зеландия?
Kolko struva da izpratya pismo/kartichka/tozi paket do Velikobritania/Irlandia/Se-Ah-Sht/Kanada/Avstralia/Nova Zelandia?

I would like one stamp/two stamps
Бих искал една марка/две марки
Bih iskal edna marka/dve marki

I'd like ... stamps for postcards to send abroad, please
Бих искал ... марки за картички за чужбина, моля
Bih iskal ... marki za kartichki za chuzhbina, molya

Phones

I would like to make a telephone call/reverse the charges to (make a collect call to) ...
Бих искал да се обадя/да се обадя за тяхна сметка до...
Bih iskal da seh obadyah do/da se obadyah za tyahna smetka do...

Which coins do I need for the telephone?
Какви монети ми трябват за телефона?
Kakvi moneti mi tryabvat za telefona?

The line is engaged (busy)
Линията е заета
Liniyata eh zaeta

The number is...
Номерът е ...
Nomerat eh ...

Hello, this is ...
Ало, обажда се ...
Alo, obazhda seh ...

Please may I speak to..?
Може ли да говоря с ..., моля?
Mozhe li da govorya s ..., molya?

He/she is not in at the moment. Please can you call back?
Той/тя не е тук в момента. Може ли да се обадите по-късно?
Toi/tya neh eh tuk v momenta. Mozheh li da se obaditeh po-kasno?

SHOPPING

Shops

Книжарница
Knizharnitsa
Bookshop/Stationery

Бижутерия/подаръци
Bizhuteria/Podaratsi
Jeweller/Gifts

Обувки
Obuvki
Shoes

Железария
Zhelezaria
Hardware

Бръснаро-фризьорски салон
Brasnaro-frizyorski salon
Hairdresser

Хлебарница
Hlebarnitsa
Baker

Супермаркет
Supermarket
Supermarket

Фото
Foto
Photo shop

Туристическа агенция
Touristicheska agentsia
Travel Agent

Аптека
Apteka
Pharmacy

In the Shops

What time do the shops open/close?
В колко часа отварят/
затварят магазините?
V kolko chasa otvaryat/zatvaryat magazinite?

Where is the nearest market?
Къде е най-близкият пазар?
Kadeh eh nai-blizkiat pazar?

Can you show me the one in the window/this one?
Може ли да ми покажете
онзи на витрината/този тук?
Mozhe li da mi pokazhete onzi na vitrinata/tozi tuk?

Can I try this on?
Може ли да го пробвам?
Mozhe li da go probvam?

What size is this?
Кой размер е това?
Koi razmer e tova?

This is too large/too small/too expensive. Do you have any others?
Това е много голямо/малко/
скъпо. Имате ли други?
Tova eh mnogo golyamo/malko/skapo. Imateh li drugi?

My size is...
Моят размер е ...
Moyat razmer eh ...

Where is the changing room/children's/cosmetic/ladieswear/menswear/food department?

B
U
L
G
A
R
I
A
N

33

B U L G A R I A N

Къде е пробната/детските
стоки/козметиката/дамското
облекло/мъжкото облекло/
хранителните стоки?
*Kadeh sa probnata/detskite
stoki/kozmetikata/damskoto
obleklo/mazhkoto obleklo/
hranitelniteh stoki?*

**I would like ... a quarter of a
kilo/half a kilo/a kilo of
bread/butter/ham/this fruit**
Бих искал ... четвърт кило/
половин кило/кило хляб/
масло/шунка/от тези плодове
*Bih iskal ... chetvart kilo/polovin
kilo/kilo hlyab/maslo/shunka/ot tezi
plodove*

How much is this?
Колко струва това?
Kolko struva tova?

I'll take this one, thank you
Ще взема този, благодаря
Shte vzema tozi, blagodarya

**Do you have a carrier
(shopping) bag?**
Имате ли торба?
Imateh li torba?

**Do you have anything
cheaper/larger/smaller/
of better quality?**
Имате ли нещо по-евтино/
по-голямо/по-малко/
по-качествено?
*Imateh li neshto po-evtino/po-
golyamo/po-malko/po-kachestveno?*

**I would like a film/to develop
this film for this camera**
Бих искал филм/да промия
филма от този апарат

Bih iskal film/da promia filma ot tozi
aparat

**I would like some batteries,
the same size as this old one**
Бих искал няколко батерии
същия размер като тази
*Bih iskal nyakolko baterii, sashtia
razmer kato tazi*

**Would you mind wrapping
this for me, please?**
Може ли да ми опаковате
това, моля?
*Mozhe li da mi opakovate tova,
molya?*

**Sorry, but you seem to have
given me the wrong change**
Извинявайте, но изглежда не
сте ми върнали точното
ресто
*Izvinyavaite, no izglezhda neh steh
mi varnali tochnoto resto*

Car Hire (Rental)

**I have ordered (rented) a car
in the name of ...**
Поръчал съм (взел съм под
наем) кола на името на ...
*Porachal sam (vzel sam pod naem)
kola na imeto na ...*

**How much does it cost to
hire (rent) a car for one day/
two days/a week?**
Колко струва да се наеме
кола за един ден/два дни/
седмица?
*Kolko struva da se naemeh kola za
edin den/dva din/sedmitsa?*

Is the tank already full of petrol (gas)?
Резервоарът пълен ли е с бензин?
Reservoarat palen li eh s benzin?

Is insurance and tax included? How much is the deposit?
Включени ли са застраховка и данъци? Колко е депозитът?
Vklyucheni li sa zastrahovka i danatsi? Kolko eh depozita?

By what time must I return the car?
Кога най-късно трябва да върна колата?
Koga nai-kasno tryabva da varna kolata?

I would like a small/large/ family/sports car with a radio/cassette
Бих искал малка/голяма/ семейна/спортна кола с радио/касетофон
Bih iskal malka/golyama/semeina/ sportna kola s radio/kasetofon

Do you have a road map?
Имате ли пътна карта?
Imateh li patna karta?

Parking

How long can I park here?
Колко време мога да паркирам тук?
Kolko vremeh moga da parkiram tuk?

Is there a car park near here?
Има ли паркинг наблизо?
Ima li parking nablizo?

At what time does this car park close?
В колко часа затваря паркингът?
V kolko chasa zatvarya parkinga?

Signs and Notices

Еднопосочна улица
Ednoposochna ulitsa
One way

Влизането забранено
Vlizaneto zabraneno
No entry

Паркирането забранено
Parkiraneto zabraneno
No parking

Отклонение
Otklonenieh
Detour (Diversion)

Стоп
Stop
Stop

Път/улица с предимство
Pat/ulitsa s predimstvo
Give way (Yield)

Хлъзгав път
Hlazgav pat
Slippery road

Изпреварването забранено
Izprevarvaneto zabraneno
No overtaking

Опасност
Opasnost
Danger

B
U
L
G
A
R
I
A
N

At the Filling Station
(В Бензиностанцията)

**Unleaded (lead free)/
standard/premium/diesel**
Безоловен/обикновен/
супер/дизел
*Bezoloven/obiknoven/
super/deezel*

Fill the tank please
Напълнете резервоара, моля
Napalneteh rezervoara, molya

Do you have a road map?
Имате ли пътна карта?
Imateh li patna karta?

How much is the car wash?
Колко струва измиването на
кола?
Kolko struva izmivaneto na kola?

Breakdowns

I've had a breakdown at …
Колата ми се повреди в …
Kolata mi seh povredi v …

**I am a member of the …
[motoring organisation]**
Аз съм член на …
Az sm chlen na …

**I am on the road
from … to …**
Аз съм на пътя от … до …
Az sam na patya ot … do …

**I can't move the car.
Can you send a tow-truck?**
Не мога да помръдна колата.
Можете ли да изпратите
аварийна кола?

Ne moga da pomradna kolata.
Mozheteh li da izpratiteh avariyina
kola?

I have a flat tyre
Спука ми се гума
Spuka mi se guma

**The windscreen (windshield)
has smashed/cracked**
Предното стъкло е счупено/
спукано
*Prednoto staklo eh
schupeno/spukano*

**There is something wrong
with the engine/brakes/
lights/steering/gearbox/
clutch/exhaust**
Имам повреда в двигателя/
спирачките/светлините/
волана/скоростната кутия/
амбреажа/ауспуха
*Imam povreda v dvigatelya/
spirachkiteh/svetliniteh/volana/
skorostnata kutia/ambreazha/
auspuha*

It's overheating
Прегрява
Pregriava

It won't start
Не пали
Ne pali

Where can I get it repaired?
Къде може да се ремонтира?
Kadeh mozhe da seh remontira?

Can you take me there?
Може ли да ме закарате там?
Mozhe li da me zakarateh tam?

36

Will it take long to fix?
Дълго време ли ще отнеме
да се ремонтира?
*Dalgo vremeh li shteh otnemeh da
seh remontirah?*

How much will it cost?
Колко ще струва?
Kolko shteh struva?

**Please can you pick me up/
give me a lift?**
Може ли да ме докарате/
закарате?
*Mozhe li da meh dokarateh/
zakarateh?*

Accidents and Traffic Offences (Violations)

**Can you help me? There has
been an accident**
Може ли да ми помогнете?
Стана катастрофа
*Mozhe li da mi pomognete? Stana
katastrofa*

**Please call the police/an
ambulance**
Моля повикайте
полиция/линейка
Molya, povikayte politsiya/lineyka

Is anyone hurt?
Има ли ранени?
Ima li raneni?

I'm sorry, I didn't see the sign
Съжалявам, не видях знака
Sazhaliavam, ne vidiah znaka

Must I pay a fine? How much?
Трябва ли да платя глоба?
Колко?
Tryabva li da platya globa? Kolko?

Покажете ми документите си
Pokazhete mi dokumentite si
Show me your documents

HEALTH

Pharmacy (Аптека)

**Do you have anything for a
stomach ache/headache/sore
throat/toothache?**
Имате ли нещо за стомашни
болки/главоболие/болно
гърло/зъбобол
*Imateh li neshto za stomashni
bolki/glavobolie/bolno garlo/zabobol*

**I need something for diar-
rhoea/constipation/a cold/a
cough/insect bites/sunburn/
travel (motion) sickness**
Трябва ми нещо за диария/
запек/настинка/кашлица/
ужилвания/изгаряне/гадене
*Triabva mi neshto za diaria/zapek/
nastinka/kashlitsa/uzhilvania/
izgariane/gadeneh*

**How much/how many do I
take?**
Колко трябва да взимам?
Kolko tryabva da vzimam?

**I am taking anti-malaria
tablets/these pills**
Аз взимам таблетки срещу
малария/тези хапчета
*Az vzimam tabletki sreshtu
malaria/tezi hapcheta*

How often do I take it/them?
Колко често трябва да го/ги
взимам?
*Kolko cheshto tryabva da go/gi
vzimam?*

B
U
L
G
A
R
I
A
N

I am/he is/she is taking this medication
Аз взимам/той/тя взима това лекарство
Az vzemam/toi/tya vzima tova lekarstvo

How much does it cost?
Колко струва?
Kolko struva?

Can you recommend a good doctor/dentist?
Може ли да ми препоръчате добър лекар/зъболекар?
Mozhe li da mi preporachate dobar lekar/zabolekar?

Is it suitable for children?
Може ли да се взима от деца?
Mozhe li da se vzima ot detsa?

Doctor (Доктор/Лекар)

I have a pain here/in my arm/leg/chest/stomach
Боли ме тук/ръката/кракът/гърдите/стомахът
Boli me tuk/rakata/kraka/gardite/stomaha

Please call a doctor, this is an emergency
Моля повикайте лекар, това е спешен случай
Molya povikaite lekar, tova e speshen sluchai

I would like to make an appointment to see the doctor
Искам да си определя час за преглед при лекаря
Iskam da si opredelya chas za

pregled pri lekaria

I am diabetic/pregnant
Аз имам диабет/Аз съм бременна
Az imam diabet/Az sam bremenna

I need a prescription for ...
Трябва ми рецепта за ...
Triabva mi retsepta za ...

Can you give me something to ease the pain?
Може ли да ми дадете нещо за болката?
Mozhe li da mi dadeteh neshto za bolkata?

I am/he is/she is/allergic to penicillin
Аз имам/той/тя има алергия към пеницилин
Az imam/toi/tya ima alergia kam penitsilin

Това боли ли?
Tova boli li?
Does this hurt?

Трябва да отидете/отиде в болницата
Tryabva da otideteh/otideh v bolnitsata
You must/he must/she must go to hospital

Вземайте ги веднъж/два пъти/три пъти на ден
Vzimaite gi vednazh/dva pati/tri pati na den
Take these once/twice/three times a day

I am/he is/she is taking this medication
Аз взимам/той/тя взима това лекарство
Az vzemam/toi/tya vzima tova lekarstvo

I have medical insurance
Аз имам здравна застраховка
Az imam zdravna zastrahovka

Dentist (Зъболекар)

I have toothache/my filling has come out
Боли ме зъб/паднала ми е пломбата
Boli me zab/padma mi plombata

I do/do not want to have an injection first
Искам/не искам първо инжекция
Iskam/ne iskam parvo inzhektsia

EMERGENCIES

Help!
Помощ!
Pomosht!

Fire!
Пожар!
Pozhar!

Stop!
Стоп!/Спри!
Stop!/Spri!

Call an ambulance/a doctor/ the police/the fire brigade!
Извикайте линейка/лекар/ полицията/пожарната!
Izvikaite lineika/lekar/politsiata/ pozharnata!

Please may I use a telephone?
Може ли използвам телефона, моля?
Mozhe li da izpolzvam telefona, molya?

I have had my traveller's cheques/credit cards/ handbag/rucksack/luggage/ wallet/passport/mobile phone stolen
Откраднаха ми пътническите чекове/кредитните карти/ чантата/раницата/багажа/ портфейла/паспорта/ мобилния телефон
Otkradnaha mi patnicheskite chekoveh/kreditniteh karti/ chantata/ranitsata/bagazha/ portfeila/pasporta/mobilniya telefon

May I please have a copy of the report for my insurance claim?
Може ли да ми дадете копие на полицейския протокол, необходим за застрахователния иск?
Mozhe li da mi dadete kopie na politseyskiya protocol, neobhodim za zastrahovatlniya isk?

Can you help me, I have lost my daughter/son/my companion(s)?
Може ли да ми помогнете, загубих дъщеря си/сина си/ приятеля/приятелите си?

B
U
L
G
A
R
I
A
N

39

B
U
L
G
A
R
I
A
N

Mozhe li da mi pomogneteh, zagubih dashteria si/sina si/ priatelya si?

Please go away/leave me alone

Идете си/оставете ме намира, моля
Idete si/ostaveteh meh namira, molya

I'm sorry

Съжалявам
Sazhalyavam

I want to contact the British/ American/Canadian/Irish/ Australian/New Zealand/ South African Consulate

Искам да се свържа с консулството на Великобритания/САЩ/ Канада/Ирландия/Австралия /Нова Зеландия/Южна Африка
Iskam da seh svarzha s konsultstvoto na Velikobritania/ Ess-Ah-Sht/Kanada/Irlandia/ Avstralia/Nova Zelandia/ Yuzhna Afrika

I'm/we're/he is/she is/they are/ill/lost/injured

Аз съм/ние сме/той е/тя е/ те са болен (болни)/ изгубен(изгубени)/ранен(и)
Az sam/nieh smeh/toy eh/tya eh/the sa bolen (bolni)/izguben (izgubeni)/ ranen(i)

CROATIAN

INTRODUCTION

Croatian should not be confused with Serbo-Croat. It comprises three main dialect groups: the main one being the Tokavian group, with the greatest number of speakers. Tokavian, in the shape of its Ijekavian dialect, is the basis for standard literary Croatian, which is used here. It will generally be understood by speakers of other dialects, including those who speak the closely-related Bosnian and Serbian languages. English, German and Italian are also spoken in tourist areas.

Addresses for Travel and Tourist Information

UK: *Croatian National Tourist Board,* 2 The Lanchesters, 162-164 Fulham Palace Road, London W6 9ER. Tel: (020) 8563 7979. Fax: (020) 8563 2616.

USA: *Croatian National Tourist Board,* 350 Fifth Avenue, Suite 4003, New York, NY 10118. Tel: 1 800 829 4416, (212) 279 8672.
Fax: (212) 279 8683.

Official tourism website: www.croatia.hr

Croatia Facts

CAPITAL: Zagreb
CURRENCY: Kuna (Kn). 1 Kuna = 100 Lipa.
OPENING HOURS: Banks: Mon–Fri 0800–1200, but may vary. Most food shops: Mon–Sat 0800–2000, closed Sun. Some shops close 1300–1700. Most open-air markets daily, mornings only. Museums vary.
TELEPHONES: To dial in, +385. Outgoing, 00 and the country code. Police, 92. Fire, 93. Ambulance, 94.
PUBLIC HOLIDAYS: Jan 1; Jan 6; Easter Mon; May 1; May 30; Jun 22; Aug 5; Aug 15; Nov 1 and Dec 25–26.

Technical Language Hints

Croatian is an easy language to spell and pronounce. Each letter is pronounced separately and clearly in any position and each word is spelt as it is pronounced. The alphabet has 30 letters.

Standard Croatian does not employ the so-called 'tonic accent' of other South Slavic dialects, but instead employs simple word stress.

In two-syllable words, stress generally falls on the first syllable; in words of three or more syllables, stress may fall on any syllable except the last. The stressed syllable in such words will be indicated by the mark (`).

Notes on Grammar

The verb forms are usually used without personal pronouns as subjects and the person is indicated by the verb ending. Sometimes the pronoun must be left out. The optionality will be indicated by brackets.
The second person plural is also used for the polite form of address. In this phrasebook, the polite form will be used. In Croatian, word forms change according to the gender. Where applicable, both masculine and feminine forms are given.

ESSENTIALS

Alphabet and Pronunciation

Name Pronounced

A a	a	like a in father
B b	be	like b in brother
C c	tse	like ts in cats
Č č	che	like ch in church
Ć ć	tche	like ty in get you, or like ch with the top of the tongue slightly forward
D d	de	like d in day
Dž dž	je	like j in jungle
Đ đ	dye	like dy in would you, or j with the top of the tongue slightly forward
E e	e	like e in bed, or like ea in head
F f	ef	like f in fast
G g	ge	like g in go
H h	ha	like h in huge, or like ch in Scottish loch
I i	i	like e in he
J j	ye	like y in yes

K k	ka	like k in key
L l	el	like l in love
Lj lj	lye	like ll in million
M m	em	like m in mother
N n	en	like n in not
Nj nj	nye	like ni onion
O o	o	like o in hot
P p	pe	like p in pet
R r	er	rolled r, like Scottish r
S s	es	like s in sin
Š š	she	like sh in shy
T t	te	like t in top
U u	u	like oo in food
V v	ve	like v in vest
Z z	ze	like z in zeal
Ž ž	zhe	like s in pleasure

CROATIAN

Basic Words and Phrases

Yes
Da
Da

No
Ne
Ne

Please
Molim
Mo-lim

Thank you
Hvala
Hva-la

Hello
Zdravo
Zdra-vo

Goodbye
Zbogom
Zbo-gom

That's O.K.
To je u redu
To ye oo re-doo

Perhaps
Možda
Mozh-da

How
Kako
Ka-ko

When
Kada
Ka-da

Why
Zašto
Za-shto

What
Što
Shto

Who
Tko
Tko

Excuse me
Oprostite
O-`pro-sti-te

Sorry
Pardon
Par-don

To
U
Oo

From
Iz
Iz

Here
Ovdje
Ov-die

There
Tamo
Ta-mo

I don't understand
Ne razumijem
Ne ra-`zoo-mi-yem

I don't speak Croatian
(Ja) ne govorim hrvatski
(Ja) ne `go-vo-rim `hr-vat-ski

Do you speak English?
Govorite li engleski?
`Go-vo-ri-te li `en-gle-ski

Can you please write it down?
Molim Vas možete li mi to napisati?
Mo-lim vas `mo-zhe-te li mi to na-`pi-sa-ti

Please can you speak more slowly?
Molim vas govorite polakše
Mo-lim vas go-`vo-ri-te po-`lak-she

Greetings

Good morning
Dobro jutro
Do-bro yoo-tro

Good afternoon
Dobar dan
Do-bar dan

Good evening
Dobra veěer
Do-bra ve-cher

Good night
Laku noć
La-koo noch

Pleased to meet you
Drago mi je
Dra-go mi ye

How are you?
Kako ste?
Ka-ko ste

I am well, thank you. And you?
Hvala, dobro. A vi?
Hva-la do-bro a vi?

My name is …
Moje ime je …
Mo-ye ime ye …

This is my friend/boyfriend/girlfriend/husband/wife/brother/sister
Ovo je moj prijatelj/momak/djevojka/suprug/supruga/brat/sestra
O-vo ye moy `pri-ya-tell/mo-mak/`die-voy-ka/soo-proog/`die-voy-ka/soo-proo-ga/brat/se-stra

Where are you travelling to?
Kamo putujete?
Ka-mo `poo-too-ye-te?

I am/we are going to …
Putujem/Putujemo u …
`Poo-too-yem/`poo-too-yemo oo …

How long are you travelling for?
Koliko dugo ostajete na putu?
`Ko-li-ko doo-go `o-sta-ye-te na poo-too?

Where do you come from?
Odakle ste?
`O-da-kle ste?

I am/we are from … Australia/Britain/Canada/America
Ja sam/mi smo iz …
Australije/Velike Britanije/Kanade/Amerike
Ya sam iz … a-oo-`stra-li-ye/`ve-li-ke bri-`ta-ni-ye/`ka-na-de/amerike

We are on holiday
Na odmoru smo
Na `od-mo-roo smo

This is our first visit here
Ovdje smo prvi put
Ov-die smo p-rvi poot

How old are you?
Koliko imate godina?
`Ko-li-ko `i-ma-te `go-di-na?

I am … years old
Imam … godina
I-mam … `go-di-na

I am a business person/doctor/journalist/manual worker/administrator/scientist/student/teacher
Ja sam poduzetnik/liječnik/novinar/radnik/upravitelj/znanstvenik/student/učitelj **(masculine)**
Ya sam `po-do-zet-nik/liech-nik/`no-vi-nar/rad-nik/`znan-stve-nik/stoo-dent/`oo-chi-tell
Ja sam poduzetnica/liječnica/novinarka/radnica/upraviteljica/znanstvenica/studentica/učiteljica. **(feminine)**
Ya sam `po-do-zet-ni-tsa/`liech-ni-tsa/`no-vi-nar-ka/`rad-ni-tsa/`znan-stve-ni-tsa/`stoo-den-ti-tsa/oo-chi-`te-lli-tsa

I am waiting for my husband/wife/boyfriend/girlfriend
Čekam svoga supruga/svoju suprugu/svoga momka/svoju djevojku
Che-kam svo-ga `soo-proo-ga/svo-yoo `soo-proo-goo/svo-ga mom-ka/svo-yoo `die-voy-koo

45

Would you like/may I have a cigarette?
Želite li/mogu li dobiti cigaretu?
`Zhe-li-te li/mo-goo li `do-bi-ti tsi-ga-`re-too?

Do you mind if I smoke?
Smijem li zapaliti?
Smi-yem li za-`pa-li-ti?

Do you have a light?
Molim Vas vatre?
Mo-lim vas va-tre?

Days

Monday
Ponedjeljak
Po-`nie-die-llak

Tuesday
Utorak
`Oo-to-rak

Wednesday
Srijeda
Srie-da

Thursday
Četvrtak
Che-`tvr-tak

Friday
Petak
Pe-tak

Saturday
Subota
`Soo-bo-ta

Sunday
Nedjelja
`Ne-die-lla

Morning
Jutro
Yoo-tro

Afternoon/Evening/Night
Popodne/večer/noč
Po-`po-dne/ve-cher/noty

Yesterday/Today/Tomorrow
Jučer/Danas/Sutra
Yoo-cher/Da-nas/Soo-tra

Numbers

Zero
Nula
Noo-la

One
Jedan
Ye-dan

Two
Dva
Dva

Three
Tri
Tri

Four
Četri
`Che-ti-ri

Five
Pet
Pet

Six
Šest
Shest

Seven
Sedam
Se-dam

Eight
Osam
O-sam

Nine
Devet
De-vet

Ten
Deset
De-set

Eleven
Jedanaest
Ye-`da-na-est

Twelve
Dvanaest
`Dva-na-est

Thirteen
Trinaest
`Tri-na-est

Fourteen
Četrnaest
Che-`tr-na-est

Fifteen
Petnaest
`Pet-na-est

Sixteen
Šesnaest
`Shes-na-est

Seventeen
Sedamnaest
Se-`dam-na-est

Eighteen
Osamnaest
O-`sam-na-est

Nineteen
Devetnaest
De-`vet-na-est

Twenty
Dvadeset
`Dva-de-set

Twenty-one
Dvadeset jedan
`Dva-de-set je-dan`

Twenty-two
Dvadeset dva
`Dva-de-set dva`

Thirty
Trideset
`Tri-de-set`

Forty
Četrdeset
`Che-tr-`de-set`

Fifty
Pedeset
Pe-`de-set`

Sixty
Šezdeset
Shez-`de-set`

Seventy
Sedamdeset
Se-dam-`de-set`

Eighty
Osamdeset
O-sam-`de-set`

Ninety
Devetdeset
De-ve-`de-set`

One hundred
Sto
Sto

Five hundred
Petsto
Pet-sto

One thousand
Tisuća
`Ti-soo-cha`

One million
Milijun
Mi-`li-yoon`

Time

What time is it?
Koliko je sati?
`Ko-li-ko ye sa-ti`

It is ...
Točno...
Toch-no...

9.00
Devet sati
De-vet sa-ti

9.05
Devet i pet
De-vet i pet

9.15
Devet i četvrt
De-vet i chet-vrt

9.20
Devet i dvadeset
De-vet i `dva-de-set`

9.30
Devet i trideset (pola deset)
De-vet i `tri-de-set (po-la de-set)`

9.35
Devet i trideset pet (dvadestet
pet do deset)
De-vet i `tri-de-set pet (`dva-de-set
pet do de-set)`

9.40
Devet i četrdest (dvadeset do
deset)
De-vet i che-tr -`de-set (`dva-de-set
do de-set)`

9.45
Devet i četrdeset pet (četvrt do
deset)
De-vet i che-tr-`de-set (chet-vrt do
de-set)`

9.50
Devet i pedeset (deset do
deset)
De-vet i pe-`de-set (de-set do
de-set)`

9.55
Devet i pedeset pet (pet do
deset)
De-vet i pe-`de-set pet (pet do
de-set)`

12.00/Midday/Midnight
Dvanaest/podne/ponoć
`Dva-na-est/pod-ne/po-noch`

CROATIAN

C
R
O
A
T
I
A
N

Money

I would like to change these traveller's cheques. I would like to change this currency
Želio bih unovčiti ove putničke čekove. Želio bih promijeniti ovaj novac
(masculine)
`Zhe-li-o bih oo-`nov-chi-ti ove `poot-nich-ke `che-ko-ve. `zhe-li-o bih pro-`mie-ni-ti o-vay no-vac
Željela bih unovčiti ove putničke čekove. Željela bih promijeniti ovaj novac
(feminine)
`Zhe-lle-la bih oo-`nov-chi-ti ove `poot-nich-ke `che-ko-ve. `zhe-lle-la bih pro-`mie-ni-ti o-vay no-vac

How much commission do you charge? (What is the service charge?)
Koliko je vaša provizija?
`Ko-li-ko ye va-sha `pro-vi-zi-ya?

Can I obtain money with my Mastercard?
Mogu li podignuti novac koristeći moju Mastercard karticu?
Mo-goo li `po-dig-noo-ti no-vac `ko-ri-ste-chi mo-yoo `ma-ster-kard `kar-ti-tsoo?

Where is the nearest ATM?
Gdje je najbliži bankomat?
Gdye ye nay-bli-zhi ban-ko-mat?

My name is ... Some money has been wired to here for me to collect
Moje ime je ... Za mene je ovdje telefonski poslan novac
Mo-ye ime ye ... Za me-ne ye ovd-ye te-le-fon-ski po-slan no-vats

Airport

Excuse me, where is the check-in desk for ...?
Oprostite, gdje se nalazi šalter prijave ...?
O-`pro-sti-te gdie se `na-la-zi shal-ter `pri-ya-ve ...?

What is the boarding gate/time for my flight?
Koji je broj izlaza za moj let? Kada je ukrcaj za moj let?
Ko-yi ye broy `iz-la-za za moy let ka-da ye `oo-kr-tsay za moy let?

How long is the delay likely to be?
Koliko otprilike će biti zakašnjenje?
`Ko-li-ko ot-`pri-li-ke che bi-ti za-ka-`shnye-nye?

Where is the duty-free shop?
Gdje se nalazi bescarinska trgovina?
Gdie se `na-la-zi `bes-tsa-rin-ska tr-`go-vi-na?

Which way is the luggage reclaim?
Gdje je izdavanje prtljage?
Gdie ye iz-`da-va-nye prt-`lla-ge?

I have lost my luggage. Please, can you help?
Izgubio (Izgubila) sam svoju prtljagu. Možete li mi pomoći? **(masculine/feminine)**
I-`zgoo-bi-o (i-`zgoo-bi-la) sam svo-yoo prt-`lla-goo `mo-zhe-te li mi `po-mo-chi?

48

I am flying to …
Letim za…
le-tim za…

Where is the bus for the city centre (downtown)?
Odakle polazi autobus za centar grada?
`O-da-kle `po.la-zi `a-oo-to-boos za tsen-tar gra-da?

Trains and Boats

Where is the ticket office/information desk?
Gdje je ured za prodaju karata/šalter za informacije?
Gdie ye oo-red za `pro-da-yoo `ka-ra-ta/shal-ter za in-for-`ma-tsie?

Which platform does the train/speedboat/ferry to … depart from?
S kojega kolosijeka polazi vlak za … Odakle polazi brzi motorni čamac/trajekt za…?
S `ko-ye-ga `ko-lo-sie-ka `po-la-zi vlak za `o-da-kle `po-la-zi br-zi `mo-tor-ni cha-mac/tra-yekt za?

Where is platform …?
Gdje je kolosijek broj …?
Gdie ye `ko-lo-siek broj…?

When is the next train/boat to …?
Kada polazi slijedeći vlak/ brod za …?
Ka-da `po-la-zi slie-de-chi vlak/ brod za …?

Is there a later train/boat to …?
Postoji li kasniji vlak/brod za …?
`Po-sto-yi li `ka-sni-yi vlak/brod za …?

Notices and Signs

Vagon-restoran
`Va-gon re-`sto-ran
Buffet (Dining) car

Autobus
`A-oo-to-boos
Bus

Voda za/nije za piće
Vo-da za/nie za pi-che
Drinking/non-drinking water

Ulaz
Oo-laz
Entrance

Izlaz
Iz-laz
Exit

Bolnica
`Bol-ni-tsa
Hospital

Informacije
In-for-`ma-ci-ye
Information

Garderoba
Gar-de-`ro-ba/
Left luggage (Baggage claim)

Garderobni ormarić
Gar-de-`rob-ni or-`ma-rich
Luggage lockers

Pošta
Po-shta
Post office

C
R
O
A
T
I
A
N

CROATIAN

Kolosijek/Peron
`Ko-lo-siek/pe-ron`
Platform

Željeznički kolodvor
`Zhe-llez-nich-ki `ko-lo-dvor`
Railway(Railroad) station

Aerodrom
`A-e-ro-drom`
Airport

Policijska stanica
Po-`li-ciy-ska `sta-ni-ca
Police station

Luka
Lu-ka
Port

Restoran
Re-`sto-ran
Restaurant

Za pušače/Za nepušače
(Zabranjeno pušenje)
Za poo-`sha-che/za `ne-poo-sha-che (`za-bra-nye-no `poo-she-nye)
Smoking/non-smoking

Telefon
Te-`le-fon
Telephone

Ured za prodaju karata
Oo-red za `pro-da-yoo `ka-ra-ta
Ticket office

Šalter za prijavu
Shal-ter za `pri-ya-voo
Check-in desk

Vozni red
Voz-ni red
Timetable (Schedule)

WC
Ve tse
Toilets (Restrooms)

Muški/Ženski
Moosh-ki/zhen-ski
Ladies/Gentlemen

Podzemna željeznica
`Pod-zem-na `zhe-llez-ni-tsa`
Underground (Subway)

Čekaonica
Che-ka-`o-ni-tsa
Waiting room

Buying a Ticket

**I would like a first-class/
second-class/third-class single
(one-way)/return (round-trip)
ticket to...**
Molim jednu kartu/povratnu
kartu prvog razreda/drugog
razreda/trećeg razreda za...
*Mo-lim yed-noo kar-tool `po-vra-tnoo
kar-too pr-vog `raz-re-da/droo-gog
`raz-re-da/tre-cheg `raz-re-da za...*

**Is it an express (fast)
train/bus?**
Je li to brzi vlak/autobus?
Ye li to br-zi vlak/`a-oo-to-boos?

**Is my rail pass valid on this
train/ferry/bus?**
Važi li moja karta za ovaj
vlak/trajekt/autobus?
*Va-zhi li mo-ya kar-ta za o-vay
vlak/tra-yekt/`a-oo-to-boos?*

50

I would like an aisle/window seat

Htio (Htjela fem.) bih mjesto kraj prolaza/prozora

Hti-o (htye-la) bih mye-sto kray `pro-la-za/`pro-zo-ra

No smoking/smoking please

Za pušače/Za nepušače, molim

Za poo-`sha-che/za `ne-poo-sha-che mo-lim

We would like to sit together

Htjeli bismo sjediti zajedno

Htye-li bis-mo `sye-di-ti `za-ye-dno

I would like to make a seat reservation

Htio (Htjela fem.) bih rezervirati sjedalo

Hti-o (htye-la) bih re-zer-`vi-ra-ti `sye-da-lo

I would like to reserve a couchette/sleeper for one person/two people/my family

Htio (Htjela fem.) bih rezervirati mjesto u kušet/spavaćim kolima za jednu osobu/dvije osobe/moju obitelj

Hti-o (htye-la) bih re-zer-`vi-ra-ti mye-sto u koo-shet/spa-va-chim ko-li-ma za yed-noo `o-so-boo/dvije `o-so-be/mo-yoo o-`bi-tell

I would like to reserve a cabin

Htio (Htjela fem.) bih rezervirati kabinu

Hti-o (htye-la) bih re-zer-`vi-ra-ti ka-`bi-noo

Timetables (Schedules)

Stiže
Sti-zhe
Arrive

Staje u
Sta-ye oo
Calls (Stops at)

Ugostiteljske usluge
Oo-`go-sti-tell-ske `oo-sloo-ge
Catering service

Presjesti u
`Pre-sye-sti oo
Change at

Preko
Pre-ko
Connection/Via

Svakodnevno
Sva-`ko-dne-vno
Daily

Svakih četrdeset minuta
Sva-kih che-tr-`de-set mi-`noo-ta
Every 40 minutes

Prvi razred
Pr-vi raz-red
First class

Svaki sat
Sva-ki sat
Hourly

Preporučamo rezervaciju sjedala
Pre-`po-roo-cha-mo re-zer-`va-tsi-yoo `sye-da-la
Seat reservations are recommended

C
R
O
A
T
I
A
N

Drugi razred
Droo-gi raz-red
Second class

Obvezna doplata
`Ob-vez-na `do-pla-ta
Supplement payable

Luggage

How much will it cost to send (ship) my luggage in advance?
Koliko košta zasebno slanje prtljage?
`Ko-li-ko kosh-ta `za-se-bno sla-nye prt-`lla-ge?

Where is the left luggage (baggage claim) office?
Gdje je garderoba?
Gdie ye gar-de`ro-ba?

What time do you open/close?
Kada otvarate/zatvarate?
Ka-da `ot-va-ra-te/`za-tva-ra-te?

Where are the luggage trolleys (carts)?
Gdje su kolica za prtljagu?
Gdie soo ko-`li-tsa za prt-`lla-goo?

Where are the lockers?
Gdje su garderobni ormarići?
Gdie soo gar-de-`ro-bni or-`ma-ri-chi?

I have lost my locker key
Izgubio (Izgubila fem.) sam ključ od moga ormarića
Iz-`goo-bio (iz-`goo-bila) sam kllooch od mo-ga or-`ma-ri-cha

On Board

Is this seat free?
Je li ovo mjesto slobodno?
Ye li ovo mie-sto `slo-bod-no?

Excuse me, you are sitting in my reserved seat
Oprostite, sjeli ste na moje mjesto
O-`pro-sti-te sie-li ste na mo-ye mie-sto

Which station is this?
Koja je ovo stanica?
Ko-ya ye ovo `sta-ni-tsa?

What time is this train/bus/ferry/flight due to arrive/depart?
Kada stiže/polazi ovaj vlak/autobus/trajekt?
Ka-da sti-zhe/`po-la-zi o-vay vlak/`a-oo-to-boos/tra-yekt?

Travelling with Children

Do you have a high chair/babysitting service/cot?
Imate li dječju stolicu/službu za čuvanje djece/dječji krevet?
`I-ma-te li die-chyoo `sto-li-tsoo/sloo-zhboo za `choo-va-nye die-tse/die-chyi kre-vet?

Where is the nursery/playroom?
Gdje je dječja soba/igraonica?
Gdie je die-chya so-ba/i-gra-`o-ni-tsa?

Where can I warm the baby's bottle?
Gdje mogu zagrijati dječju bocu?
Gdie mo-goo `za-gri-ya-ti die-chyoo bo-tsoo?

Customs and Passports

Putovnice, molim
Poo-`tov-ni-tse mo-li
Passports please

I have nothing/wine/spirits (alcohol)/tobacco to declare
Nemam ništa/Imam vino/alkohol/duhan za prijaviti
Ne-mam ni-shta/i-mam vino/`al-ko-hol/doo-han za pri-`ya-vi-ti

I will be staying for ... days/weeks/months
Ostajem ... dana/tjedana/mjeseci
`O-sta-yem ... da-na/`tye-da-na/mye-`se-tsi

SIGHTSEEING

Asking the Way

Excuse me, do you speak English?
Oprostite, govorite li engleski?
O-`pro-sti-te `go-vo-ri-te li `en-gle-ski?

Excuse me, can you help me please?
Oprostite, možete li mi pomoći?
O-`pro-sti-te `mo-zhe-te li mi `po-mo-chi?

Where is the Tourist Information Office?
Gdje se nalazi turistički ured?
Gdie se `na-la-zi too-`ri-sti-chki oo-red?

Excuse me, is this the right way to ...?
Oprostite, ide li se ovuda za ...?
O-`pro-sti-te i-de li se `o-voo-da za ...?

... the cathedral/the tourist office/the castle/the old town
... katedralu/turistički ured/zamak/stari grad
ka-te-`dra-loo/too-`ri-stich-ki oo-red/za-mak/sta-ri grad

Can you tell me the way to the railway (railroad) station/bus station/taxi rank/city centre (downtown)/beach?
Možete li mi reći kako mogu doći do željezničkog kolodvora/autobusnog kolodvora/taksi-stajalište/centra grada/plaže?
`Mo-zhe-te li mi re-chi ka-ko mo-goo do-chi do `zhe-llez-nich-kog `ko-lo-dvo-ra/`a-oo-to-boos-nog `ko-lo-dvo-ra/tak-si `sta-ya-li-shta/tsen-tra gra-da/pla-zhe?

Prva/druga/lijevo/desno/ravno
Pr-va/droo-ga/lie-vo/des-no/rav-no
First/second/left/right/straight ahead

Na uglu/na semafora
Na oog-loo/na`se-ma-fo-roo
At the corner/at the traffic lights

Where is the nearest police station/post office?
Gdje je najbliža policijska stanica/pošta?
Gdie ye `nay-bli-zha po-`li-tsiy-ska `sta-ni-tsa/po-shta?

Is it near/far?
Je li blizu/daleko?
Ye li bli-zoo/`da-le-ko?

**Do I need to take a
taxi/catch a bus?**
Trebam li poći taksijem/
autobusom?
*Tre-bam li po-chi `ta-ksi-yem/`a-oo-
to-boo-som?*

Do you have a map?
Imate li plan grada?
`I-ma-te li plan gra-da?

**Can you point to it on my
map?**
Možete li mi to pokazati na
planu grada?
*`Mo-zhe-te li mi to po-`ka-za-ti na
pla-noo gra-da?*

Thank you for your help
Hvala na pomoći
Hva-la na `po-mo-chi

**How do I reach the
motorway/main road?**
Kako se dolazi do
autoputa/glavne ceste?
*Ka-ko se `do-la-zi do `a-oo-to-poo-
ta/glav-ne tse-ste?*

**I think I have taken the
wrong turning**
Mislim da sam pogrešno skren-
uo
*Mi-slim da sam `po-gre-shno
`skre-noo-o*

I am looking for this address
Tražim ovu adresu
Tra-zhim o-voo a-`dre-soo

I am looking for the ... hotel
Tražim hotel ...
Tra-zhim ho-tel ...

How far is it to ... from here?
Koliko daleko je odavde do ...?
`Ko-li-ko `da-le-ko ye `o-dav-de do...?

Nastavite ravno... kilometara
*`Na-sta-vi-te rav-no ...
ki-`lo-me-ta-ra*
**Carry straight on for ...
kilometres**

Na slijedećem uglu skrenite
desno/lijevo
*Na `slie-de-chem oog-loo `skre-ni-te
de-sno/lie-vo*
**Take the next turning on the
right/left**

Na slijedećem raskrižju/
semaforu skrenite desno/lijevo
*Na `slie-de-chem `ras-krizh-yoo
`se-ma-fo-roo `skre-ni-te de-sno/lie-vo*
**Turn right/left at the next
crossroads/traffic lights**

Idete u pogrešnom smjeru
`I-de-te oo `po-gre-shnom smie-roo
**You are going in the wrong
direction**

**Where is the cathedral/
church/museum/pharmacy?**
Gdje se nalazi katedrala/crkva/
muzej/apoteka?
*Gdie se `na-la-zi ka-te-`dra-la/cr-
kva/moo-zey/a-po-`te-ka?*

**How much is the admission/
entrance charge?**
Koliko košta ulaznica?
`Ko-li-ko ko-shta `oo-laz-ni-tsa?

Is there a discount for children/students/senior citizens?
Dajete li popust za djecu/ studente/umirovljenike?
`Da-ye-te li po-poost za die-tsoo/stoo-`den-te/oo-mi-ro-vlle-`ni-ke?

What time does the next guided tour (in English) start?
Kada počinje vođenje (na engleskom)?
`Ka-da `po-chi-nye `vo-dye-nye (na `en-gle-skom)?

One/two adults/children please
Molim jednu/dvije za odrasle/djecu
`Mo-lim yed-noo/dvie za `od-ras-le/die-tsu

May I take photographs here?
Smijem li ovdje fotografirati?
`Smi-yem li ov-die fo-to-gra-`fi-ra-ti

At the Tourist Office

Do you have a map of the town/area?
Imate li plan grada/kartu regije?
`I-ma-te li plan gra-da/kar-too `re-gi-ye?

Do you have a list of accommodation?
Imate li spisak hotela i prenoćišta?
`I-ma-te li spi-sak ho-`te-la i `pre-no-chish-ta?

Can I reserve accommodation?
Mogu li rezervirati smeštaj?
`Mo-goo li re-zer-`vi-ra-ti smiesh-tay?

Hotels

I have a reservation in the name of...
Imam rezerviranu sobu na ime...
`I-mam re-zer-`vi-ra-noo so-boo na i-me...

I wrote to/faxed/telephoned you last month/last week
Poslao sam pismo/faks/ Telefonirao sam prošli mjesec/prošli tjedan
(masculine)
`Po-sla-o sam pi-smo/faks/te-le-fo-`ni-ra-o sam pro-shli mie-sec/pro-shli tie-dan...
Poslala sam pismo/faks/ Telefonirala sam prošli mjesec/prošli tjedan
(feminine)
`Po-sla-la sam pi-smo/faks/te-le-fo-`ni-ra-la sam pro-shli mie-sec/pro-shli tie-dan

Do you have any rooms free?
Imate li slobodnih soba?
`I-ma-te li `slo-bod-nih so-ba?

I would like to reserve a single/double room with/without a bath/shower
Htio (htjela fem) bih rezervirati jednokrevetnu/dvokrevetnu sobu s kupaonicom/tušem/bez kupaonice/tuša
Hti-o (htie-la) bih re-zer-`vi-ra-ti

C
R
O
A
T
I
A
N

`yed-no-kre-vet-noo/`dvo-kre-vet-noo so-boo s koo-pa-`o-ni-tsom/too-shem/bez koo-pa-`o-ni-tse/too-sha

I would like bed/breakfast/ (room and) full board
Htio (Htjela fem.) bih sobu s doručkom/puni pansion
Hti-o (htie-la) bih soo-boo s `do-roo-chkom/poo-ni pan-`si-on

How much is it per night?
Koliko košta jedno noćenje?
`Ko-lik-ko ko-shta yed-no `no-che-nye?

Is breakfast included?
Je li doručak uključen?
Ye li `do-roo-chak `ook-lloo-chen?

Do you have any cheaper rooms?
Imate li nešto jeftinije?
`I-ma-te li ne-shto yef-`ti-ni-ye?

I would like to see/take the room
Htio (Htjela fem.) bih vidjeti/uzeti tu sobu
Hti-o (htie-la) bih `vi-die-ti/`oo-ze-ti too so-boo

I would like to stay for ... nights
Htio (Htjela fem.) bih ostati ... noći
Hti-o (htie-la) bih `o-sta-ti ... no-chi

The shower/light/tap doesn't work. The hot water doesn't work
Tuš/svjetlo/slavina ne radi. Nema tople vode
Toosh/sviet-lo/`sla-vi-na ne ra-di. Ne-ma top-le vo-de

At what time/where is breakfast served?
Kada/gdje je doručak?
Ka-da/gdie ye `do-roo-chak?

What time do I have to check out?
Kada se moram odjaviti?
Ka-da se mo-ram od-`ya-vi-ti?

Can I have the key to room number ...?
Mogu li dobiti ključ od sobe broj ...?
Mo-goo li `do-bi-ti kllooch od so-be broy ...?

My room number is ...
Broj moje sobe je ...
Broy mo-ye so-be ye ...

My room is not satisfactory/not clean enough/too noisy. Please can I change rooms?
Moja soba/krevet nije u redu/nije dovoljno čista (čist)/je previše bučna. Mogu li dobiti drugu sobu/drugi krevet?
Mo-ya so-ba/kre-vet ni-ye oo re-doo/ni-ye `do-vo-llno chi-sta (chist)/ ye pre-vi-she booch-na. Mo-goo li `do-bi-ti droo-goo so-boo/droo-gi kre-vet?

Where is the bathroom?
Gdje je kupaonica?
Gdie ye koo-pa-`o-ni-tsa?

Do you have a safe for valuables?
Imate li sef?
`I-ma-te li sef?

Is there a laundry/do you wash clothes?
Imate li praonicu/perete li rublje?
`I-ma-te li pra-`o-ni-tsoo/`pe-re-te li roo-blle?

I would like an air-conditioned room
Htio (Htjela fem.) bih sobu s klima-uređajem
Hti-o (htie-la) bih so-boo s kli-ma `oo-re-dya-yem

Do you accept traveller's cheques/credit cards?
Mogu li platiti putničkim čekovima/kreditnom karticom?
Mo-goo li `pla-ti-ti `poot-nich-kim `che-ko-vi-ma/`kre-dit-nom `kar-ti-tsom?

May I have the bill please?
Platiti, molim
`Pla-ti-ti mo-lim

Excuse me, I think there may be a mistake in this bill
Oprostite, čini mi se da račun nije točan
O-`pro-sti-te chi-ni mi se da ra-choon ni-ye to-chan

Youth Hostels

How much is a dormitory bed per night?
Koliko košta jedno noćenje?
`Ko-li-ko ko-shta yed-no `no-che-nye?

I am/am not an HI member
Član (Članica fem.) sam/Nisam član (članica fem.) HI-a
Chlan (`chla-ni-tsa) sam/ni-sam chlan (`chla-ni-tsa) ha-`i-a

May I use my own sleeping bag?
Mogu li koristiti svoju vreću za spavanje?
Mo-goo li `ko-ri-sti-ti svo-yoo vre-choo za `spa-va-nye?

What time do you lock the doors at night?
Kada se zaključavaju vrata?
Ka-da se za-kloo-`cha-va-yoo vra-ta?

Camping

May I camp for the night/two nights?
Mogu li ostati jednu/dvije noći?
Mo-goo li `o-sta-ti jed-noo/dvie no-chi?

Where can I pitch my tent?
Gdje mogu postaviti svoj šator?
Gdie mo-goo `po-sta-vi-ti svoy sha-tor?

How much does it cost for one night/week?
Koliko košta jedna noć/tjedan dana?
`Ko-li-ko ko-shta yed-na noch/tye-dan dana?

Where are the washing facilities?
Gdje je umivaonica?
Gdie ye oo-mi-va-`o-ni-tsa?

Is there a restaurant/supermarket/swimming pool on site/nearby?
Ima li ovdje/u blizini restoran/supermarket/bazen?
I-ma li ov-die/oo bli-`zi-ni re-`sto-ran/`soo-per-mar-ket/ba-zen?

Do you have a safety deposit box?
Imate li sef?
`*I-ma-te li sef?*

EATING AND DRINKING
Cafés and Bars

I would like a cup of/two cups of/another coffee/tea
Molim jednu/dvije/još jednu kavu/jedan/dva/još jedan čaj
Mo-lim yed-noo/dvie/yosh yed-noo ka-voo/ye-dan/dva/yosh ye-dan chay

With/without milk/sugar
S/Bez mlijeka/Sa/Bez šećera
S/bez mlie-ka sa/bez `she-che-ra

I would like a bottle/glass/two glasses of mineral water/red wine/white wine, please
Molim jednu bocu/čašu/dvije čaše mineralne vode/crnog vina/bijelog vina
Mo-lim yed-noo bo-tsoo/cha-shoo/dvie cha-she `mi-ne-ral-ne vo-de/cr-nog vi-na/bie-log vi-na

I would like a beer/two beers, please
Molim jedno pivo/dva piva
Mo-lim yed-no pi-vo/dva pi-va

Please may I have some ice?
Molim malo leda?
Mo-lim ma-lo le-da?

Do you have any matches/cigarettes/cigars?
Imate li šibice/cigarete/cigare?
`*I-ma-te li `shi-bi-tse/tsi-ga-`re-te/tsi-`ga-re?*

Restaurants

Can you recommend a good/cheap restaurant in this area?
Možete li mi preporučiti dobar/jeftin restoran u blizini?
`*Mo-zhe-te li mi pre-po-`roo-chi-ti do-bar/yef-tin re-`sto-ran oo bli-`zi-ni?*

I would like a table for... people
Trebam stol za .... osoba
Tre-bam stol za ...`o-so-ba

Do you have a non-smoking area?
Imate li prostoriju za nepušače?
`*I-ma-te li pro-`sto-ri-yoo za `ne-poo-sha-che?*

Waiter! Waitress!
Konobar! Konobarica!
Ko-no-bar! ko-no-ba-ri-tsa!

Excuse me, please, may we order?
Oprostite, možemo li naručiti?
O-`pro-sti-te mo-zhe-mo li na-`roo-chi-ti?

Do you have a set menu/children's menu/wine list ... in English?
Imate li meni/dječji meni/vinsku kartu ... na engleskom?
`*I-ma-te li me-ni/di-ye-chi-yi me-ni/vin-skoo kar-too ... na `en-gle-skom?*

Do you have any vegetarian dishes?
Imate li vegetarijanskih jela?
Ima-te li ve-ge-ta-ri-yan-skih ye-la?

Do you have any local specialities?
Imate li lokalnih specijaliteta?
`I-ma-te li `lo-kal-nih spe-tsi-ya-li-`te-ta?

Are vegetables included?
Je li povrće uključeno?
Ye li `po-vr-che `oo-klloo-che-no?

Could I have it well-cooked/medium/rare please?
Molim vas za mene dobro pečeno/polupečeno/na engleski način?
Mo-lim vas za me-ne do-bro pe-che-no/`po-loo-pe-che-no/na `en-gle-ski na-chin?

What does this dish consist of?
Od čega se ovo jelo sastoji?
Od che-ga se ovo ye-lo `sa-sto-yi?

I am a vegetarian. Does this contain meat?
Ja sam vegetarijanac. Da li ovo ima mesa?
Ya sam ve-ge-ta-ri-ya-nats. Da li ovo ima me-sa?

I do not eat nuts/dairy products/meat/fish
(Ja) ne jedem orahe/mljiečne proizvode/meso/ribu
(Ya) ne ye-dem `o-ra-he/mliech-ne `pro-i-zvo-de/me-so/ri-boo

Not (very) spicy please
Molim vas, ne (vrlo) ljuto
Mo-lim vas ne (vr-lo) lloo-to

I would like the set menu, please
Uzet ću meni
Oo-zet choo me-ni

We have not been served yet
Još čekamo da nas se posluži
Yosh che-ka-mo da nas se po-sloo-zhi

Please bring a plate/knife/fork
Molim Vas, donesite tanjur/nož/vilicu
Mo-lim vas, do-ne-si-te ta-nyur/nozh/vi-li-tsoo

Excuse me, this is not what I ordered
Oprostite, ali nisam ovo naručio
O-`pro-sti-te a-li ni-sam o-vo na-`roo-chi-o

May I have some/more bread/water/coffee/tea?
Mogu dobiti malo/još kruha/vode/kave/čaja?
Mo-goo li `do-bi-ti ma-lo/yosh kroo-ha/vo-de/ka-ve/cha-ya?

May I have the bill please?
Platiti, molim?
`Pla-ti-ti mo-lim?

Does this bill include service?
Je li servis uračunat?
Ye li ser-vis oo-ra-`choo-nat?

Do you accept traveller's cheques/Mastercard/US dollars?
Mogu li platiti putničkim čekovima/Mastercard karticom/američkim dolarima?
Mo-goo li `pla-ti-ti `poot-nich-kim `che-ko-vi-ma/`ma-ster-kard kar-ti-tsom/a-`me-rich-kim `do-la-ri-ma?

Can I have a receipt please?
Mogu li dobiti račun?
Mo-goo li `do-bi-ti ra-choon?

C
R
O
A
T
I
A
N

Where is the toilet (restroom) please?
Molim vas, gdje je WC?
Mo-lim vas gdie ye ve tse?

On the Menu

Doručak/Ručak/Večera
Do-roo-chak/Roo-chak/Ve-che-ra
Breakfast/Lunch/Dinner

Predjela	Juhe
`Pred-ye-la	*Yoo-he*
First courses	**Soups**
Glavna jela	Riblja jela
Glav-na ye-la	*Rib-lla ye-la*
Main courses	**Fish dishes**
Mesna jela	Govedina
Mes-na ye-la	*Go-ve-di-na*
Meat dishes	**Beef**
Odrezak	Svinjetina
Od-re-zak	*Svi-nye-ti-na*
Steak	**Pork**
Teletina	Piletina
Te-le-ti-na	*Pi-le-ti-na*
Veal	**Chicken**
Janjetina	Ćunka
Ja-nye-ti-na	*Shoon-ka*
Lamb	**Ham**

Jela od povrća
Ye-la od `po-vr-cha
Vegetarian dishes

Povrće
Po-vr-tye
Vegetables

Pečeni krumpirići (pomfrit)
Pe-che-ni kroom-pi-ri-tyi
Chips (french fries)

Pečeni/pirjani/pire krumpir
Pe-che-ni/pir-ya-ni/pi-re kroom-pir
Boiled/sauté/mashed potatoes

Riža	Deserti
Ri-zha	*De-`ser-ti*
Rice	**Desserts**
Sladoled	Torte
Sla-do-led	*Tor-te*
Ice cream	**Cakes**
Kolači	Voće
Ko-la-chi	*Vo-tye*
Pastries	**Fruit**
Kruh	Žemlje
Krooh	*Zhe-mlye*
Bread	**Rolls**
Prepečenac	Maslac
Pre-pe-che-nats	*Mas-lats*
Toast	**Butter**
Sol/papar	Ćećer
Sol/pa-par	*She-tyer*
Salt/pepper	**Sugar**

Specijaliteti
Spe-tsi-ya-li-`te-ti
Specialities

Domaći specijaliteti
Do-ma-tyi spe-tsi-ya-li-te-ti
Local specialities

Meni	Vinska karta
Me-ni	*Vin-ska kar-ta*
Set menu	**Wine list**

C R O A T I A N

Crna vina
Tsr-na vi-na
Red wines

Bijela vina
Bi-ye-la vi-na
White wines

Rosé vina
Ro-ze vi-na
Rosé wines

Pjenušci
Pye-noosh-tsi
Sparkling wines

Pivo
Pi-vo
Beer

Flaširano pivo/točeno pivo
Fla-shi-ra-no pi-vo/to-che-no pi-vo
**Bottled beer/draught
(draft) beer**

Bezalkoholna pića
Bez-al-ko-hol-na pi-tya
Non-alcoholic drinks

Mineralna voda
Mi-ne-ral-na vo-da
Mineral water

Voćni sokovi
Voty-ni so-ko-vi
Fruit juices

Sok od naranče
Sok od na-ran-che
Orange juice

Limunada
Li-mu-na-da
Lemonade

Led
Led
Ice

Bijela kava/crna kava/
espresso
*Bi-ye-la ka-va/tsr-na
ka-va/es-pre-so*
**White coffee/black
coffee/espresso coffee**

Čaj sa mlijekom/sa limunom
Chay-sa-mli-ye-kom/sa li-moo-nom
Tea with milk/with lemon

Čokolada (napitak)
Cho-ko-la-da (na-pi-tak)
Chocolate (drink)

Mlijeko
Mli-ye-ko
Milk

Grickalice/Lagana jela
Grits-ka-li-tse/la-ga-na ye-la
Snacks/Light meals

Salate
Sa-la-te
Salads

Sendviči
Sen-dvi-chi
Sandwiches

Jaja
Ya-ya
Eggs

Kobasica
Ko-ba-si-tsa
Sausage

Pečena/pržena/tučena jaja
*Pe-che-na/pr-zhe-na/too-che-na
ya-ya*
Boiled/fried/scrambled eggs

Typical Local Dishes

Rakovice u posebnom umaku
*`Ra-ko-vi-tse oo `po-seb-nom
`oo-ma-koo*
**Boiled crabs served with
special sauce**

C
R
O
A
T
I
A
N

Dagnje na buzaru
Dag-nye na `boo-za-roo
**Boiled mussels served
with special sauce**

Teletina na žaru
`Te-le-ti-na na zha-roo
Grilled veal

Sarma
Sar-ma
**Cabbage leaves stuffed
with minced meat**

Lozovača
`L o-zo-va-cha
Grappa

GETTING AROUND

Public Transport

**Where is the bus stop/coach
stop/nearest metro (subway)
station?**
Gdje je autobusna stanica/
autobusni kolodvor/najbliža
stanica podzemne željeznice?
*Gdie ye `a-oo-to-boos-na `sta-ni-
tsa/`a-oo-to-boos-ni `ko-lo-dvor/`nay-
bli-zha `sta-ni-tsa `pod-zem-ne `zhe-
llez-ni-tse?*

**When is the next/last bus
to...?**
Kada ide slijedeći/posljednji
autobus za ...?
*Ka-da ide `slie-de-chil`po-slled-nyi
`a-oo-to-boos za...?*

**How much is the fare to the
city centre (downtown)/
railway (railroad) station/
airport?**
Koliko košta karta do centra
grada/željezničkog
kolodvora/aerodroma?
*`Ko-li-ko ko-shta kar-ta do tsen-tra
gra-da/`zhe-llez-nich-kog `ko-lo-dvo-
ra/`a-e-ro-dro-ma?*

**Will you tell me when to get
off?**
Možete li mi reći kada trebam
sići?
*`Mo-zhe-te li mi re-chi ka-da
tre-bam si-chi?*

Does this bus go to...?
Vozi li ovaj autobus za...?
Vo-zi li o-vay `a-oo-to-boos za...?

**Which number bus goes to
...?**
Koji autobus vozi za...?
Ko-yi `a-oo-to-boos vo-zi za...?

**May I have a single (one-
way)/return (round-trip)/day
ticket/book of tickets?**
Molim vas jednu/povratnu/
dnevnu kartu/jedan karnet?
*Mo-lim vas yed-noo/`po-vrat-
noo/dnev-noo kar-too/ye-dan
kar-net?*

Taxis

**I would like to go to ... How
much will it cost?**
Idem u ... Koliko će to koštati?
*I-dem oo ... `Ko-li-ko che to
`ko-shta-ti?*

Please may I stop here?
Molim vas, zaustavite ovdje?
Mo-lim vas za-`oo-sta-vi-te ov-die?

I would like to order a taxi today/tomorrow at 2pm to go from ... to ...
Htio (Htjela **fem.**) bih naručiti taksi za danas/sutra u 2 popodne iz ... u ...
Htio (htye-la) bih na-`roo-chi-ti tak-si za da-nas/soo-tra oo dva po-`po-dne iz ... oo ...

Entertainment

Can you recommend a good bar/nightclub?
Možete li mi preporučiti neki dobar bar/noćni bar?
`Mo-zhe-te li mi pre-po-`roo-chi-ti ne-ki do-bar bar/noch-ni bar?

Do you know what is on at the cinema (playing at the movies)/theatre at the moment?
Znate li što trenutno igra u kinima/kazalištima?
Zna-te li shto `tre-noot-no ig-ra oo `ki-ni-ma/`ka-za-lish-ti-ma?

I would like to book (purchase)... tickets for the matinee/evening performance on Monday
Htio (Htjela **fem.**) bih kupite karte za matineju/večernju predstavu u ponedjeljak
Htio (htye-la) bih `koo-pi-ti kar-te za ma-ti-`ne-yoo/ve-cher-nyoo `pred-sta-voo oo po-`ned-ye-llak

What time does the film/performance start?
Kada počinje ovaj film/prjedstava?
Ka-da `po-chi-nye o-vay film/`pred-sta-va?

Post

How much will it cost to send a letter/postcard/this package to Britain/Ireland/USA/Canada/Australia/New Zealand?
Koliko stoji marka za pismo/razglednicu/ovaj paket za Veliku Britaniju/Irsku/SAD/Kanadu/Australiju/Novi Zeland?
`Ko-li-ko sto-yi mar-ka za pi-smo/`raz-gled-ni-tsoo/o-vay pa-ket za `Ve-li-koo Bri-`ta-ni-yoo/Ir-skoo/ Es a de/ `Ka-na-doo/A-oo-`stra-li-yoo/ No-vi Ze-land?

I would like one stamp/two stamps
Molim jednu/dvije marke
Mo-lim yed-noo/dvie mar-ke

I'd like ... stamps for postcards to send abroad, please
Trebam ... marke za razglednice za inozemsvo
Tre-bam ... mar-ke za `raz-gled-ni-tse za `i-no-zem-stvo

CROATIAN

C
R
O
A
T
I
A
N

Phones

I would like to make a telephone call/reverse the charges to (make a collect call to) …
Htio (Htjela fem.) bih nazvati/najaviti razgovor …
Htio (htye-la) bih `na-zva-ti/na-/na-a-vi-ti er `raz-go-vor …

Which coins do I need for the telephone?
Koje kovanice trebam za telefon?
Ko-ye ko-`va-ni-tse `tre-bam za te-`le-fon?

The line is engaged (busy)
Zauzeto je
`Za-oo-ze-to ye

The number is …
Broj je…
Broj je…

Hello, this is …
Halo, ovdje…
Ha-lo ov-die…

Please may I speak to …?
Mogu li dobiti …?
Mo-goo li do-bi-ti …?

He/she is not in at the moment. Please can you call back?
On/ona nije trenutno ovdje. Možete li nazvati malo kasnije?
On/ona ni-ye `tre-noot-no ov-die. `Mo-zhe-te li `na-zva-ti ma-lo `ka-sni-ye?

Shops

Knjižara/Papirnica
`Knyi-zha-ra/pa-`pir-ni-tsa
Bookshop/Stationery

Nakit/Pokloni
Na-kit/`po-klo-ni
Jeweller/Gifts

Obuća
`O-boo-cha
Shoes

Oprema
`O-pre-ma
Hardware

Frizer
Fri-zer
Hairdresser

Pekara
`Pe-ka-ra
Baker

Supermarket
`Su-per-mar-ket
Supermarket

Fotografska radnja
Fo-`to-graf-ska rad-nya
Photo shop

Turistička agencija
Too-`ris-tich-ka a-`gen-tsi-ya
Travel agent

Apoteka
A-po-`te-ka
Pharmacy

In the Shops

What time do the shops open/close?
Kada se zatvaraju otvaraju/trgovine?
Ka-da se `zat-va-ra-yoo ot-va-ra-yoo/tr-`go-vine?

Where is the nearest market?
Gdje je najbliža tržnica?
Gdie ye `nay-bli-zha `trzh-ni-tsa?

Can you show me the one in the window/this one?
Možete li mi pokazati onaj u izlogu/ovaj ovdie?
Mo-zhe-te li mi po-`ka-za-ti o-nay oo iz-lo-goo/o-vay ov-die?

Can I try this on?
Mogu li to probati?
Mo-goo li to `pro-ba-ti?

What size is this?
Koji je to broj?
Ko-yi ye to broy?

This is too large/too small/too expensive. Do you have any others?
Ovo je preveliko/premalo/preskupo. Imate li nešto drugo?
O-vo ye `pre-ve-li-ko/`pre-ma-lo/`pre-skoo-po. `I-ma-te li ne-shto droo-go?

My size is ...
Moj broj je...
Moy broy ye...

Where is the changing room/children's/cosmetic/ladieswear/menswear/food department?
Gdje je kabina za presvlačenje/djeći odio/parfumerija/ženska odjeća/muška odjeća/namirnice?
Gdie ye ka-`bi-na za pres-`svla-che-nye/die-chyi `o-di-o/par-fu-`me-ri-ya/zhen-ska `o-die-cha/moo-shka `o-die-cha/`na-mir-ni-tse?

I would like ... a quarter of a kilo/half a kilo/a kilo of bread/butter/ham/this fruit
Molim ... četvrt kilograma/ pola kilograma/kilogram kruha/maslaca/ šunke/ovog voća
Mo-lim ... chet-vrt `ki-lo-gra-ma/po-la `ki-lo-gra-ma/`ki-lo-gram kroo-ha/`ma-sla-tsa/shoon-ke/o-vo vo-cha

How much is this?
Koliko je to?
`Ko-li-ko ye to?

I'll take this one, thank you
Hvala, uzet ću ovo
Hva-la oo-zet choo o-vo

Do you have a carrier (shopping) bag?
Imate li vrećicu?
Ima-te li vre-tyi-tsoo?

Do you have anything cheaper/larger/smaller/of better quality?
Imate li nešto jeftinje/veće/manje/kvalitetnije?
`I-ma-te li ne-shto yef-`ti-ni-ye/ve-che/ma-nye/kva-li-`tet-ni-ye?

I would like a film/to develop this film for this camera
Treba mi film/Želim da razvijete ovaj film
Tre-ba mi film/Zhe-lim da `raz-vi-ye-te o-vay film

C
R
O
A
T
I
A
N

65

C R O A T I A N

I would like some batteries, the same size as this old one
Trebam baterije iste veličine kao što je ova stara
Tre-bam `ba-te-ri-ye is-te ve-li-`chi-ne kao shto ye ova sta-ra

Would you mind wrapping this for me, please?
Molim vas, možete li mi ovo zamotati?
Mo-lim vas `mo-zhe-te li mi o-vo za-`mo-ta-ti?

Sorry, but you seem to have given me the wrong change
Oprostite, vratili ste mi pogrešan iznos
O-pro-sti-te `vra-ti-li ste mi `po-gre-shan iz-nos

MOTORING

Car Hire (Rental)

I have ordered (rented) a car in the name of ...
Unajmio sam auto na ime...
Oo-`nay-mi-o sam `a-oo-to na ime...

How much does it cost to hire (rent) a car for one day/two days/a week?
Koliko košta unajmljivanje auta za jedan dan/dva dana/tjedan dana?
`Ko-li-ko ko-shta oo-nay-`mlli-va-nye `a-oo-ta za ye-dan dan/dva da-na/tie-dan da-na?

Is the tank already full of petrol (gas)?
Je li rezervoar pun?
Ye li re-zer-`vo-ar poon?

Is insurance and tax included? How much is the deposit?
Jesu li osiguranje i porez uračunati? Koliki je polog?
Ye-soo li o-si-goo-`ra-nye i po-rez oo-ra-`choo-na-ti? `Ko-li-ki ye po-log?

By what time must I return the car?
Kada moram vratiti auto?
Ka-da mo-ram `vra-ti-ti `a-oo-to?

I would like a small/large/family/sports car with a radio/cassette
Htio (Htjela fem.) bih mali/veliki/sportski auto s radiom/kasetofonom
Htio (htie-la) bih ma-li/`ve-li-ki/spor-tski `a-oo-to s `ra-di-om/ka-se-to-`fo-nom

Do you have a road map?
Imate li auto-kartu?
`I-ma-te li `a-oo-to-kar-too?

Parking

How long can I park here?
Koliko dugo mogu ovdje ostatii?
`Ko-li-ko doo-go mo-goo ov-die `os-ta-ti?

Is there a car park near here?
Ima li blizu neko parkiralište?
I-ma li bli-zoo ne-ko par-`ki-ra-li-shte?

At what time does this car park close?
Kada se ovo parkiralište zatvara ?
Ka-da se ovo par-`ki-ra-li-shte `zat-va-ra?

C
R
O
A
T
I
A
N

Signs and Notices

Jednosmjerna ulica
`Je-dno-smier-na `oo-li-tsa
One way

Nema ulaza
Ne-ma `oo-la-za
No entry

Zabranjeno parkiranje
`Za-bra-nye-no par-`ki-ra-nye
No parking

Obilaznica
`O-bi-laz-ni-tsa
Detour (Diversion)

Stop
Stop
Stop

Daj prednost
Day pred-nost
Give way (Yield)

Klizav put
Kli-zav poot
Slippery road

Zabranjeno preticanje
`Za-bra-nye-no `pre-ti-tsa-nye
No overtaking

Opasnost!
O-`pas-nost!
Danger!

At the Filling Station
(Na Benzijskoj Pumpi)

**Unleaded (lead free)/
standard/premium/diesel**
Bezolovni/regular/super/dizel
*`Bez-o-lov-ni/`re-goo-lar/soo-per/
di-zel*

Fill the tank please
Puni rezervoar, molim
Poo-ni re-zer-`vo-ar mo-lim

Do you have a road map?
Imate li auto-kartu?
`I-ma-te li `a-oo-to-kar-too?

How much is the car wash?
Koliko košta pranje auta?
`Ko-li-ko kosh-ta pra-nye `a-oo-ta?

Breakdowns

I've had a breakdown at ...
Pokvario mi se je auto kod...
Po-`kva-ri-o mi se ye `a-oo-to kod...

**I am a member of the...
[motoring organisation]**
Ja sam član ...
Ya sam chlan ...

**I am on the road from ...
to ...**
Nalazim se na cesti ...
`Na-la-zim se na ces-ti ...

**I can't move the car. Can you
send a tow-truck?**
Ne mogu pokrenuti vozilo.
Možete li poslati vučnu službu?
*Ne mo-goo po-`kre-noo-ti `vo-zi-lo.
`Mo-zhe-te li `po-sla-ti vooch-noo
sloozh-boo?*

C R O A T I A N

I have a flat tyre
Imam praznu gumu
I-mam praz-noo goo-moo

The windscreen (windshield) has smashed/cracked
Vjetrobran je razbijen/napuknut
`Vie-tro-bran ye `raz-bi-yen/`na-pook-noot

There is something wrong with the engine/brakes/lights/steering/gearbox/clutch/exhaust
Nešto nije u redu s motorom/kočnicamasvjetlima/upravljačem/mjenjačem brzina/spojkom/ispuhom
Ne-shto ni-ye oo re-doo s mo-`to-rom/`koch-ni-tsa-ma`sviet-li-ma/oo-pra-`vlla-chem/mye-`nya-chem br-`zi-na/spoy-kom/`is-poo-hom

It's overheating
Motor se pregrijava
Mo-tor se pre-`gri-ya-va

It won't start
Neće upaliti
Ne-che oo-`pa-li-ti

Where can I get it repaired?
Gdje to mogu popraviti?
Gdie to mo-goo `pop-ra-vi-ti?

Can you take me there?
Možete li me tamo odvesti?
`Mo-zhe-te li me ta-mo `od-ve-sti?

Will it take long to fix?
Koliko dugo će trajati popravak?
`Ko-li-ko doo-go che `tra-ya-ti `pop-ra-vak?

How much will it cost?
Koliko će to koštati?
`Ko-li-ko che to kosh-ta-ti?

Please can you pick me up/give me a lift?
Molim vas možete li me povesti?
Mo-lim vas `mo-zhe-te li me `po-ve-sti?

Accidents and Traffic Offences (Violations)

Can you help me? There has been an accident
Možete li mi pomoći? Dogodila se nesreća
Mo-zhe-te li mi po-mo-tyi? Do-go-di-la se nes-re-tya

Please call the police/an ambulance
Molim Vas, zovite policiju/hitnu pomoć
Mo-lim Vas, zo-vi-te po-li-tsi-yoo/hit-noo po-moty

Is anyone hurt?
Je li netko ozlijeđen?
Ye li ne-tko oz-li-ye-dyen?

Sorry, I didn't see the sign
Žao mi je, nisam vidio znak
Zha-o mi ye ni-sam `vi-di-o znak

Must I pay a fine? How much?
Moram li platiti globu? Koliko?
Mo-ram li `pla-ti-ti glo-boo? `Ko-li-ko?

Pokažite mi vaše isprave
Po-`ka-zhi-te mi va-she `is-pra-ve
Show me your documents

HEALTH

Pharmacy (Apoteka)

Do you have anything for a stomach ache/headache/sore throat/toothache?
Imate li nešto protiv bolova u želucu/glavobolje/upale grla/zubobolje?
`I-ma-te li ne-shto pro-tiv `bo-lo-va oo `zhe-loo-tsoo/gla-`vo-bo-lle/`oo-pa-le gr-la/zoo-`bo-bo-lle?

I need something for diarrhoea/constipation/a cold/a cough/insect bites/ sunburn/travel (motion) sickness
Trebam nešto protiv proljeva/ zatvora/prehlade/kašlja/uboda insekata/opeklina od sunca/mučnine
Tre-bam ne-shto pro-tiv `pro-lle-va/`za-tvo-ra/`pre-hla-de/kash-lla/`oo-bo-da in-`se-ka-ta/`o-pe-kli-na od soon-tsa/mooch-`ni-ne

How much/how many do I take?
Koliko toga moram uzeti?
Ko-li-ko to-ga mo-ram `oo-ze-ti?

I am taking anti-malaria tablets/these pills
Uzimam tablete protiv malari-je/ove pilule
`Oo-zi-mam `ta-ble-te pro-tiv ma-`la-ri-ye/o-ve `pi-loo-le

How often do I take it/them?
Koliko često moram to uzimati?
`Ko-li-ko che-sto mo-ram to `oo-zi-ma-ti?

I am/he is/she is taking this medication
Ja uzimam/on/ona uzima ove lijekove
Ya `oo-zi-mam/on/o-na `oo-zi-ma ov-e `lle-ko-ve

How much does it cost?
Koliko to košta?
`Ko-li-ko to ko-shta?

Can you recommend a good doctor/dentist?
Možete li mi preporučiti dobrog liječnika/zubara?
`Mo-zhe-te li mi pre-po-`roo-chi-ti do-brog liech-ni-ka/zoo-`ba-ra?

Is it suitable for children?
Je li to pogodno za djecu?
Ye li to `po-god-no za die-tsoo?

Doctor (Lijeénik)

I have a pain here/in my arm/leg/chest/stomach
Boli me ovdje/u ruci/u nozi/u grudima/u želucu
Bo-li me ov-die/oo roo-tsi/oo no-zi/oo `groo-di-ma/oo `zhe-loo-tsoo

Please call a doctor, this is an emergency
Molim hitno pozovite liječnika
Mo-lim hit-no po`zo-vi-te `liech-ni-ka

I would like to make an appointment to see the doctor
Htio (Htjela fem.) bih zakazati termin kod liječnika
Htio (htie-la) bih za-`ka-za-ti ter-min kod `liech-ni-ka

CROATIAN

I am diabetic/pregnant
Ja sam dijabetičar/trudna
Ya sam di-a-`be-ti-char/trood-na

I need a prescription for ...
Trebam recept za...
Tre-bam re-tsept za...

Can you give me something to ease the pain?
Možete li mi dati nešto protiv bolova?
`Mo-zhe-te li mi da-ti ne-shto pro-tiv `bo-lo-va?

I am/he is/she is/allergic to penicillin
Ja sam alergičan/on je alergičan/ona je alergična na penicilin
Ya sam a-`ler-gi-chan/on ye a-`ler-gi-chan/o-na ye a-`ler-gich-na na pe-ni-`tsi-lin

Da li to boli?
Da li to bo-li?
Does this hurt?

Vi morate/on mora/ona mora ići u bolnicu
Vi `mo-ra-te/on mo-ra/o-na mo-ra i-chi u `bol-ni-tsoo
You must/he must/she must go to hospital

Uzmite ovo jednom/dva put/tri put dnevno
`Oo-zmi-te o-vo yed-nom/dva poot/tri poot dnev-no
Take these once/twice/three times a day

I am/he is/she is taking this medication
Ja uzimam/on/ona uzima ove lijekove
Ya`oo-zi-mam/on/o-na `oo-zi-ma ov-e `lle-ko-ve

I have medical insurance
(Ja) imam zdravstveno osiguranje
(Ya) i-mam `zdrav-stve-no o-si-goo-`ra-nye

Dentist (Zubar)

I have toothache/my filling has come out
Boli me zub/ispala mi je plomba
Bo-li me zoob/`is-pa-la mi ye `plom-ba

I do/do not want to have an injection first
Želim/Ne želim injekciju
Zhe-lim/ne zhe-lim i-`nyek-tsi-yoo

EMERGENCIES

Help!
U pomoć!
`Oo-po-moch!`

Fire!
Požar!
Po-zhar!

Stop!
Stop!
Stop!

Call an ambulance/a doctor/the police/the fire brigade!
Nazovite hitnu/liječnika/policiju/vatrogasce!
Na-`zo-vi-te hit-noo/`liech-ni-ka/po-`li-tsi-yoo/va-tro-`gas-tse!`

Please may I use a telephone?
Molim vas mogu li odavde nazvati?
Mo-lim vas mo-goo li `o-dav-de `naz-va-ti?`

I have had my traveller's cheques/credit cards/handbag/rucksack/luggage/wallet/passport/mobile phone stolen
Ukrali su mi putničke čekove/kreditne kartice/ručnu torbicu/naprtnjaču/prtljagu/novčanik/putovnicu/ mobitel
`Oo-kra-li soo mi `poo-tnich-ke `che-ko-ve/`kre-dit-ne `kar-ti-tse/roo-chnoo `tor-bi-tsoo/`na-prt-nya-choo/prt-`lla-goo/nov-`cha-nik/poo-tov-ni-tsoo/mo-bi-tel`

May I please have a copy of the report for my insurance claim?
Mogu li dobiti kopiju izvješća za moj odštetni zahtjev?
Mo-goo li do-bi-ti ko-pi-yoo iz-vyesh-cha za moj od-shtet-ni zah-tiyev?

Can you help me? I have lost my daughter/son/my companion(s)
Pomozite mi? izgubio sam kńer/sina/svoga suputnika
Po-`mo-zi-te mi? iz-`goo-bi-o sam kcher/si-na/svo-ga `soo-poo-tni-ka`

Please go away/leave me alone
Odlazite, molim vas, pustite me na miru
`O-dla-zi-te mo-lim vas `poo-sti-te me na mi-roo`

I'm sorry
Žao mi je
Zha-o mi ye

I want to contact the British/American/Canadian/Australian/New Zealand/South African Consulate
Htio (Htjela) bih stupiti u vezu s Britanskim/Američkim/Kanadskim/Australijskim/Novo zelandskim/Južnoafričkim konzulatom
Htio (htye-la) bih `stoo-pi-ti oo ve-zoo s `Bri-tan-skim/A-`me-rich-kim/`Ka-nad-skim/A-oo-`stra-liy-skim/No-vo-`ze-land-skim/Yuzh-no-`a-frich-kim kon-zoo-`la-tom`

C
R
O
A
T
I
A
N

I'm/we're/he is/she is/they are/ill/lost/injured
Ja sam bolestan/se izgubio/ozljeđen/mi smo bolesni/se izgubili/ozljeđeni/on je bolestan/se izgubio/ozljeđen/ona je bolesna/se izgubila/ozljeđena/oni su bolesni/se izgubili/ozlje eni
Ya sam `bo-les-tan/se iz-`goo-bi-ol`oz-lle-dyen/mi smo `bo-les-ni/se iz-`goo-bi-li/`oz-lle-dye-ni/on ye`bo-les-tan/se iz-`goo-bi-o/`oz-lle-dyen/o-na ye `bo-les-na/se iz-`goo-bi-la/`oz-lle-dye-na/o-ni soo `bo-les-ni/se iz-`goo-bi-li/`oz-lle-dye-ni

72

CZECH

C
Z
E
C
H

INTRODUCTION

Czech is the official language of the Czech Republic. The language spoken in neighbouring Slovakia is Slovak, but the two are so closely related that speakers of one can easily understand the other. Both belong to the Slavic family of languages that includes Russian and Polish. In larger cities, particularly in the Czech Republic, English is spoken, and German is often a second language for many Czechs. Russian is also widely understood, but not popular.

Addresses for Travel and Tourist Information

Except where stated, addresses are tourist authorities for both the Czech Republic and Slovakia.

Australia: *Czech Embassy,* 8 Culgoa Circuit, O'Malley, Canberra, ACT 2606; tel: (02) 6290 1386; fax: (02) 6290 0006. *Slovakian Embassy,* 47 Culgoa Circuit, O'Malley, Canberra, ACT 2606; tel: (02) 6290 1516; fax: (02) 6290 1755.

Canada: *Czech Tourist Authority,* 401 Bay Street, Suite #1510, Toronto, Ontario M5H 2Y4; tel:(416) 363 9928; fax:(416) 363 0239.

South Africa: *Czech Embassy,* 936 Pretorius Street, Arcadia, Pretoria; tel: (12) 342 3477. *Slovak Embassy,* 930 Arcadia Street, Arcadia, Pretoria; tel: (12) 342 2051.

UK: *Czech Tourist Authority,* Suite 29–31, 2nd Floor, Morley House, 320 Regent St, London W1B 3BG; tel: (020) 7631 0427; fax: (020) 7631 0419.

USA: *CzechTourism USA,* 1109 Madison Ave, New York, NY 10028; tel: (212) 288 0830, ext. 101, 105; fax: (212) 288 0971.

Official tourism website: www.czechtourism.com.

Czech Facts

CAPITAL: Prague (Praha, pronounced Prahah)

CURRENCY: Czech Koruna (Korroonah) or Crown (KČ);
1 Koruna = 100 Haliřú (Hallers).

OPENING HOURS: Banks: Mon–Fri 0800–1800. Shops: Mon–Fri 0900–1800, Sat 0900–1200 (longer in Prague Sat and Sun). Museums: Tues–Sun 1000–1800. Castles closed Nov–Mar.

TELEPHONES: To dial in, +420. Outgoing, 00 plus the country code. Police, Fire, Ambulance, 155.

PUBLIC HOLIDAYS: 1 Jan; Easter Monday; 1, 8 May; 5–6 July; 28 Sept; 28 Oct; 17 Nov; 24–26 Dec.

ESSENTIALS

Alphabet and Pronunciation

A few hints

- Stress the first syllable.

- T, P and K are pronounced quickly (without a drawn out 'ay' or 'ee' sound).

- Pronounce each part of the word, and pay particular attention to pronouncing vowels.

	Name	Pronounced
A a	ah	short neutral sound as in sun
Á á		long a as in father
B b	beh	like English b
C c	tsey s	sound like the c in censor
Č č	ch	as in cheap
D d	dey	like English d
Ď ď	dy	sound like the d in the British pronunciation of dew
E e	ey	short e as in get
É é		long e as in hey
Ě ě		ye sound as in yet
F f	ef	like English f

	Name	Pronounced
G g	gey	hard g as in goose
H h	hah	h as in hurry
Ch ch	khah	kh sound as in Scottish loch
I i	ee	short i as in tip
Í í		ee sound like the i in machine
J j	yeh	y sound as in yard
K k	kah	like English k
L l	el	like English l
M m	em	like English m
N n	en	like English n
Ň ň	ny	like the n in the British pronunciation of new
O o	oh	short o as in hot
Ó ó		long aw sound as in shore
P p	pey	like English p

75

C Z E C H

R r	yer	like English r
Ř ř		rzh sound as in French argent
S s	es	like English s
Š š	sh	as in sheet
T t	tey	like English t
Ť ť	ty	like the t in the British pronunciation of Tuesday
U u	oo	short u as in put
Ú ů		long u sound as in cool
V v	veh	w as in wine
W w	dvoyiteh veh	not a native Czech letter, pronounced as English w
X x	iks	not a native Czech letter, pronounced as English x
Y y	oopsilon ee	as in meet
Ý ý		as in meet
Z z	tset	like English z
Ž ž		soft zh sound like the s in measure

Basic Words and Phrases

Yes	**No**
Ano	Ne
Annoh	*Neh*
Please	**Thank you**
Prosím	Děkuji
Prosseem	*Dekooyee*
Hello	**Goodbye**
Ahoj	Nashledanou
Ahoy	*Nazhlehdano*
Excuse Me	**Sorry**
Promiňte	Pardon
Prohminyteh	*Pardohn*
How	**When**
Jak	Kdy
Yack	*Gdyh*
Why	**What**
Proč	Co
Proch	*Tsoh*
Who	
Kdo	
Gdoh	
That's O.K.	**Perhaps**
Prima	Možná
Preemmah	*Mozhnah*
To	**From**
Do	Od
Doh	*Ohd*
Here	**There**
Tady	Tam
Taddee	*Tamm*

I don't understand
Nerozumím
Nerozumeem

I don't speak Czech
Neumím česky
Neumeem cheskee

Do you speak English?
Umíte anglicky?
Oomeeteh anglitskee?

Can you please write it down?
Můžete mi to napsat, prosím?
Moozhehteh mee toh napsat, prosseem?

Please can you speak more slowly?
Můžete mluvit pomaleji prosím?
Moozhehteh mloovit pomaleyi proseem?

Greetings

Good Morning/Good Afternoon/Good Evening/Good Night
Dobrý den/Dobré odpoledne/Dobrý večer/Dobrou noc
Dobree den/Dobreh odpoledneh/Dobree vecher/Dobrow nots

Pleased to meet you
Těší mě
Tyeshee mnye

How are you?
Jak se máte?
Yak seh mahte?

I am well, thank you. And you?
Děkuji, dobře. A vy?
Dekooyi, dobrzeh. Ah vyh?

My name is ...
Jmenuji se ...
Menooyi sch ...

This is my friend/boyfriend/girlfriend/husband/wife/brother/sister
To je můj známý/přítel/přítelkyně/manžel/manželka/bratr/sestra
Toh yeh mooy znahmyh/przeetehl/przeetelkynye/manzhel/manzhelkah/bratr/sestrah

Where are you travelling to?
Kam jedete?
Kamm yedeteh?

I am/we are going to ...
Jedu/Jedeme do ...
Yedoo/Yedemeh doh ...

How long are you travelling for?
Jak dlouho cestujete?
Yack dlowhoh tsestuyeteh?

Where do you come from?
Odkud jste?
Odkood ysteh?

I am/we are from... Australia/Britain/Canada/America
Jsem/Jsme z ... Austrálie/Británie/Kanady/Ameriky
Ysem/Ysmeh z ...Austrahliye/Britahniye/Ehvropyh/Ahmerikyh

We are on holiday
Jsme na dovolené
Ysmeh nah dovoleneh

C
Z
E
C
H

77

C
Z
E
C
H

This is our first visit here
Jsme zde poprvé
Ysmeh zdeh poprveh

How old are you?
Kolik je vám let?
Kollick yeh vahm lett?

I am ... years old.
Jsem ... let starý/stará
Ysem ... lett staree/starah

**I am a business person/
doctor/journalist/manual
worker/administrator/
scientist/student/teacher**
Jsem podnikatel/doktor/
novinář/dělník/úředník/
vědec/student/učitel
*Ysem podnikatel/doktor/novinahrz
/dyelneek/oorzedneek/
vyedets/stoodent/oochitel*

**I am waiting for my husband/
wife/boyfriend/girlfriend**
Čekám na manžela/manželku/
přítele/přítelkyni
*Chekahm nah manzhella/
manzhelkoo/przeetelleh/
przeetelkeenee*

**Would you like/may I have a
cigarette?**
Chcete cigaretu/můžu si
zapálit?
*Khtsete tsigaretoo? Moozoo see
zappahleet?*

Do you mind if I smoke?
Vadí vám když kouřím?
Vadyee vahm kdeezh kowrzeem?

Do you have a light?
Máte oheň?
Mahte ohenye?

Monday
Pondělí
Pondyelee

Tuesday
Úterý
Ootehree

Wednesday
Středa
Strzehda

Thursday
Čtvrtek
Chtvrtek

Friday
Pátek
Pahtek

Saturday
Sobota
Sobotah

Sunday
Neděle
Nedyele

Morning
Ráno
Rahno

Afternoon/Evening/Night
Odpoledne/Večer/Noc
Odpoledneh/Vecher/Nots

Yesterday/Today/Tomorrow
Včera/Dnes/Zítra
Vcherah/Dnehs/Zeetrah

Zero
Nula
Noola

One
Jedna
Yednah

Two
Dvě
Dvyeh

Three
Tři
Trzhee

Four
Čtyři
Chteerzee

Five
Pět
Pyet

Six
Šest
Shest

Seven
Sedm
Sehdoom

Eight
Osm
Ohsoom

Nine
Devět
Devyet

Ten
Deset
Dessett

Eleven
Jedenáct
Yeddenahtst

Twelve
Dvanáct
Dvannahtsts

Thirteen
Třináct
Trzeenahtst

Fourteen
Čtrnáct
Chrtrnahtst

Fifteen
Patnáct
Patnahtst

Sixteen
Šestnáct
Shestnahtst

Seventeen
Sedmnáct
Sedoomnahtst

Eighteen
Osmnáct
Osoomnahtst

Nineteen
Devatenáct
Devattenahtst

Twenty
Dvacet
Dvatseht

Twenty-one
Jednadvacet
Yednadvatseht

Twenty-two
Dvádvacet
Dvahdvatseht

Thirty
Třicet
Trzheetseht

Forty
Čtyřicet
Chtyrzheetseht

Fifty
Padesát
Padehsaht

Sixty
Šedesát
Shedesaht

Seventy
Sedmdesát
Sedoomdesaht

Eighty
Osmdesát
Osoomdesaht

Ninety
Devadesát
Devahdesáht

One hundred
Sto
Stoh

Five hundred
Pět set
Pyet sett

One thousand
Tisíc
Tyiseets

One million
Milión
Milioh

Time

What time is it?
Kolik je hodin?
Kollick yeh hodyin?

It is ...
Je ...
Yeh ...

9.00
devět
devyet

9.05
je devět hodin a pět minut
yeh devyet hodyin ah pyet meenoot

9.15
je čtvrt na deset
yeh chtvert nah dessett

9.20
je devět hodin dvacet minut
yeh devyet hodyin a dvatsett meenoot

9.30
je půl desáté
yeh pool desahteh

9.35
je devět třicet pět
yeh devyet trzitsett pyet

C
Z
E
C
H

9.40
je za dvacet minut deset
yeh za dvatsett meenoot dessett

9.45
je třičtvrtě na deset
yeh trzichtrvtye nah dessett

9.50
je za deset minut deset
yeh zah dessett meenoot dessett

9.55
je za pět minut deset
yeh za pyet meenoot dessett

12.00/Midday/Midnight
dvanáct hodin/poledne/půlnoc
dvanahtst hodyin/polledneh/poolnots

Money

I would like to change these traveller's cheques/this currency
Rád/Ráda bych vyměnil/vyměnila tyto cestovní šeky/tuto měnu
Rahd/Rahdah bykh veemnyeneel/veemnyeneela teetoh tsestovnee shekyh/tutoh mnyenoo

How much commission do you charge? (What is the service charge?)
Kolik účtujete jako komisi?
Kollick oochtuyete yacko commeesee?

Can I obtain money with my Mastercard?
Můžu dostat peníze s Mastercard?
Moozhoo dostatt peneezeh s Mastercard?

Where is the nearest ATM?
Kde je nejbližší bankomat?
Gdeh yeh neyblishee bahnkomaht?

My name is ... Some money has been wired to here for me to collect
Jmenuji se ... Byly mi sem zaslány nějaké peníze na vyzvednutí
Ymenooyee seh ... Beelee mee sem zahsslahnee nyeyahkeh penyeezeh na veezvednootyee

Airport

Excuse me, where is the check-in desk for ... airline?
Prosím vás, kde je přepážka pro odbavování zavazadel?
Proseem vahs, gdeh yeh przepazhkah proh odbavovahnee zavazzadell?

What is the boarding gate for my flight?
Kterým východem mám jít k mému letadlu?
Gderzhim weekhodem maam yeet k mehmu lettadlu?

What is the time of my flight?
Kdy letí moje letadlo?
Gdee letyee moye lettadloh?

How long is the delay likely to be?
Jak dlouho bude asi zpoždění trvat?
Yack dlowhoh boodeh assee zpozhdeyene trvatt?

Where is the duty-free shop?
Kde je prodejna bezcelného
zboží?
*Gdeh yeh proddeynah beztselnehoh
zbozhee?*

**Which way is the luggage
reclaim?**
Kde se vyzvedávají zavazadla?
*Gdeh seh vyzvedahvayee
zahvazzadlah?*

**I have lost my luggage.
Please can you help?**
Ztratil/ztratila jsem zavazadla.
Můžete mi, prosím, pomoci?
*Ztrattill/ztrattillah ysemm
zavazzadlah. Moozheteh mee,
proseem, pomotsee?*

I am flying to ...
Letím do ...
Letteem doh ...

**Where is the bus for the city
centre?**
Odkud jede autobus do středu
města?
*Odkood yedeh awtoboos doh
strzeddoo myestah?*

Trains and Boats

**Where is the ticket
office?/Where is the
information desk?**
Kde je pokladna?/Kde jsou
informace?
*Gdeh yeh pockladnah?/Gdeh ysow
informatse?*

**Which platform does the
train/speedboat/ferry to ...
depart from?**
Z kterého nástupiště odjíždí

vlak/motorový člun/převozní
loď do ...?
*Z kterehhoh nahstupishtye
odyeezhdee vlack/mottorovee
chloon/przevoznee lodye doh ...?*

Where is platform ...?
Kde je nástupiště ...?
Gdeh yeh nahstupishtye ...?

**When is the next train/boat
to...?**
Kdy jede další vlak/loď do ...?
*Gdee yedeh dalshee vlack/lod
doh ...?*

**Is there a later train/boat
to...?**
Jede nějaký vlak/nějaká loď
později?
*Yedeh nyeyakee vlack/nyeyakah
lodye pozdyeyee?*

Notices and Signs

Jídelní vůz
Yeedelnee vooz
Buffet (Dining) Car

Autobus
Awtoboos
Bus

Pitná voda/Nepitná voda
*Peetnah voddah/Neppeetnah
voddah*
**Drinking/Non-drinking
water**

Vstup
Vstoop
Entrance

C
Z
E
C
H

81

C Z E C H

Východ
Veekhod
Exit

Nemocnice
Nemmotsnitse
Hospital

Informace
Informatse
Information

Úschovna zavazadel
Ooskhovnah zavazzaddel
**Left Luggage
(Baggage Claim)**

Skříňka na zavazdla
Skrzeenkah nah zavazzadlah
Luggage Lockers

Poštovní úřad
Poshtovnee oorzadd
Post Office

Nástupiště
Nahstupishtye
Platform

Železniční stanice
Zheleznichnee stanyeetseh
Railway (Railroad) Station

Letiště
Letishtye
Airport

Policejní stanice
Politseynee stanitseh
Police Station

Přístav
Przeestav
Port

Restaurace
Restawratse
Restaurant

Kuřáci/Nekuřáci
Koorzahtsi/Nekoorzahtsi
Smoking/Non Smoking

Telefón
Telefohn
Telephone

Pokladna
Pokladnah
Ticket Office

Přepážka
Przepahzhkah
Check-in desk

Cestovní řád
Tsestovnee rzahd
Timetable (Schedule)

Záchody
Zahkhodee
Toilets (Restroom)

Dámy/Páni
Dahmee/Pahnee
Ladies/Gentlemen

Podzemní dráha
Podzemnee drahhah
Underground (Subway)

Čekárna
Checkahrnah
Waiting Room

Buying a Ticket

I would like a first-class/second-class/third-class single (one-way)/return (round-trip) ticket to....
Prosím jízenku první třídy/druhé třídy/třetí třídy pouze tam/zpáteční (okružní) do ...
Prosseem yeezdenkoo prvnee trzeedee/drooheh trzeedee/trzetee trzeedee powzh tamm/zpahtechne (ockroozhnee) doh …

Is it an express (fast) train/bus?
Je to rychlín/rychlíkový autobus?
Yeh toh reekhleen/reekhleekovy awtoboos?

Is my rail pass valid on this train/ferry/bus?
Platí moje jízdenka na vlak pro tento vlak/přepravní loď/autobus?
Platee moyeh yeezdenkah nah vlack proh tentoh vlack/przepravnee lodye/awtoboos?

I would like an aisle/window seat
Přeji si sedadlo u chodbičky/u okna
Przeyee see seddahdloh u chodbichtse/oo ocknah

No smoking/smoking please
V kuřáckém/nekuřáckém oddělení prosím
V koorzahtsem/neckoorzahtsem oddelenee proseem

We would like to sit together
Přejeme si místa vedle sebe
Przeyeme see meestenkoo vedleh sebbeh

I would like to make a seat reservation
Přeji si rezervovat místenku
Przeyee see rezzervovatt meestenkoo

I would like to reserve a couchette/sleeper for one person/two people/my family
Přeji si rezervovat lehátko/místo v lehátkovém voze pro jednu osobu/dvě osoby/pro rodinu
Przeyee see rezzervovatt lehahtkoh/meestoh v lehahtkovehm vozzeh proh yednoo ossobboo /dvye ossobbee/proh rodyeenoo

I would like to reserve a cabin
Přeji si rezervovat kabinu
Przeyee see rezzervovatt kabeenoo

Timetables (Schedules)

Příjezd
Przeeyezd
Arrival

Zastavuje
Zastavooyeh
Calls (Stops)

Jídelní služby
Yeedelnee sloozhbee
Catering Service

Přesednout v
Przsesednowt v
Change at

**C
Z
E
C
H**

Spojení/přes
Spoyenee/przezz
Connection/via

Denně
Dennye
Daily

Každých čtyřicet minut
Kazdeekh chteerzitset meenoot
Every 40 minutes

První třída
Prvnee trzeedah
First Class

Každou hodinu
Kazdnow hodyinoo
Hourly

Doporučuje Vám obstarat si
místenku
*Doporoochooye Vam obstaratt see
meestenkoo*
**Seat Reservations are
recommended**

Druhá třída
Droohah trzeedah
Second Class

Příplatek
Przeeplateck
Supplement Payable

Luggage

**How much will it cost to
send (ship) my luggage in
advance?**
Kolik stojí poslat dopředu
zavazadla?
*Kollick stoyee poslatt doprzedoo
zavazzadlah?*

**Where is the left luggage
(baggage claim) office?**
Kde je úschovna zavazadel?
Gdeh yeh ooskhovnah zavazzadell?

**What time do you
open/close?**
Kdy je otvíráte/zavíráte?
Gdee yeh otveerahte/zaveerahte?

**Where are the luggage
trolleys (carts)?**
Kde jsou vozíky na zavazadla?
*Gdeh ysow vozeekee nah
zavazzadlah?*

Where are the lockers?
Kde jsou skříňky?
Gdeh ysow skrzeenkee?

I have lost my locker key
Ztratil/ztratila jsem klíč od
skříňky
*Ztrattill/ztrattillah ysemm kleech
ohd skrzeenkee*

On Board

Is this seat free?
Je toto místo volné?
Yeh tottoh meestoh volneh?

**Excuse me, you are sitting in
my reserved seat**
Promiňte, ale sedíte na místě

které jsem si rezervoval
*Promminyteh, alleh sedeeteh nah
meestye ktehreh ysehm see
rezzervovall*

Which station is this?
Jak se jmenuje tato zastávka?
Yak se ymenuyhe tattoh zastahvkah?

**What time is this train/bus/
ferry/flight due to arrive/
depart?**
V kolik hodin tenhle
vlak/tenhle autobus/tahle
loď/tohle letadlo
přijíždí/odjíždí?
*Fkollick hodyin tenhleh vluck/tenhleh
aootohbuhs/tahhleh lodye/tohhleh
lehtadloh przhiyeezhdyee/
odyeezhdyee?*

Customs and Passports

Pasy, prosím!
Passe, prosseem!
Passports please!

**I have nothing/wine/spirits
(alcohol)/tobacco to declare**
Nemám nic k procelní/víno/
lihoviny/cigarety
*Nemmahm nits k protslenee/
veenoh/leehohveenee/tsigarettee*

**I will be staying for ... days/
weeks/months.**
Zůstanu zde ... dnů/týdnů/
měsíců
*Zoostanoo zdeh ... dnoo/teednoo/
myeseetsoo*

Travelling with Children

**Do you have a high chair/
baby-sitting service/cot?**
Máte vysokou židli pro
děti/služby baby-sitting/
dětskou postýlku?
*Mahteh veesockow zhidlee proh
dyetee/sloozhbee baby-sitting/
dyetskow posteelkoo?*

**Where is the nursery/
playroom?**
Kde jsou jesle/dětská
klubovna?
*Gdeh ysow yesleh/dyetskah
kloobovnah?*

**Where can I warm the baby's
bottle?**
Kde mohu ohřát lahvičku pro
miminko?
*Gdeh mohoo ohrzaht lahvichkoo
proh meemeenkoh?*

Asking the Way

**Excuse me, do you speak
English?**
Promiňte, mluvíte anglicky?
*Prommeenyteh, mlooveeteh
anglitskee?*

**Excuse me, can you help me
please?**
Promiňte, potřebuji poradit?
Promminyteh, potrzebujee porradyit?

**Where is the Tourist
Information Office?**
Kde je turistická informační
kancelář?
*Gdeh yeh tooristitskah
informachnee kantselarz?*

85

Excuse me, is this the right way to ...?
Promiňte, jedu/jdu správně do ...?
Prommeenyteh, yeddoo/ydoo sprahvnye doh …?

... the cathedral/the tourist office/the castle/the old town
... katedrála/turistická kancelář/hrad/staré město
... katteddrahlah/tooristitskah kantselahrz/hradd/starreh myestoh

Can you tell me the way to the railway station/bus station/taxi rank/city centre/beach?
Můžete mi, prosím, ukázat kudy se jede/jde na železniční nadraží/autobusové nádraží/kde jsou taxíky/střed města/na pláž?
Moozheteh mee, proseem, ookahzatt koodee seh yeddeh nah zhelezneechnee nahdrazhee/awtoboosoveh nahdrazhee/gdeh ysow taxeekee/strzedd myestah/nah plazh?

První/druhá/do leva/do prava/přímo
Prvnee/droohah/doh levah/doh pravah/przeemoh
First/second/left/right/straight ahead

Na rohu/u dopravních světel
Nah rohhoo/oo dopravneekh svyetell
At the corner/at the traffic lights

Where is the nearest police station/post office?
Kde je nejbližší policejní stanice/poštovní úřad?
Gdeh yeh neybleezhshee poleetseynee staneetseh/poshtovnee oorzadd?

Is it near/far?
Je to blízko/daleko?
Yeh toh bleezkoh/dalekoh?

Do I need to take a taxi/catch a bus?
Musím jet taxíkem/autobusem?
Mooseem yet taxeekemm/awtoboosemm?

Do you have a map?
Máte mapu?
Mahteh mappoo?

Can you point to it on my map?
Můžete mi to ukázat na mapě?
Moozheteh mee toh ookahzatt nah mappye?

Thank you for your help
Děkuji za vaši ochotu
Dyekooyi zah vashee okhotoo

How do I reach the motorway/main road?
Jak se dostanu na dálnici/na hlavní silnici?
Yack seh dostanoo nah dahlneetsee/nah hlavnee silnitsee?

I think I have taken the wrong turning
Myslím, že jsem špatně zahnul
Meesleem, zheh ysemm shpatne zahnul

I am looking for this address
Hledám tuto adresu
Hledahm tootoh adressoo

I am looking for the ... hotel
Hledám hotel ...
Hledahm hottell ...

How far is it to ... from here?
Jak je to odtud daleko do ...?
Yack yeh toh odtood dalleckoh doh ...?

Jeďte přímo rovně ... kilometrů
Yedyteh przeemoh rovnye ... kilometroo
Carry straight on for ... kilometres

Na první křižovatce zabočte do prava/do leva
Nah prvnee krzeezhovattse zabochteh doh pravvah/doh levvah
Take the next turning on the right/left

Na příští křižovatce/u dopravních světel zabočte do prava/do leva
Nah przeeshtee krzeezhovvatse/oo dopravneekh svyetell zabochteh doh pravvah/doh levvah.
Turn right/left at the next crossroads/traffic lights

Jedete/Jdete špatně
Yedetteh/Ydetteh shpatnye
You are going in the wrong direction

Where is the cathedral/church/museum/pharmacy?
Kde je katedrála/kostel/museum/lékárna?
Gdeh yeh kattedrahlah/kostell/mooseum/lehkahrna?

How much is the admission/ entrance charge?
Kolik stojí lístky/vstupné?
Kollick stoyee leestkyh/vstoopneh?

Is there a discount for children/students/senior citizens?
Je sleva pro děti/studenty/dříve narozené?
Yeh slevah proh dyetee/stoodenteeh/drzeeveh narozeneh?

What time does the next guided tour (in English) start?
Kdy půjde příští skupina s průvodcem (mluvícím anglicky)?
Gdee poojdeh przeeshtee skoopeenah s proovodtsem (mlooveetseem anglitskee)?

One/two adults/children please.
Jeden/dva dospělí/děti prosím
Yeddenn/dvah dospyelee/dyetee proseem

May I take photographs here?
Smím tady fotografovat?
Smeem taddee phottographovatt?

At the Tourist Office

Do you have a map of the town/area?
Máte mapu města?
Mahteh mappoo myestah?

Do you have a list of accommodation?
Máte seznam ubytování?
Mahteh seznamm oobeetovahnee?

C
Z
E
H

Can I reserve accommodation?
Mohu si rezervovat ubytování?
Mohoo see rezzervovatt oobeetovahnee?

ACCOMMODATION

Hotels

I have a reservation in the name of ...
Mám rezervaci na jméno
Mahm rezervatsi nah ymehnoh ...

I wrote to/faxed/telephoned you last month/last week
Poslal/poslala jsem dopis/fax/ telefonoval/telefonovala jsem minulý měsíc/minulý týden
Poslall/poslallah ysemm doppees/ fahx/telephonnovall/telephonnovallah ysemm meenoolee myeseets/ meenoolee teedenn

Do you have any rooms free?
Máte volné pokoje?
Mahteh volneh pockoyeh?

I would like to reserve a single/double room with/ without bath/shower
Rád/Ráda bych si rezervoval/ rezervovala jednolůžkový/ dvoulůžkový pokoj s/bez koupelny/sprchy
Rahd/Rahdah beek see rezzervo- vall/rezzervoalla yednolloozhkovee/ dvowloozhkovee pockoy s/bez kowpelnee/sprkhee

I would like bed/breakfast/ (room and) full board
Přeji si lůžko se snídaní/ (pokoj) s plnou penzí
Przeyee see loozhkoh seh sneeda- nee/(pockoy) s plnow penzee

How much is it per night?
Koliks tojí pokoj na den?
Kollick stoyee pockoy nah denn?

Is breakfast included?
Zahrnuje to snídani?
Zahrnooye toh sneedanye?

Do you have any cheaper rooms?
Máte nějaké lacinější pokoje?
Mahteh nyeyakeh latsinyeyshee pockoyeh?

I would like to see/take the room
Rád/Ráda bych se na pokoj podívala
Rahd/Rahdah beek seh nah pockoy podeevallah

I would like to stay for ... nights
Zůstanu ... dnů
Zoostanoo ... dnoo

The shower/light/tap/hot water doesn't work
Sprcha/světlo/voda/horká voda nefunguje
Sperkha/svyetloh/voddah nephoongooye

At what time/where is breakfast served?
Kdy/kde se podává snídaně?
Gdee/gdeh seh podahvah sneedanye?

What time do I have to check out?
Kdy musím pokoj uvolnit?
Gdee mooseem pockoy oovolneet?

Can I have the key to room number ... ?
Přeji si klíč pokoje číslo ...?
Przeyee see kleech pockoyeh cheesloh ...?

My room number is ...
Můj pokoj má číslo ...
Mooy pockoy mah cheesloh ...

My room is not satisfactory/ not clean enough/too noisy. Please can I change rooms?
Nejsem spokojený/spokojená s Pokojem, není dost čistý/je slyšet hluk. Je možné změnit pokoj?
Neysemm spockoyenee/spockoyenah s pockoyemm, nennee dostyi cheesteh/je sleeshet hluk. Yeh mozhneh zmnyeneet pockoy?

Where is the bathroom?
Kde je koupelna?
Gdeh yeh kowpelnah?

Do you have a safe for valuables?
Máte trezor pro cennosti?
Mahteh trezohr proh tsenostee?

Is there a laundry/do you wash clothes?
Je tady prádelna/perete prádlo?
Yeh tadee prahdelnah/pereteh prahdloh?

I would like an air-conditioned room
Přeji si pokoj s klimatizací
Przeyee see pockoy s climatizatsee

Do you accept traveller's cheques/credit cards?
Berete cestovní šeky/ kreditní karty?
Berretteh tsestovnee checkee/ creditnee cartee?

May I have the bill please?
Můžu platit, prosím?
Moozhoo plateet, proseem?

Excuse me, I think there may be a mistake in this bill
Promiňte, myslím že v účtu je chyba
Prommeenyteh, meesleem zhe oochtu yeh khybah

How much is a dormitory bed per night?
Kolik stojí postel ve společné noclehárně na jednu noc?
Kollick stoyee postell veh spollechneh notslehahrnye nah yednoo nots?

I am/am not an HI member.
Jsem/Nejsem členem HI
Ysemm/Neysemm chlenemm Hah Ee

May I use my own sleeping bag?
Mohu použít vlastní spací pytel?
Mohoo powzheet vlastnee spatsee peetell?

What time do you lock the doors at night?
Kdy v noci zamykáte?
Gdee v notsee zammeekahteh?

C Z E C H

Camping

May I camp for the night/two nights?
Můžu tady kampovat jednu noc/dvě noci?
Moozhoo tadee kampovatt yednoo nots/dveh notsee?

Where can I pitch my tent?
Kde si můžu postavit stan?
Gdeh see moozhoo postavitt stann?

How much does it cost for one night/week?
Kolik to stojí na jednu noc/na jeden týden?
Kollick toh stoyee nah yednoo nots/nah yedenn teedenn?

Where are the washing facilities?
Kde je umývárna?
Gdeh yeh oomeevahrnah?

Is there a restaurant/supermarket/swimming pool on site/nearby?
Je tady/nebo blízko restaurace/supermarket/plovárna?
Yeh taddee/neboh bleezkoh restaurratse/suppermarkett/plovvahrnah?

Do you have a safety deposit box?
Máte skřínku na úschovu cenin?
Mahteh skrzeenkoo nah ooskhovoo tseneen?

EATING AND DRINKING

Cafés and Bars

I would like a cup of/two cups of/another coffee/tea
Přeji si šálek/dva šálky/ještě jednu kávu/ještě jeden čaj
Przeyee see shahleck/dvah shalckee/yeshtye yednoo kahvoo/yeshtye yedenn chay

With/without milk/sugar
S/bez mléka/cukru
S/bezz mlehkah/tsoocroo.

I would like a bottle/glass/two glasses of mineral water/red wine/white wine, please.
Přeji si láhev/sklenici/dvě sklenice minerální vody/červeného vína/bílého vína, prosím
Przeyee see lahhev/sclenitsee/dvye sclenitseh mineerahlnee vodee/chervenehhoh veenah/beelehhoh veenah, prosseem

I would like a beer/two beers, please
Přeji si pivo/dvě piva, prosím
Przeyee see peevoh/dvyeh peevah, prosseem

Please may I have some ice?
Mohu dostat prosím led?
Mohhoo dostatt prosseem ledd?

Do you have any matches/cigarettes/cigars?
Máte zápalky/cigarety/doutníky?
Mahteh zahpalkee/tsigaretee/dowtneekee?

**C
Z
E
C
H**

Restaurants

**Can you recommend a good/
cheap restaurant in this area?**
Můžete doporučit dobrou/
lacinou restauraci v okolí?
*Moozheteh dopporoocheet dobrow
/latsinow restawratsee v ockolee?*

**I would like a table for ...
people**
Přeji si stůl pro ... osob.
Przheyee see stool proh ... ossobb

**Do you have a non-smoking
area?**
Máte místnost pro nekuřáky?
*Mahte meestnost proh
nekoorzahkee?*

Waiter/waitress!
Čisniku/čisnice!
Cheeshneekoo/cheeshnitse!

**Excuse me, please may
we order?**
Promiňte, přejeme si
objednat?
*Promminyteh, przeyemmeh see
obyednatt?*

**Do you have a set menu/
children's menu/wine list
in English?**
Máte menu dne/dětské
menu/vinný lístek v angličtině?
*Mahteh menoo dneh/dyetskeh
menuh/veenee leesteck v
anglichtinye?*

**Do you have any vegetarian
dishes?**
Máte vegetariánská jídla?
Mahteh vegetahriahnskah yeedlah?

**Do you have any local
specialities?**
Máte nějaké místní speciality?
*Mahteh nyeyakeh meestnee
spetsialeetee?*

Are vegetables included?
Zahrnuje to zeleninu?
Zahrnooye toh zelleneenoo?

**Could I have it well-cooked/
medium/rare, please?**
Přeji si to dobře propečené/
středně/jen lehce propečené,
prosím
*Przeyee see toh dobrzeh
proppecheneh/strzednyeh/yen
lehtseh proppecheneh, prosseem*

**What does this dish consist
of?**
Co je v tomto pokrmu?
Tsoh yeh v tomtoh pokrmoo?

**I am a vegetarian. Does this
contain meat?**
Jsem vegetarián. Není v tom
maso?
*Ysem vegetahreeahn. Nenyee ftom
mahsoh?*

**I do not eat nuts/dairy
products meat/fish**
Nejím ořechy/mléčné výrobky/
maso/ryby
*Neyeem orzekhee/mlehchneh
veerobkee/massoh/reebee*

Not (very) spicy please
Ne (příliš) ostré, prosím
Neh (przeelish) ostreh, prosseem

**I would like the set menu
please**
Přeji si menu dne, prosím
Przeyee see menoo dneh, prosseem

C Z E C H

We have not been served yet
Jeste jsme nebyli obslouženi
Yeshtye smeh nehbyhli obslowzhenih

Please bring a plate/knife/ fork
Přineste mi, prosím talíř/nůž/ vidličku
Przeenesteh mee proseem tahleerz/noozh/veedleetchkoo

Excuse me, this is not what I ordered
Promiňte, toto jsem si neobjednal/neobjednala
Promminyteh, tottoh ysemm see neobyednall/neobyednallah

May I have some/more bread/water/coffee/tea?
Mohu dostat chleba/vodu/ kávu/čaj?
Mohoo dostatt khlebah/voddoo/ kahvoo/chay?

May I have the bill please?
Přeji si platit, prosím?
Przeyee see platteet, prosseem?

Does this bill include service?
Zahrnuje účet spropitné?
Zahrnooye oochet spropitneh?

Do you accept traveller's cheques/Mastercard/ US dollars?
Berete cestovní šeky/ Mastercard/americké dolary?
Berreteh tsestovnee shekee/ Mastercard/amerritskeh dollaree?

Can I have a receipt please?
Můžete mě dát stvrzenku, prosím vás?
Moozheteh mne daht stverzenkoo, prosseem vahs?

Where is the toilet (restroom) please?
Kde je záchod, prosím vás?
Gdeh yeh zakhod, prosseem vahs?

On the Menu

Snídaně/Oběd/Večeře
Snyeedahnyeh/Obyed/Vetchehrzeh
Breakfast/Lunch/Dinner

První chod	Polévky
Prvnee khodd	*Polehvkee*
First Courses	**Soups**
Hlavní chod	Rybí jídla
Hlavnee khodd	*Reebee yeedlah*
Main Courses	**Fish Dishes**
Chod s masem	Hovězí
Khodd s massemm	*Hovyehzee*
Meat Dishes	**Beef**
Steak	Vepřové
Steak	*Veprzoveh*
Steak	**Pork**
Telecí	Kuře
Teletsee	*Koorzeh*
Veal	**Chicken**
Jehněčí	Šunka
Yehnyetchee	*Shoonka*
Lamb	**Ham**

Jídla pro vegetariány
Yeedlah proh vegetariyahnee
Vegetarian Dishes

Zelenina	Hranolky
Zelenyeena	*Hrahnolkee*
Vegetables	**Chips (french fries)**

92

Vařené/opékané brambory/
bramborová kaše
*Varzeneh/opehkahneh brahm-
boree/brahmborovah kahsheh*
**Boiled/sauté/mashed
potatoes**

Rýže
Reezheh
Rice

Sýry
Seeri
Cheese

Zákusky
Zackooskee
Desserts

Zmrzlina
Zmrzleena
Ice cream

Cukrovinky
Tsookroveenkee
Pastries

Ovoce
Ovotseh
Fruit

Chléb
Khleb
Bread

Rohlíky
Rolleekee
Rolls

Toast
Toast
Toast

Máslo
Mahsloh
Butter

Sůl/pepř
Sooll/peprz
Salt/pepper

Cukr
Tsookrr
Sugar

Speciality
Spetsialitee
Specialities

Místní speciality
Meestnyee spetseeyahleetee
Local specialities

Jídelní lístek
*Yeedelnyee
leesteck*
Set Menu

Vinný lístek
Veeny leesteck
Wine list

Červená vína
*Chehrvenah
veena*
Red wines

Bílá vína
Beelah veena
White wines

Růžová vína
Roozhovah veena
Rosé wines

Šumivá vína
Shoomeevah veena
Sparkling wines

Pivo
Peevoh
Beer

Lahvové pivo/točené pivo
*Lahvoveh peevoh/totcheneh
peevoh*
**Bottled beer/draught (draft)
beer**

Nealkoholické nápoje
Nehalcoholeetskeh nahpoyeh
Non-alcoholic drinks

Minerální voda
Meenerahlnyee vohda
Mineral water

Ovocné džusy
Ovotsneh joosee
Fruit juices

Pomerančový džus
Pomehrahntchovee joos
Orange juice

Limonáda
Leemonahda
Lemonade

Led
Led
Ice

**C
Z
E
C
H**

Bílá káva/černá káva/espreso
*Beelah kahva/chehrnah
kahva/espresso*
**White coffee/black
coffee/espresso coffee**

Čaj s mlékem/s citrónem
Chy smlehkem/stseetronem
Tea with milk/with lemon

Čokoláda   Mléko
Chocolahda   *Mlehkoh*
Chocolate (drink)   **Milk**

Občerstvení/Lehká jídla
Obchehrstvenyee/Lehhkah yeedla
Snacks/Light meals

Saláty   Sendviče
Sahlahtee   *Sendvicheh*
Salads   **Sandwiches**

Vejce   Klobása
Veytseh   *Klohbahsa*
Eggs   **Sausage**

Vařená/smažená/
míchaná vejce
*Vahrzenah/smahzenah/
meekhahnah veytseh*
**Boiled /fried/
scrambled eggs**

Typical Local Dishes

Knedlíky
Knedleekee
Dumplings

Vepřová pečeně
Veprzovah pechenye
Roast pork

Kyselé zelí
Keeseleh zellee
**Sauerkraut (Pickled
cabbage)**

Svíčková na smetaně
Sveechkovah nah smettanye
Beef in soured cream

Řízky
Rzheezkee
Escalopes

Bramborový salát
Bramborovee salaht
Potato salad

Dort
Dort
Gateaux

Koblihy
Kobleehee
Doughnuts

Ovocné knedlíky
Ovotsneh knedleekee
Fruit dumplings

Chlebíčky
Khlebeechkee
Open sandwiches

GETTING AROUND

Public Transport

Where is the bus stop/coach stop/nearest metro (subway) station?
Kde je autobusová/autokarová zastávka/nejbližší stanice metra?
Gdeh yeh awtoboosovah/ awtocarovo zastahvkah/ neyblizhshee stannitse metrah?

When is the next/last bus to ...?
Kdy jede příští/poslední autobus do ...?
Gdee yedeh przheeshtee/poslednee awtoboos doh ...?

How much is the fare to the city centre (downtown)/ railway station/airport?
Kolik stojí jízdenka do středu města/na železniční nádraží/na letiště?
Kollick stoyee yeezdenkah doh strzedoo myestah/nah zhelleznich- nee nahdrazhee/nah letishtye?

Will you tell me when to get off?
Řeknete mně kde mám vytoupit?
Rzeknyetme mnye gdeh mahm veestowpeet?

Does this bus go to ...?
Jede tento autobus do ...?
Yedeh tentoh awtoboos doh ...?

Which number bus goes to ...?
Které číslo autobusu jede do ...?
Kterreh cheesloh awtoboosoo yeddeh doh ...?

May I have a single (one-way)/return (round-trip)/day ticket/book of tickets?
Prosím jízdenku jen tam/ zpáteční/jízdenku na celý den/ blok jízdenek?
Prosseem yeezdenkoo yenn tamm/ zpahtechnee/yeezdenkoo nah tselee denn/blohkh yeezdeneck?

Taxis (Taxíky)

I would like to go to ... How much will it cost?
Rád bych jel/jela do ...
Kolik to bude stát?
*Rahd beekh yell/yellah doh ...
Kollick toh boodeh staht?*

Please may I stop here?
Zastavíte mi zde, prosím?
Zastaveeteh mee zdeh, prosseem?

I would like to order a taxi today/tomorrow at 2pm to go from ... to ...
Rád bych/Ráda bych si objednala taxíka na dnes/na zítra ve dvě hodiny odpoledne na cestu z ... do ...
Rahd beekh/Rahdah beekh see obyednallah taxeekah nah dness/nah zeetrah veh dvye hoddee- nee odpoledneh nah tsestoo z ... doh ...

Entertainment

Can you recommend a good bar/nightclub?
Můžete doporučit dobrý bar/ nightclub?
Moozheteh dopporoochit dobree bar/nightclub?

C
Z
E
C
H

Do you know what is on at the cinema (playing at the movies)/on at the theatre at the moment?
Víte co zrovna dávají v kině/divadle?
Veeteh tsoh zrovnah dahvayee v kinye/dyivadleh?

I would like to book (purchase) ... tickets for the matinee/evening performance on Monday
Rád/Ráda bych si zamluvil/zamluvila ... lístků na odpolední/večerní představení v pondělí
Rahd/Rahdah beekh see zamlooveel/zamlooveellah ... leestkoo nah odpolednee/vechernee przedstavenee v pondyelee

What time does the film/performance start?
Kdy začíná film/představení?
Gdee zacheenah film/przeds tavenee?

Post

How much will it cost to send a letter/postcard/this package to Britain/Ireland/America/Canada/Australia/New Zealand?
Kolik stojí poslat dopis/pohlednici/tento balík do Británie/do Irska/do Ameriky/do Kanady/do Australie/na Nový Zealand?
Kollick stoyee posllat doppees/pohlednitsee/tentoh baleeck doh Britahniye/doh Irskah/doh

Americee/do Canadee/nah Novee Zehland?

I would like one stamp/two stamps
Prosím jednu známku/dvě známky
Prosseem yednoo znahmkoo/dvye znahmkee

I'd like ... stamps for postcards to send abroad, please.
Prosím ... známky pro pohlednice do zahraničí.
Prosseem ... znahmkee proh pohlednitseh doh zahraneechee.

Phones

I would like to make a telephone call/reverse the charges to (make a collect call to) ...
Rád/Ráda bych zatelefonoval/zatelefonovala na účet volaného do ...
Rahd/Rahdah beekh zattelephonnovall/zattelephonnovallah nah oochett vollannehoh do ...

Which coins do I need for the telephone?
Jaké mince na telefon potřebuji?
Yackeh meentseh nah telephonn potrzebooyee?

The line is engaged (busy)
Linka je obsazená
Linkah yeh obsazenah

The number is ...
To číslo je ...
Toh cheesloh yeh ...

Hello, this is ...
Haló, tady je ...
Halloh, taddee yeh ...

Please may I speak to ...?
Mohu, prosím, mluvit s ...?
Mohhoo prosseem, mlooveet s ...?

He/she is not in at the moment. Please can you call back?
Momentálně tady není. Můžete zavolat později, prosím vás?
Mommentalne taddee nenee. Moozhetteh zavollat pozdyeyee, prosseem vahs?

SHOPPING

Shops

Knihkupectví/Papírnické zboží
Knyihkoopetstvee/papeernitskeh zbozhee
Bookshop/Stationery

Klenotnictví/Dárky
Klenottnitstvee/Dahrkee
Jeweller/Gifts

Obuv
Obboof
Shoes

Železářské zboží
Zhelezahrzskeh zbozhee
Hardware

Kadeřník
Kaderzhneek
Hairdresser

Pekárna
Peckahrnah
Baker

Supermarket
Suppermarkett
Supermarket

Fotografický obchod
Photographitskee obkhod
Photo Shop

Cestovní kancelář
Tsestovnee kantselarz
Travel Agent

Drogerie
Droggerriye
Pharmacy

In the Shops

What time do the shops open/close?
Kdy obchody otevírají/zavírají?
Gdee obkhodee ohteveerahyee/zavveerayee?

Where is the nearest market?
Kde je nejbližší trh?
Gdeh yeh neyblizhshee terh?

Can you show me the one in the window/this one?
Můžete mi ukázat to ve výkladě/tento?
Moozheteh mee oocahzatt toh veh veeklayde/tentoh?

Can I try this on?
Můžu si to vyzkoušet?
Moozhoo see toh veezkowshett?

97

**C
Z
E
C
H**

What size is this?
Jaká je to velikost?
Yackah yeh toh velleeckost?

**This is too large/too
small/too expensive.
Do you have any others?**
To je příliš velké/příliš
malé/příliš drahé. Máte jiné?
*Toh yeh przeeleesh velckeh/
przeelish malleh/przeellish draheh.
Mahteh yeeneh?*

My size is ...
Moje velikost je ...
Moye vellickost yeh ...

**Where is the changing room/
children's/cosmetic/
ladieswear/menswear/food
department?**
Kde jsou převlékárny/dětské/
kosmetika/dámské/pánské/
potravinářské oddělení?
*Gdeh ysow przevlehkahrnee/
dyetskeh/cosmetitskeh/dahmskeh/
potraveenarzskeh oddyelenee?*

**I would like ... a quarter of a
kilo/half a kilo/a kilo of
bread/butter/ham/this fruit**
Prosím čtvrt kila/půl kila/kilo
chleba/másla/šunky/tohoto
ovoce ...
*Prosseem ... chtvert killah/pool
killah/killoh khlebah/mahslah/
shoonkee/tohotoh ovotse ...*

**Do you have a carrier
(shopping) bag?**
Máte sáček?
Mateh sahcheck?

How much is this?
Kolik je to?
Kollick yeh toh?

I'll take this one, thank you
Koupím toto, děkuji pěkně
Kowpeem totoh, dekujee pyeknye

**Do you have anything
cheaper/larger/smaller/of
better quality?**
Máte něco lacinějšího/většího/
menšího/nebo lepší kvality?
*Mahteh nyetso latsinyejsheehoh/
vyetsheehoh/mensheehoh/neboh
lepshee kvalitee?*

**I would like a film/to develop
this film for this camera**
Přeji si film/vyvolt film z této
kamery
*Przeyee see film/veevolt film z tehto
kameree*

**I would like some batteries,
the same size as this old one**
Potřebuji baterie, stejné
velikosti jako je tato stará
*Potrzebuyee batteriye, steyneh
vellickostyee yackoh yeh tatoh starah*

**Would you mind wrapping
this for me, please?**
Mužete mi to, prosím vás,
zabalit?
*Moozhete mee toh, prosseem vahs,
zabbaleet?*

**Sorry, but you seem to have
given me the wrong change**
Promiňte, ale vrátil jste mně
peníze špatně
*Promminyteh, aleh vrahtil ysteh
mnye penneezeh shpatnye*

MOTORING

Car Hire (Rental)

I have ordered (rented) a car in the name of ...
Objednal jsem si (najal) auto na jméno ...
Obyednall ysemm see (nayall) awtoh nah ymehnoh ...

How much does it cost to hire (rent) a car for one day/two days/a week?
Kolik stojí pronajmutí auta na jeden den/na dva dny/na týden?
Kollick stoyee pronnaymootee awtah nah yeddenn denn/dvah dnee/na teedenn?

Is the tank already full of petrol (gas)?
Je nádrž plná benzínu?
Yeh nahdrzh plnah benzeenoo?

Is insurance and tax included? How much is the deposit?
Zahrnuje to pojištění a daně? Kolik je záloha?
Zahrnooyeh toh poyeeshtyenee ah danye? Kollick yeh zahlohah?

By what time must I return the car?
Kdy musím auto vrátit?
Gdee mooseem awtoh vrahtyit?

I would like a small/large/family/sports car with a radio/cassette
Přeji si menší/větší/rodinné/sportovní auto s radiem/kazetou
Przeyee see menshee/vyetshee/roddeeneh/sportovnee awtoh s raddiyem/cazzettow.

Do you have a road map?
Máte silniční mapu?
Mahteh seelnichnee mappoo?

Parking

How long can I park here?
Jak dlouho tady můžu parkovat?
Yack dlowhoh taddee moozhoo parkovatt?

Is there a car park near here?
Je tady blízko parkoviště?
Yeh taddee bleezckoh parcovishtye?

At what time does this car park close?
Kdy se toto parkoviště zavírá?
Gdee seh tottoh parcovishtyeh zaveerah?

Signs and Notices

Jednosměrka
Yednosmnyerkah
One way

Zákaz vjezdu
Zahkaz vyezdoo
No entry

Zákaz parkování
Zahkaz parckovahnee
No Parking

Objížďka
Obyeezhdykah
Detour (Diversion)

C
Z
E
C
H

C Z E C H

Stop
Stop
Stop

Dejte přednost
Deyteh przednost
Give Way (Yield)

Kluzká vozovka
Kloozkah vozzovkah
Slippery Road

Zákaz předjíždění
Zahkaz przedyeezhdyenee
No overtaking

Nebezpečí !
Nebbezpechee !
Danger!

At the Filling Station
(U Benzínové Pumpy)

**Unleaded (lead free)/
standard/ premium/diesel**
Metylizovaný benzín
(bezolovnatý)/standardní/
premium/diesel
*Meteelizovannee benzeen
(bezzollovnatee)/standardnee/
deezl)*

Fill the tank please
Naplňte nádrž, prosím
Naplnyteh nahdrzh, prosseem

Do you have a road map?
Máte silniční mapu?
Mahteh seelnichnee mappoo?

How much is the car wash?
Kolik stojí umytí auta?
Kollick stoyee oomeeteey awtah?

Breakdowns

I've had a breakdown at ...
Porouchalo se mi auto u ...
Porrowkhaloh seh mee awtoh oo ...

**I am a member of the ...
[motoring organisation]**
Jsem členem ...
Ysem chlenem ...

**I am on the road from ...
to ...**
Jsem na silnici od ... do ...
Ysemm nah seelnitsee odd ... doh ...

**I can't move the car. Can you
send a tow-truck?**
Auto je nepojízdné. Můžete
poslat vlečný vůz?
*Awtoh yeh nepoyeezdneh.
Moozheteh poslatt vlechnee vooz?*

I have a flat tyre
Pneumatika je splasklá
Pneoomaticah yeh splasklah

**The windscreen (windshield)
has smashed/cracked**
Čelní sklo je rozbité/prasklé
*Chelnee skloh yeh rozbeeteh/
praskleh*

**There is something wrong
with the engine/brakes/
lights/steering/gearbox/
clutch/exhaust**
Je porouchaný motor/jsou
porouchané brzdy/světla/
řízení/převodovka/spojka/
výfuk
*Yeh porrowkhanee mottor/ysow
poroukhaneh brzdee/svyetlah/
rzeezenee/przevodovkah/spoyckah/
veefook*

100

It's overheating
Je přehřátý
Yeh przehrzahtee

It won't start
Nemohu nastartovat
Nemmohoo nastartovatt

Where can I get it repaired?
Kde to mohu nechat opravit?
Gdeh toh mohhoo nekhat opraveet?

Can you take me there?
Můžete mě tam vzít?
Moozhetteh mnye tamm vzeet?

Will it take long to fix?
Bude oprava trvat dlouho?
Boodeh opravah trvatt dlowhoh?

How much will it cost?
Kolik to bude stát?
Kollick toh boodeh staht?

**Please can you pick me up/
give me a lift?**
Prosím vás, můžete mě
vyzvednout? Vzít sebou?
*Prosseem vahs, moozhetteh mnye
veezvednowt? Vzeet sebow?*

**Can you help me?
There has been an accident.**
Můžete mi pomoct?
Stala se nehoda
*Moozheteh me pomotst?
Stahlah seh nahodah*

**Please call the police/an
ambulance**
Zavolejte, prosím,
policii/záchranku

*Zahvohlehyteh, prohseem,
pohlitssiyi/zahhrankooh.*

Is anyone hurt?
Je někdo zraněný?
Jeh nyekdoh zranyehnee?

**I'm sorry, I didn't see the
sign**
Omlouvám se, neviděl jsem
značku
*Omlowvahm seh, neveedyel ysemm
znachkoo*

**Must I pay a fine?
How much?**
Musím zaplatit pokutu?
Kolik je to?
*Mooseem zaplatteet pockootoo?
Kollick yeh toh?*

Ukažte mi dokumenty
Ookazhteh mee docoomentee
Show me your documents

**Do you have anything for a
stomach ache/headache/sore
throat/toothache?**
Máte něco na bolení žaludku/
bolení hlavy/bolení v krku/
bolení zubů?
*Mahteh nyetsoh nah bollenee
zhaloodkoo/bollenee hlavee/bolenee
v kerkoo/bollenee zooboo?*

**I need something for
diarrhoea/constipation/a
cold/a cough/insect bites/
sunburn/travel (motion)
sickness**
Potřebuji něco proti průjmu/

proti zácpě/proti rýmě/proti
kašli/na pokousání hmyzem/
na spálení sluncem/na
nevolnost při cestování
*Potrzebooyee nyetso prottee
prooymoo/prottee zatspye/prottee
reemnye/prottee kashlee/nah
pockowsahnee hmeezemm/nah
spahlenee sloontsemm/nah
nevolnost przee tsestovahnee*

How much/how many do I take?
Jaké množství/kolik jich mám brát?
Yakeh mnozhstvee/kollick yeekh mahm braht?

I am taking anti-malaria tablets/these pills
Beru tablety proti malárii/tyto tablety
Beroo tabletee prottee malahriyee/teetoh tabletee

How often do I take it/them?
Jak často to mám brát?
Yack chastoh toh mahm braht?

I am/he is/she is taking this medication
Já beru/on bere/ona bere tento lék
Yah berroo/onn berreh/onnah berreh tentoh lehk

How much does it cost?
Kolik to stojí?
Kollick toh stoyee?

Can you recommend a good doctor/dentist?
Můžete doporučit dobrého doktora/zubaře?
Moozheteh dopporoochit dobrehoh doktorah/zoobarze?

Is it suitable for children?
Je to vhodné pro děti?
Yeh toh vhodneh proh dyetee?

Doctor (Doktor)

I have a pain here/in my arm/leg/chest/stomach
Tady mě to bolí/bolí mě ruka/noha/na prsou/žaludek
Taddee mnye toh bollee/bollee mnye roockah/nohah/nah prsow/zhaloodeck

Please call a doctor, this is an emergency
Prosím zavolejte doktora, je to náhlý případ
Prosseem zavoleyteh doctorrah, yeh toh nahlee przeepadd

I would like to make an appointment to see the doctor.
Rád/Ráda bych se objednala u doktora
Rahd/Rahdah beekh seh obyednall /obyednallah oo doctorrah

I am diabetic/pregnant
Jsem diabetik/jsem těhotná
Ysemm deeyabeteeck/ysemm tyehotnah

I need a prescription for ...
Potřebuji lékařský předpis na ...
Potoeboojee lehkarzskee przedpees nah ...

Can you give me something to ease the pain?
Můžete mi dát něco aby se mi ulevilo?
Moozheteh mee daht nyetso abee seh mee ooleveeloh?

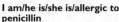
I am/he is/she is/allergic to penicillin
Jsem/on je/ona je/alergický/
alergická na penicilín
Ysemm/onn yeh/onnah yeh/
alerghitskee/alergitskah nah
pennitsileen

Bolí toto?
Bollee tottoh?
Does this hurt?

Musíte/on musí/ona musí do
nemocnice
Mooseeteh/onn moosee/ohnah
moosee doh nemmotsnitseh
**You must/he must/she must
go to hospital**

Berte tyto jednou/dvakrát/
třikrát denně
Berteh teetoh yednow/dvakraht/
trzeekraht dennye
**Take these once/twice/three
times a day**

**I am/he is/she is taking this
medication**
Já beru/on bere/ona bere
tento lék
Yah berroo/onn berreh/onnah berreh
tentoh lehk

I have medical insurance
Mám zdravotní pojištění
Mahm zdrahvotnee poyeeshtyenee

Dentist (Zubař)

**I have toothache/my filling
has come out**
Bolí mě zub/vypadla mi
plomba
Bollee mnye zoob/veepadlah mee
plombah

**I do/do not want to have an
injection first**
Přeji si/nepřeji si nejdříve
injekci
Przeyee see/neprzeyee see
neydrzeeveh inyektsee

Help!
Pomoc!
Pommots!

Fire!
Hoří!
Horzee!

Stop!
Stop!
Stop!

**Call an ambulance/a doctor/
the police/the fire brigade!**
Zavolejte sanitku/doktora/
policii/požárníky!
Zavoleyteh sanitkoo/doktorah/
politsiyee/pozhahrneeckee!

**Please may I use a
telephone?**
Mohu prosím Vás použít
telefon?
Mohu prohseem Vahs powzheet
tehlehfohn?

**I have had my traveller's
cheques/credit cards/
handbag/rucksack/luggage/
wallet/passport/mobile phone
stolen**
Byly mi ukradeny cestovní
šeky/kreditní karty/kabelka/
ruksak/zavazadla/peněženka/
pas/mobilní telefon
Beelee mee oockradenee tsestovnee

C
Z
E
C
H

C
Z
E
C
H

chekee/creditnee cartee/kabbelkah/
rooksuck/zavazzadlah/
pennyezhenkah/pahss/mobeelnyee
telefon

**May I please have a copy of
the report for my insurance
claim?**
Mohl bych dostat kopii
protokolu pro svou pojišťovnu?
*Mohl beekh dostaht kopeeyee
protokoloo proh swoe
poyeeshtyovnoo?*

**Can you help me, I have lost
my daughter/son/my
companion(s)?**
Prosím vas, pomozte mi, ztrati-
la se mi dcera/syn/společník/
společníci?
*Prosseem vahs, pommozteh mee,
ztrattilah seh mee tserah/seen/
spollechneeck/spollechneetseh?*

**Please go away/leave me
alone**
Běžte pryč/nechte mně být
Byezhteh preech/nekhteh mnye beet

I'm sorry
Promiňte
Prommeenyteh

**I want to contact the British/
American/Canadian/Irish/
Australian/New Zealand/
South African Consulate**
Rád/Ráda bych se spojil/
spojila s Britským/Americkým/
Kanadským/Irským/
Australským/Novozelandským/
Jihoafrickým Konzulátem
*Rahd/Rahdah beekh seh spoyeel/
spoyeelah s Britskeem/
Ameritskeem/Kanadskeem/
Eerskeem/Novvozehlandskeem/*

Yeehoafritskeem Konzullahtem

**I'm/we're/he is/she is/they
are/ill/lost/injured**
Jsem/jsme/on je/ona je/oni
jsou/nemocní/ztracení/
poranění
*Ysemm/ysmeh/onn yeh/onnah
yeh/onnee ysow/nemmotsnee/
ztratsenee/porannyenee*

104

ESTONIAN

E
S
T
O
N
I
A
N

INTRODUCTION

Written Estonian uses the Latin alphabet and is related to Finnish and Hungarian. However, many words in Estonian have a German, Russian or Swedish origin and may be easily recognised if you are slightly familiar with one of these languages.

Addresses for Travel and Tourist Information

Australia: *Baltic Connections,* Suite 3, 11–13 The Centre, Forestville, NSW 2087. Tel: (2) 9975 2355. Fax: (2) 9451 6446.

Canada: *Estonian Consulate,* 958 Broadview Avenue #202, Toronto, Ontario M4K 2R6. Tel: (416) 461 0764. Fax: (416) 461 0448.

UK: *Estonian Embassy,* 16 Hyde Park Gate, London SW7 5DG. Tel: (020) 7589 3428. Fax: (020) 7589 3430.

USA: *Estonian Consulate General,* 600 Third Ave, 26th Floor, New York, NY 10016. Tel: (212) 883 0636. Fax: (212) 883 0648.

Official tourism website: www.visitestonia.com

Estonia Facts

CAPITAL: Tallinn

CURRENCY: Kroon (abbreviated as EEK). 1 EEK=100 sents.

OPENING HOURS: Shops: from 0900–1800 on weekdays, and 0930–1500 Saturdays.

TELEPHONES: To dial in, +372. Outgoing, 00 + the country code. Emergency 112; Fire, 01 (in Tallinn, 001); Police, 02 (in Tallinn, 002); Ambulance, 03 (in Tallinn, 003).

PUBLIC HOLIDAYS: 1 Jan; 24 Feb; 1 May; 23, 24 June; 20 Aug; 24–26 Dec.

Technical Language Hints

- Estonian has no 'articles' ('a' or 'the'). There is no use of gender for nouns.
- There are only four tenses: one present and three past. Estonians do not believe in the future! e.g.: Ma (mina) loen (I read/I am reading/etc)
  Ma (mina) lugesin (I read (past)/I was reading/I have read/etc)
  Ma (mina) loen (I will read/etc)
- In each of the tenses, the ending of a verb depends on number and person.
- Word order is flexible: there is always a best word order for a sentence, which is used in this book, but usually the sentence will be understandable even if the word order is wrong.
- 'To' and 'from' are shown by word endings, and do not have a specific word.

In original Estonian words, stress is always placed upon the first syllable: ˋkangelane (hero), ˋvanemad (parents) (but two-stemmed words may be stressed on the second syllable): teada ˋanne (message); üksm ˋeel (agreement).

ESSENTIALS

Alphabet and Pronunciation

	Name	Pronounced	
A a	ah	long a as in father
Ä ä	a	short a as in bad
B b	beh	like English b
D d	deh	like English d
E e	eh	like e in bed
F f	ef	like English f
G g	geh	like English hard g as in go
H h	ha	like h in heal or ch in Scottish loch
I i	ee	ee like i in machine
J j	yot	like y in yes
K k	kah	like English k
L l	ell	like English l
M m	emm	like English m
N n	enn	like English n

	Name	Pronounced
O o	o	like o in hot
Õ õ	oh	oh similar to o in home
Ö ö	er	er sound like the o in word
P p	peh	like English p
R r	err	rolled r, as in Scottish English
S s	ess	like s in sit
Š š	sha	sh as in shy
T t	teh	like English t
U u	oo	u in as put
Ü ü	ew	ew like the vowel sound in hewn but with no preceding y sound
V v	veh	like English v
Z z	zeh	z as in zoo
Ž ž	zheh	zh like the s in pleasure

ESTONIAN

Basic Words and Phrases

Yes	**No**
Jah (Jaa)	Ei
Yah (Ya-a)	*Ey*

Please	**Thank you**
Palun	Tänan (Aitäh)
Pah-loon	*Ta-nan(Ay-tahh)*

Hello
Tere, tervist
Teh-reh/ter-vist

Goodbye
Nägemiseni (head aega)
Na-ghe-mi-seh-ni (he-a-d a-e-ga)

Excuse me	**Sorry**
Vabandage	Andke andeks
Vah-ban-da-gheh	*And-keh and-eks*

That's O.K.	**Perhaps**
See sobib	Võib-olla
See sobib	*Voibolla*

How	**When**
Kuidas	Millal
Kuy-das	*Mil-lal*

What	**Why**
Mis	Miks
Mis	*Miks*

Who
Kes
Kes

Here	**There**
Siin	Seal
Seen	*Se-al*

I don't understand
Ma ei saa aru
Mah ey sa-a ahroo

I don't speak Estonian
Ma ei oska eesti keelt
Mah ey os-kah e-es-ti ke-elt

Do you speak English?
Kas te räägite/oskate inglise keelt?
Kas te rae-aeghi-te/os-ka-te ing-li-seh ke-elt?

Can you please write it down?
Palun kirjutage üles
Pah-loon kir-yu-ta-ghe ew-les

Please can you speak more slowly?
Palun rääkige aeglasemalt?
Pah-loon ra-aki-ghe a-egh-la-se-mahlt?

Greetings

Good morning/Good afternoon/Good evening/Good night
Tere hommikust/tere päevast/tere õhtust/head ööd
Teh-reh hom-mi-kuhst/teh-reh pa-vahst/teh-reh oh-tuhst/he-ad urd

Pleased to meet you
Väga rõõmustav tuttavaks saada
Va-ga ro-omuhs-tav tut-tah-vahks sa-a-da

How are you?
Kuidas läheb?
Kuy-das laheb?

I am well, thank you. And you?
Tänan, hästi. Ja teil?
Ta-nan, has-ti. Ya teyl?

My name is ...
Minu nimi on...
Minu nimi on...

**This is my friend/boyfriend/
girlfriend/husband/wife/
brother/sister**
See on minu sõber/noormees/
tütarlaps/abikaasa/abikaasa/
vend/õde
*Se-e on mi-nu so-ber/no-or-me-es/
tyu-tar-laps/abi-ka-as-ah/
abi-ka-as-ah/vend/ode*

Where are you travelling to?
Kuhu te sõidate?
Ku-hu teh soy-da-teh?

I am/we are going to...
Mina sõidan/meie sõidame ...
Mi-na soy-dan/mey-e soy-da-meh ...

**How long are you travelling
for?**
Kui kaua te reisite?
Kuy kau-a teh rey-si-teh?

Where do you come from?
Kus kohast te olete?
Kus ko-hast teh oh-leh-teh

**I am/we are from...
Australia/Britain/Canada/
America**
Mina olen/meie oleme ...
Austraaliast/Inglismaalt/
Kanadast/Ameerikast
*Mi-nah ohlen/mey-e oh-leh-meh ...
A-u-s-tra-a-li-ast/Ing-lis-ma-alt/
Kah-na-a-dast/A-me-e-ri-kast*

We are on holiday
Me oleme puhkusel
Meh oh-leh-meh puhh-ku-sel

This is our first visit here
Me oleme siin esimest korda
*Meh oh-leh-meh seen esi-mest
kor-da*

How old are you?
Kui vana te olete/sa oled?
*Kuy vah-nah teh oh-leh-teh/sah
oled?*

I am ... years old
Olen ... aastane
Ol-en ... a-as-tahneh

**I am a business person/
doctor/journalist/manual
worker/administrator/
scientist/student/teacher**
Olen ettevõtja/arst/ajakirjanik/
tööline/haldustöötaja/
teadlane/üliõpilane/õpetaja
*Ol-en ette-voityah/arst/aya-kir-ya-nik/
taw-li-neh/haldoo-staw-aw-tah-yah/
teh-ahd-lah-neh/ew-li-opi-lah-neh/
ope-taya*

**I am waiting for my
husband/wife/boyfriend/
girlfriend**
Ma ootan oma abikaasat/oma
abikaasat/oma noormeest/oma
neidu
*Mah awtan omah abi-ka-as-at/
omah abi-ka-as-at/omah
no-or-me-est/ omah neydu*

**Would you like a cigarette?
May I have a cigarette?**
Kas soovite sigaretti? Kas te ei
annaks mulle sigaretti?
*Kas saw-vi-teh si-ga-ret-ti? Kas teh
ey an-naks mul-le si-ga-ret-ti?*

Do you mind if I smoke?
Kas tohib suitsetada?
Kas toh-ib suyt-seh-tah-da?

E
S
T
O
N
I
A
N

E S T O N I A N

Do you have a light?
Kas ma tohin tuld paluda?
Kas -mah toh-hin toold pah-luh-da?

Days

Monday
Esmaspäev
Es-mas-pa-ev

Tuesday
Teisipäev
Tey-si-pa-ev

Wednesday
Kolmapäev
Kol-mah-pa-ev

Thursday
Neljapäev
Nel-ya-pa-ev

Friday
Reede
Re-e-deh

Saturday
Laupäev
Lau-pa-ev

Sunday
Pühapäev
Puh-ha-pa-ev

Morning/Afternoon/Evening/Night
Hommik/Pärastlõuna/Õhtu/Öö
Hom-mik/Parastlohnah/Oh-tuh/Ur

Yesterday/Today/Tomorrow
Eile/Täna/Homme
Ey-leh/Tanah/Hom-meh

Numbers

Zero
Null
Null

One
Üks
Yuks

Two
Kaks
Kaks

Three
Kolm
Kolm

Four
Neli
Neh-li

Five
Viis
Vees

Six
Kuus
Coos

Seven
Seitse
Seyt-seh

Eight
Kaheksa
Kah-hek-sah

Nine
Üheksa
Yu-hek-sah

Ten
Kümme
Kym-meh

Eleven
Üksteist
Yuks teyst

Twelve
Kaksteist
Kaks-teyst

Thirteen
Kolmteist
Kolm-teyst

Fourteen
Neliteist
Neh-lih-teyst

Fifteen
Viisteist
Vees-teyst

Sixteen
Kuusteist
Coos-teyst

Seventeen
Seitseteist
Seyt-seh-teyst

Eighteen
Kaheksateist
Kah-hek-sah-teys

Nineteen
Üheksateist
Yu-hek-sah-teyst

Twenty
Kakskümmend
Kaks-kyum-mend

Twenty-one
Kakskümmend üks
Kaks-kyum-mend uks

Twenty-two
Kakskümmend kaks
Kaks-kyum-mend kaks

Thirty
Kolmkümmend
Kolm-kyum-mend

Forty
Nelikümmend
Neh-lik-kyum-mend

Fifty
Viiskümmend
Vees-kyum-mend

Sixty
Kuuskümmend
Coos-kyum-mend

Seventy
Seitsekümmend
Seyt-seh-kyum-mend

Eighty
Kaheksakümmend
Kah-hek-sah-kyum-mend

Ninety
Üheksakümmend
Yuh-hek-sah-kym-mend

One hundred   **Five hundred**
Sada   Viissada
Sah-da   *Vees-sah-da*

One thousand   **One million**
Tuhat   Miljon
Tuh-hat   *Mil-yon*

Time

What time is it?
Mis kell on?
Mis kell on?

It is ...
Kell on ...
Kell on ...

9.00
Täpselt üheksa
Tap-selt yuh-hek-sah

9.05
Viis minutit üheksa läbi
Vees mi-nuh-tit yuh-hek-sah la-bi

9.15
Viisteist minutit üheksa läbi
(veerand kümme)
Vees-teyst mi-nuh-tit yuh-hek-sah la-bi (ve-e-rand kyum-meh)

9.20
Üheksa kakskümmend
Yuh-hek-sah kaks-kyum-mend

9.30
Pool kümme
Pawl kyum-meh

9.35
Üheksa kolmkümmend viis
Yuh-hek-sah kolm-kyum-mend vees

9.40
Kahekümne minuti pärast kümme
Kah-hek-kyum-neh mi-nuh-ty pa-rast kyum-meh

9.45
Kolmveerand kümme
Kolm-ve-er-and kyum-meh

9.50
Kümne minuti pärast kümme
Kyum-neh mi-nuh-ty pa-rast kyum-meh

9.55
Viie minuti pärast kümme
Vee-eh mi-nuh-ty pa-rast kyum-meh

12.00/Midday/Midnight
Kaksteist/Keskpäev/Kesköö
Kaks-teyst/Kesk-pa-ev/kKesk-o-o

111

E S T O N I A N

Money

I would like to change these traveller's cheques/this currency
Ma tahaksin neid reisitšekke/
seda raha vahetada
*Mah tah-hak-sin need
rey-si-tseh-kkeh/sehdah raha
vahe-tah-dah*

How much commission do you charge? (What is the service charge?)
Kui suur on teie komisjonitasu?
*Kuy su-ur on teyeh
koh-mis-yo-nitahsu?*

Can I obtain money with my Mastercard?
Kas ma saan oma
MasterCardiga raha välja võtta?
Kas mah sa-an omah Master-kar-di-ga rah-hah val-ya voyt-tah?

Where is the nearest ATM?
Kus on lähim
sularahaautomaat?
Kus on lahim sularahah-owtomaht?

My name is ... Some money has been wired to here for me to collect
Minu nimi on ... Mulle on siia
tehtud rahaülekanne
*Minu nimi on ... Mulle on siya
tehtud raha-ewlekanne*

Airport

Excuse me, where is the check-in desk for ... ?
Vabandage, kus on ...
registreerimine?
*Vab-and-agheh kyus on ...
reh-kist-re-e-ri-mi-ne?*

What is the boarding gate for my flight?
Mitmendast väravat väljub
minu reis?
*Mitmendast varahvahst valyub
mi-nuh reys?*

What is the boarding time for my flight?
Mis kell algab minu reisile
pealeminek?
*Mis kell al-gab mi-nuh rey-si-leh
pe-aleh-mi-nek?*

How long is the delay likely to be?
Kui palju reis hilineb?
Kuy pal-yuh reys hih-li-neb?

Where is the duty-free shop?
Kus asub duty free pood?
Kyus a-sup duty free po-od?

Which way is the luggage reclaim?
Kus on pagasi kättesaamine?
Kyus on pa-kah-si kattesah-ah-mi-neh?

I have lost my luggage. Please can you help?
Ma kaotasin oma pagasi. Palun,
kas te saate mind aidata?
*Mah kao-tah-sin oh-mah pah-ga-si.
Pah-loon, kas teh sa-a-teh*

mihnd ay-da-tah?

I am flying to ...
Ma lendan ... sse.
Mah len-dan ... se.

Where is the bus for the city centre (downtown)?
Kust läheb buss kesklinna?
Kyust la-heb puss kesk-lin-nah?

Trains and Boats

Where is the ticket office/information desk?
Kus asub piletikassa/ informatsioon?
Kyus a-sup pi-leh-ti-kas-sah/ in-for-mat-sio-on?

Which platform does the train/speedboat/ferry to ... depart from?
Milliselt platvormilt väljub rong/kaater/praam ...-sse?
Milliselt plat-for-milt val-yub rong/ ka-ater/pra-am ...-seh?

Where is platform ...?
Kus asub platvorm...?
Kyus a-sup plat-form...?

When is the next train/boat to ..?
Millal väljub järgmine rong/ laev ...-sse?
Mil-lal val-yub yargh-mih-neh rong/la-ev ...-seh?

Is there a later train/boat to ...?
Kas on võimalik sõita ... -sse hilisema rongiga/laevaga?
Kas on voy-mah-lik soy-tah ... -seh hih-li-semah rongeegah/la-evah-gah?

Notices and Signs

Restoranvagun
Rest-o-rahn-vag-uhn
Buffet (Dining) car

Buss (Autobuss)
Puss (auto-puss)
Bus

Joogivesi/Tehniline vesi
Jo-oghi-veh-si/Teh-ni-li-neh veh-si
Drinking/Non-drinking water

Sissepääs
Sis-seh-pa-as
Entrance

Väljapääs
Val-yah-pa-as
Exit

Haigla
Hayg-lah
Hospital

Informatsioon
In-for-mat-si-o-on
Information

Pakkide hoiuruum
Pak-ki-deh hoy-u-room
Left luggage (Baggage claim)

Pakkide hoiukapid
Pak-ki-de hoy-u-kah-pid
Luggage lockers

Postkontor
Pohst-kon-tor
Post office

E S T O N I A N

Platvorm
Plat-form
Platform

Raudteejaam
Rowd-te-eh-ya-am
Railway (Railroad) station

Lennujaam
Len-nuh-jahm
Airport

Politsei
Polit-sey
Police station

Sadam
Sadam
Port

Restoran
Rest-o-rahn
Restaurant

Suitsetajatele/
Mittesuitsetajatele
Suyt-seh-tah-yah-the-leh/
Mit-teh-suyt-seh-tah-yah-the-leh
Smoking/Non-smoking

Telefon
Teleh-fon
Telephone

Kassa (Piletid)
Kas-sah (Pi-leh-tid)
Ticket office

Registreerimine
Regh-ist-re-eri-mi-neh
Check-in desk

Sõiduplaan
Soy-du-pla-an
Timetable (Schedule)

WC (Tualettruum)
Veh-tseh (Tu-a-lett-room)
Toilets (Restrooms)

Naistele/Meestele
Nays-the-leh/me-es-teh-leh
Ladies/Gentlemen

Ooteruum
O-oteh-room
Waiting room

Buying a Ticket

**I would like a single
(one-way)ticket/return
(round-trip) ticket to ...**
Palun mulle üheotsa
pilet/edasi-tagasi pilet ...-sse
*Pa-loon muhl-le ew-he-otsah
pi-let/eda-si - ta-ga-si pi-let ...-seh*

**Is it an express (fast) train/
bus?**
Kas see on ekspressrong/
ekspressbuss?
*Kas seh on ekspress-rong/
ekspress-puss?*

**Is my rail pass valid on this
train/ferry/bus?**
Kas minu pilet kehtib sellel
rongil/praamil/bussil?
*Kas mi-nuh pi-let kehh-tib sel-lel
ron-gil/pra-mil/pussil?*

I would like an aisle/window seat
Ma sooviks kohta vahekäigu ääres/kohta akna juures
Ma so-oviks ko-tah vahek-a-eegoo a-a-res/ko-tah ak-na yu-res

No smoking/smoking please
Mittesuitsetajatele/suitseta-jatele palun
Mit-teh-suyt-seh-tah-yah-teleh/ Suyt-seh-tah-yah-teleh pah-loon

We would like to sit together
Me tahaksime kõrvuti kohti
Meh tah-hak-si-meh kor-vu-ti kohtee

I would like to make a seat reservation
Ma tahaksin tellida koha
Mah tah-hak-sin tel-li-da ko-ha

I would like to reserve a couchette/sleeper for one person/two people/my family
Ma tahaksin tellida koha/kupee magamisvagunis ühele inimesele/kahele inimesele/perekonnale
Mah tah-hak-sin tel-li-da ko-ha/ ku-peh mah-ga-mis-vagh-unis yuh-heleh inni-me-sehleh/ka-heh-leh inni-me-sehleh/peh-reh-kon-nah-leh

I would like to reserve a cabin
Ma tahaksin tellida kajuti
Mah tah-hak-sin tel-li-da kah-yu-ti

Timetable (Schedules)

Saabub
Sa-a-boob
Arrive

Peatub
Pe-a-tuhb
Calls (Stops at)

Restoran
Rest-o-rahn
Catering service

Ümberistumine
Yum-ber-is-tuh-mi-neh
Change at

Ühendus/Läbi (Kaudu)
Yu-hen-dus/la-bi (ka-u-du)
Connection/Via

Iga päev
Yga pa-ev
Daily

Iga neljakümne minuti järel
Yga nel-yah-kyum-neh mi-nuh-ty ya-rel
Every 40 minutes

Esimene klass
Eh-si-meh-neh klass
First class

Iga tund
Yga tuhnd
Hourly

Tellige kohad õigeaegselt
Tel-li-ghe koh-had oy-ghe-a-egh-selt
Seat reservations are recommended

E
S
T
O
N
I
A
N

E S T O N I A N

Teine klass
Tey-neh klass
Second class

Lisatasu
Li-sah-tah-suh
Supplement payable

Luggage

How much will it cost to send (ship) my luggage in advance?
Kui palju maksab minu pagasi ettesaatmine?
Kuy pal-yuh mak-sab mi-nuh pah-ga-si et-teh-sa-at-mi-neh?

Where is the left luggage (baggage claim) office?
Kus asub pakkide hoiuruum?
Kus a-sup pak-ki-deh hoy-u-room?

What time do you open/close?
Mis kell te avate/panete kinni?
Mis kell teh ah-vah-the/pah-neh-teh kin-ni?

Where are the luggage trolleys (carts)?
Kus on pagasikärud?
Kus on pa-ga-si-kah-ruhd?

Where are the lockers?
Kus asuvad pakkide hoiukapid?
Kus a-suvahd pak-ki-de hoy-u-kapeed?

I have lost my locker key
Ma kaotasin hoiukapi võtme
Mah ka-o-tah-sin hoy-u-ka-pi vot-meh

On Board

Is this seat free?
Kas see koht on vaba?
Kas se-eh koht on vah-bah?

Excuse me, you are sitting in my reserved seat
Vabandage, te istute minu kohal
Vah-ban-da-ghe, teh is-tuh-teh mi-nuh koh-al

Which station is this?
Mis jaam see on?
Mis ya-am se-eh on?

What time is this train/bus/ferry/flight due to arrive/depart?
Mis kell see rong/buss/praam/reis saabub/väljub?
Mis kell se-eh rong/puss/pra-am/reys sa-a-buhb/val-yub?

Travelling with Children

Do you have a high chair/babysitting service/cot?
Kas teil on kõrget tooli/lapsehoidjateenust/lapsevoodit?
Kas teyl on kor-gheh to-ol/lap-seh-hoyd-yah te-eh-nuhs/lap-seh-vo-oh-dit?

Where is the nursery/playroom?
Kus asub ema ja lapse tuba/laste mängutuba?
Kus a-sup e-ma ya lap-seh too-bah/las-teh man-kuh-tuh-bah?

Where can I warm the baby's bottle?
Kus ma saan lapse toitu soojendada?
Kus mah sa-an lahp-seh toytu so-o-yen-da-da?

Customs and Passports

Palun esitage passid
Pah-loon eh-si-tah-ke pas-sid
Passports please

I have nothing to declare
Mul ei ole midagi deklareerida
Muhl ey o-leh mi-da-ky dek-la-re-ery-da

I have wine/spirits (alcohol)/ tobacco to declare
Ma tahan deklareerida veini/ alkoholi/tubakat
Mah tah-han dek-lah-re-e-ri-da vey-ni/alko-ho-ly/tyu-bah-kat

I will be staying for ... days/weeks/months
Ma olen selles riigis ... päeva/nädalat/kuud
Ma oh-len sel-les ry-yghis ... pa-e-vah/na-da-lat/kood

SIGHTSEEING

Asking the Way

Excuse me, do you speak English?
Vabandage, kas te oskate inglise keelt?
Vah-ban-da-ghe, kas teh os-kah-teh ing-li-seh ke-elt?

Excuse me, can you help me please?
Vabandage, kas te saaksite mind aidata?
Vah-ban-da-ghe, kas teh sa-ak-si-teh mint ay-da-tah?

Where is the Tourist Information Office?
Kus asub turismiinfopunkt?
Kus a-sup tuh-ris-mi-info-punkt?

Excuse me, is this the right way to ... the old town/tourist information office/church/ castle?
Vabandage, kas ma lähen õigesti ... vanalinna poole/ turismiinfopunkt/kiriku poole/lossi poole?
Vah-ban-da-ghe, kas mah la-hen oy-yes-ti...vah-nah-lin-nah paw-leh/ tu-ris-mi-info-punkt/ki-ri-ku paw-leh/los-si paw-leh?

Can you tell me the way to the railway (railroad) station/bus station/ taxi rank/city centre (downtown)/ beach?
Kuidas minna raudteejaama/ bussijaama/taksopeatusse/kesk linna/(supel)randa?
Kuy-das minnah rowd-te-eh-ya-a-mah/pussy-ya-a-mah/tak-soh-pe-a-tus-seh/kesk-lin-nah/(sup-el-)ran-da?

Pöörake esimesest/teisest/ tänavast vasakule/paremale/ minge otse
Poh-oh-rahkeh eh-si-meh-sest/ tey-sest/tannah-vahst vahsah-ku-leh/pa-re-mahleh/ meengeh otse
First/second/left/right/ straight ahead

Nurga peal/valgusfoori juures
*Nur-ga pe-al/val-gus-fo-o-ri
yu-u-res*
**At the corner/At the traffic
lights**

**Where is the nearest police
station/post office?**
Kus asub lähim politsei-
jaoskond/lähim postkontor?
*Kus a-sup la-him poh-li-tsey-ya-os-
kond/la-him pohst-kon-tor?*

Is it near/far?
Kas see on ligidal/kaugel?
Kas se-eh on on li-ghi-dal/ka-u-ghel?

**Do I need to take a taxi/
catch a bus?**
Kas ma pean võtma takso/
sõitma bussiga?
*Kas mah pe-an vot-mah
tak-soh/soyt-ma pussy-ga?*

Do you have a map?
Kas teil on kaart?
Kas teyl on ka-art?

**Can you point to it on my
map?**
Kas te võite näidata, kus see
on kaardi peal?
*Kas teh voy-teh nay-da-tah, kus se-e
on ka-ar-di pe-al?*

Thank you for your help
Suur tänu abi eest
Su-ur ta-nuh ah-bi e-est

**How do I reach the main
road?**
Kuidas ma saan suurele teele?
*Kuy-das mah sa-an su-u-re-leh
te-e-leh?*

**I think I have taken the
wrong turning**
Ma arvan, et ma pöörasin
valesse tänavasse
*Mah ar-van, et mah po-o-rah-sin
vah-les tannah-vah-seh*

I am looking for this address
Ma otsin seda aadressi
Mah ot-sin seh-da a-ad-res-sy

I am looking for the... hotel
Palun, kus on hotell ...
Pah-loon, kus on hot-tell ...

How far is it to... from here?
Kui kaugel on siit ...?
Kuy ka-u-ghel on seet ...

Minge otse ... kilomeetrit
Ming-eh ot-seh ...kilo-me-et-rit
**Carry straight on for...
kilometres**

Järgmisel ristmikul pöörake
paremale/vasakule
*Jarg-mi-sel rist-mi-kuhl po-o-ra-keh
pah-reh-mah-leh/va-sah-ku-leh*
**Take the next turning on the
right/left**

Pöörake paremale/vasakule
järgmisel ristmikul/valgusfoori
juures
*Po-o-ra-keh pah-reh-mah-leh/
va-sah-ku-leh yargh-mi-sel
rist-mi-kuhl/val-gus-fo-ory you-res*
**Turn right/left at the next
crossroads/traffic lights**

Te lähete (sõidate) vales suunas
*Teh la-heh-teh (soy-da-teh) vah-les
soon-as*
**You are going in the wrong
direction**

Where is the church/ museum/pharmacy?
Kus asub kirik/muuseum/ apteek?
Kus a-sup ki-rik/ mu-u-seh-um/ap-te-ek?

How much is the admission/ entrance charge?
Kui palju maksab sissepääs?
Kuy pal-yuh mak-sap sis-seh-pa-as?

Is there a discount for children/students/senior citizens?
Kas lastele/üliõpilastele/ pensionäridele on soodushind?
Kas las-teh-leh/yu-li-o-pi-las-the-leh/ pen-si-on-a-ry-de-le on saw-duhs-hint?

What time does the next guided tour (in English) start?
Millal algab järgmine ekskursioon (inglise keeles)?
Mil-lal al-gap yarg-mi-neh eks-kur-si-o-on (ing-ly-seh ke-e-les)?

One/two adults/children please
Üks/kaks täiskasvanut/last palun
Yuks/kaks tays-kas-va-nuht/last pah-loon

May I take photographs here?
Kas siin tohib pilti teha?
Kas seen to-hib pil-ti teh-ha?

At the Tourist Office

Do you have a map of the town/area?
Kas teil on linna/rajooni kaarti?
Kas teyl on lin-nah/rah-yo-o-ni ka-arti?

Do you have a list of accommodation?
Kas teil on hotellide nimekirja?
Kas teyl on hot-el-li-deh ni-meh-kir-yah?

Can I reserve accommodation?
Kas ma saaksin reserveerida hotelli (tuba)?
Kas mah sa-ak-seen re-ser-ve-e-ri-da hot-el-ly (tuh-bah)?

ACCOMMODATION

Hotels

I have a reservation in the name of ...
Mul on broneeritud tuba ... nimele
Mul on bro-ne-e-ri-tud tuh-bah ... ni-meh-leh

I wrote to you/faxed you/ telephoned you last month/ last week
Ma kirjutasin teile/saatsin teile faksi/helistasin teile eelmisel kuul/eelmisel nädalal
Mah kir-yuh-tah-sin tey-leh/sa-at-sin tey-leh fak-si/heh-lis-tah-sin tey-leh e-el-mih-sel ku-ul/e-el-mi-sel na-da-lal

Do you have any rooms free?
Kas teil on vaba tuba?
Kas teyl on vah-bah tuh-bah?

119

E S T O N I A N

I would like to reserve a single/double room with bath (shower)/without a bath (shower)
Ma tahaksin broneerida üheko-halise/kahekohalise toa vanniga (dušiga)/ilma vannita (dušita)
Mah tah-hak-sin bronneh-eh-ridda uh-heh-koh-hah-li-seh/kah-heh-koh-ha-li-seh to-ah van-ni-kah-(duh-shee-kah)/il-mah van-nih-tah (duh-shee-tah)

I would like bed and breakfast/(room and) full board
Mulle on vaja tuba hommikusöögiga/tuba koos toitlustamisega
Mul-leh on vah-yah to-bah hom-mi-kuh-so-o-gi-kah/to-bah ko-os toyt-lus-tah-mi-seh-kah

How much is it per night?
Kui palju üks öö maksab?
Kuy pal-yuh ewks o-o mak-sab?

Is breakfast included?
Kas hommikusöök on hinna sees?
Kas hom-mi-kuh-so-ok on hin-nah se-es?

Do you have any cheaper rooms?
Kas teil odavamaid tube on?
Kas teyl od-da-vah-mayd tuh-beh on?

I would like to see/take the room
Ma tahaksin vaadata seda tuba/üürida selle toa
Ma tah-hak-sin va-a-da-tah she-dah toobah/yuy-ri-da sel-leh to-ah

I would like to stay for ... nights
Ma tahaksin peatuda teil ... ööd
Mah tah-hak-sin pe-ah-tuh-da teyl ... o-od

The shower/light/tap/hot water doesn't work
Duš/lamp/kraan/kuum vesi ei tööta
Tush/lamp/kra-an/ku-um veh-si ey to-o-tah

At what time/where is breakfast served?
Mis kell/kus on hommikusöök?
Mis kell/kus on hom-mih-kuh-syo-ok?

What time do I have to check out?
Mis kellaks ma pean lahkuma?
Mis kel-laks mah pe-an lah-kuhmah?

Can I have the key to room number ...?
Ma palun ... toa võtit
Ma pah-loon ... to-a vot-it

My room number is...
Minu toa number on...
Mi-nuh to-ah num-ber on...

My room is not satisfactory/not clean enough/too noisy. Please can I change rooms?
Minu tuba ei ole rahuldav/on koristamata/on liiga mürarikas. Palun, kas ma saan teise toa?
Mi-nuh tuh-bah ey oleh rah-hul-dav/on koh-ree-stah-mah-tah/on lee-ga mew-rah-ree-kahs. Pah-loon, kas mah sa-an tey-seh to-ah?

Where is the bathroom?
Kus asub vannituba?
Kus a-sup van-ni-tu-bah?

Do you have a safe for valuables?
Palun, kas teil on seif väärtasjade hoidmiseks?
Pah-loon, kas teyl on seyf va-art-asya-deh hoyd-mees-eks?

Is there a laundry/do you wash clothes?
Kas teil on pesumaja/kas te pesete riideid?
Kas teyl on peh-suh-mah-ya/kas teh peh-seh-teh ri-id-eyd?

I would like an air-conditioned room
Ma tahan üürida tuba õhukonditsioneeriga
Mah tah-han yu-u-ri-da tuh-bah ohu-kon-dit-si-oh-ne-e-ri-ga

Do you accept traveller's cheques/credit cards?
Kas te võtate vastu reisitšekke/krediitkaarte?
Kas te vyuitate vastu rey-si-tsek-ke/kre-di-it-ka-ar-te?

May I have the bill, please?
Palun arve
Pah-loon ar-veh

Excuse me, I think there may be a mistake in this bill
Vabandage, mulle näib, et arves on viga
Vah-ban-da-ghe, mul-leh nayb, et ar-ves on vi-ga

How much is a dormitory bed per night?
Kui palju maksab koht ühiselamus üheks ööks?
Kuy pal-yuh mak-sab koht yu-his-eh-lah-muhs yu-heks o-oks?

I am/am not an HI [Hostelling International] member
Ma olen/ei ole HI liige
Mah oh-len/ey oh-leh Ha-Ee lee-ghe

May I use my own sleeping bag?
Kas ma võin oma magamiskot-ti kasutada?
Kas mah voyn omah mah-ga-mis-kot-ti kah-suh-ta-da?

What time do you lock the doors at night?
Mis kell te õhtul uksed sulgete?
Mis kell teh oh-tul uk-sed sul-gette?

May I camp for the night/two nights?
Kas ma saan siin üks/kaks päeva peatuda?
Kas mah sa-an see-een ewks/kaks pya-eh-vah pea-tu-da?

Where can I pitch my tent?
Kuhu ma võin telgi üles panna?
Kuhu mah voin tel-ghi yu-les pan-nah?

ESTONIAN

E S T O N I A N

How much does it cost for one night/week?
Kui palju see maksab päevas/nädalas?
Kuy pal-yu se-eh mak-sab pyae-vas/na-da-las?

Where are the washing facilities?
Kus asub vannituba (dušš)?
Kus a-sup van-ni-tuh-bah (tush)?

Is there a restaurant/shop/ swimming pool on site/ nearby?
Kas siin/ligidal on restoran/ kauplus/bassein?
Kas si-in/li-gi-dal on res-tor-an/ kaup-luhst/bas-seyn?

Do you have a safety deposit box?
Kas teil on seifi?
Kas teyl on sey-fee?

EATING AND DRINKING

Cafés and Bars

I would like a cup of/two cups of/another coffee/tea
Ma palun ühe tassi/kaks tassi/veel kohvi/teed
Mah pah-loon yu-heh tas-si/ kaks tas-si/ve-el koh-vi/te-ed

With/without milk/sugar
Piimaga/ilma piimata suhkrga/ ilma suhkruta
Pee-mah-ga/il-mah pee-mah-tah suhk-ruh-gah/il-mah suhk-ruh-tah

I would like a bottle/glass/two glasses of mineral water/red wine/white wine, please
Ma palun pudeli/klaasi/kaks klaasi mineraalvett/punast veini/valget veini
Mah pah-loon puh-dely/kla-a-si/kaks kla-a-si/minera-al-vett/puh-nast vey-ni/val-ghet vey-ni

I would like a beer/two beers, please
Palun üks õlu/kaks õlut
Pah-loon yuks oh-lyuh/kaks oh-lyuht

Please may I have some ice?
Palun, kas ma saaksin pisut jääd?
Pah-loon, kas mah sa-aks-een pi-sut ya-ad?

Do you have any matches/ cigarettes/cigars?
Kas teil on tikke/sigarette/ sigareid?
Kas teyl on tik-keh/si-ga-ret-teh/ si-ga-reyd?

Restaurants

Can you recommend a good/cheap restaurant in this area?
Kas te võite soovitada läheduses head/odavat restorani?
Kas teh voy-teh so-o-vih-tah-da la-heh-du-ses he-ad/o-da-vat rest-o-rah-ny?

I would like a table for ... people
Ma soovin lauda ... inimesele
Mah so-ov-in lau-da ... ih-ni-meh-seh-leh

Do you have a non-smoking area?
Kas teil on koht mittesuitseta-jatele?
Kas teyl on koht mit-teh-suyt-seh-tah-yah-teh-leh?

Waiter! Waitress!
Kelner! Ettekandja!
Kelner! Ettekandyah!

Excuse me, please may we order?
Vabandage, kas me võime tellida?
Vah-ban-da-ghe kas meh voy-meh tel-li-da?

Do you have a menu/ children's menu/wine list in English?
Kas teil on menüüd/ lastemenüüd/veinikaarti inglise keeles?
Kas teyl on men-ew-ewd/ lahste-menew-ewd/vey-ni-ka-art ing-li-seh ke-e-les?

Do you have any vegetarian dishes?
Kas teil on taimetoite?
Kas teil on taime-toit-eh?

Do you have any local specialities?
Kas teil on mingeid kohalikke toite?
Kas teyl on ming-eyd koh-ha-lik-keh toy-teh?

Are vegetables included?
Kas see on koos köögiviljadega?
Kas se-eh on ko-os koh-ohgee-vilya-deh-ga?

Please, could I have it well-cooked/medium/rare?
Palun praadige liha tugevalt/ keskmiselt/pooltooreks?
Pah-loon pra-a-di-ghe ly-hah tuh-ghe-valt/kesk-mi-selt/ poh-ohl-toh-oh-reks?

What does this dish consist of?
Millest on see toit valmistatud?
Mil-lest on se-eh toyt val-mis-tah-tud?

I am a vegetarian. Does this contain meat?
Ma olen taimetoitlane. Kas see sisaldab liha?
Ma olen tayme-toytlane. Kahs se-eh see-sahl-dahb liha?

I do not eat nuts/dairy products/meat/fish
Ma ei söö pähkleid/ piimatoite/liha/kala
Mah ey syo-oh pahk-leit/pee-mah-toy-teh/li-hah/kah-la

Not (very) spicy please
Palun, mitte (väga) vürtsitatud
Pah-loon mit-teh (vya-ga) vyurt-si-tah-tud

I would like the set menu please
Ma palun komplektlõuna
Mah pah-loon komp-lekt-low-nah

We have not been served yet
Me ootame ikka veel, et meid teenindataks
Me o-otame ikkah ve-el et meid teenindataks

123

E S T O N I A N

Please bring a plate/knife/ fork
Palun tooge mulle taldrik/ nuga/kahvel
Palun to-ogeh mulle taldrik/nugah/ kahvel

Excuse me, this is not what I ordered
Vabandage, aga ei ole see, mida ma tellisin
Vah-ban-da-ghe, ah-ga ey ohleh se-eh mi-da mah tel-li-sin

May I have some (more) bread/water/coffee/tea?
Palun, kas ma saaksin (veel) leiba/saia/vett/kohvi/teed?
Pah-loon, kas mah sa-akseen (ve-ehl) ley-bah/sayah/vett/koh-vi/te-ed?

May I have the bill please?
Ma palun arve?
Mah pah-loon ar-veh?

Does this bill include service?
Kas arve sisaldab teenindamist?
Kas ar-veh see-sahl-dahb te-nin-da-mi-st?

Do you accept traveller's cheques/Mastercard/ US dollars?
Kas te võtate vastu reisitšekke/ MasterCardi/Ameerika dollareid?
Kas teh vo-tah-teh vastu rey-si-tsek-keh/Mas-ter-ka-ar-ti/A-me-e-ri-kah dol-lah-reyd?

Can I have a receipt please?
Kas te saate anda mulle kviitungi?
Kas teh sa-at-eh an-da mul-leh kvi-it-hun-ghy?

Where is the toilet (restroom) please?
Palun, kus asub WC?
Pah-loon, kus a-sup veh-tseh?

Hommikusöök/Lõunasöök/ Õhtusöök
Hommiku-ser-erk/Louna- ser-erk/ Ohtu- ser-erk
Breakfast/Lunch/Dinner

Eelroad	Supid
E-el-roh-ad	*Sup-id*
First courses	**Soups**

Praed
Pra-ed
Main courses

Kala (Kalatoidud)
Kah-lah (kah-lah-toy-dud)
Fish dishes

Liha (Liharoad)
Li-hah (Li-hah-ro-ad)
Meat dishes

Loomaliha
Lo-omah-lihah
Beef

Praelõik	Sealiha
Prah-el-oyk	*Se-ah-lihah*
Steak	**Pork**

Vasikaliha	Kanaliha
Vasikah-lihah	*Kanah-lihah*
Veal	**Chicken**

E
S
T
O
N
I
A
N

Lambaliha
Lambah-lihah
Lamb

Sink
Sink
Ham

Taimetoidud
Tay-meh-toy-dud
Vegetarian dishes

Köögiviljad
Koh-ohgee-vilyahd
Vegetables

Friikartulid
Free-kartulid
Chips (french fries)

Keedetud kartulid/
Praekartulid/
Kartulipuder
*Ke-edetud kartulid/
Prah-eh-kartulid/Kartuli-puder*
**Boiled/sauté/mashed
potatoes**

Riis
Rees
Rice

Desserdid (magustoidud)
Des-ser-did (ma-gus-toy-dud)
Deserts

Jäätis
Ya-atis
Ice cream

Koogid
Ko-ogid
Cakes

Kondiitritooted
Kondee-trito-oted
Pastries

Puuviljad
Pu-uvilyahd
Fruit

Leib
Le-ib
Bread

Kuklid
Kuklid
Rolls

Röstsai
Rerst-sai
Toast

Või
Voi
Butter

Sool/pipar
So-ol/pipar
Salt/pepper

Suhkur
Suhkur
Sugar

Firmaroad
Fir-mah-ro-ad
Specialities

Kohalik toit
Kohalik to-it
Local specialities

Komplektlõuna
Komplekt-loh-oonah
Set menu

Veinikaart
Veini-kahrt
Wine list

Punased veinid
Punased veinid
Red wines

Valged veinid
Valged veinid
White wines

Rosé veinid
Roze veinid
Rosé wines

Vahuveinid
Vahu-veinid
Sparkling wines

Õlu
Ohlu
Beer

ESTONIAN

Pudeliõlu/vaadiõlu
Pudeli-ohlu/vahdi-ohlu
Bottled beer/draught (draft) beer

Mittealkohoolsed joogid
Mitte alkoho-olsed yoogid
Non-alcoholic drinks

Mineraalvesi
Minerahl-vesi
Mineral water

Puuviljamahlad   Jää
Pu-uvilya-mahlad   *Ya-a*
Fruit juices   **Ice**

Apelsinimahl   Limonaad
Apelseeni-mahl   *Limonahd*
Orange juice   **Lemonade**

Valge kohv/must kohv/espresso
Valge kohv/must kohv/espresso
White coffee/black coffee/espresso coffee

Tee piimaga/sidruniga
Te peemaga/sidrunigah
Tea with milk/with lemon

Šokolaad   Piim
Shokolahd   *Peem*
Chocolate   **Milk**
(drink)

Suupisted/Kerged eined
Su-upisted/Kerged e-ined
Snacks/Light meals

Salatid   Võileivad
Salatid   *Voh-eele-ivad*
Salads   **Sandwiches**

Munad   Vorst
Munahd   *Vorst*
Eggs   **Sausage**

Keedetud munad/praetud munad/munapuder
Kedetud munahd/pra-etud munahd/munah-puder
Boiled/ fried/scrambled eggs

Typical Local Dishes

Ühepajatoit
Yu-he-pah-ya-toyt
Mixed vegetable stew

Leivasupp hapukoore või keedisega
Ley-vah supp hah-pook-o-o-re voy ke-ed-ee-sega
Brown bread soup served with sour cream or jam

Kartulisalat
Kar-tuh-li sah-lat
Potato salad with salted cucumbers, green peas, sausage and soured cream

Mulgikapsad sealihaga
Mul-gi-kap-sat se-ah-li-hah-ga
Cooked soured cabbage with roast pork

Kama
Kah-mah
Ground toasted cereal mix in soured milk

Hakklihakaste
Hakk-li-hah-kas-teh
Sauce of minced meat

GETTING AROUND

Public Transport

Where is the bus stop/nearest tram stop/coach station?
Kus asub bussipeatus/lähim trammipeatus/maaliinide bussijaam?
Kus a-sup pussy-pe-at-hus/lah-him tram-mi-pe-at-hus/ma-ah-lee-ni-de pussy-ya-am?

When is the next/last bus to ...?
Millal läheb järgmine/viimane buss ...-sse?
Mil-lal la-heb yarg-mi-neh/vee-mah-neh puss ...-seh?

How much is the fare to the city centre (downtown)/railway (railroad) station/airport?
Kui palju maksab pilet kesklinna/raudteejaama/lennujaama?
Kui pal-yu mak-sab pi-let kesk-lin-nah/ra-ud-te-e-ya-am-ah/len-nuh-ya-am-ah?

Will you tell me when to get off?
Palun ütelge mulle, kus ma pean maha minema?
Pah-loon yut-el-ghe mul-leh, kus mah pe-an mah-hah mi-neh-mah?

Does this bus go to ...?
Kas see buss läheb ...-sse?
Kas se-eh puss la-heb ...-seh?

Which number bus goes to ...?
Mis number buss läheb ...-sse?
Mis num-ber puss la-heb ...-seh?

May I have one single (one-way)/return (round-trip)/day ticket/book of tickets?
Ma palun üks üheotsa pilet/pilet sinna ja tagasi/talongiraamat.
Mah pah-loon yuks ew-he-ot-sah pi-let/pi-let sin-nah ya tah-ga-si/tah-longi-ra-am-at?

Taxis (Takso)

I would like to go to ... How much will it cost?
Ma tahaksin sõita...-sse. Kui palju see maksab?
Mah ta-hak-sin soy-tah...-she. Kuy pal-yuh se-eh mak-sab?

Please may I stop here?
Palun, peatage siin
Pah-loon pe-a-tah-ge seen

I would like to order a taxi today/tomorrow at 2pm to go from ... to ...
Ma tahaksin tellida takso täna/homme kella kaheks päeval, et sõita ...-st ...-sse
Mah tah-hak-sin tel-li-da tak-soh ta-nah/hom-meh kel-lah kah-heks pya-ev-al, het soy-tah ...-st ...-seh

Entertainment

Can you recommend a good bar/nightclub?
Kas te soovitaksite head baari/ööklubi?
Kas teh so-o-vi-taksit-e he-ad baar-ri/yuo-kluh-bi?

E
S
T
O
N
I
A
N

Do you know what is on at the cinema (playing at the movies)/theatre at the moment?
Kas te teate, mis on täna kinos/teatris?
Kas teh te-a-teh, mis on tah-nah ki-nos/te-at-ris?

I would like to book (purchase) ... tickets for the matinee/evening performance on Monday
Ma tahaksin tellida (osta) ... pileteid päevasele/õhtusele etendusele esmaspäevaks
Mah tah-hak-sin tel-li-da (os-tah) ... pi-leh-tid pa-e-vah-seh-leh/yoh-tu-seh-leh eh-ten-du-seh-leh es-mas-pa-ev-aks

What time does the film/ performance start?
Mis kell film/etendus algab?
Mis kell film/et-en-dus al-gab ?

COMMUNICATIONS

Post

How much will it cost to send a letter/postcard/this package to ... Britain/Ireland/ America/Canada/Australia/ New Zealand?
Kui palju maksab kirja/ postkaardi/selle paki saatmine ... Inglismaale/Iirimaale/Ameerikasse/Kanadasse/Austraaliasse/ Uus-Meremaale?
Kuy pal-yuh mak-sab kir-yah/pohst-kaart/se-eh pakk sah-aht-mee-neh... Ing-lis-ma-a-leh/Ee-ri-ma-a-leh/ A-me-e-ri-kas-seh/Kah-na-ad-as-seh/ A-u-stra-a-li-as-seh/ U-us Meh-reh-ma-a-leh?

I would like one stamp/two stamps
Andke palun üks mark/kaks marki
And-keh pah-loon yuks mark/kaks mar-ki

I'd like ... stamps for postcards to send abroad, please
Palun ... marki postkaartide jaoks välismaale
Pah-loon...mar-ki pohst-ka-ar-ti-deh ya-oks va-lis-ma-a-leh

Phones

I would like to make a telephone call/reverse the charges to (make a collect call to)...
Ma tahaksin tellida kõne/ tellida kõne vastuvõtja arvel ...
Mah tah-hak-sin tel-li-da ko-neh/ tel-li-da ko-neh vas-tuv-oht-yah ar-vel...

Which coins do I need for the telephone?
Missuguseid münte on helistamiseks vaja?
Mis-su-guh-eyd mewnteh on heli-stami-seks vah-yah?

The line is engaged (busy)
Number on kinni
Number on kin-ni

The number is...
Number on ...
Nuhm-ber on...

Hello, this is...
Tere, siin...
Ter-eh, seen...

Hello, please may I speak to..?
Tere, palun kas ma võiksin rääkida ... -ga?
The-reh, pah-loon kas mah voykseen rya-a-ki-da ...-ga?

He/she is not in at the moment. Please can you call back?
Teda praegu ei ole. Palun helistage hiljem
Teh-da pra-e-gu ey ole. Pah-loon heh-lis-ta-ghe hil-yem

SHOPPING

Shops

Raamatud/Kirjatarbed
Ra-a-mah-tud/Keer-yah-tah-bet
Bookshop/Stationery

Ehted/Kingitused
Eh-ted/King-it-uh-set
Jeweller/Gifts

Jalatsid (Kingad)
Yah-lat-sid (King-ad)
Shoes

Tööstuskaubad (Kodutarbed)
Tyo-os-tus-ka-u-bad (Koh-duh-tar-bed)
Hardware

Juuksur
Yu-uk-suhr
Hairdresser

Leib, Sai (Kondiitritooted)
Leyb, Say, (kon-deet-ri-to-o-ted)
Baker

Supermarket
Supermarket
Supermarket

Fototarbed
Fo-to-tar-bed
Photo shop

Reisibüroo
Rey-si-byuro-oh
Travel agent

Apteek
Ap-te-ek
Pharmacy

In the Shops

What time do the shops open/close?
Mis kell kauplused avatakse/suletakse?
Mis kell kah-up-lused ahvah-tahkse/su-letahk-se?

Where is the nearest market?
Kus asub lähim turg?
Kus a-sub la-him turg?

Can you show me the one in the window/this one?
Näidake mulle palun seda vaateaknalt/seda?
Nay-da-keh mul-leh pah-loon seh-da vah-ah-te-ahk-nalt/seh-da?

E
S
T
O
N
I
A
N

Can I try this on?
Kas ma tohin seda proovida?
Kas mah toh-hin seh-da pro-o-vi-da?

What size is this?
Mis number see on?
Mis num-ber se-eh on?

This is too large/too small/too expensive. Do you have any others?
See on liiga suur/liiga väike/liiga kallis. Kas teil on midagi muud?
Se-eh on lee-ga su-ur/lee-ga vay-keh/lee-ga kal-lis. Kas teyl on mi-da-gi mood?

My size is...
Minu number on ...
Mi-nuh nub-ber on ...

Where is the changing room/children's/cosmetic/ladieswear/menswear/food department?
Kus on proovikabiin/lastekaubad/parfümeeria/naiste riided/meeste riided/toidu osakond?
Kus on pro-o-vi-kah-been/las-teh-ka-u-bad/par-fu-me-e-rya/nays-teh ree-ded/me-es-teh ree-ded/toy-du-oh-sah-kond?

I would like ... a quarter of a kilo/half a kilo/a kilo of bread/butter/ham/this fruit
Ma palun ... veerand kilo/pool kilo/üks kilo leiba/või/sinki/neid puuvilju
Mah pah-lun ... ve-e-rand kilo/po-ol kilo/yuks kilo/ley-bah/voyd/sin-ki/neid poo-vil-yuh

How much is this?
Kui palju see maksab?
Kuy pal-yu se-eh mak-sab?

I'll take this one, thank you
Aitäh, ma võtan selle
Ay-tahh, mah vo-tan sel-leh

Do you have a carrier (shopping) bag?
Kas teil on kandekotti on?
Kahs teil kande-kotti on?

Do you have anything cheaper/larger/smaller/of better quality?
Kas teil on midagi odavamat/suuremat/väikse-mat/parema kvaliteediga?
Kas teyl on mi-da-gi oh-da-va-mat/su-u-reh-mat/vayk-seh-mat/pah-reh-mah kvah-li-te-e-di-ga?

I would like a film for this camera/to develop this film
Ma tahaksin osta filmi selle aparaadi jaoks/ilmutada selle filmi
Mah tah-hak-sin os-tah filmy sel-leh ah-pah-ra-a-dih ya-oks/il-muh-ta-da sel-leh filmy

I would like some batteries, the same size as this old one
Ma soovin sama suuri patareisid kui see
Mah so-ov-in sah-mah soory pah-tah-rey-sid kuy se-eh

Would you mind wrapping this for me, please?
Palun pakkige see ära.
Pah-loon pak-ki-ghe se-eh a-rah?

Sorry, but you seem to have given me the wrong change
Andke andeks, aga te vist andsite valesti raha tagasi
And-keh an-deks, ah-ga teh vist andsi-teh vah-les-ti rah-ha tah-ga-s.

MOTORING

Care Hire (Rental)

I have ordered (rented) a car in the name of ...
Ma tellisin (rentisin) auto ... nimele
Mah tel-li-sin (ren-ti-sin) out-oh ... ni-meh-leh

How much does it cost to hire (rent) a car for one day/two days/a week?
Kui palju maksab auto rentimine üheks päevaks/kaheks päevaks/nädalaks?
Kuy pal-yuh mak-sab out-oh ren-ti-mi-neh yuh-ex pa-e-vaks/kah-heks pa-e-vaks/nya-tah-laks?

Is the tank already full of petrol (gas)?
Kas paak on bensiini täis?
Kas pa-ak on ben-see-ni tays?

Is insurance and tax included? How much is the deposit?
Kas see sisaldab kindlustust ja makse? Kui suur on tagatisraha?
Kas seh-eh see-sahl-dahb kin-dlus-tus ya mak-se? Kuy su-ur on tah-ga-tis-rah-hah?

By what time must I return the car?
Mis kell pean ma auto tagasi tooma?
Mis kell pe-an mah out-oh ta-ga-si to-o-mah?

I would like a small/large/family/sports car with a radio/cassette
Ma tahaksin võtta väikese auto/suure auto/perekonnaauto/sportauto raadioga/magnetofoniga
Mah tah-hak-sin vot-tah vay-keh-seh owtoh/soo-reh owtoh/peh-reh-konnah-owtoh/sport-owtoh ra-a-di-ohga/mag-net-of-on-yga

Do you have a road map?
Kas teil on autoteede kaart?
Kas teyl on out-oh-te-e-deh ka-art?

Parking

How long can I park here?
Kui kaua siin tohib seista?
Kuy kau-ah seen toh-hib seys-tah?

Is there a car park near here?
Kas siin ligidal on parkla?
Kas seen li-gi-dal on park-lah?

At what time does this car park close?
Mis kell see parkla suletakse?
Mis kell se-eh park-lah suh-leh-tak-seh?

ESTONIAN

E S T O N I A N

Signs and Notices

Ühesuunaline liiklus
Yu-heh-soon-ah-li-neh leek-lus
One way

Sissesõit keelatud
Sis-seh-soyt ke-e-la-tud
No entry

Parkimine keelatud
Par-ki-mi-ne ke-e-la-tud
No parking

Ümbersõit
Um-ber-soyt
Detour (Diversion)

Stopp!
Stop!
Stop!

Anna teed
An-nah te-ed
Give way (Yield)

Libe tee (Kiilasjää)
Li-beh- te-eh (Kee-las-ya-ah)
Slippery road

Möödasõit keelatud
Mo-o-da-soyt ke-e-la-tud
No overtaking

Oht! (Ettevaatust!)
Oht! (Et-teh-va-a-tust!)
Danger!

At the Filling Station
(Bensiinijaamas)

**Unleaded (lead free)/
standard/premium/diesel**
Pliivaba/standard/kõrge
kvaliteediga/diisel
*Plee-va-ba/stan-dard/ker-geh
kvahl-it-eh-ehd-eegah/dee-sel*

Fill the tank please
Terve paak, palun
Ter-veh pa-ak, pah-loon

Do you have a road map?
Kas teil on autoteede kaart?
Kas teyl on out-oh-te-e-deh ka-art?

How much is the car wash?
Kui palju maksab auto pesemine?
Kuy pal-yuh mak-sab out-oh peh-seh-mi-neh?

Breakdowns

I've had a breakdown at ...
Minu auto läks katki ...
Mi-nuh aut-oh lyaks kat-ki...

**I am a member of the ...
[motoring organisation]**
Ma olen ... liige
Ma olen ... leege

I am on the road from ... to ...
Ma asun teel ... ja ...vahel
Mah ah-suhn te-el ... ya ... va-hel

**I can't move the car. Can you
send a tow-truck?**
Minu auto ei lähe käima. Kas
te ei saadaks puksiirauto?
*Mi-nun out-oh ey lya-heh kay-mah.
Kas teh ey sa-a-daks puhk-seer-out-oh?*

I have a flat tyre
Mul läks kumm katki
Mul laks kuhmm kat-ki

The windscreen (windshield) has smashed/cracked
Minu auto tuuleklaas purunes/pragunes
Mi-nuh out-oh too-leh-kla-as puh-ru-nes/pra-kuh-nes

There is something wrong with the engine/brakes/lights/ steering/gearbox/clutch/ exhaust
Midagi juhtus mootoriga/ piduritega/tuledega/rooliga/ käigukastiga/siduriga/summutiga
Mi-da-gi yuh-tus mo-o-toh-ri-ga/ piduh-ri-the-ga/tuh-leh-deh-ga/ raw-li-ga/kay-gu-kas-ti-ga/si-duh-riga/ suhm-muh-ti-ga

It's overheating
Ta kuumeneb üle
Tah koo-meh-neb yu-leh

It won't start
Ta ei lähe käima
Tah ey la-heh kay-mah

Where can I get it repaired?
Kus oleks võimalik seda parandada?
Kus oh-leks voy-mah-lik seh-da pah-ran-da-da?

Can you take me there?
Kas te saate mind sinna viia?
Kas teh sa-a-teh mihnd sin-nah vee-ah?

Will it take long to fix?
Kui palju aega võtab remont?
Kuy pal-yuh a-e-kah vo-tab reh-mont?

How much will it cost?
Kui palju see maksab?
Kuy pal-yuh se-eh mak-sab?

Please can you pick me up/give me a lift?
Palun tulge mulle järele/viige mind kohale.
Pah-loon tul-ghe muhl-leh ya-reh-leh/vee-ghe mihnd ko-hah-leh?

Accidents and Traffic Offences (Violations)

Can you help me? There has been an accident
Kas te saate mind aidata? On juhtunud õnnetus
Kas te sah-ahte mind aidata? On yuhtunud onnetus

Please call the police/an ambulance
Palun helistage politseisse/ kiirabisse
Palun helistahge politseisse/ keer-ahbisse

Is anyone hurt?
Kas keegi on viga saanud?
Kas ke-egi on vigah sah-ahnud?

Sorry, I didn't see the sign
Andke andeks, ma ei näinud seda märki
And-keh and-ex, mah ey nay-nud seh-da mar-ki

Must I pay a fine? How much?
Kas ma pean trahvi maksma? Kui palju?
Kas mah pe-an trah-vi maks-mah? Kuy pal-yuh?

E
S
T
O
N
I
A
N

Teie dokumendid, palun
Teye do-kuh-men-did, pah-loon
Your documents, please

HEALTH

Pharmacy (Apteek)

Do you have anything for ... a stomach ache/headache/sore throat/toothache?
Kas teil on midagi kõhuvalu/
peavalu/kurguvalu/hambavalu
... vastu?
*Kas teyl on mi-da-gi koh-hu-vah-luh/
pe-a-vah-luh/kur-gu-vah-luh/
ham-bah-vah-luh ...vas-tuh?*

I need something for diarrhoea/constipation/a cold/a cough/insect bites/sunburn/travel (motion) sickness
Mulle on vaja midagi
kõhulahtisuse/kõhukinnisuse/
külmetuse/köha/putukaham-
mustuste/päikesepõletuse/reisil
tekkiva iivelduse vastu
*Mul-leh on vah-ya mi-da-gi koh-huh-
lahh-ti-suh-seh/koh-huh-kin-ni-suh-
seh/kyul-meh-tuh-she/kyo-hah/puh-
tuh-kah-ham-mus-tus-teh/pai-kese-
poele-teuse/rey-sil tek-keevah eevel-
duh-seh vas-tuh*

How much/how many do I take?
Kui palju ma pean seda võtma?
*Kuy pal-yuh mah pe-an seh-da
vot-mah?*

How often do I take it/them?
Kui tihti ma pean seda/neid
võtma?

*Kuy tih-ti ma pe-an se-dah/neyd vot-
mah?*

I am/he is (she is) taking this medication
Mina võtan/ta võtab seda
rohtu
*Mi-nah voy-tan/tah voy-tab seh-da
roh-tuh*

How much does it cost?
Kui palju see maksab?
Kuy pal-yuh se-eh mak-sab?

Can you recommend a good doctor/dentist?
Kas te võite soovitada head
arsti/hambaarsti?
*Kas teh voy-teh so-o-vi-tah-da he-ad
arsty/ham-bah-arsty?*

Is it suitable for children?
Kas see sobib lastele?
Kas se-eh so-bib lahs-te-leh?

Doctor (Arst)

I have a pain here/in my arm/leg/chest/stomach
Mul valutab siit/käsi/jalg/
rind/kõht
*Mul vah-luh-tab seet/ka-si/yalg/rind/
kyoht*

Please call a doctor, this is an emergency
Palun kutsuge arst, siin on
tarvis kiirabi
*Pah-loon kut-suh-geh arst, seen on
tar-vis keer-ah-bi*

I would like to make an appointment to see the doctor
Mul on tarvis arsti vastuvõtule

registreerida
Mul on tar-vis arsty vas-tuh-voh-tuh-leh reh-gis-tre-e-ri-da

I am diabetic/pregnant
Ma olen suhkruhaige
(diabeetik)/rase
*Mah oh-lehn suhk-ruh-hay-geh
(di-a-be-e-tik)/rah-seh*

I need a prescription for ...
Mulle on tarvis retsepti ... jaoks
Mul-leh on tar-sep-ti ... ya-oks

**Can you give me something
to ease the pain?**
Kas te saate mulle anda
valuvaigistit?
*Kas te sa-a-teh mul-leh an-da
vah-luh-vay-gis-tit?*

**I am/he is (she is) allergic to
penicillin**
Ma olen/ta on penitsiliiini
suhtes allergiline
*Mah oh-len/tah on peni-tsi-lee-ni
suh-tes al-ler-gi-li-ne*

Kas see on valus?
Kas se-eh on vah-lus?
Does this hurt?

Te peate/ta peab/minema
haiglasse
*Teh pe-a-teh/tah pe-ab mi-neh-mah
hayg-las-seh*
**You must/he must (she must)
go to hospital**

Võtke neid üks/kaks/kolm
korda päevas
*Vyot-keh neyd yuks/kaks/kolm kor-
da pa-e-vas*
**Take these once/twice/three
times a day**

**I am/he is (she is) taking this
medication**
Mina võtan/ta võtab seda
rohtu
*Mi-nah voy-tan/tah voy-tab seh-da
roh-tuh*

I have medical insurance
Mul on ravikindlustus
Mul on rah-vi-kynd-lus-tus

Dentist (Hambaarst)

**I have toothache/my filling
has come out**
Mul valutab hammas/plomm
kukkus välja
*Mul vah-luh-tab ham-mas/plomm
kuk-kus vyal-ya*

**I do/do not want to have an
injection first**
Ma tahan/ma ei taha enne
seda süsti
*Mah tah-han/mah ey tah-hah
hen-neh seh-da sys-ti*

EMERGENCIES

Help!
Appi!
Ap-pi!

Fire!
Tulekahju! (Põleb!)
Tuh-leh-kah-yuh! (Poleb!)

Stop!
Pidage kinni! (Peatuge!)
(Stopp!)
*Pi-da-ghe kin-ni! (Pe-a-tu-ghe)
(Stop!)*

E
S
T
O
N
I
A
N

Call an ambulance/a doctor/the police/the fire brigade!
Kutsuge kiirabi/arst/politsei/tuletõrje!
Kyut-su-keh keer-ah-bi/arst/po-lit-sey/tu-leh-tor-ye!

Please may I use a telephone?
Kas ma tohin teilt helistada?
Kas mah to-hin teylt heh-lis-tah-da?

I have had my traveller's cheques/credit cards/handbag/rucksack/luggage/wallet/passport/mobile phone stolen
Mul varastati ära reisitšekid/krediitkaardid/käekott/seljakott/pagas/rahakott/pass/mobiiltelefon
Myul vah-ras-tah-ti rey-si-tse-kid/kre-deet-ka-ar-did/kyae-kott/sel-yah-kott/pagas/ra-ha-kott/pass/mobeel-telefon

May I please have a copy of the report for my insurance claim?
Kas ma saaksin palun aktist oma kindlustusnõude jaoks koopia?
Kas ma saaksin pahlun aktist oh-mah kindlustus-noh-ude yaoks ko-opya?

Can you help me? I have lost my daughter/son/my companion(s)
Palun, aidake mind? Minu tütar/poeg/kaaslane (kaaslased) läks (läksid) kaduma!
Pah-loon, ay-da-ke mint? Mi-nuh tyu-tar/po-eg/ka-as-la-ne (ka-as-la-sed) laks (lak-sid) kah-du-mah!

Please go away/Leave me alone!
Palun, minge ära!/Jätke mind rahule!
Palun, ming-eh ah-rah!/Yatkeh mint rah-hu-leh!

I'm sorry!
Andestage!/Palun andeks!
An-des-ta-ghe!/Pah-loon and-ex!

I want to contact the British/American/Canadian/Irish/Australian/New Zealand/South African Consulate.
Mul soovin võtta ühendust Inglise/Ameerika/Kanada/Iiri/Austraalia/Uus Meremaa/Lõuna-Aafrika konsulaadiga
Mul so-o-vin vot-tah uh-end-uhs Ing-li-seh/A-me-e-ri-kah/Kah-nah-da/Ee-ri/A-u-s-tra-a-lya/U-us Meh-reh-ma-a/Low-nah A-af-ri-kah kon-suh-la-a-di-kah

I'm/we're/he (she) is ill/lost/injured
Ma jäin/me jäime/ta jäi/haigeks; ma eksisin ära/me eksisime ära/ta eksis ära; ma sain/me sain/me saime/ta sai vigastada
Mah-ya-in/meh ya-im-eh-tah/tah ya-I hay-geks; mah eks-is-in a-rah/meh eks-is-im-eh a-rah/mah sah-in/meh sah-im-eh/tah sah-I vi-gas-tah-da

They are/ill/lost/injured
Nad jäid haigeks/eksisid ära/said vigastada
Nad ya-id hay-gheks/eks-is-id a-rah/said vi-gas-tah-da

136

HUNGARIAN

**H
U
N
G
A
R
I
A
N**

INTRODUCTION

Hungarian, or Magyar, is distantly related to Finnish and Estonian, but is utterly unlike the languages of the other main linguistic groups of Europe. German is widespread as a second language.

Hungarian is undoubtedly a difficult language to master, and Hungarians are well aware of this, but you should nevertheless try to learn a few greetings, as silence when entering a shop, for instance, is considered rude.

Prepositions are replaced by suffixes. Each suffix has two forms: choose one that sounds harmonious with the noun/place name. There is no specific gender in the Hungarian language, therefore there is no difference in the words for 'he/she/it'.

Addresses for Travel and Tourist Information

New Zealand: *Hungarian Consulate-General,* PO Box 29-039, Wellington 6030; tel: (04) 973 7507; fax: (04) 973 7509.

UK: *Hungarian National Tourist Office,* 46 Eaton Place, London SW1X 8AL; tel: (020) 7823 1032; fax: (020) 7823 1459.

USA: *IBUSZ Hungarian Travel Company,* 1 Parker Plaza, #1104, Fort Lee, NJ 07024; tel: (201) 592 8585.

Official tourism websites: www.hungarywelcomesbritain.com (UK); www.gotohungary.com (USA).

Hungary Facts

CAPITAL: Budapest
CURRENCY: Forints (Ft); 1 Forint = 100 filler.
OPENING HOURS: Food/Tourist Shops, markets open Sun. Banks: National Bank of Hungary: Mon–Fri 1030–1400; Commercial Banks: Mon–Thur 0800–1500, Fri 0800–1300. Food shops: Mon–Fri 0700–1900; others: 1000–1800 (Thur until 1900); shops close for lunch and half-day on Sat (1300). Museums: Tues–Sun 1000–1800.
TELEPHONES: To dial in, +36. Outgoing, 00 and the country code. Police, 107. Fire, 105. Ambulance, 104.
PUBLIC HOLIDAYS: 1 Jan; 15 Mar; Easter Monday; 1, 8 May; 20 Aug; 23 Oct; 24–26 Dec.

Technical Language Hints

- You will notice there are different suffixes added onto the ends of words – e.g. -ban/-ben (in). These two options are for 'vowel harmony'. Hungarian has two kinds of vowels: open, and closed:

- Open Vowels: e, é, i, í, ö, ő, ü, and ű

  e.g.: kérem [kehrem], segítsen [shegítshen], önöknél [yuonyuoknehk], etc.

- Closed Vowels: a, á, o, ó, u, and ú

  e.g.: lámpámat [lahmpahmat], hálózsákomat [hahlohzhakomaht]

- For example, take the word "ház" (house): here you would use the ending "-ban", so that both vowels are in the "closed" group and two similar sounds are made sequentially.

ESSENTIALS

Alphabet and Pronunciation

	Name	Pronounced
A, a	o	o as in clock
Á, á	ah	ah as in father
B, b	bay	as in boy
C, c	tsay	ts as in cats
Cs, cs	chay	ch as in chug
D, d	day	d as in do
Dz, dz		ds as in feeds
Dzs, dzs		j as in jeans
E, e	eh	e as in set
É, é	eh	eh as grey
F, f	eff	f as in find
G, g	gay	hard g as in go
Gy, gy		dy as in British pronunciation of duke
I, i	ee	i as in sit
Í, í	ee	ee as in machine
J, j	yay	y as in yes
K, k	kah	k as in keep
L, l	el	l as in low

	Name	Pronounced
Ly, ly		y as in yes (the l is silent)
M, m	em	as in mother
N, n	en	n as in no
Ny, ny		ny as in canyon
O, o	o	o as clock
Ó ó	o	aw as in law
Ö, ö	oo	short oo as in zoo
Ő, ő	ur	as the vowel sound in fur
P, p	pay	as in pirate
Q, q		k sound as in cheque
R, r	air	slightly rolled rr sound
S, s	esh	sh as in sugar
Sz, sz	ess	s as in see
T, t	tay	t as in top
Ty, ty		ty as in met you
U, u	oo	short oo as in zoo
Ú, ú	ooh	long oo as in cool

ESSENTIALS

Ü, ü	ew	ew as in feud	
Ű, ű	eew	eew as in feud but longer	
V, v	vay	v as in value	
W, w	dooplo vay	v as in value	

X, x	ex	x as in tax	
Y, y	eepseelon	ee as in see	
Z, z	zat	z as in zebra	
Zs, zs		zh like the sound of the s in treasure	

HUNGARIAN

Basic Words and Phrases

Yes
Igen
Ee-gehn

No
Nem
Nehm

Please
Kérem
Kay-rehm

Thank you
Köszönöm
Kuh-suh-nuhm

Hello
Szervusz
Sehr-voos

Goodbye
Viszontlátásra
Vee-sohnt-lah-tahsh-ro

Excuse me
Elnézést
Ehl-nay-zaysht

Sorry
Bocsánat
Bo-chah-not

How
Hogyan
Hoh-djon

When
Mikor
Mee-kohr

Why
Miért
Mee-ayrt

What
Mi
Mee

Who
Ki
Kee

That's O.K.
Rendben van.
Rhend-ben von

Perhaps
Esetleg
Eh-shet-leg

To
-be/ba,-hez/hoz/höz,-ig
-beh/bo,-hehz/hohz/huhz,-eeg

From
-ből/ból,-tól/től
-burl/bohl,-tohl/turl

To & From: Always choose the vowel sound which resembles the sound of the destination

Here
Itt
Eett

There
Ott
Ohtt

I don't understand
Nem értem
Nehm ayr-tehm

I don't speak Hungarian
Nem beszélek magyarul
Nehm beh-say-lehk mo-djo-rool

Do you speak English?
Beszél angolul?
Beh-sayl on-goh-lool?

Can you please write it down?
Írja le, kérem?
Eer-yo leh, kay-rehm?

Please can you speak more slowly?
Kérem, beszéljen lassabban?
Kay-rehm, beh-sayl-yehn losh-shob-bon?

140

Greetings

Good Morning/Good Afternoon/Good Evening/Good Night
Jó reggelt/Jó napot/Jó estét/ Jó éjszakát kívánok
Joh rehg-gehlt/Joh no-poht/ Joh ehsh-tayt/Joh ahy-so-kaht kee-vah-nohk

Pleased to meet you
Örülök, hogy megismerhettem
Uh-rew-luhk hohdj mehg-eesh-mehr-heht-tehm

How are you?
Hogy van?
Hohdj von?

I am well, thank you. And you?
Köszönöm, jól. És Ön?
Kuh-suh-nuhm johl. Aysh Uhn?

My name is ...
A nevem ...
O neh-vehm ...

This is my friend/boyfriend/ girlfriend/husband/wife/ brother/sister
Ez az én barátom/udvarlóm/ barátnőm/férjem/feleségem/ fiútestvérem/lánytestvérem
Ehz oz ayn bo-rah-tohm/ood-vor-lohm/bo-raht-nurm/feh-leh-shay-gehm/fee-oo-tehsht-vay-rehm/lahnj-tehsht-vay-rehm

Where are you travelling to?
Hova utazik?
Hoo-vo oo-to-zek?

I am/we are going to ...
...-ba/be/ra/re

utazom/utazunk
...-bo/beh/ro/reh oo-to-zohm/oo-to-zoonk

How long are you travelling for?
Milyen hosszú lesz az utazása?
Mee-yehn hohs-soo lehs oz oo-to-zah-sho?

Where do you come from?
Hová valósi Ön?
Hoh-vah vo-loh-she Uhn?

I am/we are from... Australia/Britain/Canada/ America
Én/mi ...-ból/ből vagyok/ vagyunk ... Ausztráliából/ NagyBritanniából/Kanadából/ Amerikából
Eyn/mee ...-bohl/burl vo-djohk /vo-djoonk Aust-rah-lee-ah-bohl/ Nodj-Britanni-ah-bohl/Kanadah-bohl/ Amerikah-bohl

We are on holiday
Szabadságon vagyunk
So-bod-shah-gohn vo-djoonk

This is our first visit here
Először vagyunk itt
Eh-lur-suhr vo-djoonk eet

How old are you?
Hány éves Ön?
Hahnj ay-vehsh Uhn?

I am .... years old
... éves vagyok
... ay-vehsh vod-yohk

I am a business person/ doctor/journalist/manual worker/administrator/ scientist/student/teacher

H
U
N
G
A
R
I
A
N

141

Üzletember/orvos/újságíró/
munkás/adminisztrátor/tudós/
diák/tanár/vagyok
Ewz-leht-ehm-behr/ohr-vohsh/oohy-
shayg-ee-roh/moon-kahsh/od-mee-
neest-rah-tohr/too-dohsh/dee-ahk/
to-nahr/vod-yohk

I am waiting for my husband/wife/boyfriend/girlfriend
Várom a férjemet/
feleségemet/barátomat/
barátnőmet
Vah-rohm o fayr-yeh-meht/feh-leh-
shay-geh-meht/bo-rah-toh-mot/
bo-raht-nur-meht

Would you like/may I have a cigarette?
Kér egy cigarettát? Kérhetnék
egy cigarettát?
Kayr ehdj tzee-go-reht-taht?
Kayr-heht-nayk ehdj-tsee-go-reht-that?

Do you mind if I smoke?
Nem zavarja, ha rágyújtok?
Nehm zo-vor-yah, ho rah-djooy-tohk?

Do you have a light?
Adna egy kis tüzet?
Od-no ehdj keesh tew-zeht?

Days

Monday
Hétfő
Hayt-fur

Tuesday
Kedd
Kehdd

Wednesday
Szerda
Sehr-do

Thursday
Csütörtök
Chew-tuhr-tuhk

Friday
Péntek
Payn-tehk

Saturday
Szombat
Sohm-bot

Sunday
Vasárnap
Vo-shahr-nop

Morning
Reggel
Rehg-gehl

Afternoon/Evening/Night
Délután/Este/Éjszaka
Dayl-oo-tahn/Ehsh-teh/Ay-so-ko

Yesterday/Today/Tomorrow
Tegnap/Má/Holnap
Tehg-nop/ Mah/Hohl-nop

Numbers

Zero
Nulla
Nool-lo

One
Egy
Ehdj

Two
Kettő
Kayt-tur

Three
Három
Hah-rohm

Four
Négy
Naydj

Five
Öt
Uht

Six
Hat
Hot

Seven
Hét
Hayt

Eight
Nyolc
Njohlts

Nine
Kilenc
Kee-lehnts

Ten
Tíz
Teez

Eleven
Tizenegy
Tee-zehn-ehdj

Twelve
Tizenkettő
Tee-zehn-keht-tur

Thirteen
Tizenhárom
Tee-zehn-hahrohm

Fourteen
Tizennégy
Tee-zehn-naydj

Fifteen
Tizenöt
Tee-zehn-uht

Sixteen
Tizenhat
Tee-zehn-hot

Seventeen
Tizenhét
Tee-zehn-hayt

Eighteen
Tizennyolc
Tee-zehn-njolhlts

Nineteen
Tizenkilenc
Tee-zehn-kee-lehnts

Twenty
Húsz
Hoos

Twenty-one
Huszonegy
Hoo-sohn-ehdj

Twenty-two
Huszonkettő
Hoo-sohn-keht-tur

Thirty
Harminc
Hor-meents

Forty
Negyven
Nehdj-vehn

Fifty
Ötven
Urt-vehn

Sixty
Hatvan
Hot-von

Seventy
Hetven
Heht-vehn

Eighty
Nyolcvan
Njolts-von

Ninety
Kilencven
Kee-lents-vehn

One hundred
Száz
Sahz

Five hundred
Ötszáz
Uht-sahz

One thousand
Ezer
Eh-zehr

One million
Millió
Mil-lee-oh

H
U
N
G
A
R
I
A
N

Time

What time is it?
Mennyi az idő?/Hány óra van?
Menj-njee os ee-dur?/Hahnj ooh-ro von?

It is …
Most … óra van
Mosht … oh-ro von

9.00
Pontosan kilenc óra
Pohn-toh-shon kee-lehnts oh-ro

9.05
Öt perccel múlt kilenc
Uht pehrts-tsehl moolt kee-lehnts

9.15
Negyed tíz
Neh-djehd teez

9.20
Öt perccel múlt negyed tíz
Uht pehrts-tsehl moolt neh-djehd teez

9.30
Fél tíz
Fayl teez

9.35
Öt perccel múlt fél tíz
Uht pehrts-tsehl moolt fayl teez

9.40
Öt perc múlva háromnegyed tíz lesz
Uht pehrts mool-vo hah-rohm-neh-djehd teez lehs

9.45
Háromnegyed tíz
Hah-rohm-neh-djehd teez

9.50
Öt perccel múlt háromnegyed tíz
Uht pehrts-tsel moolt hah-rohm-neh-djehd teez

**H
U
N
G
A
R
I
A
N**

9.55
Öt perc múlva tíz lesz
Uht pehrts mool-vo teez lehs

Midday/Midnight
Dél/Éjfél
Dayl/Ay-fayl

Money

I would like to change these traveller's cheques/this currency
Be szeretném váltani az úticsekkeket/ezt a valutát
Beh seh-reht-naym vahl-to-nee oz oo-tee-chehk-keh-keht/ehzt o vo-loo-taht

How much commission do you charge? (What is the service charge?)
Mennyi a jutalékdíj?
Mehnj-njee o joo-to-layk-deey?

Can I obtain money with my Mastercard?
Vehetek fel pénzt a Mastercard-omról?
Veh-heh-tehk fehl paynzt o Mastercard-ohm-roohl?

Where is the nearest ATM?
Hol van a legközelebbi bankautomata?
Hol von o lehg-kew-zeh-lehbee bonk-auto-moto?

My name is ... Some money has been wired to here for me to collect
Nevem ... Ide átutaltak nekem pénzt. Fel szeretném venni
Neh-vehm ... Eedeh ayt-oo-tol-tok neh-kehm paynzt. Fehl seh-reht-nahm vehn-nee

ARRIVING AND DEPARTING

Airport

Excuse me, where is the check-in desk for ... airline?
Legyen szíves, mondja meg, hol van a regisztrálás a ... járatra?
Leh-djehn see-vehsh, mohnd-jo mehg, hohl von o reh-geest-rah-lash o ... jah-rotro?

What is the boarding gate for my flight?
Melyik kapunál kell beszállni a járatomra?
Meh-yeek ko-poo-nahl kehll beh-sahll-nee o jah-ro-tohm-ro?

What is the time for my flight?
Hánykor van a beszállás a járatomra?
Hahnj-kohr von o beh-sahl-lahsh o jah-ro-tohm-ro?

How long is the delay likely to be?
Mennyi a várható késés?
Mehnj-njee o vahr-ho-toh kay-shaysh?

Where is the duty-free shop?
Hol van a duty free üzlet?
Hohl von o duty free ewz-leht?

Which way is the luggage reclaim?
Merre kell mennem a poggyász kiadásához?
Mehr-reh kehll mehn-nehm o pohdj-djahs kee-o-dah-shah-hohz?

I have lost my luggage. Please can you help?
Elvesztettem a poggyászomat.
Tudna nekem segíteni?
Ehl-vehs-teht-tehm o pohdj-djah-soh-mot. Tood-no neh-kehm sheh-gee-teh-nee?

I am flying to …
…-ba/be repülök
…-bo/beh reh-puew-luhk

Where is the bus for the city centre?
Honnan indul a busz a városközpont felé?
Hohn-non een-dool o boos o vah-rohsh-kuhz-pohnt feh-lay?

Trains and Boats

Where is the ticket office/information desk?
Hol van a jegypénztár/
információ?
*Hohl von o yehdj-paynz-tahr/
infor-mah-tsee-oh?*

Which platform does the train/speedboat/ferry to … depart from?
Melyik peronról indul a …
-ba/be menő vonat/hajó/
komp?
Meh-yeek peh-rohn-rohl een-dool o … –bol-beh meh-nur voh-not/ho-yoh/kohmp?

Where is platform …?
Merre van a … peron?
Mehr-reh von o … peh-rohn?

When is the next train/boat to …?
Mikor indul a következő

vonat/hajó …-ba/be?
Mee-kohr een-dool o kuh-veht-keh-zur voh-not/ho-yoh … – bol/beh?

Is there a later train/boat to…?
Van későbbi vonat/hajó …
-ba/be?
Von kay-shurb-bee voh-not/ho-yoh …-bol/beh?

Notices and Signs

Büfékocsi (Étkezőkocsi)
*Bew-fay-koh-chee
(Ayt-keh-zur-koh-chee)*
Buffet (Dining) Car

Busz
Boos
Bus

Ivóvíz/nem ivóvíz
Ee-voh-veez/nehm ee-voh-veez
Drinking/Non-drinking water

Bejárat
Beh-rah-rot
Entrance

Kijárat
Kee-yah-rot
Exit

Kórház
Kohr-hahz
Hospital

Tudakozó
Too-do-koh-zoh
Information

HUNGARIAN

Poggyászmegőrző
Pohdj-djahs-mehg-urr-zur
Left Luggage (Baggage Claim)

Önkiszolgáló poggyászmegőrző
Uhn-kee-sohl-gah-loh-pohdj-djahs-meg-urr-zur
Luggage Lockers

Posta
Pohsh-to
Post Office

Peron
Peh-rohn
Platform

Vasútállomás
Vah-shooht-ahl-loh-mahsh
Railway (Railroad) Station

Repülőtér
Reh-pew-lur-tayr
Airport

Rendőrkapitányság
Rehn-dur-ko-pee-tahnj-shahg
Police Station

Kikötő
Kee-kuh-tur
Port

Étterem
Ayt-teh-rehm
Restaurant

Dohányzóknak/Nem dohányzóknak
Doh-hahnj-zohk-nok/Nehm doh-hahnj-zohk-nok
Smoking/Non Smoking

Telefon
Teh-leh-fohn
Telephone

Jegypénztár
Yehdj-paynz-tahr
Ticket Office

Check-in ablak
Check-in ob-lok
Check-in desk

Menetrend
Meh-neht-rehnd
Timetable

WC
Vay-tsay
Toilets(Restrooms)

Női/Férfi
Nyr-ee/Fayr-fee
Ladies/Gentlemen

Metró
Meht-roh
Underground(Subway)

Váróterem
Vah-roh-teh-rehm
Waiting Room

Buying a Ticket

I would like a first-class/second-class/third class-single (one-way)/return (round trip) ticket to...
Jegyet kérek első osztályra/ másodosztályra/ harmadosztályra egy irányban/oda-vissza ... ig
Yeh-djeht kay-rehk ehl-shur ohs-tahy-ro/mah-shohd-ohs-tahy-ro/hor-mod-

ohs-tayy-ro ehdj ee-rahnj-bon/oh-do-
vees-so … eeg

Is it an express (fast) train/
bus?
Ez express vonat/busz?
Ehz ehx-prehs voh-not/boos?

Is my rail pass valid on this
train/ferry/bus?
A vasúti bérletem érvényes
erre a vonatra/kompra/buszra?
*O vo-shoo-tee bayr-leh-tehm ayr-vay-
njehsh ehr-reh o voh-not-ro/kohmp-
ro/boos-ro?*

I would like an aisle/window
seat
Folyosó menti/ablak melletti
helyet kérek
*Foh-yoh-shoh mehn-tee/ob-lok mehl-
leht-tee heh-yeht kay-rehk*

No smoking/smoking please
Nemdohányzó/dohányzó
kocsiba kérek jegyet
*Nehm-doh-hahnj-zoh/doh-hanynj-zoh
koh-csee-bo kay-rehk yeh-djeht*

We would like to sit together
Egymás mellett szeretnénk ülni
*Ehdj-mahsh mehl-leht seh-reht-
naynk-eewl-nee*

I would like to make a seat
reservation
Helyjegyet szeretnék rendelni
*Hehy-yeh-djeht seh-reht-nayk
rehn-dehl-nee*

I would like to reserve a
couchette/sleeper for one
person/two people/my
family
Szeretnék helyet foglalni
couchettebe/hálókocsiba egy

személyre/két személyre/
családomnak
*Seh-reht-nayk heh-yeht fohg-lol-nee
couchette-beh/hah-loh-koh-chee-bo
ehdj seh-may-reh/kayt she-may-
reh/cho-lah-dohm-nok*

I would like to reserve a
cabin
Hajófülkét szeretnék foglalni
*Ho-yoh-fewl-kayt seh-reht-nayk
fohg-lol-nee*

Timetables (Schedules)

Érkezés
Ayr-keh-zaysh
Arrive

Megállóhelyek (Megállók)
*Mehg-ahl-loh-heh-yehk
(Mehg-ahl-lohk)*
Calls (Stops at)

Étkezés
Ayt-keh-zaysh
Catering Service

Átszállás …-ra/-re
Aht-sahl-lash … -ro/reh
Change At…

Csatlakozás/Útvonal
Chot-lo-koh-zahsh/Oht-vohh-nol
Connection/Via

Naponta
No-pohn-to
Daily

Negyven percenként
Nehdj-vehn pehr-tsehn-kaynt
Every 40 minutes

Első osztály
Ehl-shur ohs-tahy
First Class

Óránként
Oh-rahn-kaynt
Hourly

Helyjegyfoglalás ajánlott
Hehy-yehdj-fohg-lo-lahsh o-jahn-lohtt
Seat Reservations are recommended

Második osztály
Mah-shoh-deek ohs-tahy
Second Class

Kiegészítő díj fizetendő
Kee-eh-gay-see-tur deey fee-zeh-tehn-dur
Supplement Payable

Luggage

How much will it cost to send (ship) my luggage in advance?
Mennyibe kerül, ha előre küldöm a poggyászomat?
Mehnj-njee-beh keh-rewl, ho eh-lur-reh kewl-duhm o pohdj-djah-soh-mot?

Where is the left luggage (baggage claim) office?
Hol van a poggyászmegőrző?
Hohl von o pohdj-djahs-mehg-urr-zur?

What time do you open/close?
Hánykor nyitnak/zárnak?
Hahnj-kohr njeet-nok/zahr-nok?

Where are the luggage trolleys (carts)?
Hol vannak a poggyászkocsik?
Hohl von-nok o pohdj-djahs-koh-cheek?

Where are the lockers?
Hol van az önkiszolgáló poggyászmegőrző?
Hohl von oz uhn-kee-sohl-gah-loh pohdj-djahs-mehg-urr-zur?

I have lost my locker key
Elvesztettem a poggyászmegőrző kulcsomat
Ehl-vehs-teht-tehm o pohdj-djahs-meg-urr-zur kool-choh-mot

On Board

Is this seat free?
Szabad ez a hely?
So-bod ehz o hehy?

Excuse me, you are sitting in my reserved seat
Bocsánat, de Ön az én foglalt helyemen ül
Boh-chah-not, deh Uhn oz ayn fohg-lolt heh-yeh-mehn ewl

Which station is this?
Ez melyik állomás?
Ehz meh-yeek ahl-loh-mahsh?

What time is this train/bus/ferry/flight due to arrive/depart?
Hánykor érkezik/indul ez a vonat/busz/komp/repülő?

HUNGARIAN

Hahnj-kohr ayr-keh-zeek/een-dool ehz o voh-not/boos/kohmp/reh-puh-lur?

Travelling with Children

Do you have a high chair/ babysitting service/cot?
Van itt etetőszék/ gyermekvigyázó/gyermekágy?
Von eett eh-teh-tur-sayk/djehr-mehk-vee-djah-zoh/djehr-mehk-ahdj?

Where is the nursery/ playroom?
Hol van a bölcsöde/játékszoba?
Hohl von o buhl-chuh-deh/yah-tayk-soh-bo?

Where can I warm the baby's bottle?
Hol lehet felmelegíteni a cumisüveget?
Hohl leh-heht fehl-meh-leh-gee-teh-nee o tsoo-meesh-ew-veh-geht?

Customs and Passports

Kérem az útleveleket
Kay-rehm oz ooht-leh-veh-leh-keht
Passports please

I have nothing to declare
Nincs vámolnivalóm
Neench-vah-mohl-nee-vo-lohm

I have wine/spirits (alcohol)/tobacco to declare
Bor/szeszes italok/dohányáru elvámolnivalóm van
Bohr/seh-sehsh ee-to-lohk/ doh-hahny-ah-roh ehl-vah-mohl-nee-vo-lohm von

I will be staying for … days/weeks/months
… napot/hetet/hónapot szeretnék itt tartózkodni
… noh-poht/heh-teht/hoh-noh-poht seh-reht-nayk eett tor-tohz-kohd-nee

Asking the Way

Excuse me, do you speak English?
Elnézést, beszél angolul?
Ehl-nay-zaysht, beh-sayl on-goh-lool?

Excuse me, can you help me please?
Bocsánat, tudna nekem segíteni?
Boh-tsah-not, tood-no neh-kehm sheh-gee-teh-nee?

Where is the Tourist Information Office?
Hol van az Utazási Iroda?
Hohl von oz Oo-to-zah-shee Ee-roh-do?

Excuse me, is this the right way to … the cathedral/the tourist office/the castle/the old town?
Elnézést, jó felé megyek a templomhoz/utazási irodához/várhoz/belváros felé?
Ehl-nay-zaysht, joh feh-leh med-yek o tehmp-lohm-hohz/oo-to-zah-shee ee-roh-dah-hohz/vahr-hohz/behl-vah-rosh feh-lay?

Can you tell me the way to the railway station/bus station/taxi rank/city centre/beach?

Hogy jutok el a pályaud-
varhoz/autóbuszállomáshoz/ta
xiállomáshoz/belvárosba/
strandra?
*Hohdj joo-tohk ehl o pah-yo-ood-
vahr-hohz/au-toh-boos-ahl-loh-
mahsh-hohz/taxi-ahl-loh-mahsh-
hohz/behl-vah-rohsh-bo/shtrond-ro?*

Első/második forduló balra/
jobbra/egyenesen előre
*Ehl-shur/mah-shoh-deek fohr-doo-loh
bol-ro/johb-ro/eh-djeh-neh-shehn eh-
lur-reh*
**First/second/left/right/
straight ahead**

A sarkon/A lámpánál
O shor-kohn/O lahm-pah-nahl
**At the corner/At the traffic
lights**

**Where is the nearest police
station/nearest post office?**
Hol van a legközelebbi
rendőrkapitányság/legközeleb-
bi posta?
*Hohl von o lehg-kuh-zeh-lehb-bee
rehn-dur-ko-pee-tahnj-sahg/
lehg-kuh-zeh-lehb-bee pohsh-to?*

Is it near/far?
Közel/messze van?
Kuh-zehl/mehs-seh von?

**Do I need to take a
taxi/catch a bus?**
Taxival/busszal kell mennem?
Taxi-vol/boos-sol kehl mehn-nehm?

Do you have a map?
Van Önnél térkép?
Von Uhn-nayl tayr-kayp?

**Can you point to it on my
map?**

Meg tudná ezt mutatni a
térképemen?
*Mehg tood-nah ehzt moo-tot-nee o
tayr-kay-peh-mehn?*

Thank you for your help
Köszönöm a segítségét
Kuh-suh-nuhm o sheh-geet-say-gayt

**How do I reach the
motorway/main road?**
Hogyan jutok el az
autópályára/a főútra?
*Hohd-jon yoo-tohk el oz auto-pah-
yah-ro/o fur oht-ro?*

**I think I have taken the
wrong turning**
Azt hiszem, rossz helyen
kanyarodtam be
*Ozt hee-sehm, rohss heh-yehn
ko-njo-rohd-tom beh*

I am looking for this address
Ezt a címet keresem
Ehzt o tsee-meht keh-reh-shehm

I am looking for the … hotel
A … szállodát keresem
O …. sahl-loh-daht keh-reh-shehm

How far is it to … from here?
Milyen messze van ez innen …?
*Mee-yehn mehs-she von ehz
een-nehn… ?*

Menjen tovább … kilométert
egyenesen
*Mehn-yehn toh-vahbb … kee-loh-
may-tehrt eh-djeh-neh-shehn*
**Carry straight on for …
kilometres**

A következő sarkon forduljon
jobbra/balra
O kuh-veht-keh-zur shor-kohn

fohr-dool-yohn yohbb-ro/bol-ro
Take the next turning on the right/left

A következő kereszteződésnél/
lámpánál kanyarodjon jobbra/
balra
O kuh-veht-keh-zur keh-rehs-teh-zur-daysh-nayl fohr-dool-yohn yohbbro/bol-ro
Turn right/left at the next crossroads/traffic lights

Rossz irányba megy
Rohss ee-rahnj-bo mehdj
You are going in the wrong direction

**Where is the cathedral/
church/museum/pharmacy?**
Hol van a katedrális/templom/
múzeum/gyógyszertár?
Hol von o ko-tehd-rah-leesh/tehmp-lom/mooh-zeh-oom/djohdj-zehr-tahr?

**How much is the admission/
entrance charge?**
Mennyibe kerül a belépőjegy?
Mehnj-njee-beh keh-rewl o beh-lay-pur-yehdj?

**Is there a discount for
children/students/senior
citizens?**
Van engedmény
gyerekeknek/diákoknak/nyugdí
jasoknak?
Von ehn-gehd-maynj-djeh-reh-kehk-nehk/dee-ah-kohk-nok/njoog-dee-yo-shohk-nok?

**What time does the next
guided tour (in English) start?**
Mikor indul a következő
csoport (angol nyelven)?
Mee-kohr een-dool o kuh-veht-keh-

zur choh-pohrt (on-gohl njehl-vehn)?

**One/two adults/children
please**
Egy/két felnőtt/gyerek jegyet
kérek
Ehdj/kayt fehl-nurtt/djeh-rehk yeh-djet kay-rehk

May I take photographs here?
Szabad itt fényképezni?
So-bod eett faynj-kay-pehz-nee?

At the Tourist Office

**Do you have a map of the
town/area?**
Van Önöknek várostérképük/
körzeti térképük?
Von Uhn-nuhk-nehk vah-rosh-tayr-kay-pewk/kuhr-zeh-tee tayr-kay-pewk?

**Do you have a list of
accommodation?**
Van Önöknek szállodalistájuk?
Von Uh-nuhk-nehk sahl-loh-do-leesh-tah-yook?

**Can I reserve
accommodation?**
Foglalhatok szállást?
Fogh-lol-ho-tohk sahl-lahsht?

ACCOMMODATION

Hotels

**I have a reservation in the
name of..**
Szobát foglaltam ... névre
Soh-baht fogh-lol-tom ... nayv-reh

I wrote to/faxed/telephoned you last month/last week
Levelet/faxot küldtem/
telefonáltam Önöknek a múlt hónapban/múlt héten
Leh-veh-leht/fax-oht kewld-tehm/tele-foh-nahl-tom Uh-nuhk-nehk o moolt hoh-nop-bon/moolt hay-tehn

Do you have any rooms free?
Van szabad szobájuk?
Von so-bod soh-bah-yook?

I would like to reserve a single/double room with bath (shower)/without bath (shower)
Foglalni szeretnék egy egyágyas/kétágyas szobát fürdőszobával (zuhanyozóval)/fürdőszoba (zuhanyozó) nélkül
Fohg-lol-nee seh-reht-nayk ehdj ehdj-ah-djosh/kayt-ah-djosh soh-baht fewr-dur-soh-bah-vol (zoo-ho-njoh-zoh-vol) fewr-dur-soh-bah (zoo-ho-njoh-zoh) nayl-kewl

I would like bed/breakfast/ (room and) full board
Szállást/reggelit/(szobát és) teljes panziót kérek
Sahl-lahsht/rehg-geh-leet/(soh-baht aysh) tehl-yesh pon-zee-oht kay-rehk

How much is it per night?
Mennyibe kerül ez egy éjszakára?
Mehnj-njee-beh keh-rewl ehz ehdj ayy-so-kah-ro?

Is breakfast included?
A reggeli is benne van az árban?
O rehg-geh-lee eesh behn-neh von oz ahr-bon?

Do you have any cheaper rooms?
Van olcsóbb szobájuk?
Von ohl-chohbb soh-bah-yook?

I would like to see/take the room
Megnézném/kivenném a szobát
Mehg-nayz-naym/kee-vehn-naym o soh-baht

I would like to stay for ..... nights
... napot szeretnék maradni
... no-pot seh-reht-nayk mo-rod-nee

The shower/light/tap/hot water doesn't work
A zuhanyozó/villany/csap/melegvíz nem működik
O zoo-ho-njoh-zoh/veel-lonj/chop/meh-lehg-veez nehm meew-kuh-deek

At what time/where is breakfast served?
Hánykor/hol van a reggeli?
Hahnj-kohr/hohl von o rehg-geh-lee?

What time do I have to check out?
Mikor kell kijelentkeznem?
Mee-kohr kehll kee-yeh-lehnt-kehz-nehm?

Can I have the key to room number...?
Megkaphatnám a ...-as/-os/-es szoba kulcsát?
Mehg-kop-hot-nahm o ...-osh/-ohsh/-ehsh soh-bo kool-chaht?

My room number is...
A szobaszámom ...
O soh-bah-sah-mohm ...

**My room is not satisfactory/
not clean enough/too noisy.
Please can I change rooms?**
A szobám nem megfelelő/
piszkos/túl zajos. Cserélhetnék
szobát?
*O soh-bahm nehm mehg-feh-lehl-
lur/pees-kohsh/tool zo-yohsh.
Cheh-rayl-heht-nayk soh-baht?*

Where is the bathroom?
Hol van a fürdőszoba?
Hohl von o fewr-dur-soh-bo?

**Do you have a safe for
valuables?**
Van Önöknél értékmegőrző?
*Von Uh-nuhk-nayl ayr-tayk-mehg-urr-
zur?*

**Is there a laundry/do you
wash clothes?**
Van maguknál
mosoda/mosnak-e ruhát?
*Von mo-gook-nahl moh-shoh-
do/mohsh-nok-eh roo-haht?*

**I would like an
air-conditioned room**
Légkondicionált szobát
szeretnék
*Layg-kohn-dee-tsee-oh-nahlt soh-
baht seh-reht-nayk*

**Do you accept traveller's
cheques/credit cards?**
Elfogadnak úticsekkeket/
hitelkártyát?
*Ehl-foh-god-nok oo-tee-chehk-
keht/hee-tehl-kahr-tjayt?*

May I have the bill please?
Kérhetem a számlát?
Kayr-heh-tehm o sahm-laht?

**Excuse me, I think there may
be a mistake in this bill.**
Elnézést kérek, de azt hiszem,
téves a számla
*Ehl-nay-zaysht kay-rehk, deh ozt
hee-sehm, tay-vehsh o sahm-lo*

Youth Hostels

**How much is a dormitory
bed per night?**
Mennyibe kerül a hálóteremben
egy ágy egy éjszakára?
*Mehnj-njee-beh keh-rewl o hah-loh-
teh-rehm-behn ehdj ahdj ehdj ayy-
so-kah-ro?*

I am/am not an HI member.
Tagja vagyok/nem vagyok
tagja a HI-nek
*Tog-yo vo-djohk/nehm vo-djohk
tog-yo o HI-nehk*

**May I use my own sleeping
bag?**
Használhatom a saját
hálózsákomat?
*Hos-nahl-ho-tom o sho-yaht hah-loh-
zhay-koh-mot?*

**What time do you lock the
doors at night?**
Este hánykor zárják be a
kaput?
*Ehsh-teh hahnj-kohr zahr-jahk beh o
ko-poot?*

Camping

**May I camp for the night/two
nights?**
Maradhatok egy/két éjszakára?
*Mo-rod-ho-tohk ehdj/kayt ayy-so-
kah-ro?*

H
U
N
G
A
R
I
A
N

153

H U N G A R I A N

Where can I pitch my tent?
Hol üthetem fel a sátramat?
Hohl ewt-heh-tehm fehl o shaht-roh-mot?

How much does it cost for one night/week?
Mennyibe kerül ez egy éjjelre/egy hétre?
Meehnj-njee-beh keh-rewl ehz ehdj ayy-yehl-reh/ehdj hayt-reh?

Where are the washing facilities?
Hol van a fürdőszoba-zuhanyozó?
Hohl von o fewr-dur-soh-bo - zoo-ho-njoh-zoh?

Is there a restaurant/supermarket/swimming pool on site/nearby?
Van itt a közelben/a kempingben étterem/supermarket/uszoda?
Von eett o kuh-zehl-behn/o kehm-peeng-behn ayt-teh-rehm/supermar-ket/oo-soh-do?

Do you have a safety deposit box?
Van Önöknél értékmegőrző?
Von Uh-nuhk-nayl ayr-tayk-mehg-urr-zur?

Cafés and Bars

I would like a cup of/two cups of/another coffee/tea
Szeretnék egy csésze/két csésze kávét/még egy kávét/teát
Seh-reht-nayk ehdj chay-seh/kayt chay-she kah-veht/mayg ehdj kah-veht/teh-aht

With/without milk
Tejjel/tej nélkül
Tehy-yehl/tehy nayl-kewl

With/without sugar
Cukorral/cukor nélkül
Tsoo-kohr-rol/tsoo-kohr nayl-kewl

I would like a bottle/glass/two glasses of mineral water/red wine/white wine, please
Szeretnék egy üveg/pohár/két pohár ásványvizet/vörös bort/fehér bort
Seh-reht-nayk ehdj ew-vehg/poh-hahr/kayt poh-hahr ahsh-vahnj-vee-zeht/vuh-ruhsh bohrt/feh-hayr bohrt

I would like a beer/two beers, please
Szeretnék egy sört/két sört
Seh-reht-nayk ehdj suhrt/kayt suhrt

Please may I have some ice?
Kaphatnék egy kis jeget?
Kop-hot-nayk ehdj kees yeh-geht?

Do you have any matches/cigarettes/cigars?
Van Önöknél gyufa/cigaretta/szivar?
Von uh-nuhk-nayl djoo-fo/tsee-go-reht-to/see-vor?

Restaurants

Can you recommend a good/cheap restaurant in this area?
Tudna ajánlani egy jó/nem drága éttermet a környéken?

*Tood-no o-yahn-lo-nee ehdj
joh/nehm drah-go ayt-tehr-meht o
kuhr-njay-kehn?*

**I would like a table for …
people**
Szeretnék egy asztalt …
személyre
*Seh-reht-nayk ehdj os-tolt …
seh-mayy-reh*

**Do you have a non-smoking
area?**
Van maguknál nemdohányzó
terem?
*Von mo-gook-nahl nehm-doh-hahnj-
zoo teh-rehm?*

Waiter/Waitress!
Pincér/Pincérnő!
Pin-cayr/pin-cayr-nur!

**Excuse me, please may
we order?**
Kérem, rendelhetünk?
Kay-rehm, rehn-dehl-heh-tewnk?

**Do you have a set menu/
children's menu/wine list … in
English?**
Van komplett menüjük/gyer-
mek menüjük/itallapjuk?
*Von komp-lett meh-new-yewk/djehr-
mehk meh-new-yewk/ee-tol-lop-
yook?*

**Do you have any vegetarian
dishes?**
Van vegetariánus ételük?
*Von veh-geh-to-ri-ah-noosh
ay-teh-lewk?*

**Do you have any local
specialities?**
Vannak helyi specialitásaik?

*Von-nok heh-yee shpeh-tsee-o-lee-
tah-sho-eek?*

Are vegetables included?
A zöldségek benne vannak az
árban?
*O zuhld-shay-gehk behn-neh von-
nok oz ahr-bon?*

**Could I have it well-
cooked/medium rare please?**
Kaphatnám ezt jól
megsülten/félig sülten?
*Kop-hot-nahm ehzt johl mehg-shewl-
tehn/fay-leeg shewl-tehn?*

**What does this dish
consist of?**
Miből készült ez az étel?
Mee-burl kay-sewlt ehz oz ay-tehl?

**I am a vegetarian. Does this
contain meat?**
Vegetariánus vagyok. Van
ebben hús?
*Veh-geh-tah-ree-ah-nosh vodjok.
Von ehb-behn hoosh?*

**I do not eat nuts/dairy
products/meat/fish**
Nem eszem dióféléket/
tejtermékeket/húst/halat
*Nehm eh-sehm dee-oht-feh-leh-
ket/tehy-tehr-may-keh-keht/hoosht/
ho-lot*

Not (very) spicy please
Kérem, ne legyen (nagyon)
erős
*Kay-rehm, neh-leh-djehn (no-djohn)
eh-rursh*

**I would like the set menu
please**
Kérem szépen a menüt
Keh-rehm say-pehn o meh-newt

HUNGARIAN

H U N G A R I A N

We have not been served yet
Még nem szolgáltak ki minket
Mayg nem sol-gahl-tok kee meen keht

Please bring a plate/knife/fork
Kérem, hozzon tányért/
kést/villát
Kay-rehm, hoz-zon tah-njayrt/ kaysht/vee-llaht

Excuse me, this is not what I ordered
Bocsánat, de nem ezt
rendeltem
Boh-chah-not, deh nehm ehzt rehn-dehl-tehm

May I have some/more bread/water/coffee/tea?
Kérhetnék még egy kis keny-
eret/vizet/kávét/teát?
Kayr-heht-nayk mayg ehdj keesh keh-njeh-reht/vee-zeht/kah-vayt/ teh-aht?

May I have the bill please?
Kérhetem a számlát?
Kayr-heh-tehm o sahm-laht?

Does this bill include service?
A kiszolgálás benne van az
árban?
O kee-sohl-gah-lash behn-neh von oz ahr-bon?

Do you accept traveller's cheques/Mastercard/ US dollars?
Elfogadnak
úticsekkeket/Mastercard
hitelkártyát/USA dollárt?
Ehl-foh-god-nok oo-tee-chehk-keht/Mastercard hee-tehl-kahr-tjayt/ USHAH dohl-lahrt?

Can I have a receipt please?
Kaphatnék nyugtát a
számláról?
Kop-hot-nayk njoog-taht o sahm-lah-rohl?

Where is the toilet (restroom) please?
Hol van a WC?
Hohl von o aya-tsay

On the Menu

Reggeli/Ebéd/Vacsora
Rehg-geh-lee/Eh-bayd/Votso-ro
Breakfast/Lunch/Dinner

Előételek	Levesek
Eh-lur-ay-teh-lehk	*Leh-veh-shehk*
First Courses	**Soups**

Fő ételek
Fur ay-teh-lehk
Main Courses

Halételek	Húsételek
Hahl-ay-teh-lehk	*Hohsh-ay-teh-lehk*
Fish Dishes	**Meat Dishes**

Marhahús
Morho-hoo-sh
Beef

Sült (hús, hal) szelet
Shewlt (hoosh, hol) seh-leht
Steak

Disznóhús	Borjúhús
Dees-no-hoosh	*Bohr-yoo-hoosh*
Pork	**Veal**

Csirkehús
Tseer-keh-hoosh
Chicken

Bárányhús
Bah-rahnj-hoosh
Lamb

Sonka
Shon-ko
Ham

Vegetáriánus ételek
Veh-geh-tah-ree-ah-noosh ay-teh-lehk
Vegetarian Dishes

Zöldségek/Főzelékek
Zewld-shay-ghek/Fur-ze-ley-kehk
Vegetables

Rósejbni (hasábburgonya)
Rosh-ayb-nee (hoh-sayb-boor-goh-njo)
Chips (french fries)

Főtt/Hirtelen sült
burgonya/burgonyapüré
Furt/Heer-teh-lehn shewlt boor-goh-njo/boor-goh-njo-pew-ray
Boiled/sauté/mashed potatoes

Rizs
Reezh
Rice

Desszertek
Dehs-sehr-tehk
Desserts

Fagylalt
Fodj-lolt
Ice cream

Torta
Tor-to
Cakes

Sütemény
Shew-teh-may-nj
Pastries

Gyümölcs
Djew-muh-lts
Fruit

Kenyér
Kehnj-ayr
Bread

Péksütemény
(Kifli/Zsemle)
Payk-shew-teh-may-nj (Keef-lee/Zhehm-leh)
Rolls

Piritós
Pee-ree-tawsh
Toast

Vaj
Voy
Butter

Só/bors
Shaw/borrsh
Salt/pepper

Cukor
Tsoo-kohr
Sugar

Ételspecialitások
Ay-tehl-shpeh-tsee-o-lee-tah-shohk
Specialities

Helyi specialitások
Hehy-ee shpeh-tsee-o-lee-tay-shock
Local specialities

Napi menü
Nopeh meh-new
Set Menu

Borlista
Bohr-lee-shto
Wine list

Vörösbor
Vuh-ruhsh-bohr
Red wines

Fehérbor
Feh-hayr-bohr
White wines

Világos vörös bor
Vee-lah-gosh vuh-ruhsh bohr
Rosé wines

Habzóbor
Hobzo-bohr
Sparkling wines

Sör
Shuhr
Beer

Palackozott sör/Csapolt sör
Po-lots-ko-zott shuhr/Tso-polt shuhr
Bottled beer/Draught (draft) beer

Alkoholmentes italok
Ol-ko-hol-mehn-tehsh ee-to-lok
Non-alcoholic drinks

Ásványvíz
Aysh-vaynj-veez
Mineral water

HUNGARIAN

HUNGARIAN

Gyümölcslevek
Djew-muhlts-leh-vehk
Fruit juices

Narancslé
No-ronts-lay
Orange juice

Limonádé	Jég
Lee-mo-nah-day	*Jaygh*
Lemonade	**Ice**

Tejeskávé/feketekávé/
eszpresszó kávé
Teh-yesh-kah-vay/fehkehteh-kah-vay/espresso kay-vay
White coffee/black coffee/espresso coffee

Tea tejjel/citrommal
Teh-a tehj-jehl/tseet-rom-mol
Tea with milk/with lemon

Kakaó	Tej
Koko-aw	*Tehj*
Chocolate	**Milk**
(drink)	

Falatkák/Könnyű ételek
Fo-lot-kahk/Kuhnj-njew ay-teh-lehk
Snacks/Light meals

Saláták	Szendvicsek
Sho-lah-tahk	*Sehnd-vww-tschehk*
Salads	**Sandwiches**

Tojás	Kolbász/Virsli
Toy-ahsh	*Kohl-bahs/Veer-shlee*
Eggs	**Sausage**

Főtt tojás/tükörtojás/rántotta
Furt toy-asshsh/tew-kuhr tohy-ash/rahn-tot-to
Boiled/fried/scrambled eggs

Typical Local Dishes

Tyúkhúsleves
Tjohk-hohsh-leh-vesh
Chicken soup

Gyümölcsleves
Djew-muhlch-leh-vesh
Fruit Soup

Sült pisztráng
Sheewlt peest-rahng
Fried Trout

Töltött palacsinta
Tuhl-tuhltt po-lo-cheen-to
Pancakes with filling

Pálinka
Pah-leen-ko
Strong alcoholic drink

Public Transport

Where is the bus stop/coach stop/nearest metro station?
Hol van az autóbuszmegálló/
távolsági-buszmegálló/
legközelebbi metróállomás?
Hohl von oz auto-boos-mehg-ahl-loh/tah-vohl-shah-gee-boos-mehg-ahl-loh/lehg-kuh-zeh-lehb-bee metro-ahl-loh-mahsh?

When is the next/last bus to...?
Mikor indul a következő/utolsó busz ...-ba/be?
Mee-kohr een-dool a kuh-veht-keh-zur boos ... –bo/beh?

How much is the fare to the city centre (downtown)/railway station/airport?

Mennyi a viteldíj a városközpontig/pályaudvarig/repülőtérig?

Mehnj-njee o vee-tehl-deey o vah-rohsh-kuhz-pohnt-eeg/pah-yo-ood-vo-reeg/reh-pew-lur-tay-reeg?

Will you tell me when to get off?

Szólna, amikor le kell szállnom?

Sohl-no, o-mee-kohr leh kehll sahll-nohm?

Does this bus go to...?

Ez a busz megy...-ig?

Ehz o boos mehdj ...-eeg?

Which number bus goes to...?

Hányas busz megy ...-ig?

Hah-njos boos mehdj .... eeg?

May I have a single (one way)/return (round trip)/day ticket/book of tickets?

Szeretnék egy jegyet egy irány-ban/oda-vissza (menettérti jegyet)/egésznapos bérletet/jegytömböt?

Seh-reht-nayk ehdj-yeh-djeht ehdj ee-rahnj-bon/oh-do-vees-so (meh-neht-tay-ree yeh-djeht)/eh-gays-no-pohsh bayr-leh-teht/yehdh-tuhm-buht?

Taxi (Taxi)

I would like to go to ... How much will it cost?

...-ba/-be szeretnék eljutni. Mennyibe fog ez kerülni?

...-oal-beh seh-reht-nayk ehl-joot-nee. Mehnj-njee-beh fohg ehz keh-rewl-nee?

Please may I stop here?

Kérem, álljon meg itt?

Kay-rehm ahll-yohn mehg eett?

I would like to order a taxi today/tomorrow at 2pm to go from...to...

Taxit szeretnék rendelni mára/holnapra két órára, hogy ...-ból/-ből ...-ig menjek

Taxit seh-reht-nayk rehn-dehl-nee mah-ro/hohl-nop-ro kayt oh-rah-ro, hodj ... bool/bur ... eeg mehn-yehk

Entertainment

Can you recommend a good bar/nightclub?

Tudna ajánlani egy jó bárt/éjszakai klubot?

Tood-no o-yahn-lo-nee ehdj joh bahrt/ay-so-ko-ee kloob-oht?

Do you know what is on at the cinema (playing at the movies)/theatre at the moment?

Meg tudná mondani, hogy mi megy most a mozikban/színházakban?

Mehg tood-nah mohn-do-nee, hohdj mee mehdj mohsht o moh-zeek-bon/seen-hahz-ok-bon?

I would like to book (purchase) ... tickets for the matinee/evening performance on Monday

Szeretnék ... jegyet rendelni/venni a hétfő délutáni/esti előadásra

Seh-reht-nayk ... yeh-djeht rehn-dehl-nee/vehn-nee o hayt-fur dayl-oo-tah-nee eh-lur-o-dahsh-ro

What time does the film/performance start?
Hánykor kezdődik a film/az előadás?
Hahnj-kohr kehz-dur-deek o film/oz eh-lur-o-dahsh?

COMMUNICATIONS

Post

How much will it cost to send a letter/postcard/this package to Britain/Ireland/America/Canada/Australia/New Zealand?
Mennyibe kerül egy levelet/képeslapot/ezt a küldeményt feladni Angliába/Irországba/Amerikába/Kanadába/Ausztráliába/Új-Zélandba?
Mehnj-njee-beh keh-rewl ehdj leh-vehl-leht/kay-pehsh-lo-poht/ehzt o kewl-deh-maynjt fehl-od-nee Ong-lee-ah-bo/Amerikah-bo/Ko-no-dah-bo/Aoost-rah-lee-ah-bo/Ohy-zay-lond-bo?

I would like one stamp/two stamps
Kérek egy/két bélyeget
Kay-rehk ehdj/kayt bay-yeh-geht

I'd like ... stamps for postcards to send abroad, please
Kérek ... képeslapra való nemzetközi bélyeget
Kay-rehk ... kay-pehsh-lop-ro vah-loh nehm-zeht-kuh-zee bay-yeh-geht

Phones

I would like to make a telephone call/reverse the charges to (make a collect call to)...
Szeretnék telefonálni/telefonálni a hívott szám költségére ... -ba/-be
Seh-reht-nayk teh-leh-foh-nahl-nee/teh-leh-foh-nahl-nee o hee-vohtt sahm kuhlt-say-gay-reh ... -bol/-beh

Which coins do I need for the telephone?
Milyen érmékkel lehet telefonálni?
Mee-yehn ayr-mayk-kehl leh-heht telefonahl-nee?

The line is engaged (busy)
Foglalt a vonal
Fohg-lahlt o voh-nol

The number is...
A szám ...
O sahm ...

Hello, this is...
Halló, ... vagyok
Hallo, ... vah-djohk

Please may I speak to ..?
Kérem, beszélhetnék ... val/-vel?
Keh-rehm, beh-sayl-heht-nayk ... vol/-vehl?

He/she is not in at the moment. Please can you call back?
Most nincs bent. Kérem, hívja később?
Mohsht neench behnt. Kay-rehm heev-jo kay-surbb?

SHOPPING

Shops

Könyvesbolt/Papírbolt
Kuhnj-vehsh-bohlt/Pap-eer-bohlt
Bookshop/Stationery

Ékszerbolt/Ajándékbolt
Ayk-sehr-bohlt/O-yahn-dayk-bohlt
Jeweller/Gifts

Cipőbolt
Tsee-pur-bohlt
Shoes

Ruhabolt
Roo-ho-bohlt
Clothes

Mosoda
Moh-shoh-do
Laundry

Háztartási cikkek
Hahz-tor-tah-shee tseek-kehk
Hardware

Fodrász
Fohd-rahs
Hairdresser

Pék
Payk
Baker

Szupermarket
Supermarket
Supermarket

Fotóüzlet
Foh-toh-ewz-leht
Photo Shop

Utazási iroda
Oh-to-zah-shee ee-roh-do
Travel Agent

Gyógyszertár
Djohdj-zehr-tahr
Pharmacy

In the Shops

What time do the shops open/close?
Mikor nyitnak/zárnak a boltok?
Mee-kohr nn-y-eet-nok/zahr-nok o bohl-tohk?

Where is the nearest market?
Hol van a legközelebbi piac?
Hohl von o lehg-kuh-zeh-lehb-bee pee-ots?

Can you show me the one in the window/this one?
Megmutatná nekem a kirakatban levőt/ezt?
Megh-moo-tot-nah neh-kehm o kee-ro-kot-bon leh-vurt/ehzt?

Can I try this on?
Felpróbálhatom?
Fehl-proh-bahl-ho-tom?

What size is this?
Ez hányas méret?
Ehz hah-njosh may-reht?

**This is too large/too small/too expensive.
Do you have any others?**
Ez túl nagy/túl kicsi/túl drága.
Más van?
Ehz toohl nogj/tool kee-chee/tool drah-go. Mahsh von?

My size is...
Az én méretem ...
Oz ehn may-reh-tehm ...

Where is the changing room/children's/cosmetic/ladieswear/menswear/food department?
Hol van a próbafülke/gyermekosztály/parfümosztály/nőiruha osztály/férfiruha osztály/élelmiszerosztály?
Hohl von o proo-bah-fewl-keh/djehr-mehk-ohs-tahy/por-fewm-ohs-tahy/nur-ee-roo-hah ohs-tahy/ay-lehl-mee-sehr-ohs-tahy?

I would like ... a quarter of a kilo/half a kilo/a kilo of bread/butter/ham/this fruit
Kérek ... huszonöt deka/fél kiló/kiló kenyeret/vajat/sonkát/ebből a gyümölcsből
Kay-rehk ... hoo-sohn-uht deh-ko/fayl kee-loh keh-njeh-reht/vo-jot/sohn-kaht/ehb-bur o djew-muhlch-burl

How much is this?
Mennyibe kerül ez?
Mehnj-njee-beh keh-rewl ehz?

I'll take this one, thank you
Ezt megveszem, köszönöm
Ehzt mehg-veh-sehm, kuh-suh-nuhm

Do you have a carrier (shopping) bag?
Kérhetek egy nylonzacskót?
Kayrheh-tehk edj nehylon-zochkawt?

Do you have anything cheaper/larger/smaller/of better quality?
Van Önnek ennél olcsóbb/nagyobb/kisebb/jobb minőségű?
Vahn Uhn-nehk ehn-nayl ohl-csohbb/no-gyobb/kee-sehbb/johbb mee-nur-shay-geew?

I would like a film/to develop this film for this camera
Szeretnék ehhez a fényképezőgéphez filmet venni/filmet előhívatni
Seh-reht-nayk eh-hez o faynj-kay-peh-zur-gayp-hehz feel-meht vehn-nee/feel-meht elur-hee-vot-nee

I would like some batteries, the same size as this old one
A régivel azonos méretű elemet szeretnék
O ray-gee-vehl o-zoh-nohsh may-reh-teew eh-leh-meht seh-reht-nayk

Would you mind wrapping this for me, please?
Kérem, becsomagolná ezt nekem?
Kay-rehm, beh-choh-mo-gohl-nah ehzt neh-kehm?

Sorry, but you seem to have given me the wrong change
Elnézést, de úgy látszik, rosszul adott nekem vissza a pénzből
Ehl-nay-zaysht, deh oogj laht-sik, rohs-sool o-dohtt neh-kehm vees-so o paynz-burl

Car Hire (Rental)

I have ordered (rented) a car in the name of...
Rendeltem (kibéreltem) egy autót ... névre
Rehn-dehl-tehm (kee-bay-rehl-tehm) ehdj autoht ... nayv-reh

How much does it cost to hire (rent) a car for one day/two days/a week?
Mennyibe kerül az autótbérlés (kölcsönzés) egy napra/két napra/egy hétre?
Mehnj-njee-beh keh-rewl oz auto-bayr-laysh (kuhl-chuhn-zaysh) ehdj nop-ro/kayt nop-ro/ehdj hayt-reh?

Is the tank already full of petrol (gas)?
A benzintartály már tele van üzemanyaggal?
A behn-zeen-tor-tayy mahr teh-leh von ew-zehm-o-njog-gol?

Is insurance and tax included? How much is the deposit?
A biztosítás és az adó is benne van az árban? Mennyi a letét nagysága?
O beez-toh-shee-tahsh aysh oz o-doh eesh behn-neh von oz ahr-bon? Mehnj-njee o leh-tayt nogy-shah-go?

By what time must I return the car?
Hány órára kell visszahoznom az autót?
Hahnj oh-rah-ro kehll vees-so-hohz-nohm oz autoht?

I would like a small/large/family/sports car with a radio/cassette
Szeretnék egy kis/nagy/családi/sport autót kölcsönözni rádióval/magnóval
Seh-reht-nayk ehdj keesh/nodj/cho-lah-dee/shport autoht kuhl-chuhn-nuhz-nee rah-dee-oh-vol/mog-noh-vol

Do you have a road map?
Van Önöknek autótérképe?
Von Uh-nuhk-nehk autoh-tayr-kay-peh?

How long can I park here?
Meddig lehet itt állni?
Mehd-deeg leh-heht eett ahl-nee?

Is there a car park near here?
Van itt a közelben parkolóhely?
Vahn eett o kuh-zehl-behn por-koh-loh-hehy?

At what time does this car park close?
Hánykor zár ez a parkolóhely?
Hahnj-kohr zahr ehz o por-koh-loh-hehly?

Egyirányú forgalom
Ehdj-ee-rah-njoo fohr-go-lom
One way

Behajtani tilos
Beh-hoj-toh-nee tee-lohsh
No entry

Parkolni tilos
Pahr-kohl-nee tee-lohsh
No parking

Terelőút
Teh-reh-lur-oot
Detour (Diversion)

H U N G A R I A N

Stop
Shtop
Stop

Elsőbbségadás kötelező
Ehl-shurbb-shayg-o-dahsh kuh-teh-leh-zur
Give way (Yield!)

Csúszós út
Choo-soosh oot
Slippery road

Előzni tilos
Eh-lurz-nee tee-lohsh
No overtaking

Veszély!
Veh-sayy!
Danger!

At the Filling Station
(A Benzinkútnál)

Unleaded (lead free)/ standard/premium/diesel
Ólommentes/normál/szuper benzin/dízelolaj
Oh-lohm-mehn-tehsh/nohr-mahl/soo-pehr behn-zeen/dee-eh-zehl-oh-loy

Fill the tank please
Kérem, töltse tele a tankot
Kah-rehm, tuhlt-sheh teh-leh o tonkoht

Do you have a road map?
Van Önöknek autótérképe?
Von Uh-nuhk-nehk autoh-tayr-kay-peh?

How much is the car wash?
Mennyibe kerül a kocsimosás?
Mehnj-njee-beh keh-rewl o ko-chee-moh-shahsh?

Breakdowns

I've had a breakdown at …
Elromlott a kocsim …-n/-en/-on
Ehl-rohm-lohtt o koh-cheem…-n/-ehn/-ohn

I am a member of the … [motoring organisation]
A … tagja vagyok
Ah … tog-yo vodjok

I am on the road from… to…
A …-ból/-ből …-ba/-be vezető úton vagyok
A …-bohl/-burly …-bol-beh veh-zeh-tur oo-tohn vo-gyohk

I can't move the car. Can you send a tow-truck?
Nem tudom elindítani a kocsit. Tudna küldeni egy vontatót?
Nehm too-dohm ehl-een-dee-to-nee o koh-cheet. Tood-no kewl-deh-nee ehdj vohn-to-toht?

I have a flat tyre
Defektet kaptam
Deh-fehk-teht kop-tom

The windscreen (windshield) has smashed/cracked
A szélvédő eltörött/elrepedt
O sayl-vay-dur ehl-tuh-ruhtt/ehl-reh-pehdt

There is something wrong with the engine/brakes/ lights/steering/gearbox/clutch /exhaust.
Valami baj van a motorral/ fékkel/fényszórókkal/ kormánnyal/sebességváltóval/ kipufogócsővel
Vah-lo-mee boj von o moh-toh-rrol/ fayk-kehl/faynj-soh-rohk-kol/kohr-

mahnj-njol/seh-behsh-shayg-vahl-too-vol/kee-poof-foh-goh-chur-vehl

It's overheating
Túlmelegszik
Tool-meh-lehg-seek

It won't start
Nem indul
Nehm een-dool

Where can I get it repaired?
Hol lehet ezt megjavíttatni?
Hohl leh-het ehzt mehg-yo-veet-toht-nee?

Can you take me there?
Elvinne engem oda?
Ehl-veen-neh ehn-gehm ohdo?

Will it take long to fix?
Sokáig tart a javítás?
Shoh-kah-eeg tort o ja-vee-tahsh?

How much will it cost?
Mennyibe kerül a javítás?
Mehnj-njee-beh ekh-rewl o ja-vee-tahsh?

Please can you pick me up/give me a lift?
Kérem, elvinne engem?
Kay-rehm, ehl-veen-neh ehn-gehm?

Accidents and Traffic Offences (Violations)

Can you help me? There has been an accident
Tudna segíteni? Baleset történt
Tood-no sheh-gee-teh-ni? bol-eh-sheht tuhr-taynt

Please call the police/an ambulance

Kérem hívja a rendőrséget/mentőket
Kay-rehm heev-yo o rehn-dur-shay-geht/mehn-tur-keht

Is anyone hurt?
Megsebesült valaki?
Meg-she-beh-shewlt vo-loki?

I'm sorry, I didn't see the sign
Bocsánat, nem vettem észre a jelzőtáblát
Boh-chah-not, nehm veht-tehm ays-reh o yehl-zur-tahb-laht

Must I pay a fine? How much?
Büntetést kell fizetnem? Mennyit?
Bewn-teh-taysht kehl fee-zeht-nehm? Mehnj-njeet?

Kérem, mutassa az iratait
Kay-rehm, moo-to-sso oz ee-ro-to-eet
Show me your documents

Pharmacy (Gyógyszertár)

Do you have anything for a stomach ache/headache/sore throat/toothache?
Van Önnek valami hasfájás/fejfájás/torokgyulladás/fogfájás ellen?
Vahn Uhn-nehk vo-lo-mee hosh-fah-yahsh/fehy-fah-yahsh/toh-rohk-djool-lah-dahsh ehl-lehn?

I need something for diarrhoea/constipation/a cold/a cough/insect bites/sunburn/travel (motion) sickness
Nekem kell valami hasmenés/

**H
U
N
G
A
R
I
A
N**

székrekedés/megfázás/
köhögés/szúnyogcsípés/
leégés/tengeribetegség ellen
*Neh-kehm kehll vo-loh-mee hosh-
meh-naysh/sayk-reh-keh-daysh/
mehg-fah-zahsh/soo-njohg-chee-
paysh/tehn-geh-ree-beh-tehg-shayg
ehl-lehn*

How much/how many do I take?
Mennyit/hány darabot kell
bevennem?
*Mehnj-njeet/hahnj do-ro-boht kehll
beh-vehn-nehm?*

I am taking anti-malaria tablets/these pills
Malária elleni
tablettákat/ezeket és
kapszulákat szedem
*Mah-lah-ree-o ehl-lehnee tob-leht-
tah-kot/eh-zeh-keht o kop-soo-lah-
kot seh-dehm*

How often do I take it/them?
Milyen gyakran kell ezt/ezeket
bevennem?
*Mee-lyehn djok-ron kehll ehzt/eh-
zeh-keht beh-vehn-nehm?*

I am/he is/she is taking this medication
Ezt a gyógyszert szedem/szedi
*Ehzt o djoodj-sehrt seh-dehm/
seh-dee*

How much does it cost?
Mennyibe kerül ez?
Mehnj-njee-beh keh-rewl ehz?

Can you recommend a good doctor/dentist?
Tudna ajánlani egy jó
orvost/fogorvost?
*Tood-no o-jahn-lo-nee ehdj jooh ohr-
vohsht/fohg-ohr-vohsht?*

Is it suitable for children?
Ez gyerekeknek is való?
Ehz djeh-reh-kehk-nehk eesh vo-loh?

Doctor (Orvos)

I have a pain here/in my arm/leg/chest/stomach
Nekem fáj itt/a kezem/a
lábam/a mellkasom/a hasam
*Neh-kehm fahy eett/o keh-zehm/
o lah-bohm/o mehll-ko-shohm/
o ho-shohm*

Please call a doctor, this is an emergency
Kérem, hívja sürgősen az orvost
*Kay-rehm, heev-yoh shewr-gur-shehn
oz ohr-vohsht*

I would like to make an appointment to see the doctor
Szeretnék bejelentkezni az
orvoshoz
*She-reht-nayk beh-yeh-lehnt-kehz-
nee oz ohr-vohsh-hohz*

I am diabetic/pregnant
Diabetikus/terhes vagyok
Diabeti-koosh/tehr-hehsh vo-djohk

I need a prescription for...
Nekem recept kell ...-ra/re
Neh-kehm reh-tsept kehll ... ro/reh

Can you give me something to ease the pain?
Tudna nekem adni valami
fájdalomcsillapítót?
*Tood-no neh-kehm od-nee vo-lo-mee
fahy-do-lohm-cheel-lo-pee-toht?*

166

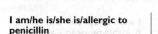
I am/he is/she is/allergic to penicillin
Nekem allergiám/neki allergiája van penicillinre
Neh-kehm allehr-gee-ahm/neh-kee allehr-gee-ahyo von penni-tsee-leen

Fáj itt?
Fahy eett?
Does this hurt?

Korházba kell mennie
Kohr-hahz-bo kehl mehn-nee-eh
You must/he must/she must go to hospital

Naponta egyszer/kétszer/háromszor vegye ezt be
No-pohn-to ehdj-sehr/kayt-sehr/hah-rohm-sohr veh-djeh ehzt beh
Take these once/twice/three times a day

I am/he is/she is taking this medication
Ezt a gyógyszert szedem/szedi
Ehzt o djoodj-sehrt seh-dehm/seh-dee

I have medical insurance
Van egészségbiztosításom
Von eh-gays-shayg-beez-toh-shee-tah-shohm

Dentist (Fogorvos)

I have toothache/my filling has come out
Fáj a fogam/kiesett a tömés
Fahy o foh-gom/kee-eh-shehtt o tuh-maysh

I do/do not want to have an injection first
Akarok/nem akarok injekciót előtte
O-ko-rohk/nehm o-ko-rohk een-yehk-tsee-oht eh-lurt-teh

EMERGENCIES

Help!
Segítség!
Sheh-geet-shayg!

Fire!
Tűz!
Teewz!

Stop!
Allj!
Ahlly!

Call an ambulance/a doctor/the police/the fire brigade!
Hívja a mentőket/orvost/rendőrséget/tűzoltókat!
Heev-yo o mehn-tur-keht/ohr-vohsht/rehn-dur-shay-geht/teewz-ohl-tooh-kot!

Please may I use a telephone?
Telefonálhatok innen?
Teh-leh-foh-nahl-ho-tok een-nehn?

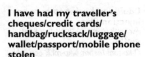

H U N G A R I A N

I have had my traveller's cheques/credit cards/handbag/rucksack/luggage/wallet/passport/mobile phone stolen

Ellopták az úticsekkjeimet/hitelkártyámat/táskámat/hátizsákomat/poggyászomat/pénztárcámat/útlevélemet/mobiltelefonomat

Ehl-lohp-tahk oz oo-tee-chehk-yeh-ee-meht/hee-tehl-kahr-tjah-mot/tahsh-kah-mot/hah-tee-zhay-koh-mot/pohdj-djah-soh-mot/paynz-tahr-tsah-mot/oot-leh-vayl-emet/mo-beel-teh-leh-fonoh-mot

May I please have a copy of the report for my insurance claim?

Megkaphatom a biztosítási igény-bejelentésem másolatát?

Mehg-kop-ho-tom o beez-to-shee-taay-shee ee-ganj-beh-jeh-lehn-tay-shehm mah-sho-lo-taht?

Can you help me, I have lost my daughter/son/my companion(s)

Kérem segítsen, nem találom a lányomat/fiamat/a társa(i)mat

Kay-rehm sheh-geet-shehn, nehm to-lah-lohm o lah-njoh-mot/fee-o-mot/o tahr-so-(ee)-mot

Please go away/leave me alone!

Menjen innen! Hagyjon engem békén!

Mehn-yehn een-nehn! Hodj-yohn ehn-gehm bay-kayn!

I'm sorry

Bocsánat

Bo-chah-not

I want to contact the British/American/Canadian/Irish/Australian/New Zealand/South African consulate

Fel akarom hívni a Brit/Amerikai/Kanadai/Ausztrál/Új-Zélandi/Dél-Afrikai Konzulátust

Fehl o-ko-rohm heev-nee o Breet/Amerika-ee/Kah-nah-dah-Eeaust-rahl/Ooy-Zay-lon-dee/Dayl-Of-ree-koee Kohn-zoo-lah-toohsht

I'm/we're/he is/she is/ill/lost/injured

Beteg vagyok/betegek vagyunk/ő beteg/eltévedtem/eltévedtünk/ő eltévedt/megsebesültem/megsebesültünk/megsebesült

Beh-tehg vo-djohk/beh-the-gehk vo-djoonk/ur beh-tehg/ehl-tay-vehd-tehm/ehl-tay-vehd-tewnk/ur ehl-tay-vehdt/mehg-sheh-beh-shewl-tehm/mehg-sheh-beh-shewl-tewnk/ur mehg-sheh-beh-shewlt

They are/ill/lost/injured

Betegek/eltévedtek/megsebesültek

Beh-the-gehk/ehl-tay-vehd-tehk/mehg-sheh-beh-shewl-tehk

LATVIAN

L
A
T
V
I
A
N

INTRODUCTION

The Latvian language is related to the majority of European languages. It belongs to the Baltic branch of the Indo-European language family, which also includes Lithuanian.

Addresses for Travel and Tourist Information

Australia: *Baltic Connections,* Suite 3, 11-13 The Centre, Forestville, NSW 2087. Tel: (2) 9975 2355. Fax: (2) 9451 6446.

Canada; *Latvian Embassy,* 350 Sparks St, Suite 1200, Ottawa, Ontario KIR 7S8. Tel: (613) 238 6014. Fax: (613) 238 7044.

South Africa: *Honorary Consulate of Latvia,* 4 Lafeyette Rd, Sandhurst, Sandton 2196. Tel: (011) 783 9445. Fax: (011) 783 9450.

UK: *Latvian Embassy,* 45 Nottingham Place, London WIU 5LR. Tel: (020) 7312 0040; Fax: (020) 7312 0042.

USA: *Latvian Embassy,* 4325 17th St, NW, Washington DC 20011. Tel: (202) 726 8213. Fax: (202) 726 6785.

Official tourism website www.latviatourism.com

Latvia Facts

CAPITAL: Riga

CURRENCY: 1 Lats = 100 santimi

OPENING HOURS: Banks: Mon–Fri 0900–1700, some Sat 0900–1230. Shops: Mon–Fri 0900/1000–1800/1900 and Sat 0900/1000–1700. Many close on Mon.
Food shops open earlier and close later. Many 24 hr food shops.
Museums: days vary, but usually open Tues/Wed–Sun 1100–1700.

TELEPHONES: To dial in, +371. Outgoing, 8 00 + the country code. Police, 02. Fire, 01. Ambulance, 03.

PUBLIC HOLIDAYS: Jan 1; Good Friday; Easter Monday; May 1; June 23–24; Nov 18; Dec 24–26, Dec 31.

Technical Language Hints

The Latvian standard alphabet is phonetic, with each of its letters corresponding to only one sound, except for two letter combinations ch, dz, dž, which mark single sounds.

ESSENTIALS

Alphabet and Pronunciation

	Name	Pronounced		Name	Pronounced
A a	ah	neutral sound as in sun; ai as i in fine; au as ow in how	Ģ ģ	mikstais gah	dy sound as in British pronunciation of duty
Ā ā	ah	long a as in car	H h	hah	kh sound as in Scottish pronunciation of loch
B b	beh	as in bed			
C c	tseh	ts sound as in bats	I i	ee	short i as in sit; ie as in tier
Č č	cheh	ch as in church	Ī ī	ee	long i as in machine
D d	deh	d as in day	J j	yot	y as in yes
Dz dz	dzeh	dz sound as at the end of lads	K k	kah	as in kind
			Ķ ķ	mikstais kah	ky sound as in queue
Dž dž	yeh	j as j in jest	L l	el	as in lemon
E e	eh	short e as in pet or short a as in bad; ei as in rein	Ļ ļ	mikstais el	ly sound as in million
			M m	em	as in mother
			N n	en	as in not
Ē ē	eh	long e sound as in air or long a as in bark	Ņ ņ	mikstais en	ny sound as in British pronunciation of new
			O o	o	as in got; oi as in loiter
F f	ef	as in fast	P p	peh	as in paper
G g	gah	as in garden	R r	er	rolled r as in Scottish pronunciation

L
A
T
V
I
A
N

S s	es		as in sit
Š š	esh		sh as in she
T t	teh		as in tick
U u	oo		short u as in put; ui as in ruin
Ū ū	oo		long u sound as in food
V v	veh		as in vote
Z z	zeh		as in zoo
Ž ž	zheh		zh sound like the s in pleasure

Basic Words and Phrases

Yes
Jā
Ja

No
Nē
Ne

Please
Lūdzu
Ludzu

Thank you
Paldies
Paldies

Hello
Sveiki
Sveiki

Goodbye
Uz redzēšanos
Uz redzeshanos

Excuse me
Atvainojiet
Atvaynoyiet

Sorry
Piedodiet
Piedodiet

That's O.K.
Tas ir labi
Tas ir labi

Perhaps
Varbūt
Varboot

How
Kā
Ka

When
Kad
Kad

What
Ko Kas
Ko Kas

Why
Kāpēc
Kapets

Who
Kas Kurš
Kas Kursh

To
Līdz
Lidz

From
No
No

Here
Šeit
Sheit

There
Tur
Tur

I don't understand
Es nesaprotu
Es nesaprotu

I don't speak Latvian
Es nerunāju latviski
Es nerunayu latviski

Do you speak English?
Vai Jūs runājat angliski?
Vai Jus runayat angliski?

Can you please write it down?
Vai jūs nevarētu lūdzu to uzrakstīt?
Vai yus nevaretu ludzu to uzrakstit?

Please can you speak more slowly?
Lūdzu, vai jūs nevarētu runāt lēnāk?
Ludzu, vai yus nevaretu runat lenak?

Greetings

Good morning/Good afternoon/Good evening/Good night
Labrīt/Labdien/Labvakar/ Ar labunakti
Labrit/labdien/labvakar/labnakti/ Ar labunakti

Pleased to meet you
Priecājos iepazīties
Priecayos iepazities

How are you?
Kā jums klājas?
Ka yums klayas?

I am well, thank you. And you?
Paldies, labi. Un jums?
Paldies, labi. Un yums?

My name is ...
Mans vārds ir ...
Mans vahrds ir ...

This is ... my friend/boyfriend/ girlfriend/husband/wife/ brother/sister
Šis ir ... mans draugs/mans draugs/mana draudzene/mans vīrs/mana sieva/mans brālis/ mana māsa
Shis ir ... mans draugs/mans draugs/ mana draudzene/mans virs/mana sieva/mans bralis/mana masa

Where are you travelling to?
Uz kurieni jūs ceļojat?
Uz kurieni yus tseloyat?

I am/we are going to ...
Es braucu/mēs braucam uz ...
Es braucu/mes brautsam uz ...

How long are you travelling for?
Cik ilgi jūs ceļojat?
Tsik ilgi yus tseloyat?

Where do you come from?
No kurienes jūs esat?
No kurienes yus esat?

I am/we are from ... Australia/Britain/Canada/ America
Es esmu/mēs esam no Austrālijas/Lielbritānijas/ Kanādas/Amerikas
Es esmu/mes esam no Australiyas/ Leelbritahniyas/Kanadas/Amerikas

We are on holiday
Mēs esam atvaļinājumā
Mes esam atvalyinayuma

This is our first visit here
Šis ir mūsu pirmais brauciens uz šejieni
Shis ir musu pirmais brauciens uz sheyieni

How old are you?
Cik jums gadu?
Tsik yums gadu?

I am ... years old
Man ir ... gadi
Man ir ... gadi

I am a business person/ doctor/journalist/manual worker/administrator/ scientist/student/teacher
Es esmu biznesmenis/ārsts/ žurnālists/strādnieks/ administrators/zinātnieks/ students/skolotājs
Es esmu biznesmenis/arsts/ zhurnalists/stradnieks/administrators/ zinatnieks/students/skolotays

I am waiting for my husband/ wife/boyfriend/girlfriend
Es gaidu savu vīru/sievu/ draugu/draudzeni
Es gaidu savu viru/sievu/draugu/ draudzeni

L
A
T
V
I
A
N

Would you like/may I have a cigarette?
Vai Jūs vēlaties/vai es varētu palūgt cigareti?
Vai Jus velaties/vai es varetu palugt cigareti?

Do you mind if I smoke?
Vai es drīkstu smēķēt?
Varu es drikstu smeket?

Do you have a light?
Vai jums ir šķiltavas?
Vai yums ir shkiltavas?

Days

Monday
Pirmdiena
Pirmdiena

Tuesday
Otrdiena
Otrdiena

Wednesday
Trešdiena
Treshdiena

Thursday
Ceturtdiena
Tseturdiena

Friday
Piektdiena
Piekdiena

Saturday
Sestdiena
Sesdiena

Sunday
Svētdiena
Svediena

Morning/Afternoon/Evening/Night
Rīts/Pēcpusdiena/Vakars/Nakts
Rits/Petspusdiena/Vakars/Nakts

Yesterday/Today/Tomorrow
Vakar/Šodien/Rīt
Vakar/Shuodien/Rit

Numbers

Zero
Nulle
Nulle

One
Viens
Viens

Two
Divi
Divi

Three
Trīs
Tris

Four
Četri
Tshetri

Five
Pieci
Pietsi

Six
Seši
Seshi

Seven
Septiņi
Septini

Eight
Astoņi
Astoni

Nine
Deviņi
Devini

Ten
Desmit
Desmit

Eleven
Vienpadsmit
Vienpatsmit

Twelve
Divpadsmit
Divpatsmit

Thirteen
Trīspadsmit
Trispatsmit

Fourteen
Četrpadsmit
Tshetrpatsmit

Fifteen
Piecpadsmit
Pietspatsmit

Sixteen
Sešpadsmit
Seshpatsmit

Seventeen
Septiņpadsmit
Septinpatsmit

Eighteen
Astoņpadsmit
Astonpatsmit

Nineteen
Deviņpadsmit
Devinpatsmit

Twenty
Divdesmit
Divdesmit

Twenty-one
Divdesmit viens
Divdesmit viens

Twenty-two
Divdesmit divi
Divdesmit divi

Thirty
Trisdesmit
Trisdesmit

Forty
Četrdesmit
Tshetrdesmit

Fifty
Piecdesmit
Pietsdesmit

Sixty
Sešdesmit
Seshdesmit

Seventy
Septiņdesmit
Septindesmit

Eighty
Astoņdesmit
Astondesmit

Ninety
Deviņdesmit
Devindesmit

One hundred
Simts
Simts

Five hundred
Pieci simti
Pietsi simti

One thousand
Tūkstots
Tukstots

One million
Miljons
Milyons

Time

What time is it?
Cik ir pulkstenis?
Tsik ir pulkstenis?

It is ...
Pulkstenis ir...
Pulkstenis ir...

9.00
Deviņi
Devini

9.05
Piecas minūtes pāri deviņiem
Pietsas minutes pari deviniem

9.15
Piecpadsmit minūtes pāri
deviņiem
Pietspatsmit minutes pari deviniem

9.20
Divdesmit minūtes pāri
deviņiem
Divdesmit minutes pari deviniem

9.30
Pusdesmit
Pusdesmit

9.35
Bez divdesmit piecām minūtēm
desmit
*Bez divdesmit pietsam minutem
desmit*

9.40
Bez divdesmit minūtēm desmit
Bez divdesmit minutem desmit

9.45
Ceturksnis pirms desmitiem
Ceturksnis pirms desmitiem

9.50
Bez desmit minūtēm desmit
Bez desmit minutem desmit

9.55
Bez piecām minūtēm desmit
Bez pietsam minutem desmit

12.00/Midday/Midnight
Divpadsmit/Dienasvidus/
Pusnakts
Divpatsmit/Dienasvidus/Pusnakts

L
A
T
V
I
A
N

175

L A T V I A N

Money

I would like to change these traveller's cheques/this currency
Es vēlos izmainīt šos ceļojumu čekus/šo valūtu
Es velos izmainit shos tselyoyumu chekus/scho valutu

How much commission do you charge? (What is the service charge?)
Cik liela ir komisijas nauda?
Tsik liela ir komisiyas nauda?

Can I obtain money with my Mastercard?
Vai es varu izņemt naudu ar savu Māsterkarti?
Vai es varu iznemt naudu ar savu Masterkarti?

Where is the nearest ATM?
Kur ir tuvākais bankas automāts?
Kur ir tuvahkais bankas automahts?

My name is ... Some money has been wired to here for me to collect
Mans vārds ir ... Man ir pārsūtīta nauda, kas man ir jāsaņem
Mans vahrds ir ... Man ir pahrsooteeta nauda, kas man ir yahsanyem

ARRIVING AND DEPARTING

Airport

Excuse me, where is the check-in desk for ...?
Atvainojiet, kur ir atrodas reģistratūra ...?
Atvainoyiet, kur ir atrodas redyistratoora ...?

What is the boarding gate/time for my flight?
Kādi ir izejas vārti/kas ir izlidošanas laiks manam lidojumam?
Kadi ir izeyas varti/kas ir izli-doshanas laiks manam lidoyumam?

How long is the delay likely to be?
Cik ilgi varētu aizkavēties?
Tsik ilgi varetu aizkaveties?

Where is the duty-free shop?
Kur atrodas beznodokļu veikals?
Kur atrodas beznodoklu veikals?

Which way is the luggage reclaim?
Kur ir bagāžas celiņš?
Kur ir bagazhas tselinsh?

I have lost my luggage. Please can you help?
Es pazaudēju savu bagāžu. Lūdzu, vai jūs nevarētu palīdzēt?
Es pazaudeyu savu bagazhu. Ludzu vai yus nevaretu palidzet?

I am flying to ...
Es lidoju uz....
Es lidoyu uz....

Where is the bus for the city centre?
Kur ir autobuss uz pilsētas centru?
Kur ir autobuss uz pilsetas tsentru?

Trains and Boats

Where is the ticket office/information desk?
Kur ir biļešu kase/uzziņu birojs?
Kur ir bilyeshu kase/uzzinu biroys?

Which platform does the train/speedboat/ferry to ... depart from?
No kura perona atiet vilciens/ātrlaiva/kuģis, prāmis uz ...?
No kura perona atiet viltsiens/atrlaiva/kudyis, pramis uz ...?

Where is platform ...?
Kur ir ... perons?
Kur ir ... perons?

When is the next train/boat to...?
Cikos atiet nākošais vilciens/kuģis uz..?
Cikos atiet nakoshais viltsiens/kudyis uz..?

Is there a later train/boat to...?
Vai ir vilciens/kuģis uz ... kas atiet vēlāk?
Vai ir viltsiens/kudyis uz...kas atiet velak?

Notices and Signs

Restorānvagons
Restoranvagons
Buffet (Dining) car

Autobuss
Autobuss
Bus

Dzeramūdens/Nav dzeramūdens
Dzeramudens/Nav dzeramudens
Drinking/Non-drinking water

Ieeja
Ieeya
Entrance

Izeja
Izeya
Exit

Slimnīca
Slimnitsa
Hospital

Informācija
Informatsiya
Information

Bagāžas glabātava
Bagazhas glabatava
Left luggage (Baggage claim)

Bagāžas skapji
Bagazhas skapyi
Luggage lockers

Pasts
Pasts
Post office

L
A
T
V
I
A
N

Dzelzceļa stacijas perons
Dzelztselya statsiyas perons
Platform

Dzelzceļa stacija
Dzelztselya statsiya
Railway (Railroad) station

Lidosta
Lidosta
Airport

Policijas iecirknis
Politsiyas ietsirknis
Police station

Osta
Osta
Port

Restorāns
Restorans
Restaurant

Smēķēt atļauts/
Smēķēt aizliegts
Smeket atlyauts/
Smeket aizliegts
**Smoking/
Non-smoking**

Telefons
Telefons
Telephone

Biļešu kase
Bilyeshu kase
Ticket office

Reģistratūra
Redyistratoora
Check-in desk

Saraksts
Saraksts
Timetable (Schedule)

Tualete
Tualete
Toilets (Restrooms)

Dāmām/Kungiem
Damam/Kungiem
Ladies/Gentlemen

Metro
Metro
Underground (Subway)

Uzgaidāmā telpa
Uzgaidama telpa
Waiting room

Buying a Ticket

**I would like a first-class/
second-class/third-class single
(one-way)/return (round-trip)
ticket to...**
Es vēlos pirmās klases/otrās
klases/trešās klases
(vienvirziena)/turp atpakaļ
biļeti uz ...
*Es velos pirmas klases/otras
klases/treshas klases (vienvirziena)
turp atpakaly bilyeti uz...*

**Is it an express (fast) train/
bus?**
Vai tas ir ātrvilciens/
autobuss-ekspresis?
*Vai tas ir atrviltsiens/
autobuss-ekspresis?*

Is my rail pass valid on this train/ferry/bus?
Vai mana vilciena biļete ir
derīga šajā vilcienā/prāmī/
autobusā?
*Vai mana vilciena bilyete ir deriga
shaya viltsiena/prami/autobusa?*

I would like an aisle/window seat
Es vēlos vietu pie ejas/pie loga
Es vçlos vietu pie eyas/pie loga

No smoking/smoking please
Nesmēķētāja vietu/smēķētāja
vietu, lūdzu
*Nesmeketaya vietu/smeketaya vietu,
ludzu*

We would like to sit together
Mes vēlamies sēdēt kopā
Mes velamies sedet kopa

I would like to make a seat reservation
Es vēlos rezervēt vietu
Es velos rezervet vietu

I would like to reserve a couchette/sleeper for one person/two people/my family
Es vēlos rezervēt kupeju/
guļamvietu vienam cilvēkam/
diviem cilvēkiem/manai
ģimenei
*Es velos rezervet kupeju/gulmvietu
vienam tsilvekam/diviem
tsilvekiem/manai dyimenei*

I would like to reserve a cabin
Es vēlos rezervēt kajīti
Es velos rezervet kayiti

Timetables (Schedules)

Pienāk
Pienak
Arrive

Pietur ...
Pietur...
Calls (Stops at)

Bufete/restorānvagons
Bufete/restoranvagons
Catering service

Pārsēšanās ...
Parseshanas
Change at

Savienojums/Caur
Savienoyums/Caur
Connection/Via

Katru dienu
Katru dienu
Daily

Ik pēc četrdesmit minūtēm
Ik pets chetrdesmit minutem
Every 40 minutes

Pirmā klase
Pirma klase
First class

Katru stundu
Katru stundu
Hourly

Rezervācijas ir ieteicamas
Rezervaciyas ir ieteitsamas
Seat reservations are recommended

L
A
T
V
I
A
N

179

Otrā klase
Otra klase
Second class

Obligāta piemaksa
Obligata piemaksa
Supplement payable

Luggage

How much will it cost to send (ship) my luggage in advance?
Cik maksā, lai iepriekš aizsūtītu manu bagāžu?
Tsik maksa, lai iepriekš aizsutetu manu bagazhu?

Where is the left luggage (baggage claim) office?
Kur ir bagāžas glabātava (bagāžas celiņš)?
Kur ir bagazhas glabatativa (bagazhas selyins)?

What time do you open/close?
Cikos Jūs atverat/slēdzat?
Tsikos yus esat atverat/slehdzat?

Where are the luggage trolleys/carts?
Kur ir bagāžas ratiņi?
Kur ir bagazhas ratini?

Where are the lockers?
Kur ir bagāžas skapji?
Kur ir bagazhas skapyi?

I have lost my locker key
Es pazaudēju bagāžas skapja atslēgu
Es pazaudeyu bagazhas skapya atslegu

On Board

Is this seat free?
Vai šī vieta ir brīva?
Vai shi vieta ir briva?

Excuse me, you are sitting in my reserved seat!
Atvainojiet, bet jūs sēžat manā rezervētajā vietā!
Atvainoyet, bet yus sezhat mana rezervetaya vieta!

Which station is this?
Kas ir šī stacija?
Kas ir shi statsiya?

What time is this train/bus/ferry/flight due to arrive/depart?
Cikos pienāk/atiet šis vilciens/autobuss/prāmis/lidmašīna?
Cikos pienak/atiet shis viltsiens/autobuss/pramis/lidmashina?

Travelling with Children

Do you have a high chair/babysitting service/cot?
Vai jums ir bērnu krēsls/bērnu aukles pakalpojumi/bērnu gultas?
Vai yums ir bernu kresls/bernu aukles pakalpoyumi/bernu gultas?

Where is the nursery/playroom?
Kur ir istaba bērniem/spēļu istaba?
Kur ir istaba berniem/spelyu istaba?

Where can I warm the baby's bottle?
Kur es varu uzsildīt bērnam pudelīti?
Kur es varu uzsildit bernam pudeliti?

Customs and Passports

Lūdzu pases
Ludsu pases
Passports please

I have nothing/wine/spirits (alcohol)/tobacco to declare
Man nav nekā/ir viņa/ir spirta dzērieni (alkohols)/ir tabaka muitas deklarācijai
Man nav neka/ir vina/ir spirta dserieni (alkohols)/ir tabaka muitas deklaratsiyai

I will be staying for … days/weeks/months
Es palikšu… dienas/nedēļas/mēnešus
Es palikshu… dienas/nedelyas/meneshus

SIGHTSEEING

Asking the Way

Excuse me, do you speak English?
Atvainojiet, vai jūs runājat angliski?
Atvainoyiet, vai yus runayat angliski?

Excuse me, can you help me please?
Atvainojiet, vai jūs nevarētu man lūdzu palīdzēt?
Atvainoyiet, vai yus nevaretu man ludsu palidze?

Where is the Tourist Information Office?
Kur atrodas tūristu informācijas birojs?
Kur atrodas turistu informaciyas biroys?

Excuse me, is this the right way to…?
Atvainojiet, vai šis ir pareizais ceļš uz…?
Atvainoyiet, vai shis ir pareizais celysh uz…?

… the cathedral/the tourist information office/the castle/the old town
…katedrāli/tūristu informācijas biroju/baznīcu/vecpilsētu
…katedrali/turistu informatsiyas biroyu/baznitsu/vetspilsetu

Can you tell me the way to the railway (railroad) station/bus station/taxi rank/city centre (downtown)/beach?
Vai jūs varētu man pateikt kā tikt uz dzelzceļa staciju/autoostu/taksometru pieturu/pilsētas centru/pludmali?
Vai yus varetu man pateikt ka tikt uz dzelztselya statsiyu/autoostu/taksometru pieturu/pilsetas tsentru/pludmali?

Pirmais/otrais/pa kreisi/pa labi/uz priekšu
Pirmais/otrais/pa kreisi/pa labi/uz priekshu
First/second/left/right/straight ahead

L
A
T
V
I
A
N

Uz stūra/pie luksofora
Uz stura/pie luksofora
At the corner/at the traffic lights

Where is the nearest police station/post office?
Kur atrodas tuvākais policijas iecirknis/pasts?
Kur atrodas tuvakais politsiyas ietsirknis/pasts?

Is it near/far?
Vai tas ir tuvu/tālu?
Vai tas ir tuvu/talu?

Do I need to take a taxi/catch a bus?
Vai man vajag braukt ar taksi/autobusu?
Vai man vayag braukt ar taksi/autobusu?

Do you have a map?
Vai jums ir karte?
Vai yums ir karte?

Can you point to it on my map?
Vai jūs varētu to parādīt uz manas kartes?
Vai yus varetu to paradit uz manas kartes?

Thank you for your help
Paldies par palīdzību
Paldies par palidzibu

How do I reach the motorway/main road?
Kā es varu tikt uz lielceļa/uz galvenā ceļa?
Ka es varu tikt uz lieltselya/uz galvena tselya?

I think I have taken the wrong turning
Man liekas, ka es nogriezos nepareizi
Man liekas, ka es nogriezos nepareizi

I am looking for this address
Es meklēju šo adresi
Es mekleyu sho adresi

I am looking for the... hotel.
Es meklēju viesnīcu...
Es mekleyu viesnitsu...

How far is it to... from here?
Cik tālu no šejienes līdz ...?
Tsik talu no sheyienes lidz ...?

Turpiniet uz priekšu ... kilometrus
Turpiniet uz priekshu ... kilometrus
Carry straight on for ... kilometres

Nākamais pa labi/pa kreisi
Nakamais pa labi/pa kreisi
Take the next turning on the right/left

Pa labi/pa kreisi pie nākošā krustojuma/luksofora
Pa labi/pa kreisi pie nakosha krustoyuma/luksofora
Turn right/left at the next crossroads/traffic lights

Jūs braucat nepareizā virzienā
Jus brautsat nepareiza virziena
You are going in the wrong direction

How much is the admission/entrance charge?
Cik ir ieejas maksa?
Tsik ir ieeyas maksa?

Is there a discount for children/students/senior citizens?
Vai ir atlaides bērniem/studentiem/pensionāriem?
Vai ir atlaides bçrniem/studentiem/pensionariem?

What time does the next guided tour in English start?
Cikos ir nākamā apskate angliski runājoša gida pavadījumā?
Tsikos ir nakama apskate angliski runayosha gida pavad'yuma?

One/two adults/children please
Viens pieaugušais/divi pieaugušie/viens bērns/divi bērni, lūdzu
Viens pieaugushais/divi pieaugushie/viens berns/divi berni, ludzu

May I take photographs here?
Vai es drīkstu šeit fotogrāfēt?
Es es drikstu sheit fotografet?

At the Tourist Office

Do you have a map of the town/area?
Vai jums ir pilsētas/rajona karte?
Vai yums ir pilsetas/rayona karte?

Do you have a list of accommodation?
Vai jums ir apmešanās vietu saraksts?
Vai yums ir apmeshanas vietu saraksts?

Can I reserve accommodation?
Vai es varu rezervēt apmešanās vietu?
Vai es varu rezervet apmeshanas vietu?

ACCOMMODATION

Hotels

I have a reservation in the name of...
Man ir rezervācija ... vārdā
Man ir rezervatsiya ... varda

I wrote to/faxed/telephoned you last month/last week
Es jums uzrakstīju/sūtīju faksu/zvanīju pagājušā mēnesī/nedēļā
Es yums uzrakstiyu/sutiyu faksu/zvaniyu pagayushaya menesi/nedelya

Do you have any rooms free?
Vai jums ir brīvi numuri?
Vai yums ir brivi numuri?

I would like to reserve a single/double room with/without a bath/shower
Es vēlos rezervēt vienvietīgu/divvietīgu numuru ar vannu/dušu/bez vannas/dušas
Es velos rezervet vienvietigu/divietigu numuru ar vannu/dushu/bez vannas/dushas

I would like bed/breakfast/(room and) full board
Es vēlos numuru ar brokastīm/numuru un pilnu pansiju
Es velos numuru ar brokastim/numuru un pilnu pansiyu

How much is it per night?
Cik maksā diennaktī?
Tsik maksa diennakti?

Is breakfast included?
Vai brokastis ir ierēķinātas
cenā?
Vai brokastis ir ierekinatas tsena?

Do you have any cheaper rooms?
Vai jums ir lētāki numuri?
Vai yums iri letaki numuri?

I would like to see/take the room
Es vēlos redzēt/rezervēt
numuru
Es velos redzet/rezervet numuru

I would like to stay for ... nights
Es vēlos palikt ... diennaktis
Es velos palikt ... diennaktis

The shower/light/tap/hot water doesn't work
Duša/gaisma/krāns/karstais
ūdens nestrādā
Dusha/gaisma/krans/karstais udens nestrada

At what time/where is breakfast served?
Cikos/kur ir brokastis?
Tsikos/kur ir brokastis?

What time do I have to check out?
Cikos man ir jāatbrīvo numurs?
Tsikos man ir yaatbrivo numurs?

Can I have the key to room number ...?
Vai es varētu dabūt atslēgu ...
numuram?
Vai es varetu dabut atslegu ... numuram?

My room number is...
Manas istabas numurs ir...
Manas istabas numurs ir...

My room is not satisfactory/not clean enough/too noisy. Please can I change rooms?
Mana istaba mani neapmieri-
na/nav pietiekami tīra/ir pārāk
trokšņaina. Vai es drīkstu
samainīt istabu?
Mana istaba mani neapmierina/nav pietiekami tira/ir parak trokshnaina. Vai es drikstu samainit istabu?

Where is the bathroom?
Kur ir vannas istaba?
Kur ir vannas istaba?

Do you have a safe for valuables?
Vai jums ir seifs dārglietām?
Vai yums ir seifs darglietam?

Is there a laundry/do you wash clothes?
Vai ir veļasmazgātuve/vai jūs
mazgājat drēbes?
Vai ir velyasmazgatuve/vai yus mazgayat drebes?

I would like an air-conditioned room
Es vēlos istabu ar gaisa
kondicionieri
Es velos istabu ar gaisa konditsionieri

L
A
T
V
I
A
N

Do you accept traveller's cheques/credit cards?
Vai jūs pieņemat ceļojumu čekus/kredītkartes?
Vai yus pienemat tselyoyumu chekus/kreditkartes?

May I have the bill please?
Lūdzu rēķinu!
Ludzu rekyinu!

Excuse me, I think there may be a mistake in this bill
Atvainojiet, man liekas, ka šajā rēķinā ir kļūda
Atvainoyiet, man liekas ka shaya rekina ir klyuda

Youth Hostels

How much is a dormitory bed per night?
Cik maksā gultasvieta diennaktī?
Tsik maksa gultasvieta diennakti?

I am/am not an HI member
Es esmu/neesmu HI biedrs
Es esmu/meesmu HI biedrs

May I use my own sleeping bag?
Vai es drīkstu lietot savu guļammaisu?
Vai es drikstu lietot savu gulyam-maisu?

What time do you lock the doors at night?
Cikos Jūs vakaros slēdzat durvis?
Tsikos yus vakaros sledsat durvis?

Camping

May I camp for the night/two nights?
Vai es drīkstu apmesties uz vienu nakti/divām naktīm?
Vai es drikstu apmesties uz vienu nakti/divam naktim?

Where can I pitch my tent?
Kur es varu novietot savu telti?
Kur es varu novietot savu telti?

How much does it cost for one night/week?
Cik maksā viena nakts/nedēļa?
Tsik maksa viena nakts/nedelya?

Where are the washing facilities?
Kur ir mazgātuves?
Kur ir mazgatuves?

Is there a restaurant/supermarket/swimming pool on site/nearby?
Vai šeit/tuvumā ir restorāns/universālveikals/peldbaseins?
Vai sheyt/tuvuma ir restorans/universalveikals/peldbaseins?

Do you have a safety deposit box?
Vai jums ir seifs?
Vai yus ir seifs?

L
A
T
V
I
A
N

**L
A
T
V
I
A
N**

EATING AND DRINKING

Cafés and Bars

I would like a cup of/two cups of/another coffee/tea
Es vēlos vienu tasi/divas tases/
vēlvienu tasi kafijas/tējas
*Es velos vienu tasi/divas tases/vel-
vienu tasi kafiyas/teyas*

With/without milk/sugar
Ar/bez krējumu/cukuru
Ar/bez kreyumu/tsukuru

I would like a bottle/glass/two glasses of mineral water/red wine/white wine, please
Es vēlos pudeli/glāzi/divas
glāzes minerālūdens/
sarkanvīnu/baltvīnu, lūdzu
*Es velos pudeli/glazi/divas glazes/
mineraludens/sarkanvinu/baltvinu,
ludzu*

I would like a beer/two beers, please
Es vēlos alu/divus alus, lūdzu
Es velos alu/divas alus, ludzu

Please may I have some ice?
Lūdzu atnesiet man ledu!
Ludzu atnesiet man ledu!

Do you have any matches/cigarettes/cigars?
Vai jums ir sērkociņi/
cigaretes/cigāri?
*Vai yums ir serkotsini/tsigaretes/
tsigari?*

Restaurants

Can you recommend a good/cheap restaurant in this area?
Vai jūs varētu ieteikt labu/lētu
restorānu šajā apkārtnē?
*Vai yus varetu ieteikt labu/letu
restoranu shaya apkartne?*

I would like a table for ... people
Es vēlos galdu ... cilvēkiem
Es velos galdu ... cilvekiem

Do you have a non-smoking area?
Vai jums ir nodalījums
nesmēķētājiem?
*Vai yums ir nodaliyums nesmeke-
tayiem?*

Waiter! Waitress!
Oficiant! Oficiante!
Ofitsant! Ofitsante!

Excuse me, please may we order?
Atvainojiet, vai mēs varētu,
lūdzu, pasūtīt?
*Atvainoyiet, vai mes varetu ludzu
pasutit?*

Do you have a set menu/children's menu/wine list in English?
Vai jums ir ēdienkarte/bērnu
ēdienkarte/vīnu karte angļu
valodā?
*Vai yums ir edienkarte/behrnu ehdi-
enkarte/vinu karte anglu valoda?*

Do you have any vegetarian dishes?
Vai jums ir veģetārie ēdieni?
Vai yums ir vedyetahrieh ehdieni?

Do you have any local specialities?
Vai jums ir kādi vietējie ēdieni?
Vai yums ir kadi vietehyieh edieni?

Are vegetables included?
Vai klāt ir dārzeņi?
Vai klat ir darzeni?

Could I have it well-cooked/ medium/rare please?
Man, lūdzu, labi izceptu/vidēji izceptu?
Man, loodzu, labi iztseptu/videyi iztseptu?

What does this dish consist of?
No kā sastāv šis ēdiens?
No ka sastav shis ediens?

I am a vegetarian. Does this contain meat?
Es esmu veģetārietis.
Vai tajā ir gaļa?
Es esmu vedyetahrietis.
Vai tayah ir galya?

I do not eat nuts/dairy products/meat/fish
Es neēdu riekstus/piena produktus/gaļu/zivis
Es needu riekstus/piena produktus/galyu/zivis

Not (very) spicy please
Ne pārāk pikantu, lūdzu
Ne parak pikantu, ludzu

I would like the set menu please
Lūdzu ēdienkarti
Ludzu edienkarti

We have not been served yet
Mēs joprojām gaidām, kad mūs apkalpos
Mehs yuopruoyahm gaidahm, kad moos apkalpos

Please bring a plate/knife/ fork
Lūdzu, atnesiet šķīvi/nazi/dakšiņu
Loodzu, atnesiet shkeevi/nazi/dakshinyu

Excuse me, this is not what I ordered
Atvainojiet, šis nav ko es pasūtīju
Atvainoyiet, shis nav ko es pasutiyu

May I have some/more bread/water/coffee/tea?
Vai drīkstu palūgt mazliet/ vairāk maizi/ūdeni/ kafiju/tēju?
Vai drikstu palugt mazliet/vairak maizi/udeni/kafiyu/teyu?

May I have the bill please?
Lūdzu rēķinu!
Ludzu rekyinu!

Does this bill include service?
Vai šajā rēķinā ir ieskaitīta apkalpošana?
Vai shaya rekyina ir ieskaitita apkalposhana?

Do you accept traveller's cheques/Mastercard/ US dollars?
Vai jūs pieņemat ceļojumu čekus/māsterkarti/ ASV dolārus?
Vai yus pienyemat tselyoyumu chekus/masterkarti/ASV dolarus?

L A T V I A N

Can I have a receipt please?
Vai es drīkstu palūgt čeku/kvīti,
lūdzu?
*Vai es drikstu palugt cheku kviti,
ludzu?*

**Where is the toilet
(restroom) please?**
Kur ir tualete?
Kur ir tualete?

On the Menu

Brokastis/Pusdienas/
Vakariņas
Bruokastis/Pusdienas/Vakarinas
Breakfast/Lunch/Dinner

Uzkodas	Zupas
Uzkodas	*Zupas*
First courses	**Soups**

Otrie ēdieni	Zivju ēdieni
Otrie edieni	*Zivyu edieni*
Main courses	**Fish dishes**

Gaļas ēdieni
Galyas edieni
Meat dishes

Liellopu gaļa	Bifšteks
Lieluopu galya	*Bifshteks*
Beef	**Steak**

Cūkas gaļa	Teļa gaļa
Tsookas galya	*Tela galya*
Pork	**Veal**

Vistas gaļa	Jēra gaļa
Vista galya	*Yehra galya*
Chicken	**Lamb**

Šķiņķis
Shkyinkyis
Ham

Veģetārie ēdieni
Vedyetarie edieni
Vegetarian Dishes

Dārzeņi
Dahrzenyi
Vegetables

Kartupeļu čipsi
Kartupelyu chipsi
Chips (french fries)

Vārīti/cepti kartupeļi/
kartupeļu biezenis
*Vahreeti/tsepti kartupelyi/
kartupelyu biezenis*
**Boiled/sauté/mashed
potatoes**

Rīsi	Deserti
Reesi	*Deserti*
Rice	**Desserts**

Saldējums	Kūkas
Saldehyums	*Kookas*
Ice cream	**Cakes**

Biskvīti	Augļi
Biskveeti	*Auglyi*
Pastries	**Fruit**

Maize	Apaļmaizītes
Maize	*Apalmaizeetes*
Bread	**Rolls**

Grauzdiņš	Sviests
Grauzdinsh	*Sviests*
Toast	**Butter**

Sāls/pipari
Sahls/pipari
Salt/pepper

Cukurs
Tsukurs
Sugar

Firmas ēdieni
Firmas edieni
Specialities

Vietējais sortiments
Vietehyais sortiments
Local specialities

Ēdienkartes komplekts
Ehdienkartes komplekts
Set menu

Vīnu saraksts
Veenu saraksts
Wine list

Sarkanvīni
Sarkanveeni
Red wines

Baltvīni
Baltveeni
White wines

Rozē vīni
Rozeh veeni
Rosé wines

Dzirkstošie vīni
Dzirkstuoshie veeni
Sparkling wines

Alus
Alus
Beer

Pudeļu alus/izlejamais alus
Pudelu alus/izleyamais alus
**Bottled beer/draught
(draft) beer**

Bezalkoholiskie dzērieni
Bezalkoholiskie dzehrieni
Non-alcoholic drinks

Minerālūdens
Minerahloodens
Mineral water

Augļu sulas
Auglyu sulas
Fruit juices

Apelsīnu sula
Apelseenu sula
Orange juice

Limonāde
Limonahde
Lemonade

Ledus
Ledus
Ice

Kafija ar pienu/melna
kafija/espresso kafija
*Kafiya ar pienu/melna
kafiya/espresso kafiya*
**White coffee/black
coffee/espresso coffee**

Tēja ar pienu/ar cukuru
Tehya ar pienu/ar tsukuru
Tea with milk/with lemon

Šokolāde
Shokolahde
**Chocolate
(drink)**

Piens
Piens
Milk

Naški/uzkodas
Nashki/uzkuodas
Snacks/Light meals

Salāti
Salahti
Salads

Sviestmaizes
Sviestmaizes
Sandwiches

Olas
Uolas
Eggs

Desa
Dehsa
Sausage

Vārītas/ceptas olas/
olu kultenis
*Vahreetas/tseptas olas/
uolu kultenis*
**Boiled/fried/
scrambled eggs**

L A T V I A N

Typical Local Dishes

Piena zupa
Piena zupa
Milk soup

Pelēkie zirņi
Pelekie zirnyi
Grey peas

Sīpolsitenis kupāti
Sipolsitenis kupati
Sausages with onions

Ceptas desiņas
Tseptas desinyas
Fried sausages

Meža zemenes ar
putukrējumu
Mezha zemenes ar putukreyumu
**Wild strawberry with
cream**

Balzāms
Balsam
Strong alcoholic drink

GETTING AROUND

Public Transport

**Where is the bus stop/coach
stop/nearest metro (subway)
station?**
Kur ir autobusu pietura/
starppilsētu autobusu pietura/
tuvākā metro stacija?
*Kur ir autobusu pietura/starppilsetu
autobusu pietura/tuvaka metro statsiya?*

**When is the next/last bus
to...?**
Cikos atiet nākošais/pēdējais
autobuss uz...?
*Cikos atiet nakoshais/pedeyais auto-
buss uz...?*

**How much is the fare to the
city centre (downtown)/
railway (railroad) station/
airport?**
Cik maksā brauciens līdz
pilsētas centram/
dzelzceļa stacijai/lidostai?
*Tsik maksa brautsiens lidz pilsetas
tsentram/dzelztselya
statsiyai/lidostai?*

**Will you tell me when to
get off?**
Vai jūs varētu man pateikt, kur
man ir jāizkāpj?
*Vai yus varetu man pateikt, kur man
ir yaizkapy?*

Does this bus go to ...?
Vai šis autobuss brauc līdz ...?
Vai shis autobuss brauts lidz ...?

**Which number bus goes
to ...?**
Kura numura autobuss brauc
līdz ...?
Kura numura autobuss brauc lids ...?

**May I have a single (one-
way)/return (round-trip)/day
ticket/book of tickets?**
Vienvirziena/turp atpakaļ
biļeti/dienas biļeti/vairākas
biļetes, lūdzu?
*Vienvirziena/turp atpakaly bilyeti/
dienas bilyeti/vairakas bilyetes,
ludzu?*

L
A
T
V
I
A
N

Taxis (Taksometru)

I would like to go to ... How much will it cost?
Es vēlos braukt uz ... Cik tas maksās?
Es velos braukt uz ...Tsik tas mak-sas?

Please may I stop here?
Lūdzu, pieturiet šeit!
Ludzu pieturiet sheit!

I would like to order a taxi today/tomorrow at 2pm to go from ... to ...
Es vēlos pasūtīt taksometru šodien/rītā pulksten divos no ... līdz ...
Es velos pasutit taksometru shodi-en/rita pulksten divos no ... lidz ...

Entertainment

Can you recommend a good bar/nightclub?
Vai jūs varētu ieteikt labu bāru/nakts klubu?
Vai yus varetu ieteikt labu baru/nakts klubu?

Do you know what is on at the cinema (playing at the movies)/theatre at the moment?
Vai jūs zināt, ko pašlaik rāda kinoteātrī/teātrī?
Vai yus zinat, ko pashlaik rada kinoteatri/teatri?

I would like to book (purchase) ... tickets for the matinee/evening performance on Monday
Es vēlos rezervēt (nopirkt) ... biļetes pēcpusdienas/vakara izrādei
Es velos rezervet (nopirkt) ...bilyetes pecpusdienas/vakara izradei

What time does the film/performance start?
Cikos sākas filma/izrāde?
Tsikos sakas filma/izrade?

COMMUNICATIONS

Post

How much will it cost to send a letter/postcard/this package to Britain/Ireland/America/Canada/Australia/New Zealand?
Cik maksā nosūtīt šo vēstuli/šo atklātni/šo paku uz Lielbritāniju/Īriju/ASV/Kanādu/Austrāliju/Jaunzēlandi?
Tsik maksa nosutit sho vestuli/sho atklahtni/sho paku uz Leelbritaniyu/Iriyu/Ameriku/Kanadu/Australiyu/Jaunzelandi?

I would like one stamp/two stamps
Es vēlos vienu pastmarku/divas pastmarkas
Es velos vienu pastmarku/divas past-markas

I'd like ... stamps for postcards to send abroad, please
Es vēlos ... pastmarkas atklātnēm uz ārzemēm
Es velos...pastmarkas atklatnem uz arzemem

191

L A T V I A N

Phones

I would like to make a telephone call/reverse the charges to (make a collect call to) ...
Es vēlos piezvanīt uz/piezvanīt ar apmaksu otrā galā ...
Es velos piezvanit uz/piezvanit ar apmaksu otra gala ...

Which coins do I need for the telephone?
Kādas monētas ir vajadzīgas telefonam?
Kadas monetas ir vayadzigas telefonam?

The line is engaged (busy)
Līnija ir aizņemta
Liniya ir aiznemta

The number is...
Telefona numurs ir...
Telefona numurs ir...

Hello, this is...
Labdien, te runā...
Labdien, te runa...

Please may I speak to...?
Vai drīkstu palūgt...?
Vai drikstu palugt...?

He/she is not in at the moment. Please can you call back?
Viņš/viņa pašlaik nav uz vietas. Lūdzu atzvaniet mazliet vēlāk?
Vinsh/vina pashlaik nav uz vietas. Ludzu atzvaniet mazliet velak?

SHOPPING

Shops

Grāmatu veikals/Kancelejas piederumi
Gramatu veikali/Kantseleyas piederumi
Bookshop/Stationery

Juvelieru izstrādājumi/dāvanas
Juvelieru izstradayumi/davanas
Jeweller/Gifts

Apavi
Apavi
Shoes

Saimniecības preces
Saimniecibas pretses
Hardware

Frizētava
Frizetava
Hairdresser

Maizes veikals
Maizes veikals
Baker

Universālveikals
Universalveikals
Supermarket

Fotopiederumi
Fotopiederumi
Photo shop

Tūrisma birojs
Turisma biroys
Travel agent

Aptieka
Aptieka
Pharmacy

In the Shops

What time do the shops open/close?
Cikos veikali tiek atvērti/slēgti?
Cikos veikali tiek atvehrti/slegti?

Where is the nearest market?
Kur ir tuvākais tirgus?
Kur ir tuvakais tirgus?

Can you show me the one in the window/this one?
Vai variet man parādīt to, kas ir logā/šo?
Vai variet man paradit to, kas ir loga/sho?

Can I try this on?
Vai drīkstu to uzmērīt?
Vai drikstu to uzmehreet?

What size is this?
Kāds izmērs tas ir?
Kads izmers tas ir?

This is too large/too small/too expensive. Do you have any others?
Šis ir pārāk liels/pārāk mazs/ļoti dārgs. Vai jums ir citi?
Shis ir parak liels/parak mazs/lyoti dargs. Vai yums ir citi?

My size is…
Mans izmērs ir….
Mans izmers ir….

Where is the changing room/children's/cosmetic/ladieswear/menswear/food department?
Kur ir uzlaikojamā kabīne/bērnu/kosmētikas/sieviešu apģērbu/vīriešu apģērbu/pārtikas nodaļa?
Kur ir uzlaikoyama kabine/bernu/kosmetiska/sievieshu apdyerbu/virieshu apdyerbu/partikas nodalya?

I would like … a quarter of a kilo/half a kilo/a kilo of bread/butter/ham/this fruit
Es vēlos. … ceturto daļu kilograma/puskilogramu/kilogramu maizes/sviesta/šķiņķa/šos augļus
Es velos … tseturto dalyu kilograma/puskilogramu/kilogramu maizes/sviesta/shkyinkya/shos auglyus

How much is this?
Cik tas maksā?
Tsik tas maksa?

I'll take this one, thank you
Šo lūdzu, paldies
Sho ludzu, paldies

Do you have a carrier (shopping) bag?
Vai jums ir maisiņš, kur ielikt pirkumus?
Vai yums ir maisinysh, kur ielikt pirkumus?

Do you have anything cheaper/larger/smaller/of better quality?
Vai jums ir kaut kas lētāks/lielāks/mazāks/labākas kvalitātes?
Vai yums ir kaut kas letaks/lielaks/mazaks/labakas kvalitates?

193

L
A
T
V
I
A
N

I would like a film/to develop this film for this camera
Es vēlos filmu/attīstīt šo filmu šim fotoaparātam
Es velos filmu/attistit sho filmu shim fotoaparatam

I would like some batteries, the same size as this old one
Es vēlos baterijas, tādā pašā izmērā kā šīs vecās
Es velos bateriyas, tada pasha izmera ka shis vetsas

Would you mind wrapping this for me, please?
Vai jūs varētu šo man, lūdzu, iesainot?
Vai yus varetu sho man, ludzu, iesainot?

Sorry, but you seem to have given me the wrong change
Atvainojiet, bet man liekas, ka jūs man nepareizi izdevāt naudu
Atvainoyiet, bet man liekas, ka yus man nepareizi izdevat naudu

MOTORING

Car Hire (Rental)

I have ordered (rented) a car in the name of...
Es esmu pasūtījis (noīrējis) automašīnu ... vārdā
Es esmu pasutiyis (noireyis) automashinu ... varda

How much does it cost to hire (rent) a car for one day/two days/a week?
Cik maksā noīrēt automašīnu uz vienu dienu/divām dienām/nedēļu?
Tsik maksa noiret automashinu uz vienu dienu/divam dienam/nedelyu?

Is the tank already full of petrol(gas)?
Vai bāka ir jau pilna?
Vai baka ir yau pilna?

Is insurance and tax included? How much is the deposit?
Vai apdrošināšana un nodokļi ir ieskaitīti cenā? Cik ir iemaksa?
Vai apdroshinashana un nodoklyi ir ieskaititi tsena? Tsik ir iemaksa?

By what time must I return the car?
Līdz cikiem man ir jāatdod automašīna?
Leedz tsikiem man ir yaatdod automashina?

I would like a small/large/family/sports car with a radio/cassette
Es vēlos nelielu/lielu/ģimenes/sporta automašīnu ar radio/kasešu magnetafonu
Es velos nelielu/lielu dyimenes/sporta automashinu ar radio/kaseshu magnetafonu

Do you have a road map?
Vai jums ir ceļa karte?
Vai yums ir tselya karte?

L A T V I A N

Parking

How long can I park here?
Uz cik ilgu laiku es drīkstu šeit
novietot automašīnu?
*Uz cik ilgu laiku es drīkstu sheit
novietot automashinu?*

Is there a car park near here?
Vai šeit tuvumā ir mašīnu
stāvvieta?
*Vai sheit tuvuma ir mashinu
stavvieta?*

**At what time does this car
park close?**
Cikos slēdz stāvvietu?
Cikos sledz stavvietu?

Signs and Notices

Vienvirziena
Vienvirziena
One way

Ieeja aizliegta
Ieeya aizliegta
No entry

Stāvēt aizliegts
Stavet aizliegts
No parking

Apkārtceļš
Apkarttselysh
Detour (diversion)

Stāt!
Stat!
Stop!

Dot ceļu
Dot celyu
Give way (Yield)

Slidens ceļš
Slidens tselysh
Slippery road

Apdzīšana aizliegta
Apdzishana aizliegta
No overtaking

Bīstami!
Bistami!
Danger!

At the Filling Station
(Degvielas uzpildes stacijā)

**Unleaded (lead free)/
standard/diesel**
Bez svina/standarta/dīzeļa
Bez svina/standarta/dizelya

Fill the tank please
Pilnu bāku, lūdzu
Pilnu baku, ludzu

Do you have a road map?
Vai jums ir ceļa karte?
Vai yums ir tselya karte?

How much is the car wash?
Cik maksā mašīnas mazgāšana?
Tsik maksa mashinas mazgashana?

Breakdowns

I've had a breakdown at ...
Man ir bijusi avārija ...
Man ir biyusi avariya ...

I am a member of the ... [motoring organisation]
Es esmu ... biedrs
Es esmu ... biedrs

I am on the road from ... to ...
Es atrodos ceļā no... uz ...
Es atrodos tselya no ... uz ...

I can't move the car. Can you send a tow-truck?
Automašīna nebrauc. Vai jūs varētu, lūdzu, atsūtīt tauvas mašīnu?
Automashina nebrauts. Vai yus varetu, ludsu, atsutit tauvas mashinu?

I have a flat tyre
Man ir mīksta riepa
Man ir meeksta riepa

The windscreen (windshield) has smashed/cracked
Priekšējais stikls ir saplīsis/ieplīsis
Prieksheyais stikls ir saplisis/ieplisis

There is something wrong with the engine/brakes/lights/steering/gearbox/clutch/exhaust
Motoram/bremzēm/gaismām/stūrei/ātrumkārbai/sajūgam/izpūtējam ir kaut kāda vaina
Motoram/bremzem/gaismam/sturei/atrumkarbai/sayugam/izputeyam ir kaut kada vaina

It's overheating
Tas ir pārkarsis
Tas ir parkarsis

It won't start
Mašīnu nevar iedarbināt
Mashinu nevar iedarbinat

Where can I get it repaired?
Kur es varu to salabot?
Kur es varu to salabot?

Can you take me there?
Vai jūs nevarētu mani tur aizvest?
Vai yus nevaretu mani tur aizvest?

Will it take long to fix?
Vai paies ilgi to salabot?
Vai paies ilgi to salabot?

How much will it cost?
Cik tas maksās?
Tsik tas maksas?

Please can you pick me up/give me a lift?
Vai jūs nevarētu mani, lūdzu, savākt/aizvest?
Vai yus nevaretu mani, ludzu, savakt/aizvest?

Accidents and Traffic Offences (Violations)

Can you help me? There has been an accident
Vai jūs varat man palīdzēt? Ir noticis nelaimes gadījums
Vai yoos varat man paleedzeht? Ir nuotitsis nelaimes gadeeyums

Please call the police/an ambulance
Lūdzu, izsauciet policiju/ātro palīdzību
Loodzu, izsautsiet politsiyu/ahtruo paleedzeebu

Is anyone hurt?
Vai ir cietušie?
Vai ir tsietushie?

Sorry, I didn't see the sign
Atvainojiet, es neredzēju zīmi
Atvainoyiet, es neredzeyu zimi

Must I pay a fine? How much?
Vai man ir jāmaksā sods? Cik
liels?
Vai man ir yamaksa sods? Tsik liels?

Parādiet man lūdzu savus
dokumentus
*Paradiet man ludzu savus
dokumentus*
Show me your documents

HEALTH

Pharmacy (Aptieka)

**Do you have anything for a
stomach ache/headache/sore
throat/toothache?**
Vai jums ir kaut kas pret
vēdera sāpēm/galvas sāpēm/
kakla iekaisumu/zobu sāpēm?
*Vai yums ir kaut kas pret vedera
sapem/galvas sapem/kakla
iekaisumu/zobu sapem?*

**I need something for
diarrhoea/constipation/a
cold/a cough/insect bites/
sunburn/travel (motion)
sickness.**
Man vajag kaut ko pret
caureju/cietu vēderu/iesnām/
klepus/insektu kodieniem/
saules apdegumu/jūras slimību
*Man vayag kaut ko pret tsaureyu/
cietu vederu/iesnam/klepu/insektu
kodieniem/saules apdegumu/yuras
slimibu*

**How much/how many do I
take?**
Cik daudz man ir jālieto?
Cik daudz man ir yalieto?

**I am taking anti-malaria
tablets/these pills**
Es lietoju pret-malāriju
tabletes/šīs zāles
*Es lietoyu pret-malariyu tabletes/shis
zales*

How often do I take it/them?
Cik bieži man tas/tās ir jālieto?
Tsik biezhi man tas/tas ir yalieto?

**I am/he is/she is taking this
medication**
Es ņemu/viņš ņem/viņa ņem
šos medikamentus
*Es nyemu/vinsh nyem/vina nyem
shos medikamentus*

How much does it cost?
Cik tas maksā?
Tsik tas maksa?

**Can you recommend a good
doctor/dentist?**
Vai jūs varētu ieteikt labu
ārstu/zobārstu?
*Vai yus varetu ieteikt labu
arstu/zobarstu?*

Is it suitable for children?
Vai tas ir piemērots bērniem?
Vai tas ir piemerots berniem?

L
A
T
V
I
A
N

197

L
A
T
V
I
A
N

Doctor (Ārsts)

I have a pain here/in my arm/leg/chest/stomach
Man sāp šeit/rokā/kājā/krūtīs/vēderā
Man sap sheit/roka/kaya/krutis/vedera

Please call a doctor, this is an emergency
Lūdzu izsauciet ārstu, šis ir kritiski
Ludzu izsautsiet arstu shis ir kritiski

I would like to make an appointment to see the doctor
Es vēlos pierakstīties pie ārsta
Es velos pierakstities pie arsta

I am diabetic/pregnant
Es esmu diabētiķis/stāvoklī
Es esmu diabetikis/stavokli

I need a prescription for...
Man ir vajadzīga recepte...
Man ir vayadziga recepte...

Can you give me something to ease the pain?
Vai jūs nevarētu man iedot kaut ko, lai noņemtu sāpes?
Vai yus nevaretu man iedot kaut ko, lai nonemtu sapes?

I am/he is/she is/allergic to penicillin
Man ir/viņam ir/viņai ir alerģija pret penicilīnu
Man ir/vinyam ir/vinyai ir alerdyiya pret penitsilinu

Vai šis sāp?
Vai shis sap?
Does this hurt?

Jums vajag/viņam vajag/viņai vajag doties uz slimnīcu
Jums vayag/vinyam vayag/vinyai vayag doties uz slimnitsu
You must/he must/she must go to hospital

Lietojiet tās vienreiz/divreiz/trīsreiz dienā
Lietoyiet tas vienreiz/divreiz/trisreiz diena
Take these once/twice/three times a day

I am/he is/she is taking this medication
Es ņemu/viņš ņem/viņa ņem šos medikamentus
Es nemu/vinsh nem/vina nem shos medikamentus

I have medical insurance
Man ir medicīniskā apdrošināšana
Man ir meditsiniska apdroshinashana

Dentist (Zobārsts)

I have toothache/my filling has come out
Man sāp zobs/man izkrita plomba
Man sap zobs/man izkrita plomba

I do/do not want to have an injection first
Es gribu/negribu injekciju
Es gribu/negribu inyekciyu

EMERGENCIES

Help!
Palīgā!
Paliga!

Fire!
Deg!
Degs!

Stop!
Stāt!
Stat!

Call an ambulance/a doctor/ the police/the fire brigade!
Izsauciet ātro palīdzību/ārstu/ policiju/ugunsdzēsēju komandu!
Izsautsiet atro palidzibu/arstu/ politsiyu/ugunsdzeseyu komandu!

Please may I use a telephone?
Vai es varu izmantot telefonu, lūdzu?
Vai es varu izmantot telefonu, ludzu?

I have had my traveller's cheques/credit cards/ handbag/rucksack/luggage/ wallet/passport/mobile phone stolen
Man nozaga ceļojumu čekus/kredītkartes/rokas somu/mugursomu/bagāžu/ kabatas portfeli/pasi/mobilo telefonu
Man nozaga tselyojumu chekus/ kreditkartes/rokas somu/ mugursomu/bagazhu/kabatas portfeli/pasi/mobilo telefonu

May I please have a copy of the report for my insurance claim?
Vai es varu saņemt ziņojuma kopiju, ko iesniegt apdrošināšanai?
Vai es varu san'emt zin'oyuma kopiyu, kuo iesniegt apdroshinahshanai?

Can you help me? I have lost my daughter/son/my companion(s)
Vai jūs varat man palīdzēt? Es pazaudēju savu meitu/dēlu/ savu(s) ceļa biedru(s)
Vai yus varat man palidzet? Es pazaudeyu savu meitu/delu/savu(s) celya biedru(s)

Please go away/leave me alone
Lūdzu ejiet prom/atstājiet mani mierā
Ludzu eyiet prom/atstayiet mani miera

I'm sorry
Piedodiet
Piedodiet

I want to contact the British/American/Canadian/ Irish/Australian/New Zealand/South African Consulate
Es gribu griezties pie Anglijas/Amerikas/Kanādas/ Īrijas/Austrālijas/Jaunzēlandes/ Dienvidāfrikas konsulāta
Es gribu griezties pie Angliyas/ Amerikas/Kanadas/Iriyas/ Australiyas/Yunzelandes/ Dienvidafrikas konsulata

L
A
T
V
I
A
N

199

I'm ill
Es esmu slims
Es esmu slims

We're ill
Mēs esam slimi
Mes esam slimi

He is ill
Viņš ir slims
Vinsh ir slims

She is ill
Viņa ir slima
Vina ir slima

They are ill
Viņi ir slimi
Vini ir slimi

I'm lost
Es esmu pazudis
Es esmu pazudusi

We're lost
Mēs esam pazuduši
Mes esam pazudushi

He is lost
Viņš ir pazudis
Vinsh ir pazudis

She is lost
Viņa ir pazudusi
Vina ir pazudusi

They are lost
Viņi ir pazuduši
Vini ir pazudushi

I'm injured
Es esmu ievainots
Es esmu ievainots

We're injured
Mēs esam ievainoti
Mes esam ievainoti

He is injured
Viņš ir ievainots
Vinsh ir ievainots

She is injured
Viņa ir ievainota
Vina ir ievainota

They are injured
Viņi ir ievainoti
Vini ir ievainoti

L
A
T
V
I
A
N

LITHUANIAN

INTRODUCTION

Lithuanian belongs to the Baltic group of the Indo-European family and is the mother tongue of about 3 million people in Lithuania. It is written using the Latin alphabet.

L
I
T
H
U
A
N
I
A
N

Addresses for Travel and Tourist Information

Australia: *Baltic Connections,* Suite 3, 11-13 The Centre, Forestville, NSW 2087. Tel: (2) 9975 2355. Fax: (2) 9451 6446.

Canada: *Lithuanian Embassy,* 130 Albert St, Suite 204, Ottawa, Ontario K1P 5G4. Tel: (613) 567 5458. Fax: (613) 567 5315.

UK: *Lithuanian Embassy,* 84 Gloucester Place, London W1U 6AU. Tel: (020) 7486 6401. Fax: (020) 7486 6403.

USA: *Lithuanian Embassy,* 2622 16th St. NW. Washington, DC 20009. Tel: (202) 234 5860. Fax: (202) 328 0466.

Official tourism website: www.tourism.lt

Lithuania Facts

CAPITAL: Vilnius

CURRENCY: 1 Litas = 100 Centas.

OPENING HOURS: Banks: mainly Mon–Fri 0900–1700, some Sat 0900–1300. Shops: (large shops) Mon–Fri 1000/1100–1900; many also open Sat until 1600. Some close for lunch 1400–1500 and also on Sun and Mon. Food shops Mon–Sat 0900–1400 and 1500–2000. Museums: days vary, most close Mon and open at least Wed and Fri; often free on Wed; hours usually at least 1100–1700, check locally.

TELEPHONES: To dial in, +370. Outgoing, 8 10 and the country code. Police, 02. Fire, 01. Ambulance, 03.

PUBLIC HOLIDAYS: 1 Jan; 16 Feb; 11 Mar; Easter Sun and Mon; the first Sun in May (Mothers' Day); 6 July; 1 Nov; 25/26 Dec.

Technical Language Hints

All consonant sounds are short, even when a Lithuanian speaks a foreign word. There is also a sound g with its soft equivalent which are used in foreign words for the letter h (himnas, herbas).
Nouns have no article.
Besides single vowels, in Lithuanian there are two complex vowels: [ie] and [uo].

Pronunciation is based on syllable similarity, i.e., an English speaker would pronounce the syllables the same way as he would pronounce them in an English text. In some cases, this requires a certain simplification of the Lithuanian pronunciation as only the sounds present in the English language may be accommodated, but this method is widely recognised as the most user-friendly way to deal with pronunciation of unfamiliar words.

Diacritical marks on vowels (ą, ę, ė, į, ų, ū) usually mean lengthening of the vowel concerned. Vowels in Lithuanian are almost never silent.
Vowels can be short or long depending on a particular word:
a will range from mud to car;
e will range from sent to man;
i is always short (as in milk),
y is always long (as in keep),
o will range from box to more,
u will range from look to cool.

Diphthongs mostly means merging of the vowels involved:
au sounds like ow as in cow,
ai is like i in line,
ie is like ee,
ei is like in day;
oi is like oi;
uo is like odd.

Diacritical marks on the syllables mean a totally different sound: s as in silk, š as in shiver; c as in rats, č as in chew; z as is zoo, ž as in jet. Letter g is always pronounced as in get and never as in gender, j is always pronounced as y in yield and never as in jet.

L
I
T
H
U
A
N
I
A
N

LITHUANIAN

ESSENTIALS

Alphabet

	Name	Pronounced
A a	*ah*	neutral sound as in sun or short a as in bad
Ą ą	*ah nohsinya*	long a as in car
B b	*beh*	as in bed
C c	*tseh*	ts sound as in bats; ch as in Scottish pronunciation of loch
Č č	*cheh*	ch as in church
D d	*deh*	d as in day; dz like sound at the end of lads; d like j in jest
E e	*eh*	short e as in pet
Ė ė		
Ę ę	*eh nohsinya*	long e sound as in air or long a as in bark
F f	*ef*	as in fast
G g	*geh*	as in garden
H h	*hash*	kh sound as in Scottish pronunciation of loch
I i	*ee trumpoyi*	short i as in sit; ie as in tier
Į į	*ee nohsinya*	long i as in machine
Y y	*ee gohyi*	long i as in machine
J j	*yot*	y as in yes
K k	*kah*	as in kind
L l	*el*	as in lemon
M m	*em*	as in mother
N n	*en*	as in not
O o	*oh*	long o as in go
P p	*peh*	as in paper
R r	*er*	rolled r as in Scottish pronunciation
S s	*es*	as in sit
Š š	*esh*	sh as in she
T t	*teh*	as in tick
U u	*oo trumpoyi*	short u as in put; ui as in ruin
Ų ų	*oo nohsinya*	long u sound as in food
Ū ū	*oo gohyi*	long u sound as in food
V v	*veh*	as in vote
Z z	*zeh*	as in zoo
Ž ž	*zheh*	zh sound like the s in pleasure

Basic Words and Phrases

Yes	**No**
Taip	Ne
Teip	*Nya*

Please	**Thank you**
Prašau	Ačiū
Pra-show	*Ah-chyu*

Hello	**Goodbye**
Labas	Viso gero
Lah-bahs	*Vee-soh geh-roh*

Excuse me/Sorry
Atsiprašau
Aht-see-prah-show

That's O.K.
Viskas gerai
Vees-kahs geh-ray

Perhaps
Galbūt
Gahl-boot

How
Kaip
Kayp

When
Kada
Kah-dah

Why
Kodėl
Koh-dell

What
Kas
Kahs

Who
Kas
Kahs

To
Į
Ee

From
Iš
Eesh

Here
Čia
Chya

There
Ten
Tyan

I don't understand
Aš nesuprantu
Ash nya-soo-prahn-tuh

I don't speak Lithuanian
Aš nekalbu lietuviškai
Ash nya-kahl-boo lye-too-vish-kay

Do you speak English?
Ar kalbate angliškai?
Ahr kahl-bah-teh angle-ish-kay?

Can you please write it down?
Ar galite užrašyti?
Ur gull-iteh oozh-rash-ee-tee?

Please can you speak more slowly?
Gal galite kalbėti lėčiau?
Gull gull-iteh kahl-beh-tee leh-chow?

Greetings

Good morning/Good afternoon/Good evening/ Good night
Labas rytas/Laba diena/Labas vakaras/Labanakt
Lah-bas ree-tas/la-bah dye-nah/lah-bas vah-car-us/lah-bah-nuct

Pleased to meet you
Malonu susipažinti
Mah-loh-nuh soo-see-pah-zhen-tee

How are you?
Kaip sekasi?
Kayp seh-kusi?

I am well, thank you. And you?
Ačiu, gerai. O Jums?
Ah-choo, geh-ray. Oh yooms?

My name is ...
Mano vardas ...
Mano vahr-dahs ...

This is my friend/boyfriend/girlfriend/ husband/wife/brother/sister
Tai mano draugas/vaikinas/ mergina/vyras/žmona/brolis/ sesuo
Tay mano drow-gahs/vay-kee-nas/mehr-ghee-na/wee-rahs/ zhmoh-nah/broh-lees/seh-soh

Where are you travelling to?
Kur jūs keliaujate?
Coor yoos keh-lee-ow-yateh?

L
I
T
H
U
A
N
I
A
N

**L
I
T
H
U
A
N
I
A
N**

I am/we are going to ...
Aš važiuoju/Mes važiuojame į ...
Ash va-zhoh-yu/Myas vah-zhoh-ya-meh ee ...

How long are you travelling for?
Ar ilgam važiuojate?
Ahr eel-gham vah-zhuo-yah-teh?

Where do you come from?
Iš kur jūs?
Esh coor yoos?

**I am/we are from ...
Australia/Britain/Canada/
America**
Aš /Mes iš ... Australijos/
Britanijos/Kanados//Amerikos
*Ash/Myas ish Aus-trah-lee-yos/
Bree-tah-nee-yos/Cah-nah-dos/
Am-er-eek-os*

We are on holiday
Mes atostogaujame
Myas ah-tos-toh-goh—yah-meh

This is our first visit here
Mes čia pirmą kartą
Myas chya peer-mah kahr-tah

How old are you?
Kiek jums metų?
Kyek yooms mya-too?

I am ... years old
Man ...
Mann ...

**I am a business person/
doctor/journalist/manual
worker/administrator/
scientist/student/teacher**
Aš verslininkas/gydytojas/
žurnalistas/darbininkas/
administratorius/mokslininkas/
studentas/mokytojas
Ash verr-slee-nin-kahs/ghee-dee-toh-yas/zhoor-nah-lees-tahs/dahr-bee-nin-kahs/ad-mee-nees-trah-tor-us/mock-slee-nin-kahs/stoo-dent-us/mock-it-oy-us

**I am waiting for my
husband/wife/boyfriend/
girlfriend**
Aš laukiu savo vyro/žmonos/
vaikino/merginos
Ash lau-kyu sah-voh vy-roh/zhmoh-nohs/wai-kee-noh/myar-ghee-nohs

**Would you like/may I have a
cigarette?**
Gal norite rūkyti/Gal
pavaišinsite mane cigarete?
Gull noh-ree-teh roo-kee-tee/Gull pah-way-shin-see-teh mah-neh tsee-gahr-ett-eh?

Do you mind if I smoke?
Ar galiu rūkyti?
Ahr gah-loo roo-kee-tee?

Do you have a light?
Gal turite ugnies?
Gull too-ree-teh oog-nee-ess?

Days

Monday
Pirmadienis
Peer-mah-dye-nees

Tuesday
Antradienis
Ant-rah-dye-nees

Wednesday
Trečiadienis
Trya-chya-dye-nees

Thursday
Ketvirtadienis
Kyat-veer-tah-dye-nees

Friday
Penktadienis
Penck-tah-dye-nees

Saturday
Šeštadienis
Shesh-tah-dye-nees

Sunday
Sekmadienis
Seck-mah-dye-nees

Morning/Afternoon/Evening/Night
Rytas/Popietė/Vakaras/Naktis
Ree-tahs/Popee-eh-teh/Wack-ahr-us/Nuck-tiss

Yesterday
Vakar
Vah-car

Tomorrow
Rytoj
Ree-toy

Today
Šiandien
Shyan-dyen

Numbers

Zero
Nulis
Noo-liss

One
Vienas
Wienn-us

Two
Du
Doo

Three
Trys
Trees

Four
Keturi
Keh-too-ree

Five
Penki
Pyan-kee

Six
Šeši
Shya-shee

Seven
Septyni
Sep-tee-nee

Eight
Aštuoni
Ash-too-nee

Nine
Devyni
Deh-wee-nee

Ten
Dešimt
Dya-shimt

Eleven
Vienuolika
Wienn-oo-lick-ah

Twelve
Dvylika
Dwee-lick-ah

Thirteen
Trylika
Tree-lick-ah

Fourteen
Keturiolika
Kett-oor-oh-lick-ah

Fifteen
Penkiolika
Penck-oh-lick-ah

Sixteen
Šešiolika
Shesh-oh-lick-ah

Seventeen
Septyniolika
Sept-een-oh-lick-ah

Eighteen
Aštuoniolika
Ash-toon-all-lick-ah

Nineteen
Devyniolika
Deh-ween-oh-lick-ah

Twenty
Dvidešimt
Dwee-deh-shimt

Twenty-one
Dvidešimt vienas
Dwee-deh-shimt wienn-us

L
I
T
H
U
A
N
I
A
N

L I T H U A N I A N

Twenty-two
Dvidešimt du
Dwee-deh-shimt doo

Thirty
Trisdešimt
Trees-dya-shimt

Forty
Keturiasdešimt
Kett-oor-us-dya-shimt

Fifty
Penkiasdešimt
Penck-yas-dya-shimt

Sixty
Šešiasdešimt
Shya-shyas-dya-shimt

Seventy
Septyniasdešimt
Syap-teen-yas-dya-shimt

Eighty
Aštuoniasdešimt
Ash-too-nyas-dya-shimt

Ninety
Devyniasdešimt
Dya-ween-yas-dya-shimt

One hundred
Šimtas
Shim-tahs

Five hundred
Penki šimtai
Pyan-kee shimt-thai

One thousand
Tūkstantis
Toocks-stahn-tiss

One million
Milijonas
Mee-lee-yo-nahs

Time

What time is it?
Kelinta valanda?
Kel-inn-tah vah-lan-dah?

It is ...
Dabar...
Dah-bahr ...

9.00
Devinta valanda
Deh-veen-tah vah-lahn-dah

12.00
Dvylikta valanda
Dwee-lick-tah vah-lahn-dah

9.05
Penkios minutės po devynių
Penck-oss mee-noo-tehs poh dya-vee-noo

9.15
Penkiolika minučių po devynių
Penck-oh-lick-ah mee-noo-choo poh dya-vee-noo

9.20
Dvidešimt minučių po devynių
Dwee-dya-shimt mee-noo-choo poh dya-vee-noo

9.30
Pusė dešimtos
Puss-eh dash-imt-oss

9.35
Penkios minutės po pusės
dešimtos
*Penck-oss mee-noo-tehs poh puss-
ess dash-im-toss*

9.40
Be dvidešimt minučių dešimt
*Beh dwee-dash-imt mee-noo-choo
dash-imt*

9.45
Be penkiolikos minučių dešimt
*Beh penck-oh-lick-os mee-noo-choo
dash-imt*

9.50
Be dešimties minučių dešimt
*Beh dash-imt-ess mee-noo-choo
dash-imt*

9.55
Be penkių minučių dešimt
Beh penck-oo mee-noo-choo dash-imt

12.00/Midday/Midnight
Dvylikta/Vidurdienis/Vidurnaktis
*Dwee-lick-tah/Wee-duhr-dye-
niss/Wee-duhr-nackt-iss*

Money

**I would like to change these
traveller's cheques/this
currency**
Aš norėčiau iškeisti kelioninius
čekius/šitą valiutą
*Ash-norr-etch-yau ish-case-tee
kyal-on-in-oos check-oos/sheet-ah
vah-loo-tah*

**How much commission do
you charge? (What is the
service charge?)**
Koks čia komisinis mokestis?

*Cocks cha commies-in-is
mok-est-ees?*

**Can I obtain money with my
Mastercard?**
Ar galiu gauti pinigų su
Mastercard kortele?
*Ur gah-loo gou-tee pee-nee-ghoo
soo Mastercard kohr-teh-leh?*

Where is the nearest ATM?
Kur artimiausias bankomatas?
*Kuhr ahr-tee-myau-syas bahn-koh-
mah-tahs?*

**My name is ... Some money
has been wired to here for
me to collect**
Mano vardas ... Čia man buvo
atsiųsta pinigų
*Mah-noh vahr-dahs ... Chya mann
boo-voh aht-soo-stah pee-nee-goo*

ARRIVING AND DEPARTING

Airport

**Excuse me, where is the
check-in desk for ... airline?**
Atsiprašau, kur registruojama į
... oro liniją?
*Ut-see-prah-show, coor regh-iss-troh-
yam-ah ee oh-roh lee-nee-ya ... ?*

**What is the boarding
gate/time for my flight?**
Kur/kada išėjimas į mano reisą?
*Koor/kada ee-she-yeem-us ee
mah-noh ray-sah?*

**How long is the delay likely
to be?**
Kiek vėluoja reisas?
Keck veh-loh-ya ray-sus?

209

L I T H U A N I A N

Where is the duty-free shop?
Kur yra neapmuitintų prekių
parduotuvė?
*Coor eer-uh neh-ap-mu-itintoo
prek-ee-oo pahr-doh-too-veh?*

Which way is the luggage reclaim?
Kur bagažo išdavimas?
Coor bug-uzh-oh eesh-dah-veem-us?

I have lost my luggage. Please can you help?
Aš pamečau savo bagažą.
Gal galite padėti?
Ash pum-etch-ow sah-voh bug-uzh-ah. Gull gull-it-teh puh-deh-tee?

I am flying to ...
Aš skrendu į ...
Ash scren-doo ee ...

Where is the bus for the city centre (downtown)?
Kur autobusas į miesto centrą?
*Coor aw-toh-boos-us ee myes-toh
tsen-trah?*

Trains and Boats

Where is the ticket office/information desk?
Kur yra kasa/informacija?
Coor eer-uh cuh-sah/een-form-aht-see-ya?

Which platform does the train/speedboat/ferry to ... depart from?
Iš kurios platformos išvyksta
traukinys/greitasis
kateris/keltas į ...?
*Eesh coor-yos plat-form-oss eesh-week-stah trow-keen-ees/gray-tuh-sis
kat-eris/celt-us ee ...?*

Where is platform ...?
Kur yra ... platforma?
Coor eer-uh plat-form-ah?

When is the next train/boat to ...?
Kada kitas traukinys/laivas į ...?
Cah-dah keet-us trow-keen-ees/lay-wuss ee ...?

Is there a later train/boat to ...?
Ar yra traukinys/laivas į ... vėliau?
*Ur eer-uh trow-keen-ees/lay-wuss
ee ... well-low?*

Notices and Signs

Vagonas-restoranas
Vah-gone-us - rest-orr-un-us
Buffet (Dining) car

Autobusas
Aw-toh-boos-us
Bus

Geriamas/negeriamas vanduo
*Gher-ya-mus/ne-gher-ya-mus
wan-doh*
Drinking/non-drinking water

Įėjimas
Ee-eh-yee-mus
Entrance

Išėjimas
Ish-eh-yee-mus
Exit

Ligoninė
Lee-goh-nee-neh
Hospital

Informacija
Een-form-aht-see-ya
Information

Saugojimo kamera
Sou-goh-yee-moh camera
**Left luggage
(Baggage claim)**

Automatinės saugojimo
kameros
Ow-toh-matt-een-es sou-goh-yee-moh cameros
Luggage lockers

Paštas
Push-tus
Post Office

Platforma
Plat-form-ah
Platform

Geležinkelio stotis
Girl-ezh-ink-ello stoh-tiss
Railway (Railroad) station

Oro uostas
Oh-roh ohs-tahs
Airport

Policijos nuovada
Poh-lee-tsee-yoss noh-vah-dah
Police station

Uostas
Ohs-tahs
Port

Restoranas
Rest-orr-un-us
Restaurant

Rūkoma/nerūkoma
Roo-koh-mah/nya-roo-koh-mah
Smoking/non-smoking

Telefonas
Teh-leh-phon-us
Telephone

Kasa
Cah-sah
Ticket office

Registravimas
Regh-is-trah-wee-mus
Check-in desk

Tvarkaraštis
Twer-kah-rash-tiss
Timetable (Schedule)

Tualetas
Too-al-et-us
Toilets

Moterų/Vyrų
Mot-err-oo/Weer-oo
Ladies/Gentlemen

Metro
Met-roh
Underground (Subway)

Laukimo salė
Low-keem-oh sah-leh
Waiting room

L
I
T
H
U
A
N
I
A
N

211

L I T H U A N I A N

Buying a Ticket

**I would like a first-class/
second-class/third-class single
(one-way)/return (round-trip)
ticket to ...**
Man reikia pirmos klasės/
antros klasės/trečios klasės
bilieto (į vieną pusę)/ten ir
atgal į ...
*Mann rake-eh peer-moss class-
ess/ant-ross class-ess/trech-oss
klass-ess bill-yet-toh (ee vye-nah
puss-eh)/tyan eer ut-gull ee ...*

**Is it an express (fast)
train/bus?**
Ar tai greitasis traukinys/
autobusas?
*Ur thai gray-tah-sis trow-keen-
ees/ow-toh-boos-us?*

**Is my rail pass valid on this
train/ferry/bus?**
Ar galioja mano bilietas šitam
traukiniui/keltui/autobusui?
*Urr ghal-oh-ya mann-uh bill-yet-tuss
shee-tamm trow-keen-oy/kehlt-
ooy/ow-toh-boos-oy?*

**I would like an aisle/window
seat**
Norėčiau kraštinės
vietos/vietos prie lango
*Norr-etch-ow krash-tee-ness
vehtos/vehtos preh lang-oh*

No smoking/smoking please
Prašom rūkomą/nerūkomą
*Prah-shom roo-comm-ah/nya-roo-
comm-ah*

We would like to sit together
Mes norėtume sėdėti kartu
*Myas norr-et-oom-eh seh-deh-tee
car-too*

**I would like to make a seat
reservation**
Norėčiau užsakyti vietas
*Norr-etch-ow oozh-sack-ee-tee
veh-tuss*

**I would like to reserve a
couchette/sleeper for one
person/two people/my family**
Norėčiau užsakyti vietą/
miegamąją vietą vienam
žmogui/dviems/mano šeimai
*Norr-etch-ow oozh-sack-ee-tee wie-
tah/mye-gah-mah-ya veh-tah wie-
nam zhmo-gooy/dveh-ms/mah-noh
shame-ay*

**I would like to reserve a
cabin**
Norėčiau užsakyti kajutę
*Noh-reh-chow oozh-sack-ee-tee
car-yu-teh*

Timetables (Schedules)

Atvyksta
Ut-weeks-tuh
Arrive

Sustoja
Soos-toh-ya
Calls (Stops at)

Maitinimas
Mate-in-im-us
Catering service

Persėsti
Per-sess-tih
Change at

Persėdimas/per
Perr-seh-dee-mus/perr
Connection/Via

Kasdien
Cuss-dyen
Daily

Kas keturiasdešimt minučių
*Cuss kett-oor-ess-dash-imt
min-ootch-oo*
Every 40 minutes

Pirma klasė
Peer-mah class-eh
First class

Kas valandą
Cuss vah-land-ah
Hourly

Rekomenduojama užsakyti
vietas
*Reck-om-end-oy-am-ah oozh-see-
sack-eet-eh vyet-us*
**Seat reservations are
recommended**

Antra klasė
Unt-rah class-eh
Second class

Primokėti
Prim-ock-et-ee
Supplement payable

L
I
T
H
U
A
N
I
A
N

Luggage

**How much will it cost to
send (ship) my luggage in
advance?**
Kiek kainuos išsiųsti mano
bagažą iš anksto?
*Keck kay-noss eesh-soos-toh mah-
noh bag-uzh-ah eesh unks-toh?*

**Where is the left luggage
(baggage claim) office?**
Kur yra saugojimo kamera?
*Coor eer-uh sou-goh-yee-moh cam-
era?*

**What time do you
open/close?**
Kada atsidarote/užsidarote?
*Kah-dah aht-see-durr-ot-teh/
oozh-see-durr-ot-teh?*

**Where are the luggage
trolleys (carts)?**
Kur bagažo vežimėliai?
Coor bag-uzh-oh vezh-im-ell-ay?

Where are the lockers?
Kur yra automatinės saugojimo
kameros?
*Coor eer-uh ow-toh-matt-in-es
sou-goh-yee-moh cameros?*

I have lost my locker key
Aš pamečiau raktą nuo
kameros
*Ush pamm-etch-ow rack-tah noh
cam-err-oss*

On Board

Is this seat free?
Ar šita vieta laisva?
Ur sheet-ah veh-tah lay-swa?

**L
I
T
H
U
A
N
I
A
N**

Excuse me, you are sitting in my reserved seat
Atsiprašau, Jūs sėdite mano vietoje
Aht-see-prah-show, yoos seh-dee-teh mah-noh veh-toh-ya

Which station is this?
Kokia čia stotis?
Cock-eh cha stoh-tiss?

What time is this train/bus/ferry/flight due to arrive/depart?
Kada šitas traukinys/autobusas/reisas atvyksta/išvyksta?
Cah-dah sheet-us trow-keen-ees/ow-toh-boos-us/ray-sus ut-weeks-tah/eesh-weeks-tuh?

Travelling with Children

Do you have a high chair/babysitting service/cot?
Ar turite kėdę vaikui/teikiate vaikų priežiūros paslaugas/vaikišką lovytę?
Ur too-ree-teh keh-deh way-cooy/way-coo pre-zhoo-ros pass-low-gas/way-kish-kah loh-wee-teh?

Where is the nursery/playroom?
Kur vaikų kambarys/žaidimų kambarys?
Coor way-coo cam-bah-rees/zhay-dee-moo cam-bah-rees?

Where can I warm the baby's bottle?
Kur galima pašildyti buteliuką vaikui?
Coor ghal-eem-ah pah-shill-dee-tee boot-ell-ook-ah way-cooy?

Customs and Passports

Prašau parodyti pasus!
Pra-show pah-roh-dee-tee pah-soos!
Passports please!

I have nothing to declare
Deklaruojamų daiktų neturiu
Deck-larr-oy-ahmoo dayck-too nya-too-roo

I have wine/spirits (alcohol)/tobacco to declare
Noriu deklaruoti vyną/stiprius gėrimus tabaką
Noh-roo deck-lahr-otte ween-ah/stip-roos ghe-ree-moos tah-bah-kah

I will be staying for ... days/weeks/months
Aš būsiu čia ... dienas/savaites/mėnesius
Ash boos-yu cha ... dye-nas/sah-way-tes/meh-neh-soos

SIGHTSEEING

Asking the Way

Excuse me, do you speak English?
Atsiprašau, Jūs kalbate angliškai?
Aht-see-prah-show, Yoos kahl-bah-teh ahng-leesh-kay?

Excuse me, can you help me please?
Atsiprašau, gal galite man padėti?
At-see-prah-show, gull gull-it-eh mann pah-deh-tee?

Where is the Tourist Information Office?
Kur yra turistų informacijos biuras?
Coor eer-uh too-rees-too een-form-ahts-ee-yos byoo-rus?

Excuse me, is this the right way to ...?
Atsiprašau, ar aš teisingai einu į ..?
Aht-see-prah-show, ur ash tey-sing-ay ay-noo ee ...?

... the cathedral/the Tourist Information Office/the castle/the old town
... katedrą/turistų biurą/pilį/senamiestį
... cutt-ed-rah/too-riss-too byoo-rah/peeli/seh-nah-myes-tee

Can you tell me the way to the railway (railroad) station/bus station/taxi rank/city centre (downtown)/beach?
Kaip nueiti į geležinkelio stotį/autobusų stotį/taksi aikštelę/miesto centrą/pliažą?
Cayp noo-ay-tee ee girl-ezh-ink-ell-oh stoh-tee/autobusoo stotee/taxi ayksh-teh-leh/myes-toh tsen-trah/plah-zhah?

Pirmas/antras posūkis/į kairę/į dešinę/tiesiai
Peer-mus/unt-russ poss-ook-iss/ee kay-reh/ee desh-in-ya/tye-si-ay
First/second/left/right/straight ahead

Ant kampo/Prie šviesoforo
Ahnt cahmp-oh/preh shve-soh-forr-oh
At the corner/At the traffic lights

Where is the nearest police station/post office?
Kur yra artimiausias policijos skyrius/paštas?
Coor eer-uh ahr-tee-myau-syas po-lee-tsee-yohs skee-ryoos/pah-shtahs?

Is it near/far?
Ar tai arti/toli?
Are thai ahr-tee/toh-lee?

Do I need to take a taxi/catch a bus?
Ar man reikia važiuoti taksi/autobusu?
Ur mann ray-kya vah-zho-tih taxi/ow-tow-boos-ooh?

Do you have a map?
Ar turite žemėlapį?
Ur toor-it-eh zhe-mell-up-ee?

Can you point to it on my map?
Ar galite parodyti žemėlapyje?
Ur gull-it-teh purr-oddity zhe-mell-uppie-ya?

Thank you for your help
Ačiū už pagalbą
Ah-chew oozh pah-gull-bah

How do I reach the motorway/main road?
Kaip išvažiuoti į autostradą/pagrindinį kelią?
Kayp eesh-vah-zho-tee ee ow-toh-strah-dah/pag-rind-in-ee kell-eh?

I think I have taken the wrong turning
Man atrodo, aš ne ten pasukau
Mann atrohdoh, ash neh ten pah-sook-ow

L
I
T
H
U
A
N
I
A
N

215

L
I
T
H
U
A
N
I
A
N

I am looking for this address
Aš ieškau šito adreso
Ash yesh-cow sheet-oh address-oh

I am looking for the ... hotel
Aš ieškau viešbučio ...
Ash yesh-cow vesh-boo-cho...

How far is it to ... from here?
Ar toli nuo čia iki ...?
Ur toh-lee noh cha ee-kee... ?

Važiuoti tiesiai ... kilometrų
Vazh-oh-tee teh-say ... kill-om-met-roo
Carry straight on for ... kilometres

Tuojau pasukite į dešinę/kairę
Toh-yau pah-soo-kit-teh ee dash-inn-neh/kay-reh
Take the next turning on the right/left

Pasukite dešinėn/kairėn kitoje sankryžoje/prie kito šviesoforo
Pasoo-kit-teh dash-in-en/kay-renn kit-oy-ya san-cree-zho-ya/preh kit-toh shve-soh-for-roh
Turn right/left at the next crossroads/traffic lights

Jūs keliaujate ne į tą pusę
Yoos keh-lowya-teh ne ee tah pusseh
You are going in the wrong direction

Where is the cathedral/church/museum/pharmacy?
Kur yra katedra/bažnyčia/muziejus/vaistinė?
Coor ee-ruh cutt-ed-rah/buzh-knee-cha/moo-zeeh-yoos/ways-teeny?

How much is the admission/entrance charge?
Kiek kainuoja įėjimas?
Keck kay-noh-ya ee-eh-yee-mus?

Is there a discount for children/students/senior citizens?
Ar yra nuolaida vaikams/studentams/pagyvenusiems?
Ur ee-ruh noh-lay-dah vay-cums/stoo-dent-ums/pah-ghee-veh-noos-ems?

What time does the next guided tour (in English) start?
Kada prasideda artimiausia ekskursija (anglų kalba)?
Cah-dah prah-see-dedd-uh ur-tee-mouse-ah ex-curse-ee-ya (ang-loo cahl-bah)?

One adult/child please
Vieną suaugusiam/vaikui
Vye-nah soo-ow-guss-iam/way-cuh

Two adults/children please
Du suaugusiems/vaikams
Doo soo-ow-ghoo-siems/way-cams

May I take photographs here?
Ar čia galima fotogrofuoti?
Ar cheeah gah-lee-mah foh-toh-graph-ott-ee?

At the Tourist Office

Do you have a map of the town/area?
Ar turite miesto/rajono žemėlapį?
Ur toor-it-teh myes-toh ray-on-oh zhem-ell-up-ee?

Do you have a list of accommodation?
Ar turite viešbučių sąrašą?
Ur toor-it-teh vyesh-boo-choo sarah-shah?

Can I reserve accommodation?
Ar galiu užsakyti kambarį?
Ur gah-loo oozh-suck-kitty cam-bah-ree?

ACCOMMODATION

Hotels

I have a reservation in the name of ...
Aš užsisakęs kambarį. Mano pavardė ...
Ash oozh-see-suck-ess cam-bah-ree. Mah-noh pah-ward-ee ...

I wrote to/faxed/telephoned you last month/last week
Aš jums rašiau/siunčiau faksą/skambinau praeitą mėnesį/praeitą savaitę
Ash yooms rash-ow/soon-chow fax-ah/skamb-inn-ow prah-eh-itah meh-nessee/prah-eh-itah sah-waitee

Do you have any rooms free?
Ar turite laisvų kambarių?
Ar toor-it-teh lays-woo cam-bah-roo?

I would like to reserve a single/double room with bath (shower)/without a bath (shower)
Norėčiau užsakyti vienvietį/ dvivietį kambarį su vonia (dušu)/be vonios (dušo)
Noh-wrech-ow oozh-suck-it-tee wien-veh-tee/dwe-veh-tee cam-bah-ree

soo voh-nya (doo-shoo)/bya voh-nyos (doo-sho)

I would like bed/breakfast/ (room and) full board
Norėčiau nakvynės/pusryčių/ (kambario ir) pilno maitinimo
Norr-etch-ow nuck-wee-ness/puss-rich-oo/(camb-urr-oh eer) pill-noh mait-in-im-oh

How much is it per night?
Kokia kaina uš parai?
Cock-ya kay-nah oozh pah-ray?

Is breakfast included?
Ar pusryčiai įtraukti į kainą?
Are puss-rich-ay eet-rowck-tee ee kay-nah?

Do you have any cheaper rooms?
Ar turite pigesnių kambarių?
Are tour-it-eh pig-esnoo cam-bah-roo?

I would like to see/take the room
Norėčiau pažiūrėti kambarį/ Man šitas kambarys tinka
Norr-etch-ow pah-zhoo-reht-tee cam-bah-ree/Mann sheet-us cam-bah-rees tinker

I would like to stay for ... nights
Norėčiau kambario ... paroms
No-reh-chow camb-urryo... pahr-oms

The shower/light/tap/hot water doesn't work
Dušas/šviesa/čiaupas neveikia/nėra karšto vandens
Doo-shas/shveh-sah/cheeowpas nya-way-kya/nehra car-shtoh van-dens

217

At what time/where is breakfast served?
Kada/kur pateikiami pusryčiai?
Kah-dah/coor pateh-ikiami poos-rich-ay?

What time do I have to check out?
Kada man reikia išsiregistruoti?
Kah-dah mann ray-kya ish-si-reg-istroo-ohtee?

Can I have the key to room number ...?
Ar galima gauti rakta nuo ... kambario?
Ur gull-imma goatee rack-tah noh ... cam-bah-ryo?

My room number is ...
Mano kambarys yra ...
Mah-noh cam-bah-rees ee-ruh ...

My room is not satisfactory/ not clean enough/too noisy. Please can I change rooms?
Mano kambarys netinkamas/ nešvarus/triukšmingas. Ar galėčiau persikelti į kitą kambarį?
Mah-noh cam-bah-rees nya-tin-kamus/nya-shva-roos/troock-shmeen-gus. Ur gull-etch-ow per-sikel-tee ee keeta cam-bah?

Where is the bathroom?
Kur yra vonia?
Coor eer-uh von-ya?

Do you have a safe for valuables?
Ar turite seifą?
Ur tour-it-teh safe-uh?

Is there a laundry/do you wash clothes?
Ar turite skalbyklą/ar skalbiate drabužius?

Ur tour-it-teh scalb-ick-lah/ur scalb-eteh drab-oozh-oos?

I would like an air-conditioned room
Norėčiau kambario su oro kondicionavimu
Norr-etch-ow cam-bah-ryo soo oh-roh con-ditsy-oh-nah-vee-moo

Do you accept traveller's cheques/credit cards?
Ar priimate kelioninius čekius/kreditines korteles?
Ur pre-eem-ut-teh cull-on-in-yus check-us/credit-iness cort-el-ess?

May I have the bill please?
Gal galima saskaitą?
Gull gull-imma sass-kay-tah?

Excuse me, I think there may be a mistake in this bill
Atsiprašau, man atrodo, kad čia yra klaida
At-see-prah-show, mann atroh-doh, kahd cha eer-uh clay-dah

Youth Hostels

How much is a dormitory bed per night?
Kiek kainuoja bendrabučio lova uš parai?
Keck kay-noh-ya bend-rob-oocho loh-vah oozh pah-rai?

I am/am not an HI member
Aš esu/nesu HI narys
Ash ess-oo/ness-oo HI nurr-ees

May I use my own sleeping bag?
Ar galiu naudotis savo miegmaišiu?

218

*Ur gull-yo now-doh-tiss savoh
meg-may-shoo?*

**What time do you lock the
doors at night?**
Kelintą valandą užrakinamos
durys vakare?
*Cull-inter val-and-ah oozh-raki-
namos doo-riss vac-ur-eh?*

Camping

**May I camp for the night/two
nights?**
Ar galima apsistoti
parai/dviems paroms?
*Ur gull-imah up-sis-toh-tee
pah-ray/dvyems pah-roms?*

Where can I pitch my tent?
Kur galiu statytis palapinę?
*Coor gull-oo stat-eat-is pah-lapp-in-
eh?*

**How much does it cost for
one night/week?**
Kiek kainuoja parai/savaitei?
*Keck kay-noh-yah pah-ray/sah-
why-tey?*

**Where are the washing
facilities?**
Kur galima nusiprausti?
Coor gull-ima noo-sip-rows-tee?

**Is there a restaurant/
supermarket/swimming pool
on site/nearby?**
Ar netoliese yra restoranas/
supermarketas/baseinas?
*Ur net-oh-leese eer-uh rest-orr-un-
us/ supermarketus/bah-say-nus?*

**Do you have a safety deposit
box?**

Ar turite seifą?
Ur tour-it-teh say-fah?

Cafés and Bars

**I would like a cup of/two cups
of/another coffee/tea**
Prašom puodelį/du
puodelius/dar kavos/arbatos
*Prash-om poh-deh-lee/doo poh-deh-
loos/dahr kah-voss/ar-bat-oss*

**With/without milk.
With/without sugar**
Su pienu/be pieno.
Su cukrum/be cukraus
*Soo pye-noo/beh pye-noh.
Soo tsook-room/beh tsoo-crows*

**I would like a bottle/glass/two
glasses of mineral water/red
wine/white wine, please**
Norėčiau butelį/stiklinę/dvi
stiklines mineralinio vandens/
raudono vyno/baltojo vyno
*Norr-etch-ow boot-ell-ee/steek-lee-
neh/dwee steek-lee-ness mineral-in-
oh van-dens/row-don-oh ween-
oh/bahl-toh-yo ween-oh*

**I would like a beer/two beers,
please**
Norėčiau alaus/du alaus
Norr-etch-aw all-ows/doo all-ows

Please may I have some ice?
Ar galima būtų ledo?
Ur gah-lee-mah boo-too leh-doh?

**Do you have any
matches/cigarettes/cigars?**
Ar turite degtukų/cigarečių/
cigarų?

219

LITHUANIAN

Ur tour-it-teh deck-took-ooh/tsig-ur-etch-oo/tsig-ur-oo?

Restaurants

Can you recommend a good/cheap restaurant in this area?
Ar galite rekomenduoti gerą/pigų restoraną netoliese?
Ur gull-it-teh rekoh-mend-ohtee gehr-ruh/peeghoo rest-orr-un-ah netto-lesser?

I would like a table for ... people
Norėčiau staliuko ... žmonėms
Norr-etch-ow stah-lyoo-koh ... zhmo-nems

Do you have a non-smoking area?
Ar yra nerūkoma salė?
Ur eer-uh nerroo-komma sah-leh?

Waiter! Waitress!
Padavėjau! Padavėja!
Pah-dah-veh-yau! Pah-dah-veh-yah!

Excuse me, please may we order?
Atsiprašau, ar galima užsakyti?
Ut-see-prah-show, ur gull-im-uh oozh-suck-it-tee?

Do you have a set menu/ children's menu/wine list in English?
Ar turite meniu/vaikišką meniu/vyno sąrašą angliškai?
Ur tour-it-teh menoo/vay-kishka meh-nyoo/ween-oh sarah-sha ang-lish-kay?

Do you have any vegetarian dishes?
Ar turite vegetariškų patiekalų?
Ahr tuh-ree-teh veh-geh-tah-reesh-koo pah-tyeh-kah-loo?

Do you have any local specialities?
Ar turite vietinių patiekalų?
Ur tour-it-teh vye-tee-noo pat-eck-aloo?

Are vegetables included?
Ar daržovės įskaitytos?
Ur darr-zho-wees ees-kay-tee-toss?

Could I have it well-cooked/ medium/rare please?
Ar galite iškepti visiškai/ vidutiniškai/su krauju?
Ur gull-it-eh ish-kept-ee wee-seesh-kay/wee-doo-teenie-shkay/soo crow-yoo?

What does this dish consist of?
Iš ko padarytas šitas patiekalas?
Eesh koh pah-dah-ree-tus shee-tus pat-eck-al-us?

I am a vegetarian. Does this contain meat?
Aš vegetaras. Ar tai su mėsa?
Ash veh-geh-tah-rahs. Ahr tay suh meh-sah?

I do not eat nuts/dairy products/meat/fish
Aš nevalgau riešutų/pieno produktų/mėsos/žuvies
Ash ne-vall-gow resh-oot-ooh/penno proh-duck-too/mess-oss/zhoo-vess

Not (very) spicy please
Padarykite ne (labai) aštriai
Pah-dah-reek-it-eh neh (lah-bay) ash-tray

I would like the set menu please
Norėčiau kompleksinio meniu
Norr-etch-ow comp-lax-inn-oh man-ooh

We have not been served yet
Mes vis dar laukiame kol mus aptarnaus
Myas vees dahr lau-kyah-myah kohl moos up-tahr-naus

Please bring a plate/knife/fork
Prašom atnešti lėkštę/peilį/šakutę
Prah-shom aht-nesh-tee lehksh-teh/pey-lee/shah-kuh-teh

Excuse me, this is not what I ordered
Atsiprašau, aš šito neužsisakiau
At-sip-rash-ow, ash sheet-oh neh-oozh-si-suck-ee-yow

May I have some/more bread/water/coffee/tea?
Gal galima šiek tiek/dar duonos/vandens/arbatos?
Gull gull-ee-mah shack tack/dahr doh-noss/van-dens/ur-bah-toss?

May I have the bill please?
Ar galite atnešti sąskaitą?
Ur gull-i-teh at-nesh-tee sass-kay-tah?

Does this bill include service?
Ar aptarnavimas įskaičiuotas?
Ur upturn-ov-im-us ees-kay-cho-tass?

Do you accept traveller's cheques/Mastercard/US dollars?
Ar priimate kelioninius čekius/Mastercard/Amerikos dolerius?
Ur pre-imm-att-eh kell-on-in-oos check-us/Mastercard/Americk-oss dollar-yus?

Can I have a receipt please?
Ar galėčiau gauti kvitą?
Ur gull-etch-ow gowtee kwee-tah?

Where is the toilet (restroom) please?
Kur yra tualetas?
Coor ee-ruh too-al-ett-us?

On the Menu

Pusryčiai/Priešpiečiai/Pietūs
Poos-ree-chey/Pryesh-pyah-chey/Pyah-toos
Breakfast/Lunch/Dinner

Pirmas patiekalas
Peer-muss pat-yeck-al-us
First courses

Žuvies patiekalai
Zhoo-vess patte-cull-ay
Fish dishes

Mėsos patiekalai
Mess-oss patte-cull-ay
Meat dishes

Sriubos *Sroo-boss* **Soups**	Jautiena *Yauh-tyah-nah* **Beef**
Kepsnys *Kehp-snees* **Steak**	Kiauliena *Kyau-lyeh-nah* **Pork**
Veršiena *Vehr-shyeh-nah* **Veal**	Vištiena *Veesh-tyeh-nah* **Chicken**

LITHUANIAN

221

L I T H U A N I A N

Ériena
Eh-ryeh-nah
Lamb

Kumpis
Coom-pees
Ham

Vegetariški patiekalai
Veghe-tar-ish-kee patte-cull-ay
Vegetarian dishes

Daržovės
Dahr-zhoh-vehs
Vegetables

Traškučiai (keptos bulvytės)
Trash-kuh-chey (kehp-tohs bool-veeh-tehs)
Chips (french fries)

Virtos bulvės/skrudintos
bulvės/bulvių košė
Veer-tohs bool-vehs/skroo-deen-tohs bool-vehs/bool-vyoo koh-sheh
Boiled/sauté/mashed potatoes

Ryžiai
Ree-zhey
Rice

Desertai
Des-err-thai
Desserts

Ledai
Leh-day
Ice cream

Pyragaičiai
Pee-rah-ghay-chey
Cakes

Tešlainiai
Tehsh-lay-ney
Pastries

Vaisiai
Vay-sey
Fruit

Duona
Duoh-nah
Bread

Bandelės
Bahn-deh-lehs
Rolls

Skrebutis
Skreh-boo-tees
Toast

Sviestas
Svyes-tahs
Butter

Druska/pipirai
Droos-kah/pee-pee-ray
Salt/pepper

Cukrus
Tsoo-kroos
Sugar

Firminiai patiekalai
Feer-mee-ney patte-cull-ay
Specialities

Vietos firminiai patiekalai
Veetohss feer-mee-ney patte-cull-ay
Local specialities

Kompleksinis meniu
Komp-lek-see-nees meh-nyoo
Set menu

Vynų sąrašas
Vee-noo sah-rah-shahs
Wine list

Raudonieji vynai
Row-doh-nye-yee vee-nay
Red wines

Baltieji vynai
Bahl-tye-yee vee-nay
White wines

Rožiniai vynai
Roh-zhee-ney vee-nay
Rosé wines

Putojantys vynai
Puh-toh-yahn-tees vee-nay
Sparkling wines

Alus
Ah-loos
Beer

Alus buteliuose/Pilstomas alus
Ah-loos booh-teh-lyuoh-sya/Peel-stoh-mas ah-loos
Bottled beer/draught (draft) beer

Nealkoholiniai gėrimai
Neh-ahl-koh-hoh-lee-ney geh-ree-may
Non-alcoholic drinks

Mineralinis vanduo
Mee-neh-rah-lee-nis vahn-doh
Mineral water

Vaisių sultys
Vay-syoo soohl-tees
Fruit juices

Apelsinų sultys
Ah-pehl-see-noo soohl-tees
Orange juice

Limonadas
Lee-moh-nah-dahs
Lemonade

Ledas
Leh-dahs
Ice

Kava su pienu/juoda kava/espresso kava
Kah-vah soo pye-noo/yuoh-dah kah-vah/ehs-prehs-oh kah-vah
White coffee/black coffee/espresso coffee

Arbata su pienu/su citrina
Ahr-bah-tah soo pye-noo/soo tsee-tree-nah
Tea with milk/with lemon

Šokoladinis gėrimas
Shoh-koh-lah-dee-nees geh-ree-mahs
Chocolate (drink)

Pienas
Pye-nahs
Milk

Užkandžiai
Oozh-kahn-dzhey
Snacks/Light meals

Salotos
Sah-loh-tohs
Salads

Sumuštiniai
Soo-moosh-tee-ney
Sandwiches

Kiaušiniai
Kyaw-shee-ney
Eggs

Dešra
Deh-shrah
Sausage

Virti kiaušiniai/kepti kiaušiniai/kiaušinienė
Veer-tee kyaw-shee-ney/kehp-tee kyaw-shee-ney/kyaw-shee-nye-neh
Boiled /fried/scrambled eggs

Typical Local Dishes

Lietuviški patiekalai
Leh-too-vish-kee patte-cull-ay
Lithuanian dishes

Vėdarai
Veh-dah-ray
Fried pork guts stuffed with mashed potato

Žemaičių blynai
Zhe-my-choo blee-nay
Potato pancakes stuffed with minced meat

L
I
T
H
U
A
N
I
A
N

223

L
I
T
H
U
A
N
I
A
N

Koldūnai
Cold-oon-ay
Lithuanian ravioli

Cepelinai
Tse-pell-een-ay
Fist-sized mashed potato dumplings filled with minced pork, served with crackling and sour cream

Šaltibarščiai
Shal-tee-bahrsh-chay
Cold beetroot soup, served with hot boiled potatoes on the side

GETTING AROUND

Public Transport

Where is the bus stop/coach stop/nearest metro (subway) station?
Kur autobusų stotelė/autobusų stotis/artimiausia metro stotis?
Coor ow-tob-oos-oo stoh-teh-leh/ow-tob-oos-oo stoh-tiss/ur-tee-mous-ah metro stoh-tiss?

When is the next/last bus to ...?
Kada kitas/paskutinis autobusas į ...?
Kah-dah keet-us/pas-coo-tin-niss aw-tob-oos-us ee ...?

How much is the fare to the city centre (downtown)/railway (railroad) station/airport?
Kiek kainuoja nuvažiuoti į miesto centrą/geležinkelio stotį/oro uostą?
Keck kay-noh-ya noo-vah-zhoo-tee ee mess-toh tsen-trah/girl-ezh-ink-ello stoh-tee/oh-row oss-tah?

Will you tell me when to get off?
Ar pasakysite, kada man išlipti?
Ur pass-uck-ees-it-teh, kah-dah mann ish-lip-tee?

Does this bus go to...?
Ar šitas autobusas važiuoja į ... ?
Ur sheet-us ow-tob-oos-us vah-zhoo-ya ee ...?

Which number bus goes to ...?
Kuris autobusas važiuoja į... ?
Coor-iss ow-tob-oos-us vah-zhoo-ya ee...?

May I have a single (one-way)/return (round-trip)/day ticket/book of tickets?
Ar galima vieną bilietą/bilietą ten ir atgal/bilietą visai dienai/bilietų knygelę?
Ur gull-im-uh vienn-uh bill-yet-tuh/bill-yet-uh tyan eer at-ghal/bill-yet-tah viss-ay dyen-ay/bill-yet-too knee-gal-eh?

Taxis (Taksi)

I would like to go to ... How much will it cost?
Aš norėčiau važiuoti iki ... Kiek kainuos?
Ash norr-etch-ow vazh-ottee icky... Keck kay-noss?

Please may I stop here?
Prašom sustoti čia
Prah-show soos-toh-tee cha

I would like to order a taxi today/tomorrow at 2pm to go from ... to ...
Norėčiau užsakyti taksi šiandienai/rytdienai antrai valandai popiet, važiuoti iš ... į ...
Norr-etch-ow oozh-suck-it-ee taxi shan-deh-nay/reet-deh-nay ant-ray val-and-ay pop-yet, vazh-ott-ee ish ... ee ...

Entertainment

Can you recommend a good bar/nightclub?
Gal galite rekomenduoti gerą barą/klubą?
Gull gull-it-teh rek-oh-mend-ohtee geh-rah bar-ah/club-ah?

Do you know what is on at the cinema (playing at the movies)/theatre at the moment?
Gal žinote, kas dabar rodoma kine/teatre?
Gull zhee-noh-teh, kass dah-bar rodohma keen-eh/teh-at-reh?

I would like to book (purchase) ... tickets for the matinee/evening performance on Monday
Norėčiau užsakyti (nupirkti) ... bilietus į dieninį/vakarinį spektaklį pirmadienį
Norr-etch-ow oozh-suck-it-ee (noo-pier-ktee) ... bill-yet-us ee dyen-in-ee/wack-ur-in-ee speck-tack-lee peer-mah-dyena

What time does the film/ performance start?
Kada prasideda filmas/spektaklis?
Kah-dah prass-id-ed-ah film-us/speck-tack-liss?

Post

How much will it cost to send a letter/postcard/this package to Britain/ America/ Canada/Australia/ New Zealand?
Kiek kainuoja išsiųsti laišką/atviruką/banderolę į Britaniją/Ameriką/Kanadą/ Australiją/Naująją Zelandiją?
Keck kay-noh-ya ish-soos-tee laysh-kah/at-wee-rook-ah/band-err-ol-eh ee Breet-an-ee-ya/Americk-ah/ Canada/Ow-stra-lee-ya/Now-ya-ya Zell-and-ya?

I would like one stamp/two stamps
Norėčiau vieną/du ženklus
Norr-etch-ow vienn-uh/doo zhen-clus

I'd like ... stamps for postcards to send abroad, please
Norėčiau ... tarptautinių ženklų atvirukams
Noh-reh-chow ... tarp-tow-tee-noo zhen-cloo at-wee-rook-ums.

Phones

I would like to make a telephone call/reverse the charges to (make a collect call to) ...
Aš norėčiau paskambinti/ paskambinti abonento sąskaitą į ...
Ash norr-etch-ow pass-cam-bin-tee/pass-cam-bin-tee oozh ab-on-ent-oh sahs-kay-tah ee ...

LITHUANIAN

Which coins do I need for the telephone?
Kokių monetų reikia telefonui?
Cock-oo moh-nett-oo ray-kya telefon-ooy?

The line is engaged (busy)
Užimta
Oozh-im-tah

The number is ...
Numeris ...
Noom-err-iss ...

Hello, this is ...
Sveiki, čia ...
Sway-kee, cha ...

Please may I speak to..?
Ar galėčiau kalbėti su...?
Ur gull-etch-ow culb-et-tee soo...?

He/she is not in at the moment. Please can you call back?
Jo/jos dabar nėra. Skambinkite vėliau?
Yo/yoss dah-bar neh-rah. Skam-bin-kit-teh vell-ow?

SHOPPING

Shops

Knygynas/Rašymo reikmenys
Knee-ghee-nuss/Rashee-moh rake-man-iss
Bookshop/Stationery

Juvelyrinės prekės/Dovanos
Yuve-leery-ness preck-ess/Dove-annos
Jeweller/Gifts

Avalynė
Ahvah-leen-eh
Shoes

Ūkinės prekės
Oo-kee–ness preck-es
Hardware

Kirpykla
Kirr-peek-lah
Hairdresser

Duoninė
Doh-knee-neh
Baker

Supermarketas
Supermarket-us
Supermarket

Fotoreikmenų parduotuvė
Foh-toh-reyk-menoo pahr-doh-too veh
Photo shop

Turistų biuras
Too-riss-too byu-russ
Travel agent

Vaistinė
Ways-teeny
Pharmacy

In the Shops

What time do the shops open/close?
Kada atidaromos/uždaromos /parduotuvės?
Kah-dah ah-teeh-dah-roh-mohs/ uzh-darr-om-oss pahr-dot-oov-ess?

Where is the nearest market?
Kur yra artimiausias turgus?
Coor eer-uh art-team-yaus-us toor-goos?

Can you show me the one in the window/this one?
Prašom parodyti man tą iš vit-rinos/šitą?
Prah-show pah-rod-it-tee mann tah ish vit-ree-noss/shee-tah?

Can I try this on?
Ar galima pasimatuoti?
Ur gull-im-uh pass-im-ah-totee?

What size is this?
Koks čia dydis?
Cocks cha deed-is?

This is too large/too small/too expensive. Do you have any others?
Per didelis/per mažas/per brangus. Ar turite ką kitų?
Perr did-el-iss/perr mazh-us/perr bran-goose. Ur toor-it-teh kah kit-oo?

My size is...
Mano numeris...
Mah-noh noo-mer-iss...

Where is the changing room/children's/cosmetic/ladieswear/menswear/food department?
Kur yra kabina pasimatavimui/ vaikiškų/moteriškų/vyriškų/ maisto skyrius?
Coor eer-uh cab-een-ah paseem-aht-ahvee-mooy/way-keesh-koo/mott-err-ish-coo/weer-ish-coo/mays-toh skee-ryoos?

I would like ... a quarter of a kilo/half a kilo/a kilo of bread/butter/ham/this fruit
Prašau ketvirtį/pusę kilogramo/kilogramą duonos/ sviesto/kumpio/šių vaisių
Pra-show kett-vir-tee/puss-eh kill-ogg-ram-oh/kill-og-ram-ah doh-nos/ sves-toh/coom-poh/shoe ways-oo

How much is this?
Kiek šitas kainuoja?
Keck sheetus kay-noh-ya?

I'll take this one, thank you
Aš šitą paimsiu. Ačiū
Ash sheet-ah pah-im-soo. Ah-choo

Do you have a carrier (shopping) bag?
Ar turite pirkinių krepšelį?
Ahr tuh-ryh-tyah peer-keeh-nyoo krehp-sheh-lee?

Do you have anything cheaper/larger/smaller/of better quality?
Ar turite ką nors pigesnio/ didesnio/mažesnio/geresnės kokybės?
Ur tour-it-eh kah nors pig-ess-noh/deed-ess-noh/mah-jest-noh/ gerr-ess-ness cock-ee-bess?

I would like a film/to develop this film for this camera
Norėčiau juostos/Norėčiau išryškinti juostą
Norr-etch-ow yoss-toss/Norr-etch-ow ish-rish-keen-tee yoss-tah

I would like some batteries, the same size as this old one
Norėčiau baterijų, tokio pat dydžio kaip šitos
Norr-etch-ow batt-err-ee-yoo, tock-yo patt dee-joe, kype sheet-os

Would you mind wrapping this for me, please?
Gal galite suvynioti?
Gull gull-i-teh suvin-eeohtee?

Sorry, but you seem to have given me the wrong change
Atsiprašau, bet man atrodo, Jūs neteisingai atidavėte grąžą
At-see-prah-show, byat mann at-roh-doh, yoos nyathai-sing-ah ati-dah-vet-teh ghrah-zhah

MOTORING

Car Hire (Rental)

I have ordered (rented) a car in the name of...
Aš užsakiau automobilį. Mano pavardė...
Ash oozh-suck-ow ow-toh-mobili. Mah-noh pah-vard-eh...

How much does it cost to hire (rent) a car for one day/two days/a week?
Kiek kainuos automobilio nuoma vienai dienai/dviems dienoms/savaitei?
Keck kay-noss ow-toh-mobili-oh

no-mah vienn-ay dye-nay/dvems dye-noms /sah-way-thei?

Is the tank already full of petrol (gas)?
Ar bakas pilnas benzino?
Ur back-us peel-nus ben-zee-noh?

Is insurance and tax included? How much is the deposit?
Ar įskaičiuotas draudimas ir mokesčiai? Koks užstatas?
Ur ees-kay-cho-tass drow-dee-muss eer mock-esh-chay? Cocks oozh-sta-tass?

By what time must I return the car?
Kelintą valandą turiu grąžinti automobilį?
Kell-int-ah val-und-ah toor-yo grazh-int-ee ow-toh-mobilee?

I would like a small/large/family/sports car with a radio/cassette
Aš norėčiau išsinuomoti mažą/didelį/šeimyninį/sportinį automobilį su radiju/magnetofonu
Ash norr-etch-ow ish-see-nom-ottee mazh-ah/deed-ellee/shame-een-in-yee/sport-in-yee ow-toh-mobilyee soo radio/magnetoh-fonoh

Do you have a road map?
Ar turite žemėlapį?
Ar toor-it-teh zhe-meh-lap-ee?

Parking

How long can I park here?
Kiek laiko čia galima stovėti?
Keek lai-koh cha gull-im-ah stoh-veh-tee?

Is there a car park near here?
Ar yra netoliese stovėjimo
aikštelė?
Ur eer-uh netto-leeseh sto-veh-yee-moh ayk-shte-leh?

At what time does this car park close?
Kelintą valandą uždaroma šita
aikštelė?
Kell-int-ah vah-land-ah uzh-dah-rom-ah sheet-tuh ayk-shte-leh?

Signs and Notices

Vienpusis eismas
Wien-puss-iss ays-muss
One way

Įvažiuoti draudžiama
Ee-vazh-oh-tee drow-jam-uh.
No entry

Stovėti draudžiama.
Stoh-veh-tee drow-jam-un.
No parking

Apylanka
Up-ilanka
Detour (Diversion)

Stop
Stop
Stop

Užleiskite kelią
Oozh-lay-skee-teh kell-yah
Give way (Yield)

Slidus kelias
Slee-doss kell-us
Slippery road

Lenkti draudžiama
Lyank-tee drow-jam-uh
No overtaking

Pavojinga!
Pah-voh-yeen-gah!
Danger!

At the Filling Station
(Degalinė)

Unleaded (lead free)/ standard/premium/diesel
Bešvinis benzinas/standartinis
benzinas/super
benzinas/dyzelinis kuras
Besh-vinn-is ben-zeen-us/standart-een-ees ben-zeen-us/super ben-zeen-us/diesel-een-iss coor-us

Fill the tank please
Pripilkite pilną baką
Pree-pill-kit-teh peel-nah bah-kah

Do you have a road map?
Ar turite žemėlapį?
Ar toor-it-teh zhe-meh-lap-ee?

How much is the car wash?
Kiek kainuoja plovimas?
Keck kay-noh-ya plo-wee-mus?

L I T H U A N I A N

Breakdowns

I've had a breakdown at ...
Mašina sugedo ...
Mashin-ah soo-ghed-oh ...

I am a member of the ...
[motoring organisation]
Aš esu ... narys
Ash eh-soo ... nah-rees

I am on the road from ...
to ...
Aš kelyje iš ... į ...
Ash kya-lee-ya ish ... ee...

I can't move the car.
Can you send a tow-truck?
Negaliu užvesti mašinos. Ar
galite atsiųsti vilkiką?
*Nya-ghal-oo oozh-vess-tee mash-
een-oss. Ur gull-it-eh at-syoos-ti
veal-kick-ah?*

I have a flat tyre
Prakiuro padanga
Praki-uroh pah-dan-gah

The windscreen (windshield)
has smashed/cracked
Priekinis stiklas sudužo/įskilo
*Prye-keen-iss steek-luss soo-doo-
zho/ees-kill-oh*

There is something wrong
with the engine/brakes/lights/
steering/gearbox/clutch/
exhaust
Kažkas atsitiko varikliui/
stabdžiams/šviesoms/vairui/
pavarų dėžei/sankabai/
išmetimo sistemai
*Kaj-kass at-see-ticko varr-ick-
looy/stab-jams/shwee-soms/vay-
rooy/pava-roo deh-jay/sahn-cab-
ay/ish-met-imoh sis-tem-ay*

It's overheating
Variklis kaista
Var-ick-liss kays-tah

It won't start
Neužsiveda
Nya-oozh-see-vya-dah

Where can I get it repaired?
Kur galima pataisyti?
Coor gull-im-ah pat-ice-eat-ee?

Can you take me there?
Ar galite mane ten nuvežti?
*Ur gull-i-teh mah-neh tehn noo-
vej-tee?*

Will it take long to fix?
Ar ilgai užtruks remontas?
Ur eel-gau uzh-troox rem-ont-us?

How much will it cost?
Kiek tai kainuos?
Keck tay kay-noss?

Please can you pick me
up/give me a lift?
Gal galite mane pavežėti?
*Gull gull-it-teh manneh pah-vezh-et-
tee?*

Accidents and Traffic
Offences (Violations)

Can you help me? There has
been an accident
Ar galite man padėti? Įvyko
nelaimingas atsitikimas
*Ur gull-i-teh mann pah-deh-tee?
Ee-vee-koh neh-lay-meen-gahs
aht-see-tee-kee-mahs*

Please call the police/an ambulance
Prašom iškviesti policiją/ greitąją pagalbą
Prah-shom eesh-kvyas-tee poh-lee-tsee-yah/grey-tah-yah pah-gahl-bah

Is anyone hurt?
Ar yra sužeistų?
Ahr ee-ruh soo-zhey-stoo?

Sorry, I didn't see the sign
Atsiprašau, aš nepamačiau ženklo
At-see-prah-show, ash nya-pa-ma-chow-zhen-cloh

Must I pay a fine? How much?
Turiu mokėti baudą? Kiek?
Too-roo mock-et-ee bow-dah? Keck?

Parodykite savo dokumentus
Pah-roh-deeck-it-eh sah-voh dock-um-en-toos
Show me your documents

Pharmacy (Vaistinę)

Do you have anything for a stomach ache/headache/sore throat/toothache?
Ar turite ką nors nuo pilvo skausmo/galvos skausmo/ gerklės skausmo/danties skausmo?
Ur toor-it-teh kah nohrs noh peel-vo scous-moh/ghal-voss scous-moh/gher-cless scous-moh/dan-ti-ess scous-moh?

I need something for diarrhoea/constipation/ a cold/a cough/insect bites/ sunburn/travel (motion) sickness
Man reikia ko nors nuo viduriavimo/viduriu uz kietejimo/slogos/kosulio/ vabzdžių įkandimo/saulės nudegimo/jūros ligos
Mann ray-kya koh nohrs noh vidoo-ria-vimoh/wee-doo-roo oozh-keh-teh-yee-moh/slo-goss/coss-ool-oh/vabz-joo ick-ann-dee-moh/sow-less noo deh-gee-moh/yoo-ros lee-goss

How much/how many do I take?
Kiek reikia išgerti?
Keck ray-kya ish-gerr-tee?

I am taking anti-malaria tablets/these pills
Aš geriu tabletes nuo maliarijos/šias piliules
Ash gher-oo tab-lett-us noh mall-ya-ree-yoss/shas pili-oo-lyas

How often do I take it/them?
Kaip dažnai jį/juos vartoti?
Kayp daj-nay yee/yos war-toh-ya-mee?

I am/he is/she is taking this medication
Aš/jis/ji vartoja šiuos vaistus
Ash/yis/yi var-toh-ya shoss vays-toos

How much does it cost?
Kiek tai kainuoja?
Keck tay kay-noh-ya?

231

L
I
T
H
U
A
N
I
A
N

Can you recommend a good doctor/dentist?
Gal galite rekomenduoti gerą gydytoją/dantistą?
Gull gull-it-teh rek-om-mend-ottee gher-ah gheed-eet-oy-ah/dahn-tiss-tah?

Is it suitable for children?
Ar galima šitą duoti vaikams?
Ur gull-im-ah sheet-uh doh-tee way-cams?

Doctor (Gydytojas)

I have a pain here/in my arm/leg/chest/stomach
Man skauda štai čia/ranką/koją/krūtinę/pilvą
Mann scoud-ah shtay cha/runk-ah/koya/croo-teen-ya/peel-wah

Please call a doctor, this is an emergency
Iškvieskite gydytoją, kuo skubiau
Ishk-wess-kit-teh ghee-dee-toya, koh scoo-byau

I would like to make an appointment to see the doctor
Norėčiau užsirašyti priėmimui
Noh-rech-ow oozh-see-rash-eetee pree-em-im-ooy

I am diabetic/pregnant
Aš diabetikas/nėščia
Ash dya-bet-ick-us/nash-cha

I need a prescription for...
Man reikia recepto...
Mann ray-kya ret-sep-toh...

Can you give me something to ease the pain?
Ar galite duoti man ką nors nuo skausmo?
Ur gull-it-eh doh-tee mann kah nors noh scows-moh?

I am/he is/she is/allergic to penicillin
Aš/jis/ji/ alergiškas penicilinui
Ash/yis/yi/aler-ghi-shkass penni-tsi-lynn-uy

Čia skauda?
Chya scow-dah?
Does this hurt?

Jums/jam/jai teks važiuoti į ligoninę
Yums/yam/yay tex vazh-oh-tee ee lig-on-in-eh
You must/he must/she must go to hospital

Vartokite vieną/du/tris kartus per dieną
Var-toh-kee-tya vienn-ah/doo/trees kahr-toos per dye-nah
Take these once/twice/three times a day

I am/he is/she is taking this medication
Aš/jis/ji vartoja šiuos vaistus
Ash/yis/yi var-toh-ya shoss vays-toos

I have medical insurance
Aš turiu medicinos draudimą
Ash too-roo me-dee-tsee-noss drow-dee-mah

Dentist (Dantistas)

I have toothache/my filling has come out
Man skauda dantį/iškrito plomba
Mann scoud-ah dunt-ee/ish-kree-toh plombah

I do/do not want to have an injection first
Aš noriu/nenoriu nuskausminimo injekcijos
Ash noh-roo/neh-noh-roo noos-kows-minimoh een-jek-tsee-yoss

EMERGENCIES

Help!
Padėkite!
Pah-deck-it-eh!

Fire!
Gaisras!
Ghays-rus!

Stop!
Stop!
Stop!

Call an ambulance/a doctor/the police/the fire brigade!
Iškvieskite greitąją pagalbą/gydytoją/policiją/gaisrininkus!
Ish-ques-kee-teh gray-tah-yah pah-gull-bah/ghee-dee-toh-yah/poh-lee-tsee-yah/ghay-sree-neen-coos!

Please may I use a telephone?
Ar galėčiau paskambinti?
Ur gull-i-chow pass-camb-in-tee?

I have had my traveller's cheques/credit cards/handbag/rucksack/luggage/wallet/passport/mobile phone stolen
Man pavogė kelioninius čekius/kreditines korteles/rankinę/kuprinę/bagažą/piniginę/pasą/mobilųjį telefoną
Man pah-voh-geh keh-lyon-in-yus check-us/credit-iness cort-ell-ess/ran-kee-neh/coop-ree-neh/bag-azh-ah/pee-nee-ghee-neh/pah-sah/moh-bee-loo-yee teh-leh-foh-nah

May I please have a copy of the report for my insurance claim?
Ar galite duoti man ataskaitos kopiją draudimo paraiškai?
Ur gull-i-teh duoh-tee man ah-tah-skay-tohs koh-pee-yah drow-dee-moh pah-raysh-kay?

Can you help me? I have lost my daughter/son/my companion(s)
Padėkite man? Aš pamečiau savo dukrą/sūnų/draugus
Pah-deck-it-eh mann? Ash pamm-ech-ow sah-voh doock-rah/soo-noo/drow-ghuss

Please go away/leave me alone
Eikite sau/Palikite mane ramybėje
Ey-kit-eh show/Pah-lick-it-eh mah-neh rah-mee-beh-ya

I'm sorry
Atsiprašau
At-see-prash-ow

LITHUANIAN

233

**L
I
T
H
U
A
N
I
A
N**

**I want to contact the
British/American/Canadian/
Australian/New Zealand/
South African Consulate**
Aš noriu susisiekti su
Britanijos/Amerikos/Kanados/
Australijos/Naujosios
Zelandijos/Pietu Afrikos
konsulatu
*Ush nori-oo soo-see-seck-tee soo
Brit-un-ee-yos/Americk-os/Cana-
doss/Ows-trah-lee-yoss/Now-yoss-
yoss Zel-and-ee-yos/Peh-tooh Af-rick-
os con-sul-aht-too*

**I'm/we're/he is/she is/they
are/ill/lost/injured**
Aš/mes/jis/ji susirgo/
pasiklydo/susižeidė
*Ush/mess/yis/yi soo-sir-goh/
pass-ick-leed-oh/soo-see-zhey-deh*

POLISH

POLISH

INTRODUCTION

Polish is a Slavic tongue and therefore related to Russian, Czech and many other Eastern European languages. English is spoken to some extent in larger cities, particularly by younger people, though older inhabitants are more likely to speak German or French as a second language. Russian is understood but unpopular.

Addresses for Travel and Tourist Information

Australia: *Embassy*, 7 Turrana St, Yarralumla, ACT 2600; tel: (02) 6273 1208.

Canada: *Embassy*, 443 Daly Ave, Ottawa, Ontario K1N 6H3; tel: (613) 789 0468; fax: (613) 789 1218.

New Zealand: *Embassy*, 17 Upland Road, Kelburn, Wellington; tel: (04) 475 9453; fax: (04) 475 9458.

South Africa: *Embassy*, 14 Amos Street, Colbyn, Pretoria; tel: (12) 430 2631.

UK: *Polish National Tourist Office*, Level 3, Westec House, West Gate, London W5 1YY; tel: 08700 675010 (brochure line); fax: 08700 675011.

USA: *Polish National Tourist Office*, 275 Madison Ave, #1711, New York, NY 10016; tel: (212) 338 9412.

Official tourism website: www.visitpoland.org.

Poland Facts

CAPITAL: Warsaw, Warsawa (pronounced Varrshaava)

CURRENCY: Złoty (Zł), pronounced zwahti. Zł 1 = 100 groszy (pronounced groshi).

OPENING HOURS: Banks: Mon–Fri 0800–1600, with some open Sat 0900–1300. Shops: Mon–Sat 1000–1900, but some shops are open 24 hours. Museums: generally 1000–1600, closed Monday.

TELEPHONES: To dial in, +48. Outgoing, 0 for dial tone, 0 again and then the country code. Police, 997. Fire, 998. Ambulance, 999.

PUBLIC HOLIDAYS: 1, 6 Jan; Easter Monday; 1, 3 May; 15 Aug; 1, 11 Nov; 25, 26 Dec.

P
O
L
I
S
H

Technical Language Hints

Polish uses the Roman alphabet, but there are a few accented characters which are considered as separate letters, and there are some complexes of consonants which at first sight look unpronounceable to English speakers – szcz, for instance. 'Unvoiced' consonants at the end of a word are pronounced in a 'harder' way than their equivalents in the middle of a word – w, for example, which is normally pronounced like an English v, is like an English f when it occurs at the end of a word.

The word 'You' is translated in these phrases as 'Pan' (for men) and 'Pani' (for women). In other phrases the feminine form is denoted by (fem.).

ESSENTIALS

Alphabet and Pronunciation

	Name	Pronounced			
A a	ah	like the u in cut	dź		like dy in would you or j in jam with the top of the tongue slightly forward
Ą ą	awng	a nasalised long a			
B b	bey	like b in butter	E e	ey	like e in bed
C c	tsey	like ts in cats	F f	ef	like f in fast
Ć ć		like ty in get you or like ch with the top of the tongue slightly forward	G g	gye	like g in go
			H h	hah	like h in head
			I i	ee	like e in he
			J j	yot	like y in yes
ch		like h in head	K k	kah	like k in key
cz		like ch in church	L l	el	like l in love
D d	dey	like d in day	Ł ł	w	like w in wine
dz		like ds in adds up	M m	em	like m in milk
			N n	en	like n in no
dż		like j in jam	Ń ń	ny	like ni in onion

P O L I S H

O o	oh	like o in not
Ó ó		like oo in boot or u in put
P p	pey	like p in pot
Q	koo	not found in Polish words
R r	air	rolled r as in Scottish pronunciation
rz		zh like s in pleasure
S s	ess	like s in stop
Ś ś	sh	like si in passion but with the top of the tongue slightly forward
sz		like sh in show
szcz	shch	as in fresh cheese
T t	tey	like t in top
U u	oo	like oo in boot or u in put
V	fow	not found in Polish words
W w	voo	like v in vest
X	iks	not found in Polish words
Y y	eegrek	like e in he
Z z	zet	like z in zest
Ż ż	zh	like s in pleasure
Ź ź		similar to ż but with the top of the tongue slightly forward

Basic Words and Phrases

Yes
Tak
Tak

No
Nie
Nyeah

Please
Proszę
Pro-sheh

Thank you
Dziękuję
Jen-koo-yair

Hello (informal)
Cześć
Cheshch

Goodbye
Do widzenia
Do vee-je-nyah

Excuse Me/ Sorry
Przepraszam
Pshe-pra-sham

How
Jak
Yak

When
Kiedy
Kye-de

Why
Dlaczego
Dla-che-goe

What
Co
Tso

Who
Kto
Ktoh

That's O.K.
To jest O.K.
Toe yest O.K.

Perhaps
Może
Mozhe

To
Do
Doe

From
Z/Skąd
Z/Skond

Here
Tutaj
Too-tigh

There
Tam
Tam

I don't understand
Nie rozumiem
Nyeah ro-zoo-myem

I don't speak Polish
Nie mówię po polsku
Nyeah moo-vyair po pols-koo

Do you speak English?
Czy mówi Pan/Pani po angielsku?
Chy moo-vee pa-nee po an-gyels-koo?

Can you please write it down?
Czy mógłby Pan/mogłaby Pani to napisać?
Chy moogw-bi pan/ mogwah-bi pa-nee toh napisach?

Please can you speak more slowly?
Proszę mówić wolniej?
Pro-shair moo-vech vol-nyey?

Greetings

Good Morning/ Good Afternoon/Good Evening/ Good Night
Dzień dobry/Dobry wieczór/ Dobranoc
Jeny dobri /do-bri vie-choor/ do-bra-nots

Pleased to meet you
Miło mi Pana/Panią poznać
Mee-wo me pana/pa-nyom po-znach

How are you?
Jak się Pan/Pani miewa?
Yak sie pan/pa-nee mye-va?

I am well, thank you. And you?
Bardzo dobrze, dziękuję. A Pan/Pani?
Bar-zo do-bje, jen-koo-yair. ar pan/pa-nee?

My name is ...
Nazywam się ...
Nazyvam shiem ...

This is my friend/ boyfriend/ girlfriend/husband/wife/ brother/sister
To mój kolega/mój chłopak/ moja dziewczyna/mój mąż/ moja żona/mój brat/moja siostra
Toe mooy kollehga/mooy hwopak/ moya dzee-evcheena/mooy monj/moya zhona/moy brat/moya syostra

Where are you travelling to?
Dokąd Pan/Pani jedzie?
Doh-kond pan/pa-nee ye-jair?

I am/ we are going to ...
Jadę/Jedziemy do ...
Ya-dair/Yedziemmy doh ...

How long are you travelling for?
Na jak długo Pan/Pani jedzie?
Na yak dwoo-go pan/pa-nee yejair?

Where do you come from?
Skąd Pan/Pani pochodzi?
Skond pan/pa-nee po-ho-jee?

I am/we are from ... Australia/Britain/Canada/ America
Pochodzę/Pochodzimy z ... Australii/ Wielkiej Brytanii/Kanady/ Ameryki

P
O
L
I
S
H

239

POLISH

Po-ho-dzair/Po-ho-dzimee z …
Aus-tra-lee/Yyel-kyey Bre-ta-nee/
Ka-na-de/Ame-ri-key

We are on holiday
Jesteśmy na wakacjach
Ye-ste-shme na va-ka-tsyah

This is our first visit here
To jest nasza pierwsza wizyta
Toh yest na-sha pier-vsha vee-ze-ta

How old are you?
Ile ma Pan/Pani lat?
Ee-lair ma pan/pa-nee lat?

I am … years old
Mam … lat
Mam … lat

**I am a business person/
doctor/journalist/manual
worker/administrator/
scientist/student/teacher**
Jestem biznesmenem
lekarzem/dziennikarzem/
robotnikiem/urzednikiem/
naukowcem/studentem/
nauczycielem
*Ye-stem bi-znes-me-nem le-ka-jem/
je-nnee-ka-jem/ ro-bo-tnee-kyem/
oo-jen-dnee-kyem/now-kov-tsem/
stoo-den-tem/now-oo-chi-chairlem*

**I am waiting for my husband/
wife/boyfriend/girlfriend**
Czekam na męża/żonę/
mojego chłopaka/moją
dziewczynę
*Che-kam na menja/zho-nair/
moyego hwopaka/moyanhg
dzee-ehvcheenen*

**Would you like a
cigarette?/May I have a
cigarette?**

Czy chciałby Pan/Pani zapalić?
Czy mogę zapalić?
*Che hchawbi pan/pa-nee zapalitsh?
/che mogair zapalitsh?*

Do you mind if I smoke?
Czy pozwoli Pan/Pani, że
zapalę?
Chy pozvoli pan/pa-nee je za-palair?

Do you have a light?
Czy mogę prosić o ogień?
Chy mo-gair proshitsh o ogieny?

Days

Monday	**Tuesday**
Poniedziałek	Wtorek
Po-niair-ja-wek	*Vto-rek*
Wednesday	**Thursday**
Środa	Czwartek
Shro-da	*Chvar-tek*
Friday	**Saturday**
Piątek	Sobota
Pyon-tek	*So-bo-ta*
Sunday	**Morning**
Niedziela	Rano
Nyair-je-la	*Rano*

Afternoon/Evening/Night
Popołudnie/Wieczór/Noc
Po-po-woo-dnye/vyair-choor/nots

Yesterday	**Tomorrow**
Wczoraj	Jutro
Vcho-ray	*Yoo-troe*

Today
Dzisiaj
Jishyay

Numbers

Zero
Zero
Zeroe

One
Jeden
Ye-den

Two
Dwa
Dva

Three
Trzy
Tshe

Four
Cztery
Chte-ri

Five
Pięć
Pyench

Six
Sześć
Shesch

Seven
Siedem
She-dem

Eight
Osiem
O-shem

Nine
Dziewięć
Je-vyench

Ten
Dziesięć
Je-shensh

Eleven
Jedenaście
Yede-nash-chair

Twelve
Dwanaście
Dva-nash-chair

Thirteen
Trzynaście
Tshe-nahsh-chair

Fourteen
Czternaście
Chtair-nash-chair

Fifteen
Piętnaście
Peeyent-nash-chair

Sixteen
Szesnaście
Shes-nash-chair

Seventeen
Siedemnaście
Shedem-nash-chair

Eighteen
Osiemnaście
Oshem-nash-chair

Nineteen
Dziewiętnaście
Jevyet-nash-chair

Twenty
Dwadzieścia
Dva-je-shchar

Twenty-one
Dwadzieścia
jeden
*Dva-je-shchar
yeden*

Twenty-two
Dwadzieścia
dwa
*Dva-je-shchar
dva*

Thirty
Trzydzieści
Tshee-je-shchee

Forty
Czterdzieści
Chtair-je-shchee

Fifty
Pięćdziesiąt
Peeyent-je-shont

Sixty
Sześćdziesiąt
Shesch-je-shont

Seventy
Siedemdziesiąt
She-dem-je-shont

Eighty
Osiemdziesiąt
Oshem-je-shont

Ninety
Dziewięćdziesiąt
Je-vyench-jeshont

One hundred
Sto
Sto

Five hundred
Pięćset
Peeyench-set

One thousand
Tysiąc
Ti-shonts

One million
Milion
Millyon

Time

What time is it?
Która jest godzina?
Ktoo-rah yest go-jee-nah?

It is ...
Jest ...
Yest ...

9.00
Dziewiąta
Je-vyon-ta

P
O
L
I
S
H

9.05
Pięć po dziewiątej/dziewiąta
pięć
*Pyench poe je-vyon-tey/je-vyon-ta
pyench*

9.15
Piętnaście po dziewiątej/
kwadrans po dziewiątej/
dziewiąta piętnaście
*Peeyent-nash-chair poe je-vyon-tey/
kva-drans poe je-vyon-tey/
je-vyon-ta peeyent-nash-chair*

9.20
Dwadzieścia po dziewiątej/
dziewiąta dwadzieścia
*Dva-je-shchar poe je-vyon-tey/
je-vyon-ta dva-je-shchar*

9.30
W pół do dziesiątej/dziewiąta
trzydzieści
*V poow doe je-vyon-tey/je-vyon-ta
tshe-je-shchee*

9.35
Pięć po wpół do dziesiątej/
dziewiąta trzydzieści pięć
*Pyench poe v poow doe je-vyon-tey/
je-vyon-ta tshe-je-shchee pyench*

9.40
Za dwadzieścia dziesiąta/
dziewiąta czterdzieści
*Za dva-je-shchar je-shont-ta/
je-vyon-ta chtair-je-shchee*

9.45
Za piętnaście dziesiąta/
za kwadrans dziesiąta/
dziewiąta czterdzieści pięć
*Za peeyent-nash-chair je-shont-ta/
za kva-drans je-shont-ta/
je-vyon-ta chtair-je-shchee pyench*

9.50
Za dziesięć dziesiąta/
dziewiąta pięćdziesiąt
*Za je-shensh je-shont-ta/
je-vyon-ta peeyent-je-shont*

9.55
Za pięć dziesiąta/dziewiąta
pięćdziesiąt pięć
*Za pyench je-shont-ta/je-vyon-ta
peeyent-je-shont pyench*

12.00/Midday/Midnight
Dwunasta w południe/północ
*Dvoo-nas-ta v po-woo-dniair/
poow-nots*

Money

**I would like to change these
traveller's cheques/ this
currency**
Chciałbym/chciałabym
wymienić te czeki podróżne/tą
walutę
*Hcha-wbem/hcha-wa-bem vem-ye-
nech teh cheke po-droo-jneh/tom
va-loo-tair*

**How much commission do
you charge? (What is the
service charge?)**
Jaka jest opłata manipulacyjna?
*Ya-ka yest opwata
mani-poo-latsiyna?*

**Can I obtain money with my
Mastercard?**
Czy mogę uzyskać pieniądze
za pomocą Mastercard?
*Che mo-gair oo-ze-skach pier-nyon-
ze za po-moe-tsom master-kard?*

Where is the nearest ATM?
Gdzie jest najbliższy bankomat?
Gur-dj-yeah yest nay-bleesh-shee bank-oh-mat?

My name is ... Some money has been wired to here for me to collect
Nazywam się ... Czy mogę odebrać przekaz pieniężny
Nazeevam see-en ... Tchee mogeh oh-debr-ach pshe-kas pee-enee-enjnee

ARRIVING AND DEPARTING

Airport

Excuse me, where is the check-in desk for ... airline?
Przepraszam, gdzie jest odprava dla linii lotniczych ...?
Pshe-pra-sham gdjair yest odprava dla lee-nee lo-tnee-cheeh ...?

What is the boarding gate for my flight?
What is the time of my flight?
Z której sali odlotu?
O której godzinie jest odlot?
Z ktoo-rey sa-lee odlo-too?
O ktoo-rey go-jee-nyair yest od-lot?

How long is the delay likely to be?
Jakie będzie opóźnienie?
Ya-kyair ben-jair o-poo-jnyair-nair?

Where is the duty-free shop?
Gdzie jest sklep wolnocłowy?
Gdjair yest sklep volnoe-tswo-ve?

Which way is the luggage reclaim?
Gdzie jest odbiór bagażu?
Gdjair yest od-buer ba-ga-joo?

I have lost my luggage. Please can you help?
Zgubiłem bagaż. Czy mógłby mi Pan/mogłaby mi Pani pomóc?
Zgoo-bee-wem ba-gaj. Che moog-wbe me pan/mog-wa-be me pa-nee poe-moots?

I am flying to ...
Lecę do ...
Lair-tsair doe ...

Where is the bus for the city centre?
Skąd odjeżdża autobus do centrum?
Skond od-yeh-jdjah awto-boos doe tse-ntroom?

Trains and Boats

Where is the ticket office/ information desk?
Gdzie jest kasa biletowa/ informacja?
Gdjair yest ka-sah bee-le-toh-va/ in-for-ma-tsya?

Which platform does the train/speedboat/ferry to ... depart from?
Z którego peronu odjeżdża pociąg do ...?
Skąd odpływa motorówka/ prom do ...?
Z ktoo-rair-go pairo-noo od-yehj-ja poe-tsyong doe ...?
Skond od-pwe-vah mo-to-roov-ka/ prom doe ...?

P
O
L
I
S
H

243

POLISH

Where is platform ...?
Gdzie jest peron ...?
Gjair yest pair-ron ...?

When is the next train/boat to ...?
O której godzinie jest następny pociąg/statek do ...?
O ktoo-rey go-jee-nyair na-stem-pne poe-tsyong/sta-tairk doe ...?

Is there a later train/boat to ...?
Czy jest późniejszy pociąg/statek do ...?
Che yest poo-jnyey-she poe-tsyong/sta-tairk doe ...?

Notices and Signs

Wagon restauracyjny
Va-gon re-sta-wra-tse-yne
Buffet (Dining) Car

Autobus
Awtoh-boos
Bus

Woda pitna/Woda niezdatna do picia
Vo-dah pee-tnah /vo-dah nyair zda-tna doe pee-chyah
Drinking/Non-drinking water

Wejście
Vey-shchair
Entrance

Wyjście
Veey-shchair
Exit

Szpital
Sh-pee-tal
Hospital

Informacja
In-for-ma-tsya
Information

Przechowalnia bagażu
Przehovalneeah bagaju
Left Luggage (Baggage Claim)

Schowki na bagaż
Se-hoe-vkee na ba-gaj
Luggage Lockers

Poczta
Po-chtah
Post Office

Peron
Pair-ron
Platform

Stacja kolejowa/ Dworzec kolejowy
Stah-tsya ko-le-yo-va/ Dvo-jets ko-le-yo-ve
Railway (Railroad) Station

Port lotniczy/Lotnisko
Port lo-tnee-che/Lot-nee-skoe
Airport

Policja
Po-lee-tsyah
Police Station

Port
Port
Port

244

Restauracja
Re-sta-wra-tsya
Restaurant

Dla palących
Dla niepalących/Zakaz palenia
Dla pa-lon-tse-h
Dla nyair pa-lon-tse-h/Za-kaz pa-lair-nyah
Smoking
Non Smoking

Telefon
Te-lair-fon
Telephone

Kasa biletowa
Ka-sa bee-lair-to-va
Ticket Office

Odprawa
Od-pra-vah
Check-in desk

Rozkład jazdy
Roz-kwad ya-zdi
Timetable

Toalety
Toe-a-lair-te
Toilets (Restrooms)

Damska/Męska
Dam-skah/Men-skah
Ladies/ Gentlemen

Metro
Metro
Underground (Subway)

Poczekalnia
Poe-chair-kal-nyah
Waiting Room (Subway)

Buying a Ticket

I would like a first-class/ second-class/third-class/single (one-way)/ return (round trip) ticket to ...
Poproszę o bilet pierwszej klasy/drugiej klasy/trzeciej klasy w jedną stronę/ powrotny do ...
Po-pro-she o bee-lairt pyer-vshey kla-si/droo-gyey kla-si/tsheh-chaey kla-si/v yednom stro-nair/po-vro-tni doe ...

Is it an express (fast) train/bus?
Czy to jest pociąg/autobus ekspresowy?
Che toh yest poe-tsyong/awtoh-boos expre-so-vi?

Is my rail pass valid on this train/ferry/bus?
Czy mój bilet jest ważny na ten pociąg/prom/autobus?
Che mooy bee-let yest va-jni na ten poe-tsyong/prom/awtoh-boos?

I would like an aisle/window seat
Chciałbym/Chciałabym (fem.) miejsce przy przejściu/przy oknie
Hcha-wbem/Hcha-wa-bim myey-stsair pshe pshey-shchoo/ pshe o-knyair

No smoking/smoking please
Zakaz palenia/Wolno palić.
Za-kaz pa-lair-nyah/Vo-lnoe pa-leech

We would like to sit together
Chcielibyśmy siedzieć razem
Hche-lee-be-shme shair-jech ra-zem

P
O
L
I
S
H

I would like to make a seat reservation
Chciałbym/Chciałabym (fem.) zarezerwować miejsce
Hcha-wbem/Hcha-wa-bim za-rair-zer-vo-vach myey-stsair

I would like to reserve a couchette/sleeper for one person/two people/my family
Chciałbym/Chciałabym (fem.) zarezerwować kuszetkę/ miejsca w wagonie sypialnym dla jednej osoby/dla dwóch osób/dla rodziny
Hcha-wbem/Hcha-wa-bim za-rair-zer-vo-vach koo-shet-kair/myey-stsah v va-goe-nyair si-pyal-nim dla ye-dney o-so-bi/dvooh o-soob/ dla ro-jeene

I would like to reserve a cabin
Chciałbym/Chciałabym (fem.) zarezerwować kajutę
Hcha-wbem/Hcha-wa-bim za-rair-zer-vo-vach ka-yoo-tair

Timetables (Schedules)

Przyjazd
Pshe-yazd
Arrive

Przez/Przystanki
Pshehs /Pshi-stan-kee
Calls (Stops at)

Możliwość zakupu posiłku.
Moj-lee-voshch za-koo-poo po-siw-koo
Catering Service

Przesiadka
Pshair-sha-dkah
Change At

Połączenie/Przez
Po-won-che-nyair/Pshehs
Connection/ Via

Codziennie
Tsoe-jen-niair
Daily

Co 40 minut
Tsoe chtair-je-shchee mee-noot
Every 40 minutes

Pierwsza klasa
Pier-vsha kl-sa
First Class

Co godzinę
Coe goe-jee-nair
Hourly

Objęty rezerwacją miejsc
O-byen-ti re-zer-va-tsyanhg myeysts
Seat reservations are recommended

Druga klasa
Droo-gah kla-sah
Second Class

Dopłata
Doe-pwa-tah
Supplement Payable

Luggage

How much will it cost to send (ship) my luggage in advance?
Ile będzie kosztowało nadanie (wysłanie) bagażu wcześniej?
Ee-lair ben-jair koe-shtoh-vawoe na-da-nyair (vi-swa-nyair) ba-ga-joo vchair-shnyair?

Where is the left luggage (baggage claim) office?
Gdzie jest przechowalnia bagażu?
Gjair yest przehovalneeah bagaju?

What time do you open/ close?
O której jest otwarte/ zamknięte?
O ktoo-rey yest o-tvar-tair/ zam-knen-tair?

Where are the luggage trolleys (carts)?
Gdzie są wózki bagażowe?
Gjair som voo-zkee ba-ga-joe-vair?

Where are the lockers?
Gdzie są schowki na bagaż?
Gjair som s-hoe-vkee na ba-gaj?

I have lost my locker key
Zgubiłem/Zgubiłam (fem.) klucz od schowka
Zgoo-bee-wem/Zgoo-bee-wahm klooch od s-hoe-vkah

On Board

Is this seat free?
Czy to miejsce jest wolne?
Che toh myey-stsair yest volnair?

Excuse me, you are sitting in my reserved seat
Przepraszam, Pan/Pani siedzi na moim zarezerwowanym miejscu
Pshe-pra-sham Pan/Pa-nee syair-jee na mo-eem zarezervovaneem myey-stsoo

Which station is this?
Która to stacja?
Ktoo-rah toh sta-tsyah?

What time is this train/bus/ ferry/flight/ due to arrive/ depart?
O której godzinie jest planowy przyjazd/odjazd pociągu/auto-busu/promu przylot/odlot?
O ktoo-rey go-jee-nyair yest plan-ovi pshi-yazd/od-yazd poe-tsyon/goo/aw-to-boo-soo/pro-moo prshe-lot/od-lot?

Travelling with Children

Do you have a high chair/babysitting service/cot?
Czy macie fotelik dla dziecka/ opiekę nad dzieckiem/kojec?
Che ma-chair fo-te-leek dla je-tskah/ opye-kair nad jair-tskyem/ko-yets?

Where is the nursery/ playroom?
Gdzie jest kącik zabaw dla dzieci?
Gjair yest kon-cheek za-bav dla je-chee?

Where can I warm the baby's bottle?
Gdzie mogę zagrzać butelkę dla dziecka?
Gjair mo-gair zagr-jach boo-tel-kair dla je-tskah?

P
O
L
I
S
H

247

Customs and Passports

Poproszę o paszporty!
Po-pro-shair o pash-por-ti!
Passports please!

**I have nothing to declare/
I have wine/spirits (alcohol)/
tobacco to declare**
Nie mam nic od oclenia/
Mam wino/alkohol/wyroby
tytoniowe do oclenia
*Nyair mam nits doe o-tsle-nyah/
Mam veenoo/alcohol/
vi-ro-bee ti-to-nyo-veh doe o-tsle-nyah*

**I will be staying for ... days/
weeks/months**
Mam zamiar zostać na ...
dni/tygodni/miesięcy.
*Mam za-myar zo-stach na ...
dnee/ti-go-dnee/mye-syen-tsi*

SIGHTSEEING

Asking the Way

**Excuse me, do you speak
English?**
Przepraszam, czy mówi
Pan/Pani po angielsku?
*Pshe-pra-sham che moo-vee Pan/Pa-
nee poe an-gyel-skoo?*

**Excuse me, can you help me
please?**
Przepraszam, czy mógłby mi
Pan/mógłaby mi Pani pomóc?
*Pshe-pra-sham che moog-wbe me
Pan/mog-wa-be me Pa-nee po-moots?*

**Where is the Tourist
Information Office?**
Gdzie jest Biuro Informacji
Turystycznej?

*Gjair yest beu-ro In-for-ma-tsyee Too-
ri-ste-chney?*

**Excuse me, is this the right
way to ...?**
Przepraszam, czy dojdę tędy
do ...?
*Pshe-pra-sham che doy-dair ten-di
doe ...?*

**... the cathedral/the tourist
Office/the castle/the old town**
... katedry/biura turystycznego/
zamku/starego miasta?
*... ka-tair-dri/byoo-rah too-ri-sti-chne-
go/zam-koo/sta-re-go mya-stah*

**Can you tell me the way to
the railway (railroad)
station/bus station/taxi
rank/city centre (downtown)/
beach?**
Jak dojść do stacji kolejowej/
dworca autobusowego/
postoju taksówek/centrum
miasta/plaży?
*Yak doyshch doe sta-tsyee ko-le-yo-
vay/dvortsah awto-boo-so-vego/
post-o-yoo tax-oovek/pla-ji?*

Pierwsza/druga w lewo/w
prawo/prosto
*Prosto pier-vshah/droo-gah v lair-vo/v
pra-vo/pro-sto*
**First/second/left/right/
straight ahead**

Na rogu/Na światłach
Na ro-goo/Na shvya-twah
**At the corner/At the traffic
lights**

**Where is the nearest police
station/post office?**
Gdzie jest najbliższy posterunek
policji/najbliższa poczta?

Gjair yest nay-blee-jshi po-ste-roo-nek po-lee-tsyee nay-blee-jshah po-chtah?

Is it near/ far?
Czy to jest blisko/daleko?
Che toh yest blee-sko/da-le-ko?

Do I need to take a taxi/catch a bus?
Czy muszę jechać taksówką/autobusem?
Che moo-shair yehach tax-oo-vkom/awto-boo-sem?

Do you have a map?
Czy ma Pan/Pani mapę?
Che ma Pan/Pa-nee ma-pair?

Can you point to it on my map?
Czy mógłby Pan/mogłaby Pani pokazać to na mapie?
Che moog-wbe Pan/mog-wa-be Pa-nee po-ka-zach na ma-pyair?

Thank you for your help
Dziękuję za pomoc
Jen-koo-yair za po-mots

How do I reach the motorway/main road?
Jak dojechać do autostrady/głównej drogi?
Yak doe-ye-hach doe autostradee/gwoo-vney dro-gee?

I think I have taken the wrong turning
Wydaje mi się, ze skręciłem w złym miejscu
Ve-da-yair me sie je skrair-chee-wem v zwem myey-stsoo

I am looking for this address
Szukam tego adresu

Shoo-kam te-go ad-re-soo

I am looking for the ... hotel
Szukam hotelu ...
Shoo-kam ho-te-loo ...

How far is it to ... from here?
Jak daleko jest do ...?
Yak da-le-ko yest doe ...?

Trzeba jechać prosto przez ... kilometrów
Tche-bah ye-hach pshez ... kee-lo-me-troov
Carry straight on for ... kilometres

Trzeba skręcić na najbliższym zakręcie w prawo/w lewo
Tche-bah skrair-cheech na nay-blee-jsheem za-krair-chair v pra-vo/v le-vo
Take the next turning on the right/left

Trzeba skręcić w prawo/w lewo na najbliższym skrzyżowaniu/na najbliższych światłach
Tche-bah skrair-cheech v pra-vo/v le-vo na nay-blee-jsheem skshe-jova-nyoo/na nay-blee-jsheeh shvia-twah
Turn right/left at the next crossroads/traffic lights

Jedzie Pan/Pani w złym kierunku
Ye-jeh pan/pa-nee v zwem kye-roon-koo
You are going in the wrong direction

Where is the cathedral/church/museum/pharmacy?
Gdzie jest katedra/kościół/muzeum/apteka?
Gje yest katedra/koshchoow/mooseum/a-pte-kah?

**How much is the admission/
entrance charge?**
Ile kosztuje bilet wstępu?
*Ee-lair ko-sh-too-yair bee-let
vstem-poo?*

**Is there a discount for
children/students/senior
citizens?**
Czy jest zniżka dla dzieci/
studentów/osób starszych?
*Che yest znee-jkah dla jair-tsee/
stoo-den-toov/o-soob star-sheh?*

**What time does the next
guided tour (in English)
start?**
O której godzinie jest następna
wycieczka z przewodnikiem
(w języku angielskim)?
*O ktoo-rey go-jee-nyair yest na-stem-
nah vi-che-chkah z pshair-vo-dnee-
kyem (v yen-zi-koo an-gyel-skim)?*

**One/two adults/children
please**
Poproszę jeden bilet/dwa bilety
dla dorosłych/dla dzieci
*Po-pro-shair yeden bee-let/dva
beeletty dla dorosweh/dla jair-tsee*

May I take photographs here?
Czy wolno tutaj fotografować?
Che vol-no too-tigh fo-to-ghra-fo-vach?

At the Tourist Office

**Do you have a map of the
town/area?**
Czy ma Pan/Pani mapę
miasta/regionu?
*Che ma Pan/Pa-nee ma-pair
mya-stah/re-g-yo-noo?*

**Do you have a list of
accommodation?**
Czy ma Pan/Pani listę miejsc
noclegowych?
*Che ma Pan/Pa-nee lee-stair myeysts
nots-le-go-veh?*

**Can I reserve
accommodation?**
Czy mogę zarezerwować
nocleg?
*Che mo-gair za-re-zer-vo-vach
nots-leg?*

ACCOMMODATION

Hotels

**I have a reservation in the
name of ...**
Mam rezerwację na nazwisko ...
Mam re-ze-rva-tsyair na naz-vis-ko ...

**I wrote to/faxed/telephoned
you last month/last week**
Napisałem list/dzwoniłem/
wysłałem faks w zeszłym
miesiącu/tygodniu
*Na-pee-sa-wem leest/zvo-nee-
wem/ve-swa-wem fax v ze-shwem
mye-syon-tsoo/ti-go-dnyoo*

Do you have any rooms free?
Czy są wolne pokoje?
Che so vo-lne po-ko-yair?

**I would like to reserve
a single/double room with a
bath/shower without a bath/
shower**
Chciałbym/Chciałabym (fem.)
zarezerwować jednoosobowy/
dwuosobowy pokój z wanną/
prysznicem bez wanny/
prysznica

Hcha-wbem/Hcha-wa-bim za-rair-
zer-vo-vach ye-dno-o-so-bo-vi/dvoo-o-
so-bo-vi po- kooy z va-nnom pri-
shnee-tsem bes va nni/pri-shnee-tsah

I would like bed/breakfast/
(room and) full board

Chciałbym/Chciałabym (fem.)
nocleg ze śniadaniem/
nocleg z pełnym wyżywieniem
Hcha-wbem/Hcha-wa-bem nots-leg
ze shnya-da-nyem/nots-leg z
pe-wnem ve-je-vye-nyem

How much is it per night?

Jaka jest cena noclegu?
Ya-ka yest tse-nah nots-le-goo?

Is breakfast included?

Czy śniadanie jest wliczone?
Che shnya-da-nyair yest vli-cho-nair?

Do you have any cheaper
rooms?

Czy są tańsze pokoje?
Che so tan-shair po-ko-yair?

I would like to see/take the
room

Chciałbym/Chciałabym (fem.)
zobaczyć/wynająć ten pokój
Hcha-wbem/Hcha-wa-bim zo-ba-
chech/vi-na-yonch ten po-kooy

I would like to stay for ...
nights

Chciałbym/Chciałabym (fem.)
zostać przez ... nocy
Hcha-wbem/Hcha-wa-bem zo-stach
pshez ... no-tse

The shower/light/tap/hot
water doesn't work

Prysznic/światło/kran/gorąca
woda nie działa

Pri-shneets/shvia-twoh/kran/go-ron-
tsa vo-da nyair ja-wa

At what time/where is
breakfast served?

O której godzinie jest
śniadanie?
O ktoo-rey go-jee-nyair yest shnya-
da-nyair?

What time do I have to
check out?

O której godzinie muszę się
wyprowadzić?
O ktoo-rey go-jee-nyair moo-shair sie
vi-pro-va-jeech?

Can I have the key to room
number ...?

Poproszę o klucz do pokoju
numer ...?
Po-pro-shair o klooch doe po-ko-yoo
noo-mair ...?

My room number is ...

Mój pokój ma numer ...
Mooy po-kooy ma noo-mair ...

My room is not satisfactory./
It is not clean enough/too
noisy. Please can I change
rooms?

Nie jestem zadowolony/
zadowolona (fem.) z mojego
pokoju./Jest brudno/zbyt
głośno. Czy mogę prosić
o inny pokój?
Nyair ye-stem za-do-vo-lo-ne/za-do-
vo-lo-na z mo-ye-go po-ko-yoo/woo-
jkah yest broo-dno/zbit gwo-shno
pro-shair o in-ne po-kooy?

Where is the bathroom?

Gdzie jest łazienka?
Gjair yest wa-zyen-kah?

P O L I S H

Do you have a safe for valuables?
Czy tutaj jest sejf?
Che too-tigh yest safe?

Is there a laundry/do you wash clothes?
Czy jest tutaj pralnia?
Che too-tigh yest pra-nyah?

I would like an air-conditioned room
Chciałbym/Chciałabym (fem.) pokój z klimatyzacją
Hcha-wbem/Hcha-wabim po-kooy z klee-ma-ti-za-tsyoh

Do you accept traveller's cheques/credit cards?
Czy mogę płacić czekami podróżnymi/kartą kredytową?
Che mo-gair pwa-cheech che-ka-mee po-droo-jne-me/kar-toh kre-de-toh-woh?

May I have the bill please?
Poproszę o rachunek?
Po-pro-shair o ra-hoo-neck?

Excuse me, I think there may be a mistake in this bill
Przepraszam, wydaje mi się, że w rachunku jest błąd
Pshe-pra-sham we-da-yair me sie je v ra-hoon-koo yest bwond

Youth Hostels

How much is a dormitory bed per night?
Ile kosztuje nocleg?
Ee-lair ko-shtoo-yair nots-leg?

I am/am not an HI member
Jestem/nie jestem członkiem

organizacji turystycznej
Ye-stem/nyair ye-stem chwon-kyem orga-nee-za-tsyee too-re-ste-chney

May I use my own sleeping bag?
Czy mogę używać własnego śpiwora?
Che mo-gair oo-je-vach v-wa-sne-go shpee-vorah?

What time do you lock the doors at night?
O której godzinie zamyka się drzwi wieczorem?
O ktoo-rey go-jee-nyair za-me-kah sie jvee vye-cho-rem?

Camping

May I camp for the night/two nights?
Czy mogę rozbić tutaj namiot na jedną noc/dwie noce?
Che mo-ghair roz-beech too-tigh na-myot na ye-dnoh nots/dvyeh no-tsair?

Where can I pitch my tent?
Gdzie mogę rozbić namiot?
Gjair mo-ghair roz-beech na-myot?

How much does it cost for one night/week?
Ile kosztuje jedna noc/jeden tydzień?
Ee-lair ko-shtoo-yair ye-dnah nots/ye-den te-jen?

Where are the washing facilities?
Gdzie są łazienki?
Gjair so wa-jen-kee?

252

Is there a restaurant/ supermarket/swimming pool on site/nearby?
Czy jest restauracja/sklep/ basen/na kempingu/w pobliżu?
Gjair yest re-staw-ra-tsyah/sklep/ba-sen na kem-peen-goo/v po-blee-joo?

Do you have a safety deposit box?
Czy jest tutaj schowek lub sejf?
Che yest too-tigh s-hoe-vek loob safe?

EATING AND DRINKING

Cafés and Bars

I would like a cup of/ two cups of/ another coffee/tea
Poproszę o jedną/dwie/jeszcze jedną kawę/herbatę
Po-pro-shair o ye-dnoh/dvyair/ye-shchair ye-dnoh ka-vair/herba-tair

With milk/sugar
Without milk/sugar
Z mlekiem/cukrem
Bez mleka/cukru
Z mle-kyem/tsoo-krem
Bez mle-kah/tsoo-kroo

I would like a bottle/glass/two glasses of mineral water/red wine/white wine, please
Poproszę o butelkę/szklankę/ dwie szklanki wody mineralnej/ butelkę/kieliszek/dwa kieliszki czerwonego wina/białego wina
Po-pro-shair o boo-tel-kair/shklan-kair/dvyair shklan-kee vo-de mee-ne-ral-nay/boo-tel-kair/kee-elishek/dva kee-elishkee cher-vo-ne-go vee-nah/bya-we-go vee-nah

I would like a beer/two beers, please
Poproszę o piwo/dwa piwa
Po-pro-shair o pee-vo/dvah pee-wah

Please may I have some ice?
Poproszę o lód?
Po-pro-shair o lood?

Do you have any matches/ cigarettes/cigars?
Czy można kupić zapałki/papierosy/cygara?
Che mo-jnah koo-peech za-paw-kee/pa-pye-ro-se/ci-ga-rah?

Restaurants

Can you recommend a good/ cheap restaurant in this area?
Czy mógłby Pan/mogłaby Pani polecić dobrą/tanią restaurację w tej okolicy?
Che moog-wbe pan/mog-wa-be pa-nee po-le-cheech do-broh/ta-nyoh re-staw-ra-tsyair v tey o-ko-lee-tse?

I would like a table for ... people
Poproszę o stolik dla ... osób.
Po-pro-shair o sto-leek dla ... o-soob

Do you have a non-smoking area?
Czy jest sala dla niepalących?
Che yest sa-la dla nyair-pa-lon-tseh?

Waiter/Waitress!
Kelner/Kelnerka!
Kelner/Kelnerka!

Excuse me, please may we order?
Przepraszam, chcielibyśmy/ chciałybyśmy **(fem.)** złożyć

253

P O L I S H

zamówienie?
Pshe-pra-sham hche-lee-be-shme/hcha-le-be-shme zwo-jech za-moo-vye-nyair?

Do you have a set menu/children's menu/wine list/in English?
Czy macie menu/menu dla dzieci/kartę win w języku angielskim?
Che ma-chair me-nee/menu dla jechee/ka-rtair veen v yen-zi-koo an-gyel-skim?

Do you have any vegetarian dishes?
Czy macie dania jarskie?
Che ma-chair da-nya yarskye?

Do you have any local specialities?
Czy macie dania kuchni polskiej?
Che ma-chair da-nya koo-hnee pol-skyey?

Are vegetables included?
Czy warzywa są wliczone?
Che va-je-vah soh vlee-cho-neh?

Could I have it well-cooked/medium/rare please?
Poproszę o dobrze/średnio/lekko wysmażone?
Po-pro-shair o do-bjeh/shre-dnyo/lek-ko ve-sma-jo-ne?

What does this dish consist of?
Jakie są składniki tej potrawy?
Ya-kye soh skwa-dnee-kee tey po-tra-ve?

I am a vegetarian. Does this contain meat?
Jestem wegetarianinem/wegetarianką (fem.). Czy w

tym daniu jest mięso?
Yestem vegetarianinem/vegetari-ankahng. Tchee fteem dah-nyoo yest myensoh?

I do not eat nuts/dairy products/meat/fish
Nie mogę jeść orzechów/produktów mlecznych/mięsa/ryb
Nyair mo-ghair ye-shch o-je-hoof/pro-doo-ktoof mle-chneh/myair-sah/rib

Not (very) spicy please
Proszę, żeby nie było (zbyt) pikantne
Pro-shair, je-be nyair be-woh (zbit) pee-kan-tne

I would like the set menu please
Poproszę o zestaw obiadowy
Po-pro-shair o ze-stav obiadove

We have not been served yet
Nie obsłużono nas jeszcze
Nye obswoozhono nas yeshche

Please bring a plate/knife/fork
Poproszę o talerz/nóś/widelec
Poh-proshair oh tah-lesh/noosh/vee-deh-lets

Excuse me, this is not what I ordered
Przepraszam, to nie jest to co zamówiłem/zamówiłam (fem.)
Pshe-pra-sham toh nyair yest toh coh za-moo-vee-wem/za-moo-vee-wam

May I have some/more bread/water/coffee/tea?
Poproszę o więcej chleba/wody/kawy/herbaty?
Po-pro-shair o vyen-tsey hle-bah/vo-de/ka-ve/herba-te?

May I have the bill please?
Poproszę o rachunek?
Po-pro-shair o ra-hoo-neck?

Does this bill include service?
Czy opłata za obsługę jest
wliczona?
*Che o-pwa-tah za ob-swoo-ghair
yest vlee-chonah?*

**Do you accept traveller's
cheques/Mastercard/
US dollars?**
Czy mogę zapłacić czekami
podróżnymi/Mastercard/
dolarami amerykańskimi?
*Che mo-gair pwa-cheech che-ka-
mee po-droo-jne-me/master-kard/
dola-ramee ameri-kan-skeemee?*

Can I have a receipt please?
Poproszę o pokwitowanie/
paragon?
*Po-pro-shair o po-kvee-toh-va-
nyair/pa-ra-ghon?*

**Where is the toilet
(restroom) please?**
Przepraszam, gdzie jest
toaleta?
*Pshe-pra-sham ghjair yest toe-a-lair-
tah?*

On the Menu

Śniadanie/obiad/kolacja
*Shnyah-dah-nyeah/oh-b-yahd/
koh-latsyah*
Breakfast/Lunch/Dinner

Pierwsze danie   Zupy
Pier-vsheh da-nyair   *Zoo-pe*
First Courses   **Soups**

Główne danie   Dania rybne
Gwoo-vneh da-nyair   *Da-nyair rib-ne*
Main Courses   **Fish Dishes**

Dania mięsne   Wołowina
Da-nyair myair-snair   *Vo-woe-veenah*
Meat Dishes   **Beef**

Stek   Wieprzowina
Stehk   *Wyep-shoh-veenah*
Steak   **Pork**

Cielęcina   Kurczak
Cheh-len-chee-nah   *Koor-chuck*
Veal   **Chicken**

Jagnięcina   Szynka
Yag-nyen-chee-nah   *Sheen-kah*
Lamb   **Ham**

Dania wegetariańskie
Da-nyair ve-ge-ta-ryan-skyair
Vegetarian Dishes

Warzywa   Frytki
Vah-zhee-vah   *Freet-key*
Vegetables   **Chips
(french fries)**

Ziemniaki gotowane/sauté/
puree
*Zyem-nyah-key goh-toh-vah-
neh/sauté/pew-reh*
**Boiled/sauté/mashed
potatoes**

Ryż   Desery
Reezh   *De-se-re*
Rice   **Desserts**

Lody   Ciasta
Loh-dee   *Chas-tah*
Ice cream   **Cakes**

P
O
L
I
S
H

POLISH

Ciastka
Chast-kah
Pastries

Owoce
O-voh-tseh
Fruit

Chleb
H-lep
Bread

Bułki
Boow-key
Rolls

Tosty
Tohsteh
Toast

Masło
Mah-swoh
Butter

Sól/pieprz
Sool/pyepsh
Salt/pepper

Cukier
Tsoo-kier
Sugar

Specjalność
Spe-tsyal-noshch
Specialities

Miejscowe dania
Mye-ys-tso-veh da-nyah
Local specialities

Zestaw obiadowy
Zestaf ob-ya-do-vee
Set Menu

Karta win
Kartah veen
Wine list

Wina czerwone
Vee-nah cher-vo-neh
Red wines

Wina białe
Veenah byaweh
White wines

Wina różowe
Veenah roozhoveh
Rosé wines

Wina musujące
Veenah moo-soo-yon-tseh
Sparkling wines

Piwo
Peevoh
Beer

Piwo w butelkach/Piwo z beczki
Peevo vboo-tell-kah/peevoh zbech-key
Bottled beer/Draught (draft) beer

Napoje bezalkoholowe
Nah-poyeh bez-alko-holo-veh
Non-alcoholic drinks

Woda mineralna
Vodah mee-neh-ralnah
Mineral water

Soki owocowe
Soh-key ovotsove
Fruit juices

Sok pomarańczowy
Sok poh-maran-choh-vee
Orange juice

Lemoniada
Leh-moh-nyah-dah
Lemonade

Lód
Lood
Ice

Kawa z mlekiem/czarna kawa/espresso
Kavah z mleh-kyem/char-nah kavah/espresso
White coffee/black coffee/espresso coffee

Herbata z mlekiem/z cytryną
Her-bah-tah z mleh-kyem/s tsit-rinom
Tea with milk/with lemon

Czekolada na gorąco
Cheh-koh-lah-dah nah go-rontsoh
Chocolate (drink)

Mleko
Mlekoh
Milk

Przekąski/Lekkie posiłki
Pshe-konskey/lek-kye poh-sheew-key
Snacks/Light meals

Sałatki	Kanapki
Sah-wat-key	*Kah-nap-key*
Salads	**Sandwiches**

Jajka	Kiełbasa
Yay-kah	*Kye-w-bah-sah*
Eggs	**Sausage**

Jajka gotowane/sadzone/
jajecznica
*Yay-kah goh-toh-vah-neh/sah-dzoh-
neh/ya-yech-nee-tsah*
Boiled/fried/scrambled eggs

Typical Local Dishes

Rosół
Ro-soow
**Broth, usually served with
noodles**

Śledź w śmietanie
Shlej v shmye-ta-nyair
Herring in sour cream

Karp gotowany w jarzynach
Karp go-toh-va-ne v ya-jee-nah
**Steamed carp with vegeta-
bles**

Bigos
Bee-gos
**Sauerkraut with mixed
meats stew**

Kotlet schabowy z kapustą
Kot-let sha-bo-ve s ka-poo-stoh
**Breaded pork cutlet,
traditionally served with
cabbage**

Pierogi
Pier-oghee
**Dumplings stuffed with
cabbage, mushrooms, meat
or various fruits**

Kasza gryczana z kwaśnym
mlekiem
*Kasha ghre-cha-nah s kva-shnim
mle-kyem*
**Buckwheat with sour milk
or buttermilk**

Makowiec
Ma-ko-vyets
Traditional poppy seed roll

GETTING AROUND

Public Transport

**Where is the bus stop/coach
stop/nearest metro station?**
Gdzie jest najbliższy przystanek
autobusowy/metra?
*Ghjair yest nay-blee-jshe pshe-sta-
nek awto-boo-so-ve/metrah?*

**When is the next/last bus
to ...?**
O której godzinie jest następ-
ny/ostatni autobus do ...?
*O ktoo-rey go-jee-nyair yest na-stem-
pne/o-sta-tnee awto-boos doe ...?*

257

How much is the fare to the city centre (downtown)/railway station/airport?
Ile kosztuje bilet do centrum miasta/dworca kolejowego/na lotnisko?
Ee-lair kosh-too-yeh bee-let doe tse-ntroom mya-stah/dvor-tsah ko-le-yo-ve-go/na lot-nis-koh?

Will you tell me when to get off?
Czy powie mi Pan/Pani kiedy wysiąść?
Che po-vye me pan/pa-nee kye-de ve-syonshch?

Does this bus go to ...?
Czy ten autobus jedzie do ...?
Che ten awto-boos ye-je doe ...?

Which number bus goes to ...?
Którym autobusem dojadę do ...?
Ktoo-rem awto-boo-sem do-ya-dair doe ...?

May I have a single (one way)/return (round trip)/day ticket/book of tickets?
Poproszę o bilet w jedną stronę/powrotny/bilet dzienny/karnet?
Po-pro-shair o bee-let v ye-dnoh stro-nair/po-vrot-ne/bee-let jen-ne/kar-net?

Taxis (Taxi)

I would like to go to ... How much will it cost?
Chciałbym/Chciałabym (fem.) dojechać do ... Ile będzie wynosić opłata?

Hcha-wbem/Hcha-wa-bem doe-ye-hach doe ... ee-lair beir-jair ve-no-sheech o-pwa-tah?

Please may I stop here?
Proszę się tu zatrzymać?
Pro-shair sheh too za-tshe-mach?

I would like to order a taxi today/tomorrow at 2pm to go from ... to ...
Chciałbym/Chciałabym (fem.) zamówić taksówkę na dzisiaj/jutro o godzinie drugiej z ... do ...
Hcha-wbem/Hcha-wa-bem za-moo-veech tax-oo-vkair na jee-shaigh/yoo-tro o goe-jee-nyair droo-ghey z ... doe

Entertainment

Can you recommend a good bar/nightclub?
Czy mógłby Pan/mogłaby Pani polecić dobry bar/klub nocny?
Che moog-wbe pan/mog-wa-be pa-nee po-le-cheech do-bre bar/kloob notsne?

Do you know what is on at the cinema (playing at the movies)/theatre at the moment?
Co jest teraz w kinach?
Co grają w teatrze?
Tso yest te-ras v kee-nah? tso ghra-yom v teh-ah-tshe?

I would like to book (purchase) ... tickets for the matinee/evening performance on Monday
Chciałbym/Chciałabym (fem.) zarezerwować/kupić ...

bilety na poranne/wieczorne
przedstawienie w poniedziałek
*Hcha-wbem/Hcha-wa-bimza-rair-
zer-vo-vach/koo-peech ... bee-le-te
na po-ran-ne/vye-chor-ne pshed-sta-
vye-nyeh v po-nyair-ja-wek*

What time does the film/
performance start?
O której zaczyna się
film/przedstawienie?
*O ktoo-rey za-che-nah sheh film/
pshed-sta-vye-nyeh?*

Post

How much will it cost to
send a letter/postcard/this
package to Britain/Ireland/
America/Canada/Australia/
New Zealand?
Ile kosztuje wysłanie listu/
pocztówki/tej paczki do
Wielkiej Brytanii/Irlandii/Stanów
Zjednoczonych/Kanady/
Australii/Nowej Zelandii?
*Ee-lair ko-shtoo-yeh ve-swa-nyair lee-
stoo/po-chtoo-vkee/tey pa-chkee doe
vye-lkyey bre-ta-nee/ee-rlan-dee/sta-
noov zye-dno-cho-neh/ka-na-de/aus-
tra-lee/novey ze-lan-dee?*

I would like one stamp/two
stamps
Poproszę o jeden znaczek/dwa
znaczki
*Po-pro-shair o ye-den zna-chek/dva
zna-chkee*

I'd like ... stamps for
postcards to send abroad,
please
Poproszę o ... znaczki na

pocztówki za granicę
*Po-pro-shair o ... zna-chkee zah
gra-nee-tsair*

Phones

I would like to make a
telephone call/reverse the
charges to (make a collect
call to) ...
Chciałbym/Chciałabym (fem.)
zadzwonić ... na koszt odbiorcy
*Hcha-wbem/Hcha-wabem za-jvo-
neech ... nah kosht od-byor-tse*

Which coins do I need for
the telephone?
Których monet używa się do
telefonu?
*Ktoo-reh mo-net oo-je-vah sheh doe
te-le-fo-noo?*

The line is engaged (busy)
Linia jest zajęta
Lee-nyah yest za-yen-tah

The number is ...
To numer ...
Toh noo-merh ...

Hello, this is ...
Halo, mówi ...
Hah-loh, moo-vee ...

Please may I speak to ...?
Czy mogę rozmawiać z ...?
Che mo-ghair ro-zma-vyach z ...?

He/she is not in at the
moment. Please can you call
back?
Nie ma go/jej teraz w domu.
Proszę zadzwonić później?
*Nyair mah go/yey te-raz v do-moo
Pro-shair za-jvo-neech poo-jney?*

259

Where can I buy phone tokens or a phone card?
Gdzie mogę kupić żetony telefoniczne lub kartę telefoniczną?
Gjair mo-ghair koo-peech je-toh-ne te-le-fo-nee-chneh loob ka-rtair te-le-fo-nee-chnair?

SHOPPING

Shops

Księgarnia/Sklep papierniczy
Kshair-ghar-nyah/Sklehp pa-pier-neeche
Bookshop/Stationery

Jubiler/Pamiątki
Yoo-bee-lair/Pa-myont-kee
Jeweller/Gifts

Obuwie
O-boo-vyeh
Shoes

Odzież/Galanteria
O-djej/ga-lan-te-ryah
Clothes

Pralnia
Pral-nyah
Laundry

Artykuły metalowe
Arte-koo-we me-ta-lo-veh
Hardware

Fryzjer
Frez-yerr
Hairdresser

Piekarnia
P-ye-kar-nyah
Baker

Supermarket
Super-market
Supermarket

Fotograf
Fo-to-graf
Photo shop

Agencja turystyczna
A-ghen-tsyah too-re-ste-chnah
Travel Agent

Apteka
A-pte-kah
Pharmacy

In the Shops

What time do the shops open/close?
O której godzinie otwierają/zamykają sklepy?
O ktoo-rey go-jee-nyair otvyerayom/ za-me-ka-yom skhle-pe?

Where is the nearest market?
Gdzie jest najbliższy targ?
Ghair yest nay-blee-jshe targ?

Can you show me the one in the window/ this one?
Proszę mi to pokazać/
Proszę mi pokazać to z wystawy?
Pro-shair me toh po-ka-zach/ pro-shair me po-ka-zach toh s ve-stah-ve?

Can I try this on?
Czy mogę to przymierzyć?
Che mo-ghair toh pshe-mye-jech?

What size is this?
Jaki to jest rozmiar?
Ya-kee toh yest roz-myarh?

This is too large/too small/too expensive. Do you have any others?
To jest zbyt duże/zbyt małe/zbyt drogie. Czy macie coś innego?
Toh yest zbit doo-jeh/zbit ma-weh/zbit dro-ghyeh. Che ma-che cosh in-ne-go?

My size is ...
Mój rozmiar to ...
Mooy roz-myarh toh ...

Where is the changing room/ children's/cosmetic/ ladieswear/menswear/food department?
Gdzie jest przymierzalnia?
Gdzie jest dział dziecięcy/ kosmetyczny/damski/męski/ spożywczy?
Gjair yest pshe-mye-jal-nyah/ Gjair yest jyaw jair-chyen-tse/ ko-sme-te-chne/dam-skee/ men-skee/spo-je-vche?

I would like ... a quarter of a kilo/ half a kilo/ a kilo of bread/butter/ham/this fruit
Poproszę ... o ćwierć kilo/pół kilo/chleba/masła/szynki/tych owoców
Po-proshair ... o chvyerch kee-loh/ poow kee-loh/hle-bah/ma-swah/ she-nkee/teh o-vo-tsoov

How much is this?
Ile to kosztuje?
Ee-lair toh ko-shtoo-yeh?

I'll take this one, thank you
Poproszę o to
Po-pro-shair o toh

Do you have a carrier (shopping) bag?
Czy mogę prosić o torbę?
Chi mogem proshich o torbem?

Do you have anything cheaper/larger/smaller/ of better quality?
Czy macie coś tańszego/ większego/mniejszego/lepszej jakości?
Che ma-che cosh ta-nsheh-go/vyair- kshair-go/le-pshey ya-ko-shchee?

I would like a film for this camera. I would like this film developed
Poproszę o film do tego aparatu. Chciałbym/chciałabym (fem.) wywołać film
Po-pro-shair o film doh te-go a-pa-ra-too hcha-wbem/hcha-wa- bem ve-vo-wach film

I would like some batteries, the same size as this old one
Poproszę o kilka baterii tego samego rodzaju, jak te zużyte
Po-pro-shair o keel-kah ba-te-ree te-go sa-me-go ro-za-joo, yak teh zoo-je-teh

Would you mind wrapping this for me, please?
Czy byłby Pan uprzejmy/byłaby Pani uprzejma zapakować?
Che be-wbe pan uprzeymee/ beewabee/pa-nee oo-pshey-mah za-pa-ko-vach?

P
O
L
I
S
H

P
O
L
I
S
H

Sorry, but you seem to have given me the wrong change
Przepraszam, wydaje mi się, że pomylił się Pan/pomyliła się pani przy wydawaniu
Pshe-pra-sham ve-da-ye me sheh je po-me-leew sheh Pan/po-me-leewah sheh pa-nee pshe ve-da-va-nyoo

MOTORING

Car Hire (Rental)

I have ordered (rented) a car in the name of ...
Zamówiłem (wynająłem) samochód na nazwisko ...
Za-moo-vee-wem (ve-na-yair-wem) sa-mo-ho-d nah na-zvee-sko ...

How much does it cost to hire (rent) a car for one day/ two days/ a week?
Ile kosztuje wynajęcie samochódu na jeden dzień/dwa dni/tydzień?
Ee-lair ko-shtoo-yeh ve-na-yair-chair sa-mo-ho-doo na ye-den jen/dva dnee/te-jen?

Is the tank already full of petrol (gas)?
Czy bak jest pełny?
Che bak yest pe-wne?

Is insurance and tax included? How much is the deposit?
Czy wliczono ubezpieczenie i podatek? Ile wynosi kaucja?
Che vlee-cho-no oo-bez-pye-che-nyeh ee po-da-tek? Ee-lair ve-no-shee kaw-tsyah?

By what time must I return the car?
O której godzinie muszę zwrócić samochód?
O ktoo-rey go-jee-nyair moo-shair zvroo-cheech sa-mo-hood?

I would like a small/large/ family/sports car with a radio/ cassette
Chciałbym/chciałabym (fem.) mały/duży/rodzinny samochód z radiem/magnetofonem
Hcha-wbem/hcha-wa-bem ma-we/doo-je/ro-jeen-ne sa-mo-hood s ra-dyem/ma-gne-toh-fo-nem

Do you have a road map?
Czy ma Pan/Pani mapę drogową?
Che ma pan/pa-nee ma-pair dro-go-vom?

Parking

How long can I park here?
Jak długo można tu parkować?
Yak dwoo-go mo-jnah too par-ko-vach?

Is there a car park near here?
Czy jest tu parking w pobliżu?
Che yest too par-keeng v po-blee-joo?

At what time does this car park close?
O której godzinie zamyka się parking?
O ktoo-rey go-jee-nyair za-me-kah sheh par-keeng?

Signs and Notices

Droga jednokierunkowa
Dro-gah ye-dno kye-roon-ko-vah
One way

Zakaz wjazdu
Za-kaz vya-zdoo
No entry

Zakaz parkowania
Za-kaz par-ko-va-nyah
No parking

Objazd
Ob-yazd
Detour (Diversion)

Stop
Stop
Stop

Dać pierwszeństwo
przejazdu.
Dach pier-vshen-stvo pshe-yaz-doo
Give way (Yield)

Śliska droga
Shlee-skah dro-gah
Slippery road

Zakaz wyprzedzania
Za-kaz ve-pshe-za-nyah
No overtaking

Niebezpieczeństwo!/Uwaga!
Nyair-bez-pye-chen-stvo!/
Oo-va-gah!
Danger!

At the Filling Station
(Stacja Bōżynowa)

**Unleaded (lead free)/
standard/premium/diesel**
Bezołowiowa/zwyczajna/
super/diesel
Bez-owo-vyo-vah/zve-chay-nah/
soo-per/dee-zel

Fill the tank please
Pełny bak proszę
Pew-ne bak pro-shair

Do you have a road map?
Czy ma Pan/Pani mapę
drogową?
Che ma pan/pa-nee ma-pair
dro-go-vom?

How much is the car wash?
Ile kosztuje mycie samochodu?
Ee-lair ko-shtoo-yair me-chair sa-mo-
ho-doo?

Breakdowns

I've had a breakdown at ...
Zepsuł mi się samochód w ...
Ze-psoow me sheh sa-mo-hood v ...

**I am a member of the ...
[motoring organisation]**
Jestem członkiem ...
Yestem chwon-kyem ...

**I am on the road from ...
to ...**
Jestem na drodze z ... do ...
Ye-stem nah dro-zair z ... doh ...

I can't move the car. Can you send a tow-truck?
Nie mogę ruszyć. Czy może Pan/Pani przysłać samochód do holowania?
Nyair mo-ghair roo-shech. Che mo-jeh Pan/Pa-nee psh-swach sa-mo-hood doh ho-lo-va-nayah?

I have a flat tyre
Mam przebitą oponę
Mam pshe-bee-tom o-po-nair

The windscreen (windshield) has smashed/ cracked
Rozbiła się/pękła przednia szyba
Roz-bee-wah sheh/pen-kwah pshe-dnyah she-bah

There is something wrong with the engine/brakes/lights/ steering/gearbox/clutch/ exhaust
Coś się zepsuło w silniku/ hamulcach/światłach/kierowni-cy/skrzyni biegów/sprzęgle/ rurze wydechowej
Tsosh sheh ze-psoo-woh v sheel-nee-koo/ha-mool-tsah/shvya-twah/ kye-ro-vnee-tse skshe-ne bye-goof/ spshen-gleh/roo-jeh ve-de-ho-vey

It's overheating
Przegrzało się
Pshe-gja-wo sheh

It won't start
Nie chce zapalić
Nyair htseh za-pa-leech

Where can I get it repaired?
Gdzie to można naprawić?
Ghje toh mo-jnah na-pra-veech?

Can you take me there?
Czy może mnie Pan/Pani tam zawieźć?
Che mo-jeh mnyeh Pan/Pa-nee tam za-vyeshch?

Will it take long to fix?
Czy naprawa będzie długo trwała?
Che na-pra-vah ben-jeh dwoo-go trva-wah?

How much will it cost?
Ile to będzie kosztowało?
Ee-lair toh ben-jeh ko-sh-toh-va-woh?

Please can you pick me up/ give me a lift?
Czy mógłby Pan/czy mogłaby Pani mnie podwieźć?
Che moog-wbe Pan/mog-wa-be Pa-nee mnyeh pod-vye-shch?

Accidents and Traffic Offences (Violations)

Can you help me? There has been an accident
Proszę mi pomóc. Chodzi o wypadek
Proshem mi pomootz? Hodzhi o vipadek

Please call the police/an ambulance
Proszę wezwać policję/ pogotowie
Proshem vezvach policyem/ pogotohye

Is anyone hurt?
Czy ktoś jest ranny?
Chi ktosh yest rannee?

I'm sorry, I didn't see the sign
Przepraszam, nie zauważyłem
/zauważyłam (fem.) znaku
Pshe-pra-sham nyair za-oo-va-je-wem/za-oo-va-je-wam zna-koo

Must I pay a fine? How much?
Czy muszę zapłacić mandat? Ile to wynosi?
Che moo-shair za-pwa-cheech mandat? Ee-lair to ve-no-shee?

Proszę pokazać dokumenty
Pro-shair po-ka-zach do-koo-men-te
Show me your documents

HEALTH

Pharmacy (Apteka)

Do you have anything for a stomach ache/ headache/ sore throat/ toothache?
Czy ma Pan/Pani coś na ból brzucha/ból głowy/ból gardła/ból zęba?
Che ma Pan/Pa-nee tsosh nah bool bjoo-hah/bool gwo-ve/bool gar-dwah/bool zem-bah?

I need something for diarrhoea/constipation/a cold/a cough/insect bites/ sunburn/travel (motion) sickness
Chciałbym/chciałabym (fem.) coś na biegunkę/zatwardzenie/ przeziębienie/kaszel/ukąszenie owada/oparzenie słoneczne/ chorobę lokomocyjną
Hcha-wbem/hcha-wa-bem tsosh nah bye-goon-kair/za-tvar-ze-nyeh/ pshe-jem-bye-nyeh/ka-shel/ oo-kon-sheh-nyeh o-va-dah/

o-pa-je-nyeh swo-ne-chneh/ ho-ro-bair lo-ko-mo-tsey-nom

How much/how many do I take?
W jakiej ilości mam to zażywać?
Y ya-kyey ee-lo-shchee toh za-je-vach?

I am taking anti-malaria tablets/these pills
Zażywam tabletki przeciw malarii/te tabletki
Za-je-vam ta-blet-kee pshe-cheef ma-la-ree/teh ta-ble-tkee

How often do I take it/them?
Jak często mam to zażywać?
Yak chen-sto mam toh za-je-vach?

I am/he is/she is taking this medication
Zażywam/on zażywa/ona zażywa to lekarstwo
Za-je-vam/on za-je-vah/onah za-je-vah toh le-kar-stvoh

How much does it cost?
Ile to kosztuje?
Ee-lair toh ko-shtoo-yeh?

Can you recommend a good doctor/dentist?
Czy mógłby Pan/mogłaby Pani polecić mi dobrego lekarza/dentystę?
Che moog-wbe pan/mog-wa-be pa-nee po-le-cheech me do-bre-go le-kajah/den-tes-tair?

Is it suitable for children?
Czy to można podawać dzieciom?
Che toh mo-jnah po-da-vach jaircham?

P
O
L
I
S
H

Doctor (Lekarz)

I have a pain here/in my arm/ leg/chest/stomach
Boli mnie tutaj/ramię/noga/w klatce piersiowej/żołądek
Po-lee mnyeh too-tigh/ra-myeh/ no-ghah/v klat-tse pier-syo-vey/ jo-won-dek

Please call a doctor, this is an emergency
Proszę wezwać lekarza, to jest nagły przypadek
Pro-shair ve-zvach le-ka-jah, toh yest na-gwe pshe-pa-dek

I would like to make an appointment to see the doctor
Chciałbym/chciałabym (fem.) uzgodnić wizytę lekarską
Hcha-wbem/hcha-wa-bem oo-zgo-dneech vee-ze-tair le-kar-skom

I am diabetic
Mam cukrzycę
Mam tsoo-kshe-cair

I am pregnant
Jestem w ciąży
Ye-stem v tson-je

I need a prescription for ...
Potrzebuję receptę na ...
Po-tshe-boo-yair re-tse-ptair nah ...

Can you give me something to ease the pain?
Czy mógłbym/mogłabym (fem.) dostać coś przeciw-bólowego?
Che moog-wbem/mog-wa-bem doh-stach tsosh pshe-tseev-boo-lo-ve-go?

I am/he is/she is allergic to penicillin
Jestem/on jest/ona jest uczulony/uczulona (fem.) na penicylinę
Ye-stem/on yest/onah yest oo-choo-lo-nah na pe-nee-tse-lee-neir

Czy to boli?
Che toh bo-lee?
Does this hurt?

Musi Pan/Pani iść do szpitala
Moo-shee pan/pa-nee ee-shch doh sh-pee-ta-lah
You must/ he must/ she must go to hospital

Zażywać raz/dwa razy/trzy razy dziennie
Za-je-vach ras/dva ra-ze/tshe ra-ze jen-nyeh
Take these once/twice/three times a day

I am/he is/she is taking this medication
Zażywam/on zażywa/ona zażywa to lekarstwo
Za-je-vam/on za-je-vah/onah za-je-vah toh le-kar-stvoh

I have medical insurance
Jestem ubezpieczony/ ubezpieczona (fem.)
Ye-stem oo-bez-pye-cho-ne/oo-bez-pye-cho-nah

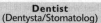

Dentist
(Dentysta/Stomatolog)

I have toothache/my filling has come out
Boli mnie ząb/Wypadła mi plomba
Bo-lee mnyeh zomb/ve-pa-dwa me plombah

I want to have an injection first
I do not want to have an injection first
Chciałbym/Chciałabym (fem.) dostać najpierw zastrzyk.
Nie chciałbym/chciałabym (fem.) dostawać zastrzyku
Hcha-wbem/Hcha-wa-bem do-stach nay-pierf za-stshek.
Nyair hcha-wbem/hcha-wa-bem do-sta-vach za-stshe-koo

EMERGENCIES

Help!
Pomocy!
Po-mo-tse!

Fire!
Pożar!
Po-jar!

Stop!
Stop! Stój!
Stop/Stooy!

Call an ambulance/a doctor/ the police/the fire brigade!
Wezwać pogotowie/lekarza/ policję/straż pożarną!
Ve-zvach po-go-toh-vyeh/ le-ka-jah/po-lee-tsyehstraj po-jar-nom!

Please may I use a telephone?
Czy mogę skorzystać z telefonu?
Che mo-ghair sko-je-stach s te-le-fo-noo?

I have had my travellers' cheques/credit cards/ handbag/rucksack/luggage/ wallet/passport/mobile phone stolen
Skradziono moje czeki podróżne/moje karty kredytowe/moją torebkę/mój plecak/mój bagaż/mój portfel/ paszport/telefon komórkowy
Skra-jo-noh mo-yeh che-kee po-droo-jneh/mo-yeh kar-te kre-de-toh-veh/mo-yoh to-reb-kair/mooy ple-tsak/mooy ba-gaj/mooy port-fel/ pash-port/teh-lefon koh-moor-koh-vee

May I please have a copy of the report for my insurance claim?
Poproszę kopię raportu dla mojego towarzystwa ubez-pieczeniowego?
Poh-proshair oh kopyeh rah-portoo dlah moyego toh-vah-zhees-tvah oo-bes-pye-che-nyo-vegoh?

Can you help me?
I have lost my daughter
I have lost my son
I have lost my companion
I have lost my companions
Proszę mi pomóc?
Moja córka zgubiła się
Mój syn zgubił się
Mój znajomy zgubił się.
Moi znajomi zgubili się

*Pro-shair me po-moots? /Mo-yah
tsoor-kah zgoo-bee-wah sheh /Mooy
sen zgoo-beew sheh /Mooy znay-
omee zgoo-beew sheh/Mo-yee znay-
omee zgoo-bee-leeh sheh*

Please go away!/Leave me alone
Proszę odejść!/Proszę mnie
zostawić w spokoju
*Pro-shair o-dey-shch!/Pro-shair
mnyeh zo-sta-veech v spo-ko-yoo*

I'm sorry
Przepraszam
Pshe-pra-sham

I want to contact the British/American/Canadian/Irish/Australian/New Zealand/South African Consulate
Chciałbym się skontaktować z
Konsulatem Brytyjskim/
Amerykańskim/Kanadyjskim/
Irlandzkim/Australijskim/
Nowozelandzkim/RPA
*Hcha-wbem sheh skon-tak-toh-vach
s Kon-soo-la-tem Bre-tey-skem/
Ame-re-kan-skem/Ka-na-dey-skem/
Eer-land-skem/Aus-tra-leey-skem/
No-vo-ze-land-skem/Air-Pey-Ah*

I'm ill/we're ill/he is ill/she is ill/they are ill
Jestem chory/chora (fem.)/
jesteśmy chorzy/ona jest
chora/on jest chory/oni są
chorzy
*Yestem ho-re /ho-rah./ye-ste-shme
ho-je/onah yest ho-rah/on yest
ho-re/onee soh ho-je*

I'm lost/we're lost/he is lost/she is lost/they are lost
Zgubiłem/zgubiłam (fem.) się/
zgubiliśmy się/ona zgubiła się/
on zgubił się/oni zgubili się
*Zgoo-bee-wem /zgoo-bee-wam
sheh/zgoo-bee-lee-shme sheh/onah
zgoo-bee-wa sheh/on zgoo-beew
sheh/onee zgoo-bee-lee sheh*

I'm injured/we're injured/he is injured/she is injured/they are injured
Jestem ranny/ranna (fem.)/
jesteśmy ranni/on jest ranny/
ona jest ranna/oni są ranni
*Yestem ran-ne/ran-nah/ye-ste-shme
ran-nee/onah yest ran-nah/on yest
ran-ne/onee soh ran-nee*

POLISH

ROMANIAN

INTRODUCTION

Alone among the languages of Eastern Europe, Romanian is a Romance tongue, descended from Latin and therefore a distant cousin of French, Italian, Spanish and Portuguese. This is of more than academic interest, since the basic meaning of many words in written Romanian can be understood by someone with a knowledge of one of these other languages. Spoken Romanian is reminiscent of French, which is the most likely second language you will encounter, at least among older and better-educated Romanians. In some regions of the country Hungarian or German will be understood.

Addresses for Travel and Tourist Information

Australia: *Embassy*, 4 Dalman Crescent, O'Malley, Canberra, ACT 2606; tel: (02) 6286 2343; fax: (02) 6286 2433.

UK: *Romanian Tourist Office*, 22 New Cavendish St, London WIM 7LH; tel: (020) 7224 3692; fax: (020) 7935 6435.

USA: *Romanian Tourist Office*, 355 Lexington Ave, 19th Floor, New York, NY 10017; tel: (212) 545 8484; fax: (212) 251 0429.

Official tourism websites: www.VisitRomania.com (UK); www.RomaniaTourism.com (USA).

Romania Facts

CAPITAL: Bucharest, Bucureşti (pronounced Boocooreshti)
CURRENCY: Leu (plural Lei). I Leu = 100 bani.
OPENING HOURS: Banks: Mon–Thur 0800–1600, Fri 0800–1300.
Shops: Mon–Fri 0700–1900, Sat 0700–1400. Some shops open 24 hrs including Sundays. Museums: Tues–Sun 1000–1800.
TELEPHONES: To dial in, + 40. Outgoing, 00 plus the country code.
Police, 955. Fire, 981. Medical emergency, 961. (These numbers are being replaced by a single number for all emergencies, 112.)
PUBLIC HOLIDAYS: 1, 2 Jan; Orthodox Easter Monday (Apr/May); 1 May; 1, 25, 26 Dec.

ROMANIAN

Technical Language Hints

There are three grammatical genders, masculine, feminine, and neutral (masculine in the singular and feminine in the plural).

Consonant clusters in Romanian occur at the beginning of syllables, which is again unusual among Romance languages.

Stress can occur on any syllable, but be careful to follow the phonetics accurately, as varying the stressed syllable can change meaning.

ESSENTIALS

Alphabet and Pronunciation

	Name	Pronounced
A a	ah	long a as in father
Ă ă		neutral sound like the o in other
Â â		no equivalent in English
B b	beh	b as in bed
C c	cheh	k as in keep or ch as in check
D d	deh	d as in delta
E e	eh	short e as in bell or eh sound as in way
F f	eff	f as in far
G g	djeh	j sound as in gesture
H h	hash	aspirated h as in Scottish loch
I i	ee	i as in pit
Î î		no equivalent in English
J j	zheu	soft zh like the s of pleasure

	Name	Pronounced
K k	kah	k as in keep
L l	ell	l as in elf
M m	em	m as in mother
N n	en	n as in no
O o	oh	o as in old
P p	peh	p as in pelt
Q q	kew	like the qu of queen
R r	air	r as in rock
S s	ess	s as in sit
Ş ş		sh as in shelf
T t	teh	t as in tick
Ţ ţ		ts as in hats
U u	oo	oo as in boot
V v	veh	v as in velvet
W w	doobl-ooveh	w as in wet
X x	icks	x as in fix
Y y	eegrek	y as in yellow
Z z	zed	z as in zoo

Basic Words and Phrases

Yes	No
Da	Nu
Dah	*Noo*

ROMANIAN

Please
Vă rog
Vah rohg

Thank you
Mulţumesc
Mooltzoomesc

Hello
Bună ziua
Boonah zeeooa

Goodbye
La revedere
La revedereh

Excuse me
Scuzaţi-mă
Scoozatz-mah

Sorry
Pardon
Pardon

How
Cum
Coom

When
Când
Cund

Why
De ce
Deh cheh

What
Ce
Cheh

Who
Cine
Cheene

That's O.K.
E în regulă
Eh an rehgoolah

Perhaps
Poate
Pwahteh

To
Către
Cahtreh

From
De la
Deh lah

Here
Aici
Aich

There
Acolo
Acohlo

I don't understand
Nu înţeleg
Noo untzehleg

I don't speak Romanian
Nu înţeleg româneşte
Noo untzeleg romaneshteh

Do you speak English?
Vorbiţi englezeşte?
Vorbeetz englezeshteh?

Can you please write it down?
Scrieţi, vă rog?
Screeyetz, vah rohg?

Please can you speak more slowly
Vorbiţi mai rar, vă rog
Vobeetz my rar, vah rohg

Greetings

Good morning/ Good afternoon/ Good evening/Good night
Bună dimineaţa/Bună ziua/ Bună seara/Noapte bună
Boonah deemeeneyatza/Boonah zeeooa/Boonah sara/Nwapteh boonah

Pleased to meet you
Mă bucur de cunoştinţă
Mah boocoor deh coonoshteentzah

How are you?
Ce mai faceţi?
Cheh my fachetz?

I am well, thank you, and you?
Bine, mulţumesc. Şi dumneavoastră?
Beeneh, mooltzoomesc. She doomneyahvwastrah?

My name is ...
Mă numesc ...
Mah noomesc ...

272

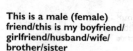
This is a male (female) friend/this is my boyfriend/girlfriend/husband/wife/brother/sister
Acesta (aceasta) este un prieten (o prietenă)/acesta (aceasta) este prietenul (prietena)/soţul/soţia/fratele/sora mea (meu)
Achesta (acheyasta) esteh oon pree-eten (oh pree-etenah) … achesta (acheyasta) esteh pree- etenool (pree-etenah) sotzo-ol/sotzeya/frateleh/sora meha (meyoo)

Where are you travelling to?
Unde călătoriţi?
Oondeh cahlahtoreetz?

I am/we are going to …
Merg/mergem la …
Merg/merdjehm lah …

How long are you travelling for?
Cât timp va dura călătoria?
Cuht teemp vah doorah cahlahtoreeya?

Where do you come from?
De unde sunteţi?
Deh oondeh soontetz?

I am/we are from …
Australia/Britain/Canada/America
Eu sunt/noi suntem din …
Australia/Marea Britanie/Canada/America
Eoo soont/noy soontem deen … Aoostraleyah/Mareya/Breetaneeye/Canadah/Amereecah

We are on holiday
Suntem în concediu

Soontem un conchedeeyoo

This is our first visit here
Este prima noastră vizită aici
Esteh preemah nwastrah veezeetah aich

How old are you?
Câţi ani aveţi?
Cutz ahny avetz?

I am … years old
Am … ani
Am … ahny

I am a business person/doctor/journalist/manual worker/administrator/scientist/student/teacher
Sunt om de afaceri/doctor/ziarist/muncitor/administrator/om de ştiinţă/student/profesor
Soont ohm deh afachery/doctor/zeeyareest/moonchee-tor/administratohr/ohm deh shteentzah/student/profesor

I am waiting for my husband/wife/boyfriend/girlfriend
Îl (o) aştept pe soţul/soţia/pri-etenul/prietena mea (meu)
Ul (oh) ashtept peh sotzool/sotzeeya/pree-etenool/pree-etenah meha

Would you like/may al have a cigarette?
Doriţi/Îmi puteţi da o ţigară?
Doreetz/Um pootezi dah oh tzeegarah?

Do you mind if I smoke?
Vă deranjează dacă fumez?
Vah deranjeyazah dacah foomez?

ROMANIAN

Do you have a light?
Aveţi un foc?
Avetz oon fohc?

Days

Monday
Luni
Loony

Tuesday
Marţi
Marti

Wednesday
Miercuri
Me-ehrcooree

Thursday
Joi
Zhoy

Friday
Vineri
Vinehry

Saturday
Sâmbătă
Sumbahtah

Sunday
Duminică
Doomeeneeka

Morning
Dimineaţa
Deemeeneyatzah

Afternoon/Evening/Night
După amiaza/Seara/Noapte
Doopah ameyazah/Sara/Nwapteh

Yesterday
Ieri
Yeree

Today
Azi
Ahzee

Tomorrow
Mâine
Mu-yneh

Numbers

Zero
Zero
Zehro

One
Unu
Oonoo

Two
Doi
Doy

Three
Trei
Tray

Four
Patru
Patroo

Five
Cinci
Chinc

Six
Şase
Shaseh

Seven
Şapte
Shapteh

Eight
Opt
Opt

Nine
Nouă
Nowah

Ten
Zece
Zecheh

Eleven
Unsprezece
Oonsprezeche

Twelve
Doisprezece
Doysprezecheh

Thirteen
Treisprezece
Traysprezecheh

Fourteen
Paisprezece
Pie-sprezeche

Fifteen
Cincisprezece
Chinchsprezecheh

Sixteen
Şaisprezece
Shy-sprezecheh

Seventeen
Şaptesprezece
Shaptesprezecheh

Eighteen
Optsprezece
Optsprezecheh

Nineteen
Nouăsprezece
Nowahsprezecheh

Twenty
Douăzeci
Dowahzech

Twenty-one
Douăzeci şi unu
Dowahzech she oonoo

Twenty-two
Douăzeci şi doi
Dowahzech she doy

Thirty
Treizeci
Trayzech

Forty
Patruzeci
Patroozech

Fifty
Cincizeci
Chinchzech

Sixty
Şaizeci
Shy-zech

Seventy
Şaptezeci
Shaptezech

Eighty
Optzeci
Optzech

Ninety
Nouăzeci
Nowahzech

One hundred
O sută
Oh sooter

Five hundred
Cinci sute
Chinch sooteh

One thousand
O mie
Oh meeyeh

One million
Un milion
Oon milion

Time

What time is it?
Cât este ceasul?
Cuht esteh cheyasool?

It is ...
Este ora ...
Esteh orah ...

9.00
Nouă
Nowoa

9.05
Nouă şi cinci
Nowa she chinch

9.15
Nouă şi un sfert
Nowa she oon sfehrt

9.20
Nouă şi douăzeci
Nowa she dowahzech

9.30
Nouă şi jumătate
Nowa she joomahtateh

9.35
Nouă şi treizeci şi cinci
Zecheh she treyzech she chinch

9.40
Nouă şi patruzeci
Zecheh she patroozech

9.45
Nouă şi patruzeci şi cinci
Zecheh she patroozech she chinc

9.50
Nouă şi cincizeci
Zecheh she chinchzech

9.55
Nouă şi cincizeci şi cinci
Zecheh she chinchzech she chinc

12.00/Midday/Midnight
Ora douăsprezece/Amiază/
Miezul nopţii
*Orah dowahsprezecheh/
Amiazah/Mee-ehzool noptzee*

Money

I would like to change these traveller's cheques/this currency
Vreau să schimb aceste cecuri de călătorie/valuta aceasta
Vreyahoo sah skimb achesteh checooree de kerlertoreeyeh/valoota acheyasta

How much commission do you charge? (What is the service charge?)
Cât este comisionul?
Cuht esteh comeeseeohnool?

R
O
M
A
N
I
A
N

Can I obtain money with my Mastercard?
Pot să obţin bani cu Mastercard?
Pot sah obtzeen banee coo Mastercard?

Where is the nearest ATM?
Unde este cel mai apropiat ATM?
Oondeh esteh chehl mahy apropyat ATM?

My name is … Some money has been wired to here for me to collect
Numele meu este … Mi s-au trimis nişte bani aici
Noomele meoo esteh … Mee saoo trymys nyshteh bany aychy

ARRIVING AND DEPARTING

Airport

Excuse me, where is the check-in desk for … airline?
Scuzaţi-mă, unde este ghişeul check-in pentru linia aeriană …?
Scoozatz-mah, oondeh esteh gishehool check-in pentroo liniah ayeree-anah …?

What is the boarding gate/time for my flight?
Care este poarta/ora de îmbarcare pentru cursa mea?
Careh esteh pwartah/orah de uhmbarcareh pentroo coorsa meya?

How long is the delay likely to be?
Cam cât o să dureze întârzierea?
Cam cuht oh sah doorezeh untuhrzeeyereya?

Where is the duty-free shop?
Unde este magazinul „duty free"?
Oonde esteh magazeenool deh duty-free?

Which way is the baggage reclaim?
De unde se ridică bagajele?
Deh oonde she ridiker bagazheleh?

I have lost my luggage. Please can you help?
Mi-am pierdut bagajul. Mă puteţi ajuta, vă rog?
Mee-am pee-erdoot bagazhool. Mah pootetz ajootah, vah rohg?

I am flying to …
Merg cu avionul la …
Merg coo aveeohnool lah …

Where is the bus for the city centre?
Unde este autobuzul pentru centrul oraşului?
Oondeh esteh aootoboozool pentroo chentrool orashoolooi?

Trains and Boats

Where is the ticket office/information desk?
Unde este ghişeul de bilete/biroul de informaţii?
Oondeh esteh gishehool deh bileteh/birohool de infor matzee?

Which platform does the train/speedboat/ferry to ... depart from?
De la ce peron pleacă trenul/vaporul/feribotul?
Deh lah cheh pehron pleyacah trenool/vaporool/feribotool?

Where is platform ... ?
Unde este peronul ... ?
Oondeh esteh pehronool ...?

When is the next train/boat to ...?
Când este următorul tren/vapor spre ...?
Cund esteh oormahtorool tren/vapor spre ...?

Is there a later train/boat to ...?
Este un tren/vapor mai târziu?
Esteh oon tren/vapor my turzeeyoo?

Notices and Signs

Vagon restaurant
Vagon restaoorant
Buffet (Dining) car

Autobuz
Aootobooz
Bus

Apă potabilă/nepotabilă
Apah potabilah/nepotabilah
Drinking/non-drinking water

Intrare
Intrareh
Entrance

Ieșire
Yehsheereh
Exit

Spital
Spital
Hospital

Informaţii
Informatzee
Information

Biroul de bagaje
Birohool de bagazhe
Left luggage (Baggage claim)

Dulăpioare pentru bagaje
Doolahpeeyowareh pentroo bagazhe
Luggage lockers

Oficiul poştal
Ofeecheeool poshtal
Post office

Peron
Perohn
Platform

Gară
Garah
Railway (Railroad) station

Aeroport
Aeroport
Airport

Circa de poliţie
Chircah deh politzye
Police station

R
O
M
A
N
I
A
N

277

**R
O
M
A
N
I
A
N**

Port
Port
Port

Restaurant
Restaoorant
Restaurant

Fumători/Nefumători
Foomahtoree/Nefoomahtoree
Smoking/Non smoking

Telefon
Telephon
Telephone

Ghișeu de bilete
Gishehoo deh bileteh
Ticket office

Ghișeu check-in
Gishehoo check-in
Check-in desk

Orar
Orar
Timetable (Schedule)

Toalete
Twaleteh
Toilets

Femei/Bărbați
Femay/Bahrbatz
Ladies/Gentlemen

Metrou
Metro
Underground (Subway)

Sala de așteptare
Salah de ashteptareh
Waiting room

Buying a Ticket

**I would like a first-class/
second-class/third-class/
single (one-way)/return
(round trip) ticket to ...**
Un bilet clasa întâi/clasa a
doua/clasa a treia dus/dus
întors până la ...
*Oon bilet clasah untuy/clasah ah
dowa/clasah ah tray-ah doos/untors
punah lah ...*

**Is it an express (fast)
train/bus?**
Este un tren/autobuz express?
Esteh oon tren/aootobooz express?

**Is my rail pass valid on this
train/ferry/bus?**
Este valabil abonamentul meu
de tren pentru trenul/feribot-
ul/autobuzul acesta?
*Esteh valabil abonamentool meyoo
deh tren pentroo trenool/feree-
botool/aootoboozool achestah?*

**I would like an aisle/window
seat**
Doresc un loc lângă coridor/la
fereastră
*Doresc oon loc lungah coridor/lah
ferehastrah*

No smoking/smoking please
Nefumători/fumători, vă rog
*Nefoomahtoree/foomahtoree,
vah rohg*

**We would like to sit
together**
Dorim să stăm împreună
Dorim sah stahm umpreoonah

**I would like to make a seat
reservation**

Doresc să rezerv un loc
Doresc sah rezerv oon loc

I would like to reserve a couchette/sleeper for one person/two people/my family
Doresc să rezerv o cuşetă pentru o persoană/două persoane/familia mea
Doresc sah rezerv oh coshetah pentroo oh perswanah/dowoah perswaneh/fameeleeya meya

I would like to reserve a cabin
Doresc să rezerv o cabină
Doresc sah rezerv oh cabeenah

Timetables (Schedules)

Soseşte
Soseshteh
Arrives

Opreşte la
Opresheteh lah
Calls (stops) at

Bufet - Restaurant
Boofet Restaoorant
Catering service

Cu schimbare la
Coo skeembareh lah
Change at

Legătură/Prin
Legahtoorah/Prin
Connection/Via

Zilnic
Zilnic
Daily

La fiecare 40 de minute
Lah fiehcareh 40 deh minooteh
Every 40 minutes

Clasa întâi
Clasah untuy
First class

La fiecare oră
Lah fiehcareh orah
Hourly

Se recomandă să rezervaţi locuri
Se recomandah sah rezervatz locooree
Seat reservations are recommended

Clasa a doua
Clasah ah dowah
Second class

Se plăteşte supliment
Seh plahteshteh soopliment
Supplement payable

Luggage

How much will it cost to send (ship) my luggage in advance?
Cât costă să trimit bagajul în avans?
Cuht costah sah trimit bagazhool uhn avans?

Where is the left luggage (baggage claim) office?
Unde este biroul de bagaje?
Oonde esteh birohool deh bagazheh?

R O M A N I A N

What time do you open/close?
La ce oră deschideți/închideți?
Lah cheh orah deskidetz/unkidetz?

Where are the luggage trolleys (carts)?
Unde sunt cărucioarele de bagaje?
Oondeh sunt cahroochiwareleh deh bagazheh?

Where are the lockers?
Unde sunt dulăpioarele de bagaje?
Oonde sunt doolahpeewareleh de bagezheh?

I have lost my locker key
Am pierdut cheia de la dulăpior
Am piehrdoot kaya deh lah doolahpeeor

On Board

Is this seat free?
E liber locul acesta?
Eh liber locool achestah?

Excuse me, you are sitting in my reserved seat
Scuzați-mă, dar stați pe locul meu rezervat
Scoozatz-mah, dar statz pe locool meyoo rezervat

Which station is this?
La ce gară ne aflăm?
Lah cheh garah neh aflahm?

What time is this train/bus ferry/flight due to arrive/depart?
La ce oră urmează să

sosească/plece trenul/auto-buzul/feribotul/avionul acesta?
Lah cheh orah oormeyazah sah soseyascah/plecheh/aootoboozool/feribotool/avionool achestah?

Travelling with Children

Do you have a high chair/babysitting service/cot?
Aveți un scaun pentru copil/serviciu de babysitting/pătuț pentru copil?
Avetz oon scaoon pentroo copil/servicheeoo deh baby sittining/pahtootz pentroo copil?

Where is the nursery/playroom?
Unde e camera copilului/camera de joacă?
Oonde e camera copiloolooi/camerah deh zhoacah?

Where can I warm the baby's bottle?
Unde pot să încălzesc biberonul copilului?
Oondeh pot sah uncahlzesc biberonool copiloolooi?

Customs and Passports

Pașapoartele, vă rog!
Pashapoarteleh, vah rohg!
Passports please!

I have nothing/wine/spirits (alcohol) tobacco to declare
Nu am nimic/vin/alcool/tutun de declarat
Noo am neemeek/veen/alcol/tootoon deh declarat

I will be staying for ... days/weeks/months
Voi sta ... zile/săptămâni/luni
Voy stah ... zeele/sahptahmuny/loony

SIGHTSEEING

Asking the Way

Excuse me, do you speak English?
Scuzați-mă, vorbiți engleză?
Scoozatz-mah, vorbitz englehzah?

Excuse me, can you help me please?
Scuzați-mă, mă puteți ajuta vă rog?
Scoozatz-mah, mah pootetz azhootah vah rohg?

Where is the Tourist Information Office?
Unde este Biroul de Informații Turistice?
Oondeh esteh Birohool deh Informatzee Tooristicheh?

Excuse me, is this the right way to ... ?
Scuzați-mă, acesta este drumul spre ... ?
Scoozatz-mah, achestah esteh droomool spreh ...?

... the cathedral/the Tourist Office/the castle/the old town
... catedrala/Biroul de Turism/castelul/orașul vechi
... catedralah/Birohool deh Toorism/castelool/orashool veki

Can you tell me the way to the railway station/bus

station/taxi rank/city centre/beach?
Puteți să-mi spuneți cum să ajung la gară/stația de autobuz/stația de taxi/centru/plajă?
Pootetz sah-me spoonetz coom sah azhoong lah garah/statzia deh aootobooz/statzia deh taxi/chentroo/plazhah?

First/second/left/right/straight ahead
Prima/a doua/stânga/dreapta/drept înainte
Preemala dowah/stungah/dreyaptah/drept unainteh

At the corner/At the traffic lights
La colț/La semafor
Lah coltz/lah semafor

Where is the nearest police station/post office?
Unde este cea mai apropiată circă de poliție/cel mai apropiat oficiu poștal?
Oonde esteh cheah my apropiatah chircah deh politzye/chel my apropiat ofeecheeoo poshtal?

Is it near/far?
Este aproape/departe?
Esteh aprwapeh/departeh?

Do I need to take a taxi/catch a bus?
Este nevoie să iau un taxi/autobuzul?
Esteh nevoyeh sah iaw oon taxi/aootobooz?

Do you have a map?
Aveți o hartă?
Avetz o hartah?

R O M A N I A N

Can you point to it on my map?
Puteți să-mi arătați pe hartă?
Pootetz sah-mee arahtatz pe har-tah?

Thank you for your help
Mulțumesc pentru ajutor
Mooltzoomesc pentroo azhootor

How do I reach the motorway/main road?
Cum ajung la autostradă/drumul principal?
Coom azhoong lah aootostradah/droomool princhipal?

I think I have taken the wrong turning
Cred că am greșit drumul
Cred cah am greshit droomool

I am looking for this address
Caut adresa aceasta
Caoot adresah acheyastah

I am looking for the ... hotel
Caut hotelul ....
Caoot hotelool ....

How far is it to ... from here?
Cât de departe este de aici până la ...
Cuht deh departeh esteh deh aich punah la ...

Continuați drept înainte încă ... kilometri
Continooatz drept unainteh uncah ... kilometree
Carry straight on for ... kilometres

Faceți prima la dreapta/stânga
Fachetz primah la dreaptah/stunga

Take the next turning on the right/left

La prima intersecție/primul semafor luați-o la dreapta/stânga
Lah primah intersectzieh/primool semafor/looatz-oh lah dreaptah/stungah
Turn right/left at the next crossroads/traffic lights

Mergeți în direcție greșită
Merdjetz un directzieh greshitah
You are going in the wrong direction

Where is the cathedral/church/museum/pharmacy?
Unde este catedrala/biserica/muzel/farmacie?
Oondeh esteh catedrahla/bisehrica/moozeul/farmachye?

How much is the admission/entrance charge?
Cât costă intrarea?
Cuht costah intrareyah?

Is there a discount for children/students/senior citizens?
Există reducere pentru copii/studenți/persoane în vârstă?
Existah redoocherah pentroo copee/stoodentz/perswaneh un vurstah?

What time does the next guided tour (in English) start?
La ce oră începe următorul tur cu ghid (în engleză)?
Lah cheh orah unchepeh oormah-torool toor coo gid (un englehzah)?

One/two adults/children please
Un/doi adulţi/copii, vă rog
Oon/doy adooltz/copee, vah rohg

May I take photographs here?
Am voie să fac poze aici?
Am voyeh sah fahc pozeh aich?

At the Tourist Office

Do you have a map of the town/area?
Aveţi o hartă a oraşului/ regiunii?
Avetz oh hartah a orashoolooi/ redjeeoonee?

Do you have a list of accommodation?
Aveţi o listă cu locuri disponibile?
Avetz o listah coo locoori deesponeebeelee?

Can I reserve accommodation?
Pot să rezerv cazarea?
Pot sah rezerv cazareya?

ACCOMMODATION

Hotels

I have a reservation in the name of ...
Am făcut o rezervare pe numele de ...
Am fahcoot oh rezervare peh noomeleh deh ...

I wrote to/faxed/telephoned you last month/last week
V-am scris/trimis un fax/tele-fonat/luna trecută/săptămâna trecută
V-am screes/treemees oon fax/tele-phonat/loonah trecootah/sahptah-munah trecootah

Do you have any rooms free?
Aveţi camere libere?
Avetz camereh leebereh?

I would like to reserve a single/double room with/without a bath/shower
Doresc să rezerv o cameră pentru o persoană/două persoane cu/fără baie/duş
Doresc sah rezerv oh camerah pentroo oh perswanah/dowah per-swaneh coo/fahrah baeeyeh/doosh

I would like bed/breakfast (room and) full board
Doresc o cameră cu micul dejun/pensiune
Doresc oh camerah coo meecool dezhoon/penseeooneh

How much is it per night?
Cât costă pe noapte?
Cuht costah peh nowapteh?

Is breakfast included?
Este inclus micul dejun?
Esteh incloos meecool dezhoon?

Do you have any cheaper rooms?
Aveţi camere mai ieftine?
Avetz camereh my yehfteeneh?

R
O
M
A
N
I
A
N

R
O
M
A
N
I
A
N

I would like to see/take the room
Doresc să văd/închiriez camera
Doresc sah vahd/unkeeryez camerah

I would like to stay for ... nights
Doresc să stau .... nopţi
Doresc sah staoo ... noptz

The shower/light/tap/hot water doesn't work
Nu merge duşul/lumina/robinetul/apa fierbinte
Noo merdje dooshool/loominah/robeenetool/apa fierbinteh

At what time/where is breakfast served?
La ce oră/unde se serveşte micul dejun?
Lah cheh orah/oondeh se serveshteh meecool dezhoon?

What time do I have to check out?
Când trebuie să eliberez camera?
Cund trebooyeh sah eleeberez camerah?

Can I have the key to room number ...?
Doresc cheia de la camera numărul ...?
Doresc kaya deh lah camerah noomahrool ...?

My room number is ...
Stau la camera numărul ...
Stau lah camerah noomahrool ...

My room is not satisfactory/not clean enough/too noisy. Please can I change rooms?
Camera mea nu este satisfăcătoare/curată/e prea zgomotoasă. Vă rog, pot să schimb camera?
Camerah meya noo esteh sateesfahcahtoareh/cooratah/eh preah zgomotwasah. Vah rohg, pot sah skimb camerah?

Where is the bathroom?
Unde este baia?
Oonde esteh ba-ya?

Do you have a safe for valuables?
Aveţi un seif pentru lucruri de valoare?
Avetz oon sayph pentroo loocroory deh valowareh?

Is there a laundry/do you wash clothes?
Aveţi o spălătorie/primiţi haine la spălat?
Avetz oh spahlahtoreeye/preemeetz roofeh lah spahlat?

I would like an air-conditioned room
Doresc o cameră cu aer condiţionat
Doresc oh camerah coo aer condizzonat

Do you accept traveller's cheques/credit cards?
Acceptaţi cecuri de călătorie/cărţi de credit?
Akcheptatz checoory de kerlertoreeyeh/cahrtz deh credit?

May I have the bill please?
Îmi puteţi da nota de plată?
Umy pootetz dah notah deh platah?

Excuse me, I think there may be a mistake in this bill
Scuzaţi-mă, cred că e o greşeală în nota de plată
Scoozatz-mah, cred cah eh oh gresheyalah um notah deh platah

Youth Hostels

How much is a dormitory bed per night?
Cât costă un pat pe noapte în dormitorul comun?
Cuht costah oon pat peh nowapteh un dormeetorool comoon?

I am/am not an HI member
Sunt/nu sunt membru în HI
Soont/noo soont membroo HI

May I use my own sleeping bag?
Pot să folosesc sacul meu de dormit?
Pot sah folosesc sacool meyoo deh dormeet?

What time do you lock the doors at night?
La ce oră se încuie uşa seara?
Lah cheh orah se unkooye oosha sara?

Camping

May I camp for the night/two nights?
Pot să pun cortul pentru noaptea asta/două nopţi?
Pot sah poon cortool pentroo nwapteah astah/dowoah noptz?

Where can I pitch my tent?
Unde pot să pun cortul?
Oondeh pot sah poon cortool?

How much does it cost for one night/week?
Cât costă pe noapte/săptămână?
Cuht costah peh nwapteh/sahptahmunah?

Where are the washing facilities?
Unde sunt lavabourile?
Oonde sunt lavaboureeleh?

Is there a restaurant/supermarket/swimming pool on site/nearby?
Este un restaurant/magazin alimentar/bazin de înot aici/în apropiere?
Esteh oon restaoorant/magazeen aleementar/bazeen deh unot aich/un apropiereh?

Do you have a safety deposit box?
Unde pot fi păstrate lucrurile de valoare?
Ondeh pot fi pahstrate loocrooreeleh deh valwareh?

Cafés and Bars

I would like a cup of/two cups of/another coffee/tea
Mai doresc o ceaşcă/două ceşti de cafea/ceai
My doresc oh cheyashcah/dowoah cheshty deh cafeya/cheyai

**R
O
M
A
N
I
A
N**

With/without milk/sugar
Cu/fără lapte/zahăr
Cool/fahrah lapteh/zahahr

I would like a bottle/glass/two glasses of mineral water/red wine/white wine, please
Doresc o sticlă/un pahar/două pahare de apă minerală/vin roșu/vin alb, vă rog
Doresc oh steeclah/oon pahar/dowah pahare deh apah meeneralah/veen roshoo/veen alb, vah rohg

I would like a beer/two beers, please
Doresc o bere/două beri, vă rog
Doresc oh bereh, dowah beree, vah rohg

Please, may I have some ice?
Gheață, vă rog?
Gheyatzah, vah rohg?

Do you have any matches/cigarettes/cigars?
Aveți chibrituri/țigări/trabucuri?
Avetz keebreetooree/tzigahree/trabookoori?

Restaurants

Can you recommend a good/cheap restaurant in this area?
Îmi puteți recomanda un restaurant bun/ieftin în zona asta?
Umi pootetz recomandah oon restaoorant boon/yefteen un zona asta?

I would like a table for ... people
Doresc o masă pentru .... persoane
Doresc oh masah pentroo .... perswaneh

Do you have a non-smoking area?
Aveți locuri pentru nefumători?
Avetz locooree pentroo nefoomahtoree?

Waiter/Waitress!
Chelner/Chelneriță!
Kelner/Kelnehritsa!

Excuse me, please may we order?
Scuzați-mă, putem să comandăm?
Scoozatz-mah, pootem sah comandahm?

Do you have a set menu/children's menu/wine list ... in English?
Aveți un meniu fix/un menu pentru copii/o listă de vinuri ... în engleză?
Avetz oon menyoo fix/oon mehnoo pentroo copii/o listah deh veenooree ... un englehzah?

Do you have any vegetarian dishes?
Aveți mâncăruri pentru vegetarieni?
Avetz muncuroori pentroo vegetaryehnee?

Do you have any local specialities?
Aveți specialități locale?
Avetz spechialitahtz lokahleh?

Are vegetables included?
Sunt incluse legumele?
Sunt inclooseh legoomeleh?

Could I have it well-cooked/ medium/rare please?
Doresc carnea bine prăjită/nu foarte prăjită/în sânge?
Doresc carneya beeneh prahzhee-tah/noo fwarteh prahzheetah/un sundjeh?

What does this dish consist of?
Din ce constă felul acesta de mâncare?
Deen cheh constah felool achesta deh muncareh?

I am a vegetarian. Does this contain meat?
Sunt vegetarian. Conţine carne?
Soont vegetaryan. Kontzyneh carneh?

I do not eat nuts/dairy products/meat/fish
Nu mănânc nuci/produse lactate/carne/peşte
Noo mahnunc noochi/prodooseh lactateh/carneh/pehshteh

Not (very) spicy please
Nu (foarte) condimentat, vă rog
Noo (fwarteh) condeementat, vah rog

I would like the set menu, please
Doresc meniul fix, vă rog
Doresc menyool fix, vah rohg

We have not been served yet
N-am fost serviţi încă

Nam fost serveetz uncah

Please bring a plate/knife/fork
Vă rog să aduceţi o farfurie/un cuţit/o furculiţă
Vah rog sah adoocetzy oh far-fooryeh/oon cootzyt/o foorkoolitzah

Excuse me, this is not what I ordered
Scuzaţi-mă, eu nu am comandat asta
Scoozatz-mah, eoo noo am comandat asta

May I have some/more bread/water/coffee/tea?
Îmi mai puteţi da pâine/apă/cafea/ceai?
Umi my pootetz dah puyneh/apah/cafeya/cheyai?

May I have the bill please?
Nota de plată, vă rog?
Notah deh platah, vah rohg?

Does this bill include service?
Nota de plată include bacşişul?
Notah deh platah incloodeh bak-shishool?

Do you accept traveller's cheques/Mastercard/US dollars?
Acceptaţi cecuri de călătorie/Mastercard/dolari americani?
Akcheptatz checooree de kerlertoreeyeh/Mastercard/dolaree americanee?

Can I have a receipt please?
Îmi puteţi da o chitanţă, vă rog?
Umi pootetz dah o kitantzah, vah rohg?

ROMANIAN

Where is the toilet (rest room) please?
Unde este toaleta, vă rog?
Oondeh este twaleta, vah rohg?

On the Menu

Mic dejun/Prânz/Cină
Mik dejoon/Prunz/Chynah
Breakfast/Lunch/Dinner

Felul întâi
Felool untuy
First Courses

Supe
Soopeh
Soups

Felul doi
Felool doy
Main Courses

Mâncăruri cu peşte
Muncahrooree coo pehshteh
Fish dishes

Mâncăruri cu carne
Muncahrooree coo carneh
Meat Dishes

Carne de vacă
Karneh deh vakah
Beef

Friptură
Friptoorah
Steak

Carne de porc
Karneh deh pork
Pork

Carne de viţel
Karneh deh vitzel
Veal

Carne de pui
Karneh deh pooy
Chicken

Carne de miel
Karneh deh myehl
Lamb

Şuncă
Shooncah
Ham

Mâncăruri vegetariene
Muncahrooree vedjetarieneh
Vegetarian Dishes

Legume
Lehgoomeh
Vegetables

Cartofi prăjiţi
Kartofy prahdjitzi
Chips (french fries)

Cartofi natur/sauté/piure
Kartofy natoor/sohteh/pyooreh
Boiled/sauté/mashed potatoes

Orez
Ohrehz
Rice

Deserturi
Desertooree
Desserts

Îngheţată
Ungetzatah
Ice cream

Fursecuri
Foorsehkoory
Cakes

Clătite
Klahtyteh
Pastries

Fructe
Froocteh
Fruit

Pâine
Punyneh
Bread

Ruladă
Roolahduh
Rolls

Pâine prăjită
Punyneh prahdjitah
Toast

Unt
Oont
Butter

Sare/piper
Sareh/pypehr
Salt/pepper

Zahăr
Zahahr
Sugar

Specialităţi
Spechialeetahtz
Specialities

Specialităţi locale
Spechalytahtzy localeh
Local specialities

Meniu fix
Menyu fix
Set menu

Lista de vinuri
Listah deh vynoory
Wine list

Vinuri roşii   Vinuri albe
Vynoory roshy Vynoory albeh
Red wines   White wines

Vinuri rosé
Vynoory rohzeh
Rosé wines

Vinuri spumoase
Vynoory spoomoahseh
Sparkling wines

Bere
Behreh
Beer

Bere îmbuteliată/halbă
Behreh unmbootehlyatah/halbah
**Bottled/Draught (draft)
beer**

Băuturi nealcoolice
Bahootoory nehalkoliche
Non-alcoholic drinks

Apă minerală
Apah mineralah
Mineral water

Sucuri de fructe
Sookoory de frookteh
Fruit juices

Suc de portocale
Sook de portokaleh
Orange juice

Limonadă   Gheaţă
Lymonadah   Geahtzah
Lemonade   Ice

Cafea cu lapte/cafea
simplă/esspresso
*Cafeah coo lapteh/cafeah
symplah/esspresso*
**White coffee/black
coffee/espresso coffee**

Ceai cu lapte/cu lămâie
Cheay coo lapteh/coo lahmunyeh
Tea with milk/with lemon

Ciocolată lichidă
chyocolaatah liquidah
Chocolate (drink)

Lapte
Lapteh
Milk

Gustări/Mâncăruri uşoare
*Goostahri/Muncahroory
ushooahreh*
Snacks/Light meals

Salate   Sandvişuri
Salateh   Sandvishoori
Salads   Sandwiches

Ouă
Oh-uah
Eggs

Ouă fierte/ochiuri/omletă
Oh-uah fyerteh/okyoory/omletah
Boiled/fried/scrambled eggs

Typical Local Dishes

Ciorbă de perişoare
Cheeorbah deh pereeshoareh
Meatball Soup (sour soup with tomato and meat-balls)

Sarmale
Sarmaleh
Stuffed Cabbage Leaves (cabbage leaves stuffed with a mixture of pork mince and rice, in sauce)

Mititei
Meeteetei
Grilled Minced Meat Rolls (spicy meat and garlic rolls)

Borş de miel
Borsh deh miehl
Sour Lamb Soup

Musaca
Moosacah
Minced Meat Pie (layers of potato slices, minced meat and vegetables)

Ardei umpluţi
Ardei oomplootz
Stuffed Peppers (large peppers stuffed with rice, vegetables and/or minced meat, in sauce)

Mămăliguţă
Mahmahleegootzah
Maize Polenta (traditional Romanian dish, can be served as a starter, with yoghurt or sour cream, or on its own as an accompaniment to 'sarmale')

GETTING AROUND

Public Transport

Where is the bus stop/coach stop/nearest metro station?
Unde este staţia de autobuz/autocar/cea mai apropiată staţie de metro?
Oondeh esteh statzia deh aooto-booz/aootocar/cheya my apropiatah statzyeh deh metro?

When is the next/last bus to ...?
Când este următorul/ultimul autobuz spre ... ?
Cund esteh oormahtorool/ooltimool aootobooz spreh ...?

How much is the fare to the city centre (downtown)/railway station/airport?
Cât este biletul până în centru/la gară/aeroport?
Cuht esteh beeletool punah un chentroo/lah garah/aeroport?

Will you tell me when to get off?
Îmi puteți spune unde să cobor?
Umi pootetz spooneh oondeh sah cobor?

Does this bus go to...?
Autobuzul acesta merge la ...?
Aootoboozool achesta merdje lah. . ?

Which number bus goes to ...?
Ce autobuz merge la ...?
Cheh aootobooz merdje lah ...?

May I have a single (one-way)/return (round-trip)/day ticket/book of tickets?
Doresc un bilet dus/ dus - întors/abonament pe o zi/carnet de bilete?
Doresc oon bilet doos/doos - untors/abonament peh oh zee/carnet deh bileteh?

Taxis (Taxiuri)

I would like to go to ... How much will it cost?
Doresc să merg la ... Cât costă?
Doresc sah merg lah ... Cuht costah?

Please may I stop here?
Vă rog, ne putem opri aici?
Vah rohg, neh pootem opree aich?

I would like to order a taxi today/tomorrow at 2pm to go from ... to ...
Doresc să comand un taxi pen-tru astăzi/mâine la ora 2 după amiază, de la ...... pâna la ....

Doresc sah comand oon taxi pen-troo astahzee/muyeeneh lah orah dowah doopah ameeazah, deh lah ... punah lah ...

Entertainment

Can you recommend a good bar/night club?
Puteți să îmi recomandați un bar/club bun de noapte?
Pootetz sah umi recomandatz oon bar/cloob boon deh nwapteh?

Do you know what is on at the cinema (playing at the movies)/theatre at the moment?
Știți ce se joacă acum la cinema/teatru?
Shteetz cheh se zhoacah acoom lah cheenemah/teyatroo?

I would like to book (purchase) ... tickets for the matinee/evening performance on Monday
Doresc să rezerv (cumpăr) bilete pentru luni, la matineu/spectacolul de seară
Doresc sah rezerv (coompahr) beeleteh pentroo loony, lah mateeneyoo/spectacolool deh sara

What time does the film/performance start?
La ce oră începe filmul/spectacolul?
Lah cheh orah unchepeh filmool/spectacolool?

ROMANIAN

Post

How much will it cost to send a letter/postcard/this package to Britain/Ireland/America/Canada/Australia/New Zealand?
Cât costă să trimit o scrisoare/vedere/un pachet în Marea Britanie/Irlanda/America/Canada/Austrilia/Noua Zeelandă?
Cuht costah sah treemeet oh screesoareh/vedereh/oon paket un Mareya Breetanyeh/Irlanda/Amereecah/Canadah/Aoostrayleeah/Nowa Zeehlandah?

I would like one stamp/two stamps
Doresc un timbru/două timbre.
Doresc oon teembroo/dowah teembreh

I'd like … stamps for postcards to send abroad, please
Doresc … timbre de străinătate pentru vederi, vă rog
Doresc …teembreh deh straheenahtateh pentroo vederee, vah rohg

Phones

I would like to make a telephone call/reverse the charges to (make a collect call to)…
Doresc să dau un telefon/cu taxă inversă la …
Doresc sah daoo oon telephon/coo taxah inversah lah …

What coins do I need for the telephone?
Ce monezi îmi trebuie pentru telefon?
Cheh monezee umy trebooye pentroo telephon?

The line is engaged (busy)
E ocupat
E ocoopat

The number is …
Numărul este …
Noomahrool esteh …

Hello, this is …
Alo, …. la telefon.
Alo, … lah telephon.

Please may I speak to …?
Pot să vorbesc cu …, vă rog?
Pot sah vorbesc coo … vah rohg?

He/she is not in at the moment. Please can you call back?
El/ea nu este aici. Telefonaţi mai târziu, vă rog?
El/ea noo esteh aich. Telefonatsi my turzeeyoo, vah rohg?

SHOPPING

Shops

Librărie/Papetărie
Leebrahryeh
Bookshop/Stationery

Bijuterii/Cadouri
Beedjooteree/Cadowree
Jeweller/Gifts

Încălțăminte
Uncahltzahmeenteh
Shoes

Confecții
Confectzee
Clothes

Spălătorie
Spahlahtoryeh
Laundry

Articole de menaj
Arteecoleh deh menadj
Hardware

Coafor
Cwafor
Hairdresser

Brutărie
Brootahryeh
Baker

Supermarket
Soopermarkeet
Supermarket

Magazin foto
Magazeen photo
Photo shop

Agenție de voiaj
Adjentzyeh deh voyadj
Travel agent

Farmacie
Farmachye
Pharmacy

In the Shops

What time do the shops open/close?
La ce oră se deschid/închid magazinele?
Lah cheh orah she deskid/unkid magazeeneleh?

Where is the nearest market?
Unde e cea mai apropiată piață?
Oondeh eh chyea my apropiatah piatzah?

Can you show me the one in the window/this one?
Puteți să mi-o arătați pe cea din vitrină/cel din vitrină/aceasta (acesta)?
Pootetz sah mee-oh arahtatz peh cheah deen veetreenah/chel deen veetreenah/achesta (acheyasta)?

Can I try this on?
Pot să o (îl) probez?
Pot sah oh (ul) probez?

What size is this?
Ce mărime e aceasta (acesta)?
Cheh mahreemeh eh acheyasta (achesta)?

R
O
M
A
N
I
A
N

293

This is too large/too small/too expensive. Do you have any others?
Acesta (acesta) e prea mare/
prea mic (mică)/prea scump
(scumpă). Mai aveţi şi altele?
*Achesta (acheyasta) eh preya mareh/
preha meec (meecah)/preha scoomp
(scoompah). My avetz she alteleh?*

My size is …
Am mărimea …
Am mahreemeya …

Where is the changing room/children's/cosmetic/ ladieswear/menswear/food department?
Unde este camera de
probă/departamentul pentru
copii/cosmetice/femei/bărbaţi/
raionul alimentar?
*Oondeh esteh camerah deh
probah/departamentool pentroo
copee/cosmeteecheh/femay/
bahrbatz/raionool aleementar?*

I would like … a quarter of a kilo/half a kilo/a kilo of bread/butter/ham/this fruit
Doresc … un sfert de kilogram/o
jumătate de kilogram/un kilogram de pâine/unt/şuncă/din
fructele acestea
*Doresc … oon sfert deh kilogram/
oh zhoomahtateh deh kilogram/
oon kilogram deh puyneh/oont/
shooncah/deen froocteleh achestea*

How much is this?
Cât costă?
Cuht costah?

I'll take this one, thank you
O iau pe aceasta, mulţumesc
Oh iaoo peh acheyasta, mooltzoomesc

Do you have a carrier (shopping) bag?
Aveţi o pungă de plastic?
Avetz oh pungah deh plastic?

Do you have anything cheaper/larger/smaller/of better quality?
Aveţi ceva mai ieftin/mare/mic
(mică)/de calitate mai bună?
*Avetz cheva my yefteen/
mareh/meec (meecah)/deh
caleetateh my boonah?*

I would like a film/to develop this film for this camera
Doresc un film/să developez
filmul acesta pentru acest
aparat
*Doresc oon film/sah developez
filmool achesta pentroo achest
aparat*

I would like some batteries, the same size as this old one
Doresc nişte baterii, de aceeaşi
mărime ca aceasta
*Doresc neeshteh bateree, deh
acheyash mahreemeh ka acheyasta*

Would you mind wrapping this for me, please?
Vreţi să mi-l (mi-o)
împachetaţi, vă rog?
*Vretz sah mee-l (mee-o)
umpahetatz, vah rohg?*

Sorry, but you seem to have given me the wrong change
Îmi pare rău, dar se pare că
mi-aţi dat restul greşit
*Umi pareh row, dar se pareh cah
mee-atz dat restool greshit*

MOTORING

Car Hire (Rental)

I have ordered (rented) a car in the name of ...
Am comandat (închiriat) o maşină pe numele de ...
Am comandat (ernchiriat) oh masheenah peh noomeleh deh ....

How much does it cost to hire (rent) a car for one day/two days/a week?
Cât costă să închiriez o maşină pentru o zi/două zile/o săptămână?
Cuht costah sah unkiriez oh masheenah pentroo oh zee/dowah zeeleh/oh sahptahmunah?

Is the tank already full of petrol (gas)?
E plin rezervorul cu benzină/motorină?
E pleen rezervorool coo benzeenah/motoreenah?

Is insurance and tax included? How much is the deposit?
E inclusă asigurarea şi taxa? Cât este depozitul?
E incloosah aseegoorareya she taxa? Cuht esteh depozeetool?

By what time must I return the car?
La ce oră trebuie să aduc maşina înapoi?
Lah cheh orah trebooyeh sah adook masheena unapoy?

I would like a small/large/family/sports car with a radio/cassette
Doresc o maşină mică/mare/de familie/sport cu radio/casetofon
Doresc oh masheenah meecah/mareh/deh fameelyeh/sport coo radio/casetophon

Do you have a road map?
Aveţi o hartă rutieră?
Avetz oh hartah rootyehrah?

Parking

How long can I park here?
Cât timp pot să parchez aici?
Cuht teemp pot sah parkez aich?

Is there a car park near here?
E o parcare în apropiere?
E oh parcare un apropyehreh?

At what time does this car park close?
La ce oră se închide parcarea?
Lah cheh orah se unkideh parcareya?

Signs and Notices

Sens unic
Sens ooneec
One way

Intrarea interzisă
Intrareya interzeesah
No entry

Parcarea interzisă
Parcareya interzeesah
No parking

ROMANIAN

ROMANIAN

Detur
Detoor
Detour (Diversion)

Stop
Stop
Stop

Acordați prioritate
Acordatz preeoreetateh.
Give way (Yield)

Drum alunecos
Droom aloonecos.
Slippery road

Depășirea interzisă
Depahshireya interzeesah.
No overtaking

Pericol!
Pereecol!
Danger!

At the Filling Station
(La Benzinărie)

**Unleaded (lead free)/
standard/premium/diesel**
Fără plumb/standard/
premium/diesel
*Fahrah ploomb/standard/
premyoom/deezel*

Fill the tank please
Umpleți rezervorul, vă rog
Oompletz rezervorool, vah rohg

Do you have a road map?
Aveți o hartă rutieră?
Avetz oh hartah rootyehrah?

How much is the car wash?

Cât costă un spălat de mașină?
*Cuht costah oon spahlat deh
masheenah?*

Breakdowns

I've had a breakdown at ...
Am făcut pană la ...
Am fahkoot panah lah ...

**I am a member of the ...
[motoring organisation]**
Sunt un membru al ...
Soont oon membroo al ...

I am on the road from... to ...
Sunt pe drumul de la ... la ...
Soont peh droomool deh lah.. lah ...

**I can't move the car. Can you
send a tow truck?**
Nu pot să mișc mașina. Puteți
trimite o mașină să mă
remorcheze?
*Noo pot sah meeshk masheena.
Pootetz treemeeteh oh masheenah
sah mah remorkezeh?*

I have a flat tyre
Am făcut pană de cauciuc
Am fahkoot panah deh cowchyooc

**The windscreen (windshield)
has smashed/cracked**
S-a spart/crăpat parbrizul
S-a spart/crahpat parbreezool

**There is something wrong
with the engine/brakes/
lights/steering/gearbox/
clutch/exhaust**
E o problemă cu motorul/
frânele/farurile/volanul/cutia de
viteze/ambreiajul/țeava de
eșapament

*E oh problemah coo motorool/
fruneleh/farooreeleh/volanool/cootya
deh veetezeh/ambrehyazhool/tzeya-
va deh eshapament*

It's overheating
Se încălzeşte prea tare
Se uncahlzeshteh preya tareh

It won't start
Nu porneşte
Noo porneshteh

Where can I get it repaired?
Unde pot să o repar?
Ondeh pot sah oh repar?

Can you take me there?
Mă puteţi duce acolo?
Mah pootetz doocheh acoloh?

Will it take long to fix?
O să dureze mult reparaţia?
Osah doorezeh moolt reparatzya?

How much will it cost?
Cât o să coste?
Cuht oh sah costeh?

**Please can you pick me
up/give me a lift?**
Vă rog, mă puteţi lua/duce cu
maşina?
*Vah rohg, mah pootetz doocheh coo
masheenah?*

Accidents and Traffic
Offences (Violations)

**Can you help me? There has
been an accident**
Vreţi să mă ajutaţi vă rog? Am
avut un accident
*Vretz sah mah azhootatz vah rohg?
Am avoot oon akcheedent*

**Please call the police/an
ambulance**
Chemaţi vă rog poliţia/salvarea
*Kehmatz vah rohg poleetzia/
salvareya*

Is anyone hurt?
Sunt răniţi?
Sunt rahneetz?

Sorry, I didn't see the sign
Îmi pare rău, nu am văzut
tăbliţa indicatoare
*Umi pareh row, noo am vahzoot
tahbleetza indicatwareh*

Must I pay a fine? How much?
Trebuie să plătesc amendă?
Cât?
*Trebooyeh sah plahtesc amendah?
Cuht?*

Arătaţi-mi actele
Arahtatz-me acteleh
Show me your documents

HEALTH

Pharmacy (Farmacie)

**Do you have anything for a
stomach ache/headache/sore
throat/toothache?**
Aveţi ceva pentru durere de
stomac/cap/usturime de
gât/dinţi?
*Avetz cheva pentroo doorereh deh
stomac/cap/oostooreemeh deh
guht/deentz?*

R
O
M
A
N
I
A
N

I need something for diarrhoea/constipation/ a cold/a cough/insect bites/sunburn/travel (motion) sickness
Am nevoie de ceva pentru diaree/constipație/răceală/ tuse/mușcătură de insecte/ arsură de soare/rău de mașină
Am nevoye deh chevah pentroo dyaryeh/consteepatzye/rahcheyalah/ mooshcahtoorah deh insecteh/ arsoorah deh sohareh/row deh masheenah

How much/how many do I take?
Cât/câte să iau?
Cuht/cuhteh sah iaoo?

I am taking anti-malaria tablets/these pills
Iau tablete anti-malarie/ pastilele acestea
Iaoo tableteh antee - malaryeh/ pasteeleleh achestea

How often do I take it/them?
De câte ori o/le iau?
Deh cuhteh ory oh/leh iaoo?

I am/he is/she is taking this medication
Eu iau/el/ea ia medicamentele acestea
Eoo iaoo/el/ea ia medeecamenteleh achestea

How much does it cost?
Cât costă?
Cuht costah?

Can you recommend a good doctor/dentist?
Puteți recomanda un doctor/dentist bun?

Pootetz recomanda oon doctor/ dentist boon?

Is it suitable for children?
E bun pentru copii?
Eh boon pentroo copee?

Doctor (Doctor)

I have a pain here/in my arm/leg/chest/stomach
Mă doare aici/brațul/ piciorul/pieptul/stomacul
Mah doareh aich/bratzool pee- chiorool/pee-eptool/stomacool

Please call a doctor, this is an emergency
Vă rog să chemați un doctor de urgență
Vah rohg sah kematz oon doctor deh oordjentzah

I would like to make an appointment to see the doctor
Doresc să fac programare la doctor
Doresc sah fahc oh programareh lah doctol

I am diabetic/pregnant
Am diabet/sunt gravidă
Am deyabet/soont gravidah

I need a prescription for ...
Am nevoie de o rețetă pentru ...
Am nevoyeh deh oh retzetah pen- troo ...

Can you give me something to ease the pain?
Îmi puteți da ceva pentru durere?
Umi pootetz dah cheva pentroo doorereh?

I am/he is/she is allergic to penicillin
Eu sunt/el/ea este alergică la penicilină
Eoo soont/el/ea esteh alerdjeecah la penichilinah

Doare aici?
Doareh aich?
Does this hurt?

Dumneavoastră trebuie să mergeți/el/ea trebuie să meargă la spital
Doomneyavwastrah trebooyeh sah mergetz/el/ea/trebooyeh sah meargah lah spital
You must/he must/she must go to hospital

Luați astea o dată/de două/de trei ori pe zi
Looatz asteya oh datah/deh dowah/deh tray oree peh zee
Take these once/twice/three times a day

I am/he is/she is taking this medication
Eu iau/el/ea ia medicamentele acestea
Eoo iaoo/el/ea ia medeecamenteleh achestea

I have medical insurance
Am asigurare medicală
Am aseegoorareh medicalah

Dentist (Dentist)

I have toothache/my filling has come out
Mă doare o măsea/a căzut plomba
Mah dwareh oh mahseya/a cahzoot plombah

I do/do not want to have an injection
Vreau/nu vreau injecție
Vrehaoo/noo vrehaoo injectzyeh

EMERGENCIES

Help!
Ajutor!
Ajootor!

Fire!
Foc!
Fohc!

Stop
Stop!
Stop!

Call an ambulance/ a doctor/the police/the fire brigade!
Chemați salvarea/doctorul/ poliția/pompierii!
Kematz salvareya/doctorool/poleet-zya/pompee-eree!

Please may I use a telephone?
Vă rog, pot să folosesc telefonul?
Vah rohg, pot sah folosesc telephonool?

ROMANIAN

R
O
M
A
N
I
A
N

I have had my traveller's cheques/credit cards/handbag/rucksack/luggage/wallet/passport/mobile phone stolen
Mi s-au furat cecurile de călătorie/cărţile de credit/geanta/rucsacul/bagajul/portofelul/paşaportul/telefonul mobil
Me s-aw foorat checooreele de kerlertoreeyeh/cahrtzeeleh deh credeet/roocsacool/bagazhool /portofelool/pashaportul/telefonul mobyl

May I please have a copy of the report for my insurance claim?
Îmi daţi vă rog o copie a raportului pentru cererea mea de asigurare?
Unmy datzy vah rog oh kopye ah rahportoolooy pentroo cherereah meah deh asygoorare?

Can you help me I have lost my daughter/son/my companion(s)?
Mă puteţi ajuta, mi-am pierdut fiica/fiul/însoţitorul (însoţitorii)?
Mah pootetz ajoota, me-am pee-ehrdoot feeca/feeool/unsotzeetorool (unsotzeetoree)?

Please go away/leave me alone
Vă rog să plecaţi/lăsaţi-mă în pace
Vah rohg sah plecatz/lahsatz-mah uhn pacheh

I'm sorry
Îmi pare rău
Umi pareh row

I want to contact the British/American/Canadian/Irish/Australian/New Zealand/South African consulate
Vreau să contactez Consulatul Marii Britanii/American/Canadian/Irlandez/Australian/Noii Zeelande/Africii de Sud
Vreaoo sah contactez Consoolatool Maree-ee Britanee-ee/Amereecan/Canadeean/Irlandez/Aoostraleean/No-ee-ee Zehlandeh/Africhee-ee deh Sood

I'm ill/injured/lost
Sunt bolnav/lovit/m-am rătăcit
Soont bolnav/lovit/m-am rahtahcheet

We're ill/injured/lost
Suntem bolnavi/loviţi/ne-am rătăcit
Soontem bolnavee/lovitz/ne-am rahrahcheet

He is ill/injured/lost
El este bolnav/lovit/s-a rătăcit
El esteh bolnav/lovit/s-a rahtahcheet

She is ill/injured/lost
Ea este bolnavă/lovită/s-a rătăcit
Ea esteh bolnavah/lovitah/s-a rahtahcheet

They are/ill/injured/lost
Ei sunt bolnavi/loviţi/s-au rătăcit
Ey sunt bolnavee/lovitz/s-aoo rahtahcheet

RUSSIAN

INTRODUCTION

Russian is the official language of Russia, and it is still used as a second language in the other former Soviet republics. Along with Belarusian and Ukrainian, it forms the eastern branch of the Slavic languages.

Russian includes three groups of dialects: northern, southern, and the central dialect, which combines both northern and southern features. In particular, the southern and central dialects are distinguished by "*akan'je*" - coalescence of certain vowels outside of stress.

e.g.: Приятно познакомиться! [pri`yatna pazna`komitsa] (Nice to meet you!)

Word order in Russian is "free" and depends on what the speaker wants to emphasise. There are also some slight differences in meaning depending on the phrasal stress.

e.g.: There are six variants of different word order for the simple phrase "I love you"! These are as follows:

Я тебя люблю! (just the fact) - most frequent word order

`Тебя люблю! (I love you but not anybody else!)

`Люблю я тебя! (I feel love (but not hate or irritation, very often ironically))

`Тебя люблю! (I love only you)

Я `люблю тебя! (I'm mad about you)

Люблю тебя я! is another possible word order, but it is rarely used because of an inconvenient combination of vowels.

The Standard Russian used in this phrasebook is based on a central dialect of Moscow, and is one of the five official languages of the United Nations.

Addresses for Travel and Tourist Information

Australia: *Russian Consulate-General,* 7-9 Fullerton St, Woollahra NSW 2025, Tel: (2) 9326 1188. Fax: (2) 9327 5065.

Canada: *Russian Embassy*, 285 Charlotte St, Ottawa.
Tel: (613) 235 4341. Fax: (613) 236 6342.

UK: *Russian National Tourist Office*, 70 Piccadilly, London WIJ 8HP.
Tel: (020) 7495 7555. Fax: (020) 7495 8555.

USA: *Russian National Tourist Office*, 130 West 42nd St, Suite 1804, New
York, NY 10036. Tel: (212) 575 3431. Fax: (212) 575 3434.

Official tourism website: www.russia-travel.com

Russia Facts

CAPITAL: Moscow
CURRENCY: Rouble (Rb) (1Rb=100 kopeks)
OPENING HOURS: Banks: vary, but mostly Mon–Fri 0900–1700
and Sat 0900–1300. In the large cities there are 24-hr exchanges.
Shops: mostly Mon–Sat 1000–1300, 1500–1900. Sunday opening seems
to be quite erratic.
TELEPHONES: To dial in, Int. Access Code +78. Outgoing, 8 (pause) +10
and the country code.
PUBLIC HOLIDAYS: Jan 1–New Year's Day, Jan 7–Orthodox Christmas;
Feb 23–Defenders of the Motherland Day;
Mar 8–International Women's Day; May 1/2–International Labour Day;
May 9–Victory Day; Jun 12–Russian Day; Nov 7–Public Holiday.

Technical Language Hints

- Russian is a complex East Slav language but any attempt you make to
  speak it will be very much appreciated. It will make a considerable
  difference to your stay if you can master the basics of the Cyrillic
  alphabet so that you can understand road names, stations and signs.

- Russian depends upon stress: and unfortunately there is no hard and
  fast rule that dictates where the stress in a word will lie. In this guide,
  the phonetic transcriptions are split up with apostrophes to help
  show which letter combinations are stressed. When you get to a
  stressed syllable, place far more emphasis upon it than you would if
  stressing in English – Russian is a much stronger, more "harsh"-sound-
  ing language than English and this will make you more easily
  understood.

R
U
S
S
I
A
N

ESSENTIALS

Alphabet and Pronunciation

	Name	Pronounced	
А а	ah	like a in father
Б б	be	like b in but
В в	ve	like v in vine
Г г	ge	like g in great
Д д	de	like d in down
Е е	ye	like e in pen
Ё ё	yo	like yo in yoghurt
Ж ж	zhe	zh, like s in pleasure
З з	ze	like z in zoo
И и	i	like i in pin
Й й	iyu	like y in boy
К к	ka	like k in key
Л л	el'	like l in lamp
М м	em	like m in mother
Н н	en	like n in nice
О о	o	like o in cot
П п	pe	like p in pack
Р р	er	like r in right
С с	es	like s in sun
Т т	te	like t in tank
У у	u	like u in put
Ф ф	ef	like f in fun
Х х	ha	like h in hide
Ц ц	tse	like ts in cats
Ч ч	che	like ch in chicken
Ш ш	sha	like sh in shock
Щ щ	scha	like ss ch in cross check
Ъ ъ	tverdyi znak	by like b in beautiful
Ы ы	yui	like i in ill
Ь ь	myagki znak	softens consonants like m in meal
Э э	e	like a in man

Ю ю	yu	yoo like u in unit
Я я	ya	like ya in yard

Basic Words and Phrases

Yes
Да
Da

No
Нет
N'et

Please
Пожалуйста
Po`zh'alusta

Thank you
Спасибо
Spa`siba

Hello
Здравствуйте
Zdr`astvuit'e

Goodbye
До свидания
Da svi`dan'ya

Excuse me
Извините
Izvi`nit'e

Sorry
Простите
Pras`tit'e

That's O.K.
Хорошо
Harasho

Perhaps
Возможно
Vazmozhna

How
Как
Kak

When
Когда
Ka`gda

Why
Почему
Poche`mu

What
Что
Shto

Who
Кто
Kto

To
В, К, До
V, K, Do

From
Из, От
Iz, Ot

Here
Здесь
Zdes'

There
Там
Tam

I don't understand
Я не понимаю
Ya n'e pani`mayu

I don't speak Russian
Я не говорю по-русски
Ya n'e govor`yu pa `ruski

Do you speak English?
Вы говорите по-английски?
Vy govo`rit'e pa ang`liyski?

Can you please write it down?
Запишите, пожалуйста
Zapi`shit'e pa`zhalusta

Please can you speak more slowly?
Пожалуйста, говорите медленнее
Pa`zhalusta gava`rit'e `medlen'ee

Greetings

Good morning/Good afternoon/Good evening/Good night
Доброе утро/Добрый день/Добрый вечер/Спокойной ночи
`Dobroe `utra/`Dobryi den'/`Dobryi vecher/Spa`koinai `nochi

Pleased to meet you
Приятно познакомиться
Pri`yatna pazna`komitsa

How are you?
Как дела?
Kak d'ela?

I am well, thank you. And you?
Спасибо, хорошо. А у вас?
Spa`sibà hara`sho? A u vas?

My name is …
Меня зовут …
Minya zavut …

This is my friend/boyfriend/girlfriend/husband/wife/brother/sister
Это мой (моя) друг (подруга)/парень/девушка/муж/жена/брат/сестра
Eto moj (moja) drug (pad`ruga)/`paren'/`devushka/muzh/zhe`na/brat/siest`ra

Where are you travelling to?
Куда вы едете?
Kuda vy `edete?

I am/we are going to…
Я еду/мы едем в…
Ya edu/my edem v…

How long are you travelling for?
Как долго вам ехать?
Kak `dolgo vam ehat'?

Where do you come from?
Откуда вы?
At`kuda vy?

I am/we are from Australia/Britain/Canada/America
Я/Мы из Австралии/Британии/Канады/Америки
Ya/My iz Afs`traliyi/Bri`taniyi/Ka`nady/A`meriki

We are on holiday
Мы в отпуске
My v `otpuske

This is our first visit here
Мы здесь впервые
My sdes' vper`vye

How old are you?
Сколько вам лет?
`Skol'ka vam l'et?

I am ... years old
Мне ... лет
Mn'e ... l'et

**I am a business person/
doctor/journalist/manual
worker/administrator/
scientist/student/teacher**
Я бизнесмен/врач/
журналист/рабочий/
администратор/ученый/
студент/преподаватель
*Yabiznes`men/vrach/zhurna`list/ra`b
ochiy/admini`stratar/uchi`onyi/stu`de
nt/pripada`vatel'*

**I am waiting for my husband/
wife/boyfriend/girlfriend**
Я жду своего мужа/свою
жену/своего парня/свою
девушку
*Ya zhdu svoe`vo muzha/sva`yu
zhenu/svae`vo `parnya/sva`yu
`devushku*

**Would you like/may I have a
cigarette?**
Не хотите ли закурить/не
дадите ли вы мне сигарету?
*N'e ha`tit'e li zaku`rit'/ne da`dit'e li
vy mn'e siga`retu?*

Do you mind if I smoke?
Вы не возражаете, если я
закурю?
*Vy n'e vazra`zhayet'e esli ya
zaku`r'u?*

Do you have a light?
Разрешите прикурить?
Razre`shit'e priku`rit'?

Days

Monday	Tuesday
Понедельник	Вторник
Pane`del'nik	*Ftornik*

Wednesday	Thursday
Среда	Четверг
Sre`da	*Chet`verg*

Friday	Saturday
Пятница	Суббота
`Pyatnitsa	*Su`bota*

Sunday	Morning
Воскресенье	Утро
Vaskre`sen'e	*Utra*

Afternoon/Evening/Night
День/Вечер/Ночь
Den'/`Vecher/Noch'

Yesterday	Today
Вчера	Сегодня
Fche`ra	*Sevodnya*

Tomorrow
Завтра
`Zaftra

Numbers

Zero	**One**
Ноль	Один
Nol'	*A`din*
Two	**Three**
Два	Три
Dva	*Tri*
Four	**Five**
Четыре	Пять
Che`tyr'e	*Pyat'*
Six	**Seven**
Шесть	Семь
Shest'	*Sem'*
Eight	**Nine**
Восемь	Девять
`Vosem'	*`Devyat'*
Ten	**Eleven**
Десять	Одиннадцать
`Desyat'	*A`dinatsat'*
Twelve	**Thirteen**
Двенадцать	Тринадцать
Dve`natsat'	*Tri`natsat'*
Fourteen	**Fifteen**
Четырнадцать	Пятнадцать
Che`tyrnatsat'	*Pyat`natsat'*
Sixteen	**Seventeen**
Шестнадцать	Семнадцать
Shes`natsat'	*Sem`natsat'*
Eighteen	**Nineteen**
Восемнадцать	Девятнадцать
Vasem`natsat'	*Devyat`natsat'*
Twenty	**Twenty-one**
Двадцать	Двадцать один
`Dvatsat'	*`Dvatsat' adin*

Twenty-two	**Thirty**
Двадцать два	Тридцать
Dvatsat' dva	*`Tritsat'*
Forty	**Fifty**
Сорок	Пятьдесят
`Sorak	*Pede`syat*
Sixty	**Seventy**
Шестьдесят	Семьдесят
Shesde`syat	*`Semdesyat*
Eighty	**Ninety**
Восемьдесят	Девяносто
`Vosemdesyat	*Devya`nosta*
One hundred	**Five hundred**
Сто	Пятьсот
Sto	*Pyat`sot*
One thousand	**One million**
Тысяча	Миллион
`Tysyacha	*Mili`on*

Time

What time is it?
Который час?
Ka`toryi chas?

It is ...
Сейчас ... часов
Se`chas ... cha`sof

9.00
Ровно девять
`Rovna `devyat'

9.05
Девять ноль пять
`Devyat' nol' pyat'

9.15
Девять пятнадцать/четверть десятого

307

`Devyat' pyat`natsat'/`chetvert`
de`syatava

9.20
Девять двадцать
`Devyat' `dvatsat'

9.30
Половина десятого
Pala`vina de`syatava

9.35
Девять тридцать пять
`Devyat' `tritsat' pyat'

9.40
Без двадцати десять
Bez dvatsa`ti `desyat'

9.45
Без пятнадцати десять
Bez pyat`natsati `desyat'

9.50
Без десяти десять
Bez desya`ti `desyat'

9.55
Без пяти десять
Bez pya`ti `desyat'

12.00/Midday/Midnight
Двенадцать/Полдень/
Полночь
Dve`natsat'/`Polden'/`Polnach

I would like to change these traveller's cheques/this currency
Я хотел бы обменять дорожные чеки/эту валюту
Ya ha`tel by abme`nyat' da`rozhnye `cheki/etu va`l'utu

How much commission do you charge? (What is the service charge?)
Сколько вы берёте комиссионных?
`Skol'ka vy be`r'ot'e kamisi`onykh?

Can I obtain money with my Mastercard?
Могу ли я снять деньги с Мастеркард?
Magu li ya `snyat' den'gi s `Masterkard?

Where is the nearest ATM?
Где здесь ближайший банкомат?
Gde zdes' blizhayshiy bankamat?

My name is ... Some money has been wired to here for me to collect
Меня зовут ... Для меня сюда были переведены деньги
Minya zavut ... Dlya minya syuda byli perevedeny den'gi

ARRIVING AND DEPARTING

Airport

Excuse me, where is the check-in desk for ... airline?
Извините, где проходит регистрация на рейс ...?
Izvi`nit'e gd'e pra`hodit regist`ratsiya na reis ...?

What is the boarding gate for my flight?
Через какой выход идёт посадка на рейс?
`Cherez ka`koi `vykhad id'et pa`satka na reis?

What is the boarding time for my flight?
В какое время производится посадка на рейс?
F ka`koye `vremya praiz`voditsa pa`satka na reis?

How long is the delay likely to be?
Насколько задерживается рейс?
Na`skol'ka za`derzhivaetsa reis?

Where is the duty-free shop?
Где находится магазин беспошлинной торговли?
Gde na`hoditsa maga`zin bes`poshi-nai tar`govli?

Which way is the luggage reclaim?
Как пройти к выдаче багажа?
Kak prai`ti k `vydache baga`zha?

I have lost my luggage. Please can you help?
Я потерял/потеряла свой багаж. Вы не могли бы мне помочь?
Ya pate`ryal/pater`yala svoi ba`gash. Vy n'e mag`li by mn'e pa`moch?

I am flying to ...
Я лечу в ...
Ya le`chu v ...

Where is the bus for the city centre?
Откуда идет автобус в центр города?
At`kuda id'ot aftobus v `tsentr `gorada?

Trains and Boats

Where is the ticket office/information desk?
Где находится билетная касса/информационная служба?
Gde na`hoditsa bi`letnaya kasa/infarmatsy`onaya `sluzhba?

Which platform does the train/speedboat/ferry to ... depart from?
С какой платформы отправляется поезд/катер/паром?
S ka`koi plat`formy atpravl`yaetsa `poezd/`kater/pa`rom?

Where is platform ...?
Где находится платформа ...?
Gde na`hoditsa plat`forma ...?

When is the next train/boat to ...?
Когда отправляется следующий поезд/корабль в ...?
Kagda atprav`lyaetsa `sleduschiy `poezd/ka`rabl' v ...?

R
U
S
S
I
A
N

R
U
S
S
I
A
N

**Is there a later train/boat
to ...?**
Есть ли поезд/корабль позже
до ...?
Est' li `poezd/ka`rabl' `pozhe do ...?

Notices and Signs

Вагон – буфет/Вагон
ресторан
Va`gon bu`fet/Va`gon resta`ran
Buffet (Dining) car

Автобус
Af`tobus
Bus

Питьевая/техническая вода
Pit'e`vaya/teh`nicheskaya va`da
**Drinking/Non-drinking
water**

Вход
Fhot
Entrance

Выход
`Vyhat
Exit

Больница
Bal`nitsa
Hospital

Информационная служба
Infamatsy`onaya `sluzhba
Information

Камера хранения
`Kamera hra`neniya
**Left luggage
(Baggage claim)**

Автоматическая камера
хранения
*Aftama`ticheskaya `kamera
hra`neniya*
Luggage lockers

Почта
`Pochta
Post office

Платформа
Plat`forma
Platform

Железнодорожный вокзал
Zheleznada`rozhnyi vak`zal
Railway (Railroad) station

Аэропорт
Aera`port
Airport

Отделение милиции
Atde`leniye mi`litsyi
Police station

Порт
Port
Port

Ресторан
Resta`ran
Restaurant

Для курящих/Для
некурящих
*Dlya kur`yaschih/Dlya
nekur`yaschih*
Smoking/Non-smoking

Телефон
Tele`fon
Telephone

Билетная касса
Bi`letnaya `kasa
Ticket office

Окно регистрации
Ak`no regist`ratsyi
Check-in desk

Расписание
Raspi`saniye
Timetable (Schedule)

Туалеты
Tua`lety
Toilets (Restrooms)

Женский/мужской
`Zhenskiy/Mushs`koi
Ladies/Gentlemen

Метро
Met`ro
Underground (Subway)

Зал ожидания
Zal azhi`daniya
Waiting room

Buying a Ticket

**I would like a first-class/
second-class/third-class single
(one-way)/return (round-trip)
ticket to...**
Мне нужен билет первого
класса/второго класса/
третьего класса в одну
сторону/обратный (туда и
обратно) до (в) ...
*Mn`e `nuzhen bi`let `pervava
`klasa/ fta`rova `klasal`tret`eva
`klasa v adnu `storanu/ab`ratnyi
(tu`da i ad`ratna) do (v)...*

**Is it an express (fast)
train/bus?**
Это скорый поезд/
автобус-экспресс?
Eta `skoryi `poezd/aftobus-eksp`res?

**Is my rail pass valid on this
train/ferry/bus?**
Мой проездной действителен
на этом поезде/пароме/
автобусе?
*Moi praezd`noi dest`vit`el`en na
`etam `poezde/pa`rome/af tobus`e?*

**I would like an aisle/window
seat**
Я хотел(а) бы боковое
место/место у окна
*Ya by hat`el (hat`ela) by baka`voe
`m`esta/`m`esta u ak`na*

No smoking/smoking please
Места для некурящих/
курящих, пожалуйста
*M`es`ta dlya nekur`yaschih/
kur`yaschih pa`zhalusta*

We would like to sit together
Мы хотели бы места рядом
My hat"`eli by m`es`ta `ryadam

**I would like to make a seat
reservation**
Я хотел(а) бы заказать места
*Ya ha`t`el (ha`t`ela) by zaka`zat'
m`es`ta*

**I would like to reserve a
couchette/sleeper for one
person/two people/my family**
Я хотел(а) бы место/купе в
спальном вагоне для одного
человека/двух человек/моей
семьи
*Ya ha`t`el (ha`t`ela) by `m`esta/
ku`pe fl `spal`nam va`gon`e dlya*

311

adna`vo chela`veka/dvuh
chela`vek/ma`ei se`m'i

I would like to reserve a cabin
Я хотел(а) бы заказать каюту
Ya ha`t'el (ha`t'ela) by zaka`zat'
ka`yutu

Timetables (Schedules)

Прибытие
Pri`bytie
Arrival

Стоянки (Остановки)
Sta`yanki (asta`nofki)
Calls (Stops) at

Питание
Pi`tanie
Catering service

Пересадка на
Pere`satka na
Change at

Сообщение/По маршруту
Saaps`chenie/Pa marsh`rutu
Connection/Via

Ежедневно
Ezhed`nevna
Daily

Каждые сорок минут
`Kazhdye `sorak mi`nut
Every 40 minutes

Первый класс
`Pervyi klas
First class

Каждый час
`Kazhdyi chas
Hourly

Желательно бронировать места
Zhe`lat'el'na bra`niravat' mes`ta
Seat reservations are recommended

Второй класс
Fta`roi klas
Second class

Оплачивается дополнительно
Ap`lachivaetsa dapal`nit'el'na
Supplement payable

Luggage

How much will it cost to send (ship) my luggage in advance?
Сколько будет стоить отправить (погрузить) мой багаж заранее?
S`kol'ka `budet `stoit' atp`ravit'
(pagru`zit') moi ba`gash za`raneye?

Where is the left luggage (baggage claim) office?
Где находится камера хранения багажа?
Gde na`hoditsa `kamera hra`n'eniya
baga`zha?

What time do you open/close?
Во сколько вы открываете/закрываете?
Va `skol'ka vy
atkry`vaet'e/zakry`vaete?

Where are the luggage trolleys (carts)?
где находятся тележки для багажа?
Gde na`hodyatsa te`leshki dlya baga`zha?

Where are the lockers?
Где находятся автоматические камеры хранения?
Gd'e na`hodyatsa aftama`ticheskie `kamery hra`n'eniya?

I have lost my locker key
Я потерял ключ от ячейки (автоматической) камеры хранения
Ya pater`yal `klyuch at ya`cheiki (aftama`ticheskai) `kamery hra`n'eniya

On Board

Is this seat free?
Это место свободно?
Eta `mesta sva`bodna?

Excuse me, you are sitting in my reserved seat
Извините, вы сидите на моем месте
Izvi`nit'e vy si`dit'e na may`om `mest'e

Which station is this?
Какая это станция?
Ka`kaya eta `stantsiya?

What time is this train/bus/ferry/flight due to arrive/depart?
Во сколько должен прибыть/отправиться этот поезд/автобус/паром/рейс?

Va `skol'ka `dolzhen pri`byt'/ atp`ravitsa `etat `poezd/ af`tobus/ pa`rom/reis?

Travelling with Children

Do you have a high chair/ babysitting service/cot?
У вас есть высокий стульчик/служба по уходу за детьми/детская кроватка?
U vas est' vy`sokiy `stul`chik/`sluzhba pa u`hodu za d'et''mil`detskaya kra`vatka?

Where is the nursery/ playroom?
Где находится комната матери и ребенка/комната для игр?
Gd'e na`hoditsa `komnata `mat'eri i re`b'enka/ `komnata igr?

Where can I warm the baby's bottle?
Где можно подогреть детское питание?
Gd'e `mozhna pada`gret' `detskae pi`tanie?

Customs and Passports

Пожалуйста, предъявите паспорта
Pa`zhalusta predya`vite paspar`ta
Passports please

I have nothing to declare
Мне нечего декларировать
Mn'e `necheva dekla`riravat'

I have wine/spirits (alcohol)/tobacco to declare
Я хочу задекларировать

R
U
S
S
I
A
N

вино/алкогольные
напитки/табачные изделия
*Ya ha`chu zadekla`riravat'
vi`no/alka`gol'nye na`pitki/ta`bach-
nye iz`deliya*

**I will be staying for …
days/weeks/months**
Я буду находиться в стране …
дней/недель/месяцев
*Ya `budu naha`ditsa v stra`n'e …
dnei/ne`del'/`mesyatsef*

SIGHTSEEING

Asking the Way

**Excuse me, do you speak
English?**
Извините, вы говорите по-
английски?
Izvi`nit'e vy gava`rit'e pa ang`liyski?

**Excuse me, can you help me
please?**
Извините, не могли бы вы
мне помочь?
*Izvi`nit'e ne mag`li by vy mn'e
pa`moch'?*

**Where is the tourist
information office?**
Где находится служба
информации для туристов?
*Gd'e na`hoditsa `sluzhba infar`mat-
sii dlya tu`ristaf?*

**Excuse me, is this the right
way to…**
Извините, я правильно иду к …
Izvi`nit'e ya `pravil'na idu k …

**…the cathedral/the tourist
information office/the
castle/the old town?**

… собору/службе
информации для туристов/
замку/старому городу?
*…sa`boru/sluzhbe informatsii dlya
turistov/`zamku/`staramu`goradu?*

**Can you tell me the way to
the railway (railroad) station/
bus station/taxi rank/city
centre (downtown)/beach?**
Как пройти к
железнодорожному
вокзалу/автовокзалу/стоянке
такси/центру города/пляжу?
*Kak prai`ti k zhel`eznada`rozhnamu
vak`zalu/aftavak`zalu/sta`yank'e
tak`sil/`tsentru `gorada/pl`yazhu?*

Первый/Второй поворот/
налево/направо/прямо
*`P'ervyi/Fta`roi pava`rot na`leva/
na`praval`pryama*
**First/second/left/right/
straight ahead**

На углу/около светофора
Na ug`lu/`okala sveta`fora
**At the corner/at the traffic
lights**

**Where is the nearest police
station/post office?**
Где находится ближайшее
отделение милиции/
ближайшая почта?
*Gde na'hoditsa blizhaisheye atdeleniye
militsii/pachtavaye atdeleniye?*

Is it near/far?
Это близко/далеко?
Eta `bliska/dal`e`ko?

**Do I need to take a
taxi/catch a bus?**
Мне нужно взять такси/ехать
на автобусе?

R
U
S
S
I
A
N

Mn'e `nuzhna vzyat' tak`si/`ehat' na af tobus'e?

Do you have a map?
У вас есть карта?
U vas est' `karta?

Can you point to it on my map?
Вы можете показать, где это на карте?
Vy `mozhet'e paka`zat' gd'e eta na `kart'e?

Thank you for your help
Спасибо за помощь
Spa`siba za `pomasch'

How do I reach the motorway/main road?
Как выехать на шоссе/главную дорогу?
Kak `vyehat' na sha`se/`glavnuyu da`rogu?

I think I have taken the wrong turning
Мне кажется, я не там повернул
Mn'e `kazhetsya ya n'e tam paver`nul

I am looking for this address
Я ищу этот адрес
Ya is`chu `etat `adres

I am looking for the ... hotel
Я ищу гостиницу ...
Ya is`chu gas`tinitsu ...

How far is it to ... from here?
Как далеко до ... отсюда?
Kak dal'e`ko do ... ats`yuda?

Ехать прямо ... километров
`Yehat'`pryama...kila`metraf
Carry straight on for ... kilometres

Следующий поворот направо/налево
`Sl'eduschiy pava`rot nap`rava/na`leva
Take the next turning on the right/left

Поверните направо/налево на следующем перекрестке/светофоре
Paver`nit'e nap`rava/na`leva na `sleduschem perekrestke/svetofore
Turn right/left at the next crossroads/traffic lights

Вы едете (идете) не в том направлении
Vy `ed'et'e (id`'ot'e) n'e v tom naprav`l'enii
You are going in the wrong direction

Where is the cathedral/church/museum/pharmacy?
Где находится собор/церковь/музей/аптека?
Gd'e na`hoditsa sa`bor/`tserkaf'/mu`zei/ap`t'eka?

How much is the admission/entrance charge?
Сколько стоит вход?
`Skol'ka `stoit vhot?

Is there a discount for children/students/senior citizens?
Есть ли скидка для детей/студентов/пожилых?
Est' li `skitka dlya d'et'ei/stu`dentaf/pazhy`lyh?

What time does the next guided tour (in English) start?
Когда начинается следующая экскурсия (на английском языке)?
Kag`da nachi`naetsa `sleduschaya eks`kursiya (na ang`liyskam yazy`ke)?

One adult/child please
Один взрослый/ребёнок
A`din vz`roslyi/re`b'onak

Two adults/children please
Двое взрослых/детей
Dvoe vz``roslyh/d`e`t'ei

May I take photographs here?
Здесь можно фотографировать?
Z`d'es` `mozhna fatagra`firavat'?

At the Tourist Office

Do you have a map of the town/area?
У вас есть карта города/района?
U vas yest' `karta `gorada/ra`yona?

Do you have a list of accommodation?
У вас есть список гостиниц?
U vas yest' `spisak gas`tinits?

Can I reserve accommodation?
Могу ли я снять жилье?
Ma`gu li ya sn``yat`zhil``ye?

ACCOMMODATION

Hotels

I have a reservation in the name of...
У меня забронирован номер на имя ...
U me`nya zabra`niravan `nomer na `im'ya ...

I wrote to/faxed/telephoned you last month/last week
Я присылал(а) вам письмо/факс/звонил(а) по телефону в прошлом месяце/на прошлой неделе
Ya prisy`lal (a) vam pis``mo/faks/zvo`nil(a) po t`ele`fonu f `proshlam `m'esyatse/na `proshloi n`e`del`e

Do you have any rooms free?
У вас есть свободные комнаты?
U vas est' sva`bodnye `komnaty?

I would like to reserve a single/double room with/ without a bath/shower
Я бы хотел(а) снять одноместный/двухместный номер с ванной/душем/без ванной/душа
Ya by ha`t'el(a) `snyat' adna`mes-nyi/dvuh`mesnyi `nomer s `vannoi/`dushem/bez `vannoi/`dusha

I would like bed/breakfast/ (room and) full board
Мне нужно место/завтрак/(комната и) полный пансион
Mn'e `nuzhna `m'esta/ `zaftrak/(`komnata i) `polnyi pansi`on

How much is it per night?
Сколько это стоит в сутки?
`Skol'ka eta `stoit v `sutki?

Is breakfast included?
Входит ли завтрак в стоимость?
`Fhodit li `zaftrak f `stoimast'?

Do you have any cheaper rooms?
Есть ли у вас комнаты подешевле?
Yest' li u vas `komnaty pod'e`shevl'e?

I would like to see/take the room
Я бы хотел(а) посмотреть/снять комнату
Ya by ho`t'el(a) pasmat`r'et'/`sn'yat' `komnatu

I would like to stay for ... nights
Я бы хотел(а) остановиться на ... суток
Ya by ho`t'el(a) astana`vit'sa na…`sutak

The shower/light/tap/hot water doesn't work
Душ/свет/кран/горячая/вода не работает
Dush/sv'et/kran/ga`ryachaya va`da n'e ra`botaet.

At what time/where is breakfast served?
Во сколько/куда подают завтрак?
Va `skol'ka/kuda pada`yut `zaftrak?

What time do I have to check out?
Когда мне нужно выехать?

Kag`da mn'e `nuzhna `vyehat'?

Can I have the key to room number ...?
Я могу получить ключ от комнаты номер ...?
Ya ma`gu palu`chit' `kl'uch at `komnaty `nomer ...?

My room number is ...
Номер моей комнаты ...
`Nomer ma`ei `komnaty ...

My room is not satisfactory/not clean enough/ too noisy.
Please can I change rooms?
Моя комната в плохом состоянии/грязная/ слишком шумная.
Я могу поменять комнату?
Ma`ya `komnata v pla`hom sasta`yanii/`gryaznaya/`slishkam `shumnaya.Ya ma`gu pame`nyat' `komnatu' ?

Where is the bathroom?
Где находится ванная?
Gd'e na`hoditsa `vannaya?

Do you please have a safe for valuables?
Скажите, у вас есть сейф для ценностей?
Ska`zhit'e u vas yest' seif dlya `tsennost'ei?

Is there a laundry/do you wash clothes?
Есть ли у вас прачечная/вы стираете одежду?
Yest' li u vas `prachechnaya/vy sti`rayet'e a`dezhdu?

R
U
S
S
I
A
N

I would like an air-conditioned room

Я хочу снять комнату с кондиционером
Ya ha`chu `snyat' `komnatu s kanditsia`n'eram

Do you accept traveller's cheques/credit cards?

Вы принимаете дорожные чеки/кредитные карточки?
Vy prini`mayt'e da`rozhnye cheki/kreditnye `kartachki?

May I have the bill please?

Я могу получить счёт?
Ya magu palu`chit' schiot?

Excuse me, I think there may be a mistake in this bill.

Извините, мне кажется в счёте ошибка
Izvi`nit'e mn'e `kazhetsa v `schiot'e a`shipka

Youth Hostels

How much is a dormitory bed per night?

Сколько стоит место в общежитии за сутки?
`Skol'ka `stoit `mesta v apsche`zhytii za `sutki?

I am/am not an HI member

Я/Я не являюсь членом эйч-ай
Ya/Ya n'e yav`lyayus' `chlenam eitch ai

May I use my own sleeping bag?

Я могу пользоваться своим спальным мешком?
Ya ma`gu `pol'zavat'sa sva`im `spal'nym mesh`kom?

What time do you lock the doors at night?

Во сколько вы запираете бвери вечером?
Va `skol'ka vy zapi`rayet'e `dveri `vecheram?

Camping

May I camp for the night/two nights?

Я могу остановиться на день/два дня?
Ya ma`gu astana`vitsa na den'/dva dnya?

Where can I pitch my tent?

Где я могу разбить палатку?
Gd'e ya ma`gu raz`bit' pa`latku?

How much does it cost for one night/week?

Сколько это стоит в сутки/неделю?
`Skol'ka eta `stoit f `sutki/n'ed`eliu?

Where are the washing facilities?

Где находится ванная (душ)?
Gd'e na`hoditsa `vannaya (dush)?

Is there a restaurant/supermarket/swimming pool on site/nearby?

Здесь есть ресторан/супермаркет/бассейн недалеко/поблизости?
Zdes' est' resta`ran/super`market/ba`sein n'edale`ko/pab`lizasti?

Do you have a safety deposit box?

У вас есть камера хранения?
U vas est' `kamera hra`n'eniya?

EATING AND DRINKING

Cafés and Bars

I would like a cup of/two cups of/another coffee/tea
Пожалуйста, принесите
чашку/две чашки/еще
кофе/чая
Pa`zhalusta prin'e`sit'e
`chashku/dv'e `chashki/yes`cho
`kofe/`chaya

With/without milk
С молоком/без молока
S mala`kom/bes mala`ka

With/without sugar
С сахаром/без сахара
S `saharam/bes `sahara

I would like a bottle/glass/two glasses of mineral water/red wine/white wine, please
Пожалуйста, принесите
бутылку/стакан/два стакана
минеральной воды/красного
вина/белого вина
Pa`zhalusta prine`sit'e bu`tylku/sta
`kan/dva sta`kana mine`ral'noi
va`dy/`krasnava vi`na/`belava vi`na

I would like a beer/two beers, please
Пожалуйста, принесите
пиво/два пива
Pa`zhalusta prin'e`sit'e piva/dva piva

Please may I have some ice?
Пожалуйста, принесите льда
Pa`zhalusta prin'e`sit'e l'da

Do you have any matches/cigarettes/cigars?
У вас продаются
спички/сигареты/сигары?

U vas prada`yutsa
`spichki/siga`r'ety/si`gary?

Restaurants

Can you recommend a good/cheap restaurant in this area?
Вы можете порекомендовать
здесь хороший/недорогой
ресторан?
Vy mozhet'e parekamenda`vat'
zdes' ha`roshyi/nedara`goi resta`ran?

I would like a table for ... people
Я хочу заказать столик на ...
человек
Ya ha`chu zaka`zat' `stolik na ...
chela`vek

Do you have a non-smoking area?
У вас есть зал для
некурящих?
U vas yest' zal dlya neku`ryaschih?

Waiter! Waitress!
Официант! Официантка!
Afitsiant! Afitsiantka!

Excuse me, please may we order?
Извините, мы можем сделать
заказ?
Izvi`nit'e my `mozhem `sdelat'
za`kas?

Do you have a set menu/children's menu/wine list in English?
У вас есть меню/детское
меню/список вин на
английском?
U vas yest' men'u/detskaye
menu/`spisak vin na ang`liyskam?

319

R
U
S
S
I
A
N

Do you have any vegetarian dishes?
У вас есть какие-нибудь вегетарианские блюда?
U vas est' kakiye-nibud' vegetarian-skiye blyuda?

Do you have any local specialities?
У вас есть какие-нибудь местные блюда?
U vas yest' ka`kie ni`but' `mesnye `bl'uda?

Are vegetables included?
Включены ли овощи в счёт?
Fkl'uche`ny li `ovoschi v sch'ot?

Could I have it well-cooked/medium/rare please?
Можно поджарить хорошо/средне/с кровью?
`Mozhna pad`zharit' hara`sho/`srednе/s `krov'yu?

What does this dish consist of?
Из чего приготовлено это блюдо?
Is che`vo priga`tovlena eta `bl'uda?

I am a vegetarian. Does this contain meat?
Я вегетарианец. Здесь есть мясо?
Ya vegetarianets. Zdes' est' myasa?

I do not eat nuts/dairy products/meat/fish
Я не ем орехи/молочные продукты/мясо/рыбу
Ya ne yem a`rehi/ma`lochnye pra`dukty/`myasa/`rybu

Not (very) spicy please
Не (очень) острый (ое), пожалуйста
N'e (`otchen') `ostryi(aya) pa`zhalusta

I would like the set menu please
Принесите, пожалуйста, меню
Prin'e`sit'e pa`zhalusta me`n'u

We have not been served yet
Мы все еще ожидаем обслуживания
My fsyo escho azhidaem absluzhivaniya

Please bring a plate/knife/fork
Пожалуйста, принесите тарелку/нож/вилку
Pazhalusta, prinesite tarelku/nosh/vilku

Excuse me, this is not what I ordered
Извините, это не то, что я заказывал(а)
Izvinit'e eta ne to shto ya za`kazy-val(a)

May I have some/more bread/water/coffee/tea?
Можно мне (ещё) хлеба/воды/кофе/чая?
`Mozhna mn'e es`cho `hl'eba/va`dy/kafe/chaya?

May I have the bill please?
Я могу получить счёт?
Ya ma`gu palu`chit' schiot?

Does this bill include service?
Стоимость обслуживания входит в счёт?

320

`Stiomast' ap`sluzhyvaniya `fhodit f `schiot?

Do you accept traveller's cheques/Mastercard/ US dollars?
Вы принимаете дорожные чеки/Мастер кард/ американские доллары?
Vy prini`mayet'e da`rozhnye `cheki/Master`kard/ameri`kanskie `dolary?

Can I have a receipt please?
Вы можете дать чек?
Vy `mozhet'e dat' chek?

Where is the toilet (restroom) please?
Где находится туалет?
Gd'e na`hoditsa tua`let?

On the Menu

Завтрак/Обед/Ужин
Zaftrak/Abet/Uzhin
Breakfast/Lunch/Dinner

Первые блюда
`Pervye `bl'uda
First courses

Супы
Su`py
Soups

Основные блюда
Asnav`nye `bl'uda
Main courses

Рыбные блюда
`Rybnye `bl'uda
Fish dishes

Мясные блюда
Myas`nye `bl'uda
Meat dishes

Говядина
Gavyadina
Beef

Стейк
Steik
Steak

Свинина
Svinina
Pork

Телятина
Telyatina
Veal

Цыпленок
Tsyplenak
Chicken

Ягненок
Yagnyonak
Lamb

Ветчина
Vechina
Ham

Вегетарианские блюда
Vegetari`anskiye `bl'uda
Vegetarian dishes

Овощи
Ovaschi
Vegetables

Жареный картофель/фри
Zharenyi kartofel'/fri
Chips (french fries)

Картофель
отварной/соте/пюре
Kartofel' atvarnoy/sote/pyure
Boiled/sauté/mashed potatoes

Рис
Ris
Rice

Десерты
De`serty
Desserts

R
U
S
S
I
A
N

321

**R
U
S
S
I
A
N**

Мороженое
Marozhenaye
Ice cream

Торты
Tarty
Cakes

Пирожные
Pirozhnyye
Pastries

Фрукты
Frukty
Fruit

Хлеб
Hlep
Bread

Булочки
bulachki
Rolls

Тост
Tost
Toast

Масло
Masla
Butter

Соль/перец
Sol'/perets
Salt/pepper

Сахар
Sahar
Sugar

Фирменные блюда
`Firmennye `bl'uda
Specialities

Местные национальные
блюда
Mesnyye natsianal'nyye blyuda
Local specialities

Утвержденное меню
Utverzhdyonnaye menu
Set menu

Карта вин
Karta vin
Wine list

Красные вина
Krasnyye vina
Red wines

Белые вина
Belyye vina
White wines

Розовые вина
Rozavyye vina
Rosé wines

Игристые вина
Igristyye vina
Sparkling wines

Пиво
Piva
Beer

Пиво в бутылках/ Бочковое
пиво
Piva v butyilkah/bachkavoye piva
**Bottled beer/draught
(draft) beer**

Безалкогольные напитки
Bezalkagol'nyye napitki
Non-alcoholic drinks

Минеральная вода
Mineral'naya vada
Mineral water

Фруктовые соки
Fruktovyye soki
Fruit juices

Апельсиновый сок
Apil'sinavyi sok
Orange juice

Лимонад
Limanat
Lemonade

Лед
Lyot
Ice

Кофе с молоком/черный
кофе/кофе эспрессо
*Kofe s malakom/chornyi kofe/kofe
espresso*
**White coffee/black
coffee/espresso coffee**

Чай с молоком/с лимоном
Chay s malakam/s limonam
Tea with milk/with lemon

Шоколад
Shakalat
Chocolate (drink)

Молоко
Malako
Milk

Закуски
Zakuski
**Snacks/
Light meals**

Салаты
Salaty
Salads

Бутерброды
Buterbrody
Sandwiches

Яйца
Yaitsa
Eggs

Сосиска
Sasiska
Sausage

Яйца вареные/
жареные/омлет
Yaitsa varyonyye/ zharenyye/amlet
Boiled/fried/scrambled eggs

Typical Local Dishes

Щи
S`chi
Schi (soup made of sour cabbage)

Блины
Bli`ny
Bliny (a kind of pancake)

Пельмени
Pel`meni
Pelmeni (boiled dough with meat filling)

Черная/красная икра
`Ch'ornaya/`Krasnaya Ik`ra
Black/Red caviar

Растегаи
Rast'e`gai
Rastegai (rich dough filled with meat and baked)

Пирожки
Pirazh`ki
Pirozhki (rich dough filled with meat/cabbage/fruit baked or fried)

Сметана
Sme`tana
Soured cream

GETTING AROUND

Public Transport

Where is the bus stop/coach stop/nearest metro (subway) station?
Где находится остановка автобуса/междугородного автобуса/ближайшая станция метро?
Gd'e na`hoditsa asta`nofka af tobusa/ mezhduga`rodnava af tobusa/ `blizhayshaya `stantsya met`ro?

When is the next/last bus to ...?
Когда идет следующий/ последний автобус в ...?
Kag`da i`d'ot `sleduschiy/pas`ledniy af tobus f...?

How much is the fare to the city centre (downtown)/ railway (railroad) station/ airport?
Сколько стоит доехать до центра города/ железнодорожного вокзала/аэропорта?
`Skol'ka stoit da`ehat' da `tsentra `gorada/zheleznada`rozhnava vak`zala/aera`porta?

R
U
S
S
I
A
N

Will you tell me when to get off?
Вы скажете, когда мне выходить?
Vy `skazhet'e, kag`da mn'e vyha`dit'?

Does this bus go to...?
Этот автобус идет в ...?
`Etat af tobus i`d'ot f...?

Which number bus goes to..?
Какой номер автобуса идет в ...?
Ka`koi `nomer af tobusa i`d'ot f...?

May I have a single (one-way)/return (round-trip)/day ticket/book of tickets?
Дайте, пожалуйста билет на одну поездку/туда и обратно/ проездной на один дэнь/ билетную книжку
`Daite, pa`zhalusta bi`l'et na `adnu pa`estku/tu`da i ab`ratna/ praezd`noi na a`din d'en'/bi`l'etnuyu `knishku

---

Taxis (Такси)

I would like to go to... How much will it cost?
Я бы хотел(а) доехать до ... сколько это стоит?
Ya by ha`tel(a) da`ehat' do... `skol`- ka `eta `stoit?

Please may I stop here?
Остановите, пожалуйста, здесь
Astana`vit'e pa`zhalusta zd'es'

I would like to order a taxi today/tomorrow at 2pm to go from...to...
Я бы хотел(а) заказать такси сегодня/завтра в два часа дня, чтобы доехать из ... до ...
Ya by ha`tel(a) zaka`zat' tak`si se`vodnya/`zaftra f dva cha`sa dnya `shtoby da`ehat' iz...do

---

Entertainment

Can you recommend a good bar/nightclub?
Вы можете пореко мендовать хороший бар/ночной клуб?
Vy `mozhet'e parekamenda`vat' ha`roshiy bar/nach`noy klub?

Do you know what is on at the cinema (playing at the movies)/theatre at the moment?
Вы не знаете, что сейчас идет в кино/театре?
Vy n'e `znayet'e shto sey`chas id'ot f kino/`tyatr'e?

I would like to book (purchase) ... tickets for the matinee/evening performance on Monday
Я бы хотел(а) заказать (купить) билеты на утреннее/вечернее представление в понедельник
Ya by ha`tel(a) zaka`zat' (ku`pit') bi`l'ety na `utren'nyeye/ve`chernyeye pretsta`vleniye f pane`del'nik

What time does the film/ performance start?
Во сколько начинается фильм/спектакль?

*Va `skol'ka nachi`nayetsa
fil'm/sp`ek`takl'?*

COMMUNICATIONS

Post

**How much will it cost to
send a letter/postcard/this
package to Britain/Ireland/
America/Canada/Australia/
New Zealand?**

Сколько стоит отправить
письмо/открытку/эту
посылку в Британию/
Ирландию/Америку/Канаду/
Австралию/Новую Зеландию?

*`Skol'ka `stoit atp`ravit'
pis''mo/atk`rytku/etu pa`sylku f
Bri`taniyu/ir`landiyu/A`m'eriku/
Ka`nadu/Afst`raliyu/`Novuyu
Z'e`landiyu?*

**I would like one stamp/two
stamps**

Дайте, пожалуйста, одну/две
марки

`Dait'e, pa`zhalusta, ad`nu/dvye `marki

**I'd like ... stamps for post-
cards to send abroad, please**

Дайте, пожалуйста, ...
международных марок для
открыток

*`Dayt'e, pa`zhalusta, ... m'ezh-
duna`rodnyh `marok dlya atk`rytak*

Phones

**I would like to make a
telephone call/reverse the
charges to (make a collect
call to)...**

Я бы хотел(а) позвонить/за
счет вызываемого абонента
в ...

*Ya by ha`tel(a) pazva`nit'/za schiot
vyzy`vayemava aba`nenta v...*

**Which coins do I need for
the telephone?**

Какие монеты нужны для
телефона?

*Ka`kiye ma`nety nuzh`ny dlya
t'el'e`fona?*

The line is engaged (busy)

Линия занята

`Liniya zanya`ta.

The number is ...

Номер ...

`Nomer...

Hello, this is ...

Здравствуйте, это ...

`Zdrastvuit'e, eta...

Please may I speak to ..?

Извините, я могу поговорить
с ...?

Izvi`nit'e, ya ma`gu pagava`rit' s ...?

**He/she is not in at the
moment. Please can you call
back?**

Его/её сейчас нет.
Пожалуйста, перезвоните
позже

*Ye`vo se`chas ne't. Pa`zhalusta,
p'erezva`nit'e `pozhe*

R
U
S
S
I
A
N

SHOPPING

Shops

Книги/канцтовары
`Knigi/kantsta`vary
Bookshop/stationery

Ювелирный/подарки
Yuve`lirniy/pa`darki
Jeweller/Gifts

Обувь
`Obuf'
Shoes

Хозтовары
Hosta`vary
Hardware

Парикмахерская
Parik`maherskaya
Hairdresser

Булочная
`Bulachnaya
Baker

Супермаркет
Super`market
Supermarket

Фототовары
Fotota`vary
Photo shop

Туристическое бюро
Turis`ticheskaye byu`ro
Travel agent

Аптека
Ap`t'eka
Pharmacy

In the Shops

What time do the shops open/close?
Во сколько открываются/
закрываются магазины?
*Va `skol'ka atkryvayutsya/
zakry`vayutsa maga`ziny?*

Where is the nearest market?
Где находится ближайший
рынок?
Gd'e na`hoditsa bli`zhayshiy `rynak?

Can you show me the one in the window/this one?
Вы можете показать мне это
на витрине/это?
*Vy `mozhet'e paka`zat' mnye eta
na vit`rinye/`eta?*

Can I try this on?
Я могу это примерить?
Ya ma`gu `eta pri`m'erit'?

What size is this?
Какой это размер?
Ka`koi raz`mer?

This is too large/too small/ too expensive. Do you have any others?
Это слишком большого
размера/слишком
маленького размера/
слишком дорого.
У вас есть другие?
*`Eta `slishkam bal`shova
rahzmyerah/`slishkam `mal'en'kava
raz`mera/`slishkam `doraga. U vas
yest' dru`gie?*

**R
U
S
S
I
A
N**

My size is…
Мой размер …
Moi raz`mer…

Where is the changing room/children's/cosmetic/ladieswear/menswear/food department?
Где примерочная/детский/парфюмерный/женский/мужской/продовольственный отдел?
Gd'e pri`merachnaya/ `d'etskiy/parfyu`merniy/zhenskiy/muzhskoy/prada`vol`stvenniy at`del?

I would like a quarter of a kilo/half a kilo/a kilo of bread/butter/ham/this fruit
Дайте, пожалуйста, двести пятьдесят граммов/полкилограмма/килограмм хлеба/масла/ветчины/этих фруктов
`Dait'e, pa`zhalusta, `dvesti pyade`syat `grammav/polkilagrama/kilagram `hl'eba/`masla/vetchniyi/`etih `fruktaf

How much is this?
Сколько это стоит?
`Skol'ka eta `stoit?

I'll take this one, thank you
Я возьму это, спасибо
Ya va`z`mu eta, spa`siba

Do you have a carrier (shopping) bag?
У вас есть пакет (хозяйственная сумка)?
U vas est' paket (hazyaistvennaya sumka)?

Do you have anything cheaper/larger/smaller/of better quality?
У вас есть что-нибудь дешевле/больше/меньше/лучшего качества?
U vas yest' shtoni`bud' de`shevl' e/ `bol'she/`men'she/`lutsheva `kachestva?

I would like a film/to develop this film for this camera
Я бы хотел купить пленку/проявить эту пленку из этого фотоаппарата
Ya by ha`t'el ku`pit' `pl'onku/praya`vit' `pl'onku iz `etava fotapa`rata

I would like some batteries, the same size as this old one
Дайте, пожалуйста, батарейки такого же размера, как вот эта старая
`Dait'e, pa`zhalusta, bata`reiki ta`kova zhe raz`mera, kak vot `eta `staraya

Would you mind wrapping this for me, please?
Пожалуйста, заверните это
Pa`zhalusta, zaver`nit'e `eta

Sorry, but you seem to have given me the wrong change
Простите, но, кажется, вы неправильно дали мне сдачу
Pras`tit'e no `kazhetsa vy n'ep `ravil'na `dali mnye `sdachu

MOTORING

Car Hire (Rental)

I have ordered (rented) a car in the name of...
Я заказал (взял напрокат)
машину на имя ...
*Ya zaka`zal (vzyial na pra`kat)
ma`shinu na `imya…*

How much does it cost to hire (rent) a car for one day/two days/a week?
Сколько стоит нанять (взять
напрокат) машину в день/за
два дня/за неделю?
*`Skol'ka stoit na`nyat' (vzyat'
napra`kat) ma`shinu v den'/za dva
dnya/za ne`delyu?*

Is the tank already full of petrol (gas)?
Бак уже заправлен
бензином?
Bak uzhe zap`ravl'en ben`zinam?

Is insurance and tax included? How much is the deposit?
Включена ли страховка и
налоги? Каков размер
залога?
*Fklyuche`na li stra`hofka i na`logi?
Ka`kof raz`mer za`loga?*

By what time must I return the car?
К которому часу я должен
(должна) вернуть машину?
*F ka`toram cha`su ya `dolzhen
(dalzh`na) ver`nut' ma`shinu?*

I would like a small/large/ family/sports car with a radio/cassette
Я бы хотел взять
небольшую/большую/
семейную/спортивную
машину с радио/
магнитофоном
*Ya by ha`tel vzyat' nebal`shuyu/bal'
`shuyu/semeinuyu/spar`tivnuyu
ma`shinu s `radio/magnita`fonam*

Do you have a road map?
У вас есть карта
автомобильных дорог?
*U vas `yest' `karta aftama`bilnyh
da`rog?*

Parking

How long can I park here?
Как долго здесь можно
стоять?
Kak `dolga zdes' `mozhna sta`yat'?

Is there a car park near here?
Есть ли автостоянка
недалеко?
Yest' li aftasta`yanka n'edal'e`ko?

At what time does this car park close?
Во сколько закрывается эта
стоянка?
*Va `skol'ka zakry`vaetsa eta
sta`yanka?*

Signs and Notices

Одностороннее движение
Adnasta`ron'nyee dvi`zhenie
One way

Въезд запрещен
`Vyezd zapr`es`chon
No entry

Парковка запрещена
Par`kofka zapresche`na
No parking

Объезд
Ab``yezd
Detour (Diversion)

Стоп
Stop
Stop

Уступи дорогу
Ustu`pi da`rogu
Give way (Yield)

Гололёд
Gala`l'od
Slippery road

Обгон запрещен
Ab`gon zapr`es`ch'on
No overtaking

Опасность!
Apasnast'!
Danger!

At the Filling Station
(На Автозаправке)

**Unleaded (lead free)/
standard/premium/diesel**
Неэтилированный/обычный/
высшево качества/дизельное
топливо
*Ne`eeti`lirovannyi/a`bychnyi/`vysheva
`kachestva/`diz`el'naye `topliva*

Fill the tank please
Заправьте, пожалуйста, бак
Zap`raf't'e, pa`zhalusta bak

Do you have a road map?
У вас есть карта
автомобильных дорог?
*U vas `yest' `karta aftama`bilnyh
da`rog?*

How much is the car wash?
Сколько стоит помыть
машину?
`Skol'ka `stoit pa`myt' ma`shinu?

Breakdowns

I've had a breakdown at...
У меня поломалась машина
на ...
*U me`nya pala`malas' ma`shina
na...*

**I am a member of the ...
[motoring organisation]**
Я являюсь членом ...
Ya yavlyayus' chlenom ...

**I am on the road from ...
to...**
Я нахожусь на дороге из ...
в ...
*Ya naha`zhus' na da`rog'e iz ...
v ...*

I can't move the car.
Can you send a tow-truck?
Я не могу завести машину.
Вы можете прислать тягач?
Ya n'e ma`gu zave`sti ma`shinu vy `mozhet'e pri`slat' tya`gach?

I have a flat tyre
Я проколол шину
Ya praka`lol `shinu

The windscreen (windshield) has smashed/cracked
Лобовое стекло разбилось/треснуло
Laba`voye stek`lo raz`bilas'/`tresnula

There is something wrong with the engine/brakes/lights/steering/gearbox/clutch/exhaust
Что-то слуилось с двигателем/тормозами/фарами/рулевым управлением/коробкой передач/сцеплением/глушителем
'Shtota slu'chilas' s 'dvigat'elem/tormozami/farami/rulevim upravleniem/ka'ropkaiper,e,dach/stsep'lyeniem/glu'shityel'em

It's overheating
Он перегревается
On peregre`vayetsa

It won't start
Он не заводится
On n'e za`voditsa

Where can I get it repaired?
Где это можно починить?
Gd'e eta `mozhna pachi`nit'?

Can you take me there?
Вы можете отбуксировать меня туда?
Vy `mozhet'e atbuk`sirovat' me`nya tu`da?

Will it take long to fix?
Много ли времени уйдёт на ремонт?
`Mnoga li `vrem'eni ui`d'ot na re`mont?

How much will it cost?
Сколько это будет стоить?
`Skol'ka eto `budit `stoit'?

Please can you pick me up/give me a lift?
Подвезите меня, пожалуйста
Padve`zit'e me`nya, pa`zhalusta

Accidents and Traffic Offences (Violations)

Can you help me? There has been an accident
Вы можете мне помочь?
Произошла авария
Vy mozhete mne pamoch?
Praizashla avariya

Please call the police/an ambulance
Пожалуйста, вызовите милицию/скорую помощь
Pazhalusta, vyzavite militsiyu/skoruyu pomasch

Is anyone hurt?
Кто-нибудь пострадал?
Kto-nibud' pastradal?

I'm sorry, I didn't see the sign
Простите, я не увидел знака
Pras`tit'e ya n'e u`videl `znaka

Must I pay a fine? How much?
Я должен заплатить штраф?
Сколько?
*Ya `dolzhen zapla`tit' shtraf
`Skol'ka?*

Предъявите ваши документы
Predyavit'e vashi dakumenty
Show me your documents

HEALTH

Pharmacy (Аптека)

Do you have anything for a stomach ache/headache/sore throat/toothache?
У вас есть что-нибудь от боли в животе/головной боли/ангины/зубной боли?
U vas yest' shtoni`bud' at `boli v zhiva`t'e/galav`noy `boli/an`giny/zub`noy `boli?

I need something for diarrhoea/constipation/a cold/a cough/insect bites/sunburn/travel (motion) sickness
Мне нужно что-нибудь от поноса/запора/простуды/кашля/укусов насекомых/солнечного ожога/укачивания
Mne `nuzhna sntoni`bud' at pa`nosa/za`pora/pras`tudy/`kashlya/u`kusaf nase`komyh/`solnechnava `azhoga/`ukachivaniya

How much/how many do I take?
Сколько нужно принимать?
`Skol'ka `nuzhna prini`mat'?

I am taking anti-malaria tablets/these pills
Я принимаю таблетки против малярии/эти капсулы
Ya prini`mayu tab`letki `protiv malya`rii/`eti `kapsuly

How often do I take it/them?
Как часто их нужно принимать?
Kak `chasta ih `nuzhna prini`mat'?

I am/he is/she is taking this medication
Я/он/она принимает это лекарство
Ya/on/a`na prini`mayet `eta le`karstva

How much does it cost?
Сколько это стоит?
`Skol'ka `eta `stoit?

Can you recommend a good doctor/dentist?
Вы можете порекомендовать хорошего врача/зубного врача?
Vy `mozhet'eparekamenda`vat' `harosheva vra`cha/zub`nova vra`cha?

Is it suitable for children?
Это подходит для детей?
`Eta pat`hodit dlya d'e`tey?

Doctor (Врач)

I have a pain here/in my arm/leg/chest/stomach
У меня болит здесь/рука/нога/грудь/живот
U me`nya ba`lit zdes'/ru`ka/na`ga/grud'/zhi`vot

R
U
S
S
I
A
N

Please call a doctor, this is an emergency

Пожалуйста, срочно вызовите врача

Pa`zhalusta, `srochna `vyzavit'e vra`cha

I would like to make an appointment to see the doctor

Мне нужно записаться на прием к врачу

Mnye `nuzhna zapi`satsa na pri`yom k vra`chu

I am diabetic/pregnant

Я диабетик/беременна

Ya dia`betik/b'e`remena

I need a prescription for…

Мне нужен рецепт для …

Mnye nuzhen ret`sept dlya…

Can you give me something to ease the pain?

Вы можете дать мне что-нибудь болеутоляющее?

Vy `mozhet'e dat' mnye shtoni`bud' bol'eut`lyayuschee?

I am/he is/she is/allergic to penicillin

У меня/него/неё/аллергия на пенициллин

U me`nya/ne`vo/ne`yo/aler`giya na penitsy`lin

Здесь болит?

Zdes' ba`lit?

Does this hurt?

Вы должны/он должен/она должна обратиться в больницу

Vy dolzh`ny/on `dolzhen/a`na dolzh`na abra`titsa v bal``nitsu

You must/he must/she must go to hospital

Принимайте это один/два/три раза в день

Prini`mayt'e `eto ad`in/deva/tri raz v den'

Take these once/twice/three times a day

I am/he is/she is taking this medication

Я/он/она принимает это лекарство

Ya/on/a`na prini`mayet `eta le`karstva

I have medical insurance

У меня есть медицинская страховка

U me`nya yest' medit`synskaya stra`hofka

Dentist (Зубной Врач)

I have toothache/my filling has come out

У меня болит зуб/выпала пломба

U me`nya ba`lit zub/`vypala `plomba

I do/do not want to have an injection first

Я хочу/не хочу, чтобы мне сначала сделали укол

Ya ha`chu/n'e ha`chu, `ch'toby mne sna`chala `sdelali u`kol

EMERGENCIES

Help!
Помогите!
Pama`git'e!

Fire!
Пожар!
Pa`zhar!

Stop!
Стой!
Stoy!

Call an ambulance/a doctor/the police/the fire brigade!
Вызовите скорую/врача/милицию/пожарных!
`Vyzavit'e `skoruyu/vra`cha/mi`lit-siyu/pa`zharnyh!

Please may I use a telehone?
Я могу от вас позвонить?
Ya ma`gu at vas pazva`nit'?

I have had my traveller's cheques/credit cards/handbag/rucksack/luggage/wallet/passport/mobile phone stolen
У меня украли дорожные чеки/кредитные карточки/сумочку/рюкзак/багаж/кошелёк/паспорт/мобильный телефон
U me`nya uk`rali da`rozhnye `cheki/kre`ditnye `kartachki/ `sumachku/ryuk`zak/ba`gash/kashe`l'yok/paspart/mabil'nyi telefon

May I please have a copy of the report for my insurance claim?
Можно мне взять копию протокола для подачи страхового иска?
Mozhna mne vzyat' kopiyu pratako-la dlya padachi strahavova iska?

Can you help me? I have lost my daughter/son/my companion(s)
Помогите, пожалуйста, моя дочь/мой сын/товарищ/потерялся (лась)
Pama`gite, pa`zhalusta, ma`ya doch'/moy syn/ta`varisch/pat'er`yalsya (las')

Please go away/leave me alone!
Уходите! Оставьте меня в покое!
Uha`dit'e! As`taf't'e me`nya f pa`koye!

I'm sorry
Простите (Мне очень жаль)
Pras`titye (Mn'e `ochen' zhal')

I want to contact the British/American/Canadian/Australian/New Zealand/South African Consulate
Мне нужно связаться с Британским/Американским/Канадским/Австралийским/Новозеландским/Южноафриканским Консульством
Mn'e `nuzhna svya`zatsa s Britaniys'kym/Ameri`kanskim/Ka`natskim/Afstra`liyskim/Navaze`landskim/Yuzhnaafri`kan-skim `Konsul'stvam

I'm/we're/he is/she is/ill/lost/injured
Я/мы/он/она/заболел(а)/
потерялся(лась)/пострадал(а)
*Ya/my/on/a`na/zaba`lel(a)/
pat'e`ryalsya(las')/pastra`dal(a)*

They are/ill/lost/injured
Они/заболели/потерялись/
пострадали
A`ni/zabal``eli/pate`r'yalis'/pastra`dali

SLOVENIAN

SLOVENIAN

INTRODUCTION

Slovenian is the official language of Slovenia. In spite of the country's small size, the dialects are numerous and differ greatly. The oldest identifiable text dates from about 1000 AD, and regular writing and printing in the language began in 1551 AD. After about 1600 AD, it declined in use until the 19th century, but nowadays it is spoken by nearly 2 million people in Slovenia alone.

Addresses for Travel and Tourist Information

Australia: *Slovenian Consulate General,* 86 Parramatta Rd, Camperdown, Sydney NSW 2050. Tel: (2) 9517 1591. Fax: (2) 9519 8889.

Canada: *Slovenian Consulate,* 8 King St East, Suite 1800, Toronto, Ontario M5C 1B5.

UK: *Slovenian Tourist Office,* The Barns, Woodlands End, Mells, Frome, Somerset BA11 3QD. Tel: (01373) 814233. Fax: (01373) 813444.

USA: *Slovenian Tourist Office,* 2929 East Commercial Bvd, Suite 201, Fort Lauderdale, FL 33308. Tel: (954) 491 0112. Fax: (954) 771 9841.

Official tourism website: www.slovenia-tourism.si.

Slovenia Facts

CAPITAL: Ljubljana
CURRENCY: Tolar (SIT); 1 SIT = 100 stotins.
OPENING HOURS: Banks: vary, but mostly Mon–Fri 0900–1200 and 1400–1630, Sat 0900–1100. Shops: mostly Mon–Fri 0700–1900, Sat 0730–1300. Museums: larger ones 1000–1800, many smaller ones 1000–1400; some close Mon.
TELEPHONES: To dial in, +386. Outgoing, 00 and the country code. Police, 113. Fire, Ambulance 112.
PUBLIC HOLIDAYS: 1–2 Jan; 8 Feb; Easter Sun–Mon; 27 Apr; 1–2 May; 25 June; 15 Aug; 31 Oct; 1 Nov; 25–26 Dec.

Technical Language Hints

- Slovenian uses the Latin alphabet, with diacritic marks on letters c, s and z. These letters need care in pronunciation:
- The diacritic c: pronounced as 'ch' in 'chop',
- The diacritic s: pronounced as 'sh' in 'shall',
- The diacritic z: pronounced as 'zh' in 'Doctor Zhivago' or 'su' in 'measure' or 'leisure'.

Slovenian has masculine, feminine and neuter endings for verbs, adjectives and some nouns. Where appropriate the feminine ending (a) has been added and should be used. In other places plural verb endings are offered.

ESSENTIALS

Alphabet and Pronunciation

	Name	Pronounced
A a	ah	ah as in father
B b	beh	b as in bet
C c	tseh	ts as in cats
Č č	ch	ch as in check
D d	deh	d as in door
E e	eh	e as in bed
F f	eff	f as in fast
G g	geh	g as in got
H h	hah	h as in house
I i	ee	ee sound like the i in machine
J j	yuh	y as in yes
K k	kah	k as in king; kd together are pronounced as gd
L l	ell	l as in like
M m	em	m as in mother
N n	en	n as in not
O o	o	aw sound like the o in bored
P p	peh	p as in paste
R r	err	rolled r as found in Scottish English

	Name	Pronounced
S s	es	s as in sit
Š š	sh	sh as in shut
T t	te	t as in ton
U u	oo	oo sound as in boot
V v	veh	v as in vest; but v before a consonant makes a w sound
Z z	zeh	z as in zoo
Ž ž	zh	zh sound like the s in pleasure
Q q	koo	not a native Slovenian letter
X x	iks	not a native Slovenian letter
W w	dvoyny veh	not a native Slovenian letter
Y y	ypsylon	not a native Slovenian letter

**S
L
O
V
E
N
I
A
N**

Basic Words and Phrases

Yes
Ja
Ya

No
Ne
Neh

Please
Prosim
Prosseem

Thank you
Hvala
Khvala

Hello
Zdravo
Zdravo

Goodbye
Nasvidenje
Nassveedenyeh

Excuse me
Prosim
Prosseem

Sorry
Oprostite
Oprossteeteh

That's O.K.
V redu je
Oo-reh-doo yeh

Perhaps
Morda
Mor-duh

How
Kako
Kako

When
Kdaj
Gday (pron. g'die)

Why
Zakaj
Zakay

What
Kaj
Kay

Who
Kdo
Gdo

To
Do
Do (as in dot)

From
Od
Od

Here
Tukaj
Tookay

There
Tam
Tam

I don't understand
Ne razumem
Neh razoomem

I don't speak Slovenian
Ne govorim slovensko
Neh govoreem slovensko

Do you speak English?
Govorite angleško?
Govoreeteh angleshko?

Can you please write it down?
Lahko to napišete, prosim?
Lakhko to napeesheteh, prosseem?

Please can you speak more slowly?
Lahko govorite počasneje, prosim?
Lakhko govoreeteh pochasneyeh, prosseem?

Greetings

**Good morning/
Good afternoon/
Good evening/Good night**
Dobro jutro/Dober dan/Dober večer/Lahko noč
Dobro yootro/dobber dan/dobber vecher/lakhko noch

Pleased to meet you
Me veseli/Veseli me, da sem vas spoznal(a)
Meh vesselee/vesselee da sem vass spoznal(a)

How are you?
Kako ste?
Kako steh?

I am well, thank you. And you?
Dobro, hvala. Pa vi?
Dobro, khvala. Pa vee?

My name is ...
Ime mi je ...
Eemeh mee yeh ...

This is my friend/boyfriend/ girlfriend/husband/wife/ brother/sister
To je moj (a) prijatelj (ica)/ (moj) fant/(moje) dekle/ (moj) mož/(moja) žena/(moj) brat/(moja) sestra
To yeh moy (a) preeyatel (yitsa)/(moy) fant/(moyeh) dekleh/(moy) mozh/(moya) zhenna/(moy) brat/(moya) sesstra

Where are you travelling to?
Kam potujete?
Kam potooyeteh?

I am/we are going to...
Potujem/o v...
Potooyem/o v...

How long are you travelling for?
Koliko časa boste na potovanju?
Koleeko chassa bossteh na potovanyoo?

Where do you come from?
Od kod ste?
Od kod steh?

I am/we are from ... Australia/Britain/Canada/ America
Sem iz/Smo iz ... Avstralije/ Anglije/ Kanade/Amerike
Sem eez/Smo eez ... Owstraleeyeh/ Angleeyeh (Breetaneeyeh)/Kanadeh/ Amereekeh

We are on holiday
Smo na počitnicah
Smo na pocheetneetsakh

This is our first visit here
Prvič smo tu
Prhveech smo too

How old are you?
Koliko ste stari?
Koleeko steh staree?

I am ... years old
(Imam) ... let
(Eemam) ... let

I am a business person/ doctor/journalist/manual worker/administrator/ scientist/student/teacher
Sem poslovnež/zdravnik/ novinar/fizični delavec/upravni delavec/znanstvenik/študent/ učitelj
Sem posslovnezh/zdrovneek/ noveenar/fizzichnee delavets/ ooprovni delavets/znanstveneek/ shtoodent/oocheetel

I am waiting for my husband/wife/boyfriend/ girlfriend
Čakam na svojega moža/ (svojo) ženo/(svojega) fanta/ (svoje) dekle
Chakam na svoyega mozha/(svoyo) zheno/(svoyega) fanta/(svoyeh) dekleh

Would you like/may I have a cigarette?
Boste cigareto?/Vas lahko prosim za cigareto?
Bossteh tseegareto?/Vass lahkho prosseem za tseegareto?

Do you mind if I smoke?
Vas moti, če kadim?
Vass motee cheh kadeem?

339

S L O V E N I A N

Do you have a light?
Imate ogenj?
Eemathe ogen?

Days

Monday
Ponedeljek
Ponedelyek

Tuesday
Torek
Torek

Wednesday
Sreda
Sreda

Thursday
Četrtek
Chetrhtek

Friday
Petek
Petek

Saturday
Sobota
Sobota

Sunday
Nedelja
Nedelya

Morning/Afternoon/Evening/ Night
Jutro/Popoldne/Večer/Noč
Yootro/Popohdneh/Vecher/Noch

Yesterday/Today/Tomorrow
Včeraj/Danes/Jutri
Oocheray/Dah-nes/Yootree

Numbers

Zero
Nič
Neech

One
Ena
Ena

Two
Dva
Dva

Three
Tri
Tree

Four
Štiri
Shteeree

Five
Pet
Pet

Six
Šest
Shest

Seven
Sedem
Sedem

Eight
Osem
Ossem

Nine
Devet
Devet

Ten
Deset
Desset

Eleven
Enajst
Enayst

Twelve
Dvanajst
Dvanayst

Thirteen
Trinajst
Treenayst

Fourteen
Štirinajst
Shteereenayst

Fifteen
Petnajst
Petnayst

Sixteen
Šestnajst
Shestnayst

Seventeen
Sedemnajst
Sedemnayst

Eighteen
Osemnajst
Ossemnayst

Nineteen
Devetnajst
Devetnayst

Twenty
Dvajset
Dvayset

Twenty-one
Enaindvajset
Enaeendvayset

Twenty-two
Dvaindvajset
Dvaeendvayset

Thirty
Trideset
Treedesset

Forty
Štirideset
Shteereedesset

Fifty
Petdeset
Pedesset

Sixty
Šestdeset
Shesdesset

Seventy
Sedemdeset
Sedemdesset

Eighty
Osemdeset
Ossemdesset

Ninety
Devetdeset
Devedesset

One hundred
Sto
Sto

Five hundred
Petsto
Petsto

One thousand
Tisoč
Teesoch

One million
Milijon
Meeleeyon

Time

What time is it?
Koliko je ura?
Koleeko yeh oora?

It is ...
(Ura je) ...
Oora yeh...

9.00
Devet
Devet

9.05
Pet čez devet
Pet chezz devet

9.15
Četrt/petnajst čez devet/četrt
na deset
*Chetrht/petnayst chezz
devet/chetrht na desset*

9.20
Dvajset čez devet
Dvayset chezz devet

9.30
Devet in trideset/pol desetih
Devet een treedesset/pol desseteekh

9.35
Devet in petintrideset
Devet een peteentreedesset

9.40
Devet in štirideset/dvajset do
desetih
*Devet een shteereedesset/dvayset
do desseteekh*

9.45
Petnajst do desetih/tri četrt
na deset
*Petnayst do desseteekh/tree chetrht
na desseteekh*

9.50
Devet in petdeset/deset do
desetih
*Devet een pehdesset/desset do des-
seteekh*

9.55
Pet do desetih
Pet do desseteekh

12.00/Midday/Midnight
Dvanajst/Poldne/Polnoč
Dvanayst/pohdne/pohnoch

Money

**I would like to change these
traveller's cheques/this
currency**
Rad(a) bi zamenjal(a) te
potovalne čeke/to valuto
*Rad(a) bee zamenyal(a) teh
potovalneh chekeh/to valooto*

341

S L O V E N I A N

How much commission do you charge? (What is the service charge?)
Kolikšno provizijo jemljete?
Koleekshno proveezeeyo yemlyeteh?

Can I obtain money with my Mastercard?
Ali lahko dvignem denar z Mastercardom?
Alee lakhko dveegnem denar z Mastercardom?

Where is the nearest ATM?
Kje je najbližji bankomat?
Kyeh yeh nuy-blee-zhyee bahn-koh-maht?

My name is ... Some money has been wired to here for me to collect
Ime mi je ... Čaka me nakazani denar
Eemeh mee yeh ...Chaka meh nah-kah-zah-nee deh-nar

ARRIVING AND DEPARTING

Airport

Excuse me, where is the check-in desk for ... airline?
Oprostite, kje je okence za prijavo letalske družbe ... ?
Oprossteeteh, kyeh yeh okentseh za preeyavo letalskeh droozhbeh ...?

What is the boarding gate/ time for my flight?
Kje/Kdaj se vkrcamo za ta polet?
Kyeh/Gday se ookrhtsamo za ta polet?

How long is the delay likely to be?
Koliko časa bo najverjetneje trajala zamuda?
Koleeko chassa bo nayveryetneyeh trayala zamooda?

Where is the duty-free shop?
Kje je brezcarinska prodajalna?
Kyeh yeh brezztsareenska prodayalna?

Which way is the luggage reclaim?
Kje je izdaja prtljage?
Kyeh yeh eezdaya prhtlyageh?

I have lost my luggage. Please can you help?
Izgubil(a) sem svojo prtljago. Mi lahko pomagate, prosim?
Eezgoobil(a) sem svoyo prhtlyago. Mee lakhko pomagateh, prosseem?

I am flying to ...
Letim v ...
Leteem v ...

Where is the bus for the city centre?
Od kod odpelje avtobus v središče mesta?
Od kod odpelyeh owtobooss v sredeeshche messta?

Trains and Boats

Where is the ticket office/information desk?
Kje je okence za prodajo vozovnic/informacije?
Kyeh yeh okentseh za prodayo vozovneets/eenformatseeyeh?

342

Which platform does the train/speedboat/ferry to ... depart from?
S katerega perona odpelje vlak/hidrogliser/trajekt do ...
S katerega perona odpelyeh vlak/heedrogleesser/trayekt do ...

Where is platform ...?
Kje je peron številka...?
Kyeh yeh peron shteveelka...?

When is the next train/boat to...?
Kdaj pelje naslednji vlak/ naslednja ladja do...?
Gday pelyeh nasslednyi vlak/ nasslednya ladya do...?

Is there a later train/boat to...?
Ali vozi še kakšen poznejši vlak/poznejša ladja do...?
Alee vozee seh kakshen poznyeshee vlak/poznaysha ladya do...?

Notices and Signs

Jedilni vagon
Yedeelnee vagon
Buffet (Dining) car

Avtobus
Owtobooss
Bus

Pitna/Nepitna voda
Peetna/nepeetna voda
Drinking/Non-drinking water

Vhod
Ookhod
Entrance

Izhod
Eezkhod
Exit

Bolnišnica
Bolneeshneetsa
Hospital

Informacije
Eenformatseeyeh
Information

Garderoba
Garderoba
Left luggage (Baggage claim)

Omarice za prtljago
Omareetseh za prhtlyago
Luggage lockers

Pošta
Poshta
Post office

Peron
Peron
Platform

Železniška postaja
Zhelezneeshka postaya
Railway (Railroad) station

Letališče
Letaleeshcheh
Airport

Policijska postaja
Poleetseeska postaya
Police station

S L O V E N I A N

Pristanišče
Preestaneeshcheh
Port

Restavracija
Restowratseeya
Restaurant

Kadilci/Nekadilci
Kadeeltsee/nekadeeltsee
Smoking/Non-smoking

Telefon
Telefon
Telephone

Prodaja vozovnic
Prodaya vozohnits
Ticket office

Okence za prijavo potnikov
Okentseh za preeyavo potneekoh
Check-in desk

Vozni red
Voznee red
Timetable (Schedule)

Sanitarije
Saneetareeyeh
Toilets (Restrooms)

Ženske/Moški
Zhenskeh/Moshkee
Ladies/Gentlemen

Čakalnica
Chakalneetsa
Waiting room

Buying a Ticket

I would like a first-class/second-class/third-class single (one-way)/return (round-trip) ticket to …
Rad(a) bi enosmerno/povratno vozovnico za prvi/drugi/tretji razred do …
Rad(a) bee enosmerno/povratno vozohneetso za prhvee/droogee/tretyee razred do …

Is it an express (fast) train/bus?
Je to ekspresni vlak/avtobus?
Yeh to ekspressnee vlak/owtobooss?

Is my rail pass valid on this train/ferry/bus?
Je moja vozovnica veljavna na tem vlaku/tej ladji/tem avtobusu?
Yeh moya vozohneetsa velyowna na tem vlakoo/tey ladyee/tem owtobooss?

I would like an aisle/window seat
Rad(a) bi sedež ob prehodu/oknu
Rad(a) bee sedezh ob prekhodoo/oknoo

No smoking/smoking please
Nekadilci/kadilci, prosim
Nekadeeltsee/kadeeltsee prosseem

We would like to sit together
Radi bi sedeli skupaj
Radee bee sedelee skoopay

I would like to make a seat reservation
Rad(a) bi rezerviral(a) sedež
Rad(a) bee rezerveeral(a) sedezh

I would like to reserve a couchette sleeper for one person two people/my family
Rad(a) bi rezerviral(a) ležalni vagon/spalnik za eno osebo/dve osebi/celo družino
Rad(a) bee rezerveeral(a) lezhalnee vagon/spalneek za eno osebo/dveh osebee/tselo droozheeno

I would like to reserve a cabin
Rad(a) bi rezerviral(a) kabino
Rad(a) bee rezerveeral(a) kabeeno

Timetables (Schedules)

Prihod
Preekhod
Arrive

Postaja
Postaya
Calls (Stops at)

Strežba
Strezhba
Catering service

Prestop v
Prestop v
Change at

Prek
Prek
Connection/Via

Vozi vsak dan
Vozee oosak dan
Daily

Vozi vsakih 40 minut
Vozee oosakeekh shteereedesset meenoot
Every 40 minutes

Prvi razred
Prhvee razred
First class

Vozi vsako uro
Vozee oosako ooro
Hourly

Priporočene rezervacije
Preeporocheneh rezervatseeyeh
Seat reservations are recommended

Drugi razred
Droogee razred
Second class

Plača se dodatek
Placha se dodatek
Supplement payable

Luggage

How much will it cost to send (ship) my luggage in advance?
Koliko stane, če pošljem svojo prtljago naprej?
Koleeko staneh cheh poshlyem svoyo prhtlyago naprey?

Where is the left luggage (baggage claim) office?
Kje je garderoba?
Kyeh yeh garderoba?

S
L
O
V
E
N
I
A
N

345

**S
L
O
V
E
N
I
A
N**

What time do you open/close?
Ob kateri uri odprete/zaprete?
Ob kateree ooree odpreteh/zapreteh?

Where are the luggage trolleys(carts)?
Kje so vozički za prtljago?
Kyeh so vozeechkee za prhtlyago?

Where are the lockers?
Kje so omarice za prtljago?
Kyeh so omareetseh za prhtlyago?

I have lost my locker key
Izgubil(a) sem ključ omarice za prtljago
Eezgoobil(a) sem klyooch omareetseh za prhtlyago

On Board

Is this seat free?
Je ta sedež prost?
Yeh ta sedezh prost?

Excuse me, you are sitting in my reserved seat
Oprostite, ta sedež sem rezerviral(a)
Oprosteeteh, ta sedezh sem rezerveeral(a)

Which station is this?
Na kateri postaji smo?
Na kateree postayee smo?

What time is this train/bus/ferry/flight due to arrive/depart?
Kdaj ima ta vlak/avtobus/ladja/let prihod/odhod?
Gday eema ta vlak/owtobooss/ladya/let preekhod/odkhod?

Travelling with Children

Do you have a high chair/babysitting service/cot?
Imate visok otroški stol/varuško/otroško posteljico?
Eemateh veesok otroshkee stol/varooshko/otroshko postel yeetso?

Where is the nursery/playroom?
Kje so jasli/Kje je igralnica?
Kyeh so yaslee/Kyeh yeh eegralneetsa?

Where can I warm the baby's bottle?
Kje lahko pogrejem stekleničko za dojenčka?
Kyeh lakhko pogreyem stekleneechko za doyenchka?

Customs and Passports

Potne liste, prosim
Potneh listeh, prosseem
Passports please

I have nothing to declare/ I have wine/spirits (alcohol)/ tobacco to declare
Nimam ničesar za prijaviti/Prijavil bi vino/žgane pijače (alkohol)/tobak
Neemam neechessar za preeyavee-tee/preeyaveel bee veeno/zhganeh peeyacheh (alkokhol)/tobak

I will be staying for ... days/weeks/months
Ostal(a) bom ... dni/tednov/mesecev
Osstal(a) bom ... dnee/tednoh/messetsew

SIGHTSEEING

Asking the Way

Excuse me, do you speak English?
Oprostite, ali govorite angleško?
Oprossteeteh, alee govoreeteh angleshko?

Excuse me, can you help me please?
Oprostite, mi lahko pomagate?
Oprossteeteh, mee lahko pomagateh?

Where is the Tourist Information Office?
Kje je turistično-informacijski center?
Kyeh yeh tooreesteechno eenformatseeskee tsenter?

Excuse me, is this the right way to ...
Oprostite, je to prava pot do ...
Oprossteeteh, yeh to prava pot do ...

... the cathedral/the Tourist Information Office/the castle/the old town?
Katedrale/turističnega urada/starega mesta?
Katedraleh/tooreesteechnega oorada/starega messta?

Can you tell me the way to the railway (railroad) station/bus station/taxi rank/city centre (downtown)/beach?
Mi lahko poveste, kako pridem do železniške postaje/avtobusne postaje/parkirnega prostora za taksije/središča mesta/plaže?
Mee lahko povessteh kako preedem do zhelezneeshkeh postayeh/owtoboossneh postaye/parkeernega prostora za takseeyeh/sredeeshcha messta/plazheh?

Prva/druga/levo/desno/naravnost
Prhva/drooga/levo/dessno/narownost
First/second/left/right/straight ahead

Na vogalu/pri semaforju
Na vogaloo/pree semaforyoo
At the corner/at the traffic lights

Where is the nearest police station/post office?
Kje je najbližja policijska postaja/pošta?
Kyeh yeh nuy-bleezh-yah poleetseeka poh-stah-yah/poh-shtah?

Is it near/far?
Je blizu/daleč?
Yeh bleezoo/dalech?

Do I need to take a taxi/catch a bus?
Ali moram iti s taksijem/z avtobusom?
Alee moram eete s takseeyem/z owtoboossom?

Do you have a map?
Imate karto mesta?
Eemate karto messta?

**S
L
O
V
E
N
I
A
N**

Can you point to it on my map?
Mi lahko pokažete na karti mesta?
Mee lakhko pokazheteh na kartee messta?

Thank you for your help
Hvala lepa za pomoč
Khvala lepa za pomoch

How do I reach the motorway/main road?
Kako pridem do avtoceste/glavne ceste?
Kako preedem do owtotsesteh/glowneh tsesteh?

I think I have taken the wrong turning
Mislim da sem narobe zavil(a)
Meesleem da sem narobeh zaveel(a)

I am looking for this address
Iščem tale naslov
Eeshchem taleh nasloh

I am looking for the ... hotel
Iščem hotel ...
Eeshchem khotel ...

How far is it to... from here?
Kako daleč je od tu do ...?
Kako dalech yeh od too do ...?

Peljite po isti poti naravnost še ... kilometrov
Pelyeeteh po eestee potee narownost sheh ... keelometroh
Carry straight on for ... kilometres

Na naslednjem odcepu zavijte na desno/levo
Na nasslednyem odsepoo zaveeteh na dessno/levo
Take the next turning on the right/left

Na naslednjem križišču/pri naslednjem semaforju zavijte desno/levo
Na Nasslednyem kreezheeshchoo/pree nasslednyem semaforoo zaveeteh dessno/levo
Turn right/left at the next crossroads/traffic lights

V napačno smer peljete
V napachno smer pelyeteh
You are going in the wrong direction

Where is the cathedral/church/museum/pharmacy?
Kje je katedrala/cerkev/muzej/lekarna?
Kyeh yeh katedrala/tserkew/moozey/lekarna?

How much is the admission/entrance charge?
Koliko je vstopnina?
Koleeko yeh oostopneena?

Is there a discount for children/students/senior citizens?
Imajo otroci/študentje/upokojenci popust?
Eemayo otrotsee/shtoodentyeh/oopokoyentsee popoost?

What time does the next guided tour (in English) start?
Kdaj se začne naslednji organizirani ogled (v angleščini)?
Gday se zachneh naslednyee organeezeeranee ogled (v angleshcheenee)?

One/two adults/children please
Eno/dve za odrasle/otroke, prosim
Eno/dve za odrasleh/otrokeh, prosseem

May I take photographs here?
Lahko tu fotografiram?
Lakhko too fotografeeram?

At the Tourist Office

Do you have a map of the town/area?
Imate karto mesta/območja?
Eemateh karto messta/obmochya?

Do you have a list of accommodation?
Imate seznam prenočišč?
Eemate seznam prenocheeshch?

Can I reserve accommodation?
Rad(a) bi rezerviral(a) prenočišče?
Rad(a) bee rezerveeral(a) prenocheeshcheh?

Hotels

I have a reservation in the name of ...
Imam rezervacijo na ime ...
Eemam rezervatseeyo na eemeh ...

I wrote to/faxed/telephoned you last month/last week
Pisal(a) sem vam/Poslal(a) sem vam faks/Telefoniral sem prejšnji mesec/teden
Peesal(a) sem vam/Posslal(a) sem vam faks/telefoneeral sem preyshnyee messets/teden

Do you have any rooms free?
Imate kakšno prosto sobo?
Eemateh kakshno prosto sobo?

I would like to reserve a single/double room with/without a bath/shower
Rad(a) bi rezerviral(a) enoposteljno/dvoposteljno sobo s kopalno kadjo/prho/brez kopalne kadi/prhe
Rad(a) bee rezerveeral(a) enoposstelno/dvoposstelno sobo s kopalno kadyo/prhkho/brez kopalneh kadee/prhkhe

I would like bed/breakfast/room (and) full board
Rad(a) bi posteljo/zajtrk/sobo (s polnim penzionom)
Rad(a) bee posstelyo/zaytrhk/sobo (s polneem penzeeonom)

How much is it per night?
Koliko stane na noč?
Koleeko staneh na noch?

S L O V E N I A N

Is breakfast included?
Je zajtrk vključen v ceno?
Yeh zaytrhk ooklyoochen v tseno?

Do you have any cheaper rooms?
Imate kakšno cenejšo sobo?
Eemateh kakshno tseneysho sobo?

I would like to see/take the room
Rad(a) bi sobo videl(a)/Sobo bom vzel(a)
Rad(a) bee sobo veedel(a)/Sobo bom oozel(a)

I would like to stay for ... nights
... krat bom prenočil(a)
... krat bom prenocheel(a)

The shower/light/tap doesn't work. The hot water doesn't work
Prha/Luč/Pipa/ne deluje.
Topla voda ne teče
*Prhkha/looch/peepa/ne delooyeh.
Topla voda ne techeh*

At what time/where is breakfast served?
Ob kateri uri/kje postrežete z zajtrkom?
Ob kateree ooree/kyeh posstrezheteh z zaytrhkom?

What time do I have to check out?
Ob kateri uri se moram odjaviti?
Ob kateree ooree se moram odyaveetee?

Can I have the key to room number ...?
Ključ sobe ... prosim
Klyooch sobe ... prosseem

My room number is ...
Številka moje sobe je ...
Shteveelka moyeh sobeh yeh ...

My room is not satisfactory/not clean enough/too noisy. Please can I change rooms?
Moja soba/postelja ni zadovoljive kakovosti/dovolj čista/je hrupna. Bi (jo) lahko sobo/posteljo zamenjal(a)?
Moya soba/posstelya nee zadovoly-eeveh kakovostee/dovol cheesta/yeh khroopna. Bee (yo) lahko sobo/posstelyo zamenyal(a)?

Where is the bathroom?
Kje je kopalnica?
Kyeh yeh kopalneetsa?

Do you have a safe for valuables?
Imate morda sef za vrednostne predmete?
Eemateh morda sef za vrednosstneh predmeteh?

Is there a laundry/do you wash clothes?
Je tu kakšna čistilnica/ali pri vas perete perilo?
Yeh too kakshna cheesteel neetsa/alee pree vass pereteh pereelo?

I would like an air-conditioned room
Rad(a) bi sobo s klimatsko napravo
Rad(a) bee sobo s kleematsko napravo

Do you accept traveller's cheques/credit cards?
Sprejemate potovalne
čeke/kreditne kartice?
*Spreyemateh potovalneh
chekeh/kredeetneh karteetseh?*

May I have the bill please?
Račun, prosim
Rachoon prosseem

Excuse me, I think there may be a mistake in this bill
Oprostite, mislim, da je v tem
računu napaka
*Oprossteeteh, meessleem, da yeh v
tem rachoonoo napaka*

Youth Hostels

How much is a dormitory bed per night?
Koliko stane prenočitev v
skupni spalnici?
*Koleeko staneh prenocheetew v
skoopnee spalneetsee?*

I am/I am not an HI member
Sem/Nisem član HI
Sem/Neesem chlan Kh Ee

May I use my own sleeping bag?
Lahko uporabljam svojo spalno
vrečo?
*Lahkko ooporablyam svoyo spalno
vrecho?*

What time do you lock the doors at night?
Ob kateri uri ponoči zaklepate
vrata?
*Ob kateree ooree ponochee
zaklepateh vrata?*

Camping

May I camp for the night/two nights?
Rad bi kampiral eno noč/dve
noči
*Rad bee kampeeral eno noch/dve
nochee*

Where can I pitch my tent?
Kam lahko postavim šotor?
Kyeh lahkko postaveem shotor?

How much does it cost for one night/week?
Koliko stane na noč/na teden?
Koleeko staneh na noch/na teden?

Where are the washing facilities?
Kje so santarije?
Kyeh so saneetareeyeh?

Is there a restaurant/ supermarket/swimming pool on site/nearby?
Je v kampu/v bližini kampa
restavracija/supermarket/
bazen?
*Yeh v kampoo/v bleezheenee
kampa restowratseeya/
soopermarket/bazen?*

Do you have a safety deposit box?
Imate sef?
Eemateh sef?

S
L
O
V
E
N
I
A
N

**S
L
O
V
E
N
I
A
N**

EATING AND DRINKING

Restaurants

Cafés and Bars

I would like a cup of/two cups of/another coffee/tea
Kavo/čaj, prosim. Dve kavi/dva čaja, prosim. Se eno kavo/še en čaj, prosim
Kavo/chay prosseem. Dve kavee/dva chaya, prosseem. Sheh eno kavo/sheh en chay, prosseem

With/without milk/sugar
Z mlekom/sladkorjem. Brez mleka/sladkorja
Z mlekom/sladkoryem. Brez mleka/sladkorya

I would like a bottle/glass/two glasses of mineral water/red wine/white wine, please
Steklenico/kozarec/dva kozarca mineralne vode/rdečega vina/belega vina, prosim
Stekleneetso/kozarets/dva kozartsa meeneralne vode/rhdechega veena/belega veena prosseem

I would like a beer/two beers, please
Pivo/dve pivi, prosim
Peevo/dve peevee prosseem

Please may I have some ice?
Bi lahko dobil(a) malo ledu, prosim?
Bee lahkho dobil(a) malo ledoo prosseem?

Do you have any matches/cigarettes/cigars?
Imate vžigalice/cigarete/cigare?
Eemateh oozheegaleetseh/tseegareteh/tseegareh?

Can you recommend a good/cheap restaurant in this area?
Mi lahko priporočite dobro/poceni restavracijo v bližini?
Mee lakhko preeporocheeteh dobro/potsenee restowratseeyo v bleezheenee?

I would like a table for ... people
Rad(a) bi mizo za ...
Rad(a) bee meezo za ...

Do you have a non-smoking area?
Imate prostor za nekadilce?
Eemateh prostor za nekadeeltseh?

Waiter! Waitress!
Natakar! Natakarica!
Nah-tah-kar! Nah-tah-kar-itsah!

Excuse me, please may we order?
Oprostite, lahko naročimo?
Oprossteeteh, lahkho narocheemo?

Do you have a set menu/children's menu/wine list in English?
Imate jedilni list/otroški meni/vinsko karto v angleščini?
Eemateh yedeelnee leest/ot-roh-shkee meh-nee/veensko karto v engleshcheenee?

Do you have any vegetarian dishes?
Ali imate kake vegetarijanske jedi?
Ah-lee eemah-teh kah-keh veh-geh-tah-ree-yahn-skeh yeh-dee?

Do you have any local specialities?
Imate kakšne lokalne specialitete?
Eemateh kakshneh lokalneh spetseealeeteteh?

Are vegetables included?
Ima ta jed prilogo?
Eema ta yed preelogo?

Could I have it well-cooked/ medium/rare please?
Rad(a) bi dobro/pečen zrezek/ zrezek po angleško
Rad(a) bee dobro/pechen zrezek/zrezek po angleshko

What does this dish consist of?
Iz česa je sestavljena ta jed?
Eez chessa yeh sestowlyena ta yed?

I am a vegetarian. Does this contain meat?
Vegetarijanec sem/ Vegetarijanka sem. (fem.)
Ali ta jed vsebuje meso?
Veh-geh-tar-yahnets sehm/ Veh-geh-tar-yahn-kah sehm. Ah-lee tah yed vseh-boo-yeh meh-saw?

I do not eat nuts/dairy products/meat/fish
Ne jem oreškov/mlečnih izdelkov/mesa/rib
Neh yem oreshkoh/mlechneekh eezdelkoh/messa/reeb

Not (very) spicy please
Ne preveč pekoče, prosim
Neh prevech pekoch prosseem

I would like the set menu please
Kosilo, prosim
Kosseelo prosseem

We have not been served yet
Še vedno čakamo na postrežbo
Sheh ved-noh chah-kah-moh nah poh-strezh-boh

Please bring a plate/knife/ fork
Prosim, prinesite krožnik/ nož/vilice
Proh-seem pree-nes-ee-teh krozh-neek/nohzh/vee-lee-tse

Excuse me, this is not what I ordered
Oprostite, to ni jed, ki sem jo naročil(a)
Oprossteeteh, to nee yed kee sem yo narocheel(a)

May I have some/more bread/water/coffee/tea?
Lahko dobim malo/še malo kruha/vode/kave/čaja?
Lakhko dobeem malo/sheh malo krookha/vodeh/kaveh/chaya?

May I have the bill please?
Račun, prosim
Rachoon prosseem

Does this bill include service?
Je postrežnina všteta v račun?
Yeh postrezhneena ooshteta v rachoon?

Do you accept traveller's cheques/Mastercard/ US dollars?
Sprejemate potovalne čeke/Mastercard/ameriške dolarje?
Spreyemateh potovalneh chekeh/Mastercard/Amereeshkeh dolaryeh?

S L O V E N I A N

Can I have a receipt please?
Mi lahko izstavite račun?
Mee lakhko eestaveeteh rachoon?

Where is the toilet (restroom) please?
Oprostite, kje je stranišče (toaleta)?
Oprossteeteh, kyeh yeh stra-neeshcheh (toaleta)?

On the Menu

Zajtrk/Kosilo/Večerja
Zuy-turk/Koh-see-loh/Veh-cher-yah
Breakfast/Lunch/Dinner

Predjedi	Juhe
Predyedee	*Yookheh*
First courses	**Soups**

Glavne jedi	Ribje jedi
Glownee yedee	*Reebyeh yedee*
Main courses	**Fish dishes**

Mesne jedi
Messnee yedee
Meat dishes

Govedina	Zrezek
Goh-veh-dee-nah	*Zreh-zek*
Beef	**Steak**

Svinjina	Teletina
Sveen-yee-nah	*Telleh-teen-ah*
Pork	**Veal**

Piščanec	Ovčetina
Peesh-chah-nets	*Ov-cheh-teen-ah*
Chicken	**Lamb**

Šunka
Shoon-kah
Ham

Vegetarianske jedi
Vegetareeyanskeh yedee
Vegetarian dishes

Zelenjava
Zellen-yah-vah
Vegetables

Pečen krompir
Petch-en krom-peer
Chips (french fries)

Kuhan/pražen/pire krompir
Koo-hun/prah-zhen/peereh krom-peer
Boiled/sauté/mashed potatoes

Riž	Sladice
Reezh	*Sladeetseh*
Rice	**Desserts**

Sladoled	Torte
Slah-doh-led	*Tor-teh*
Ice cream	**Cakes**

Pecivo	Sadje
Petseevoh	*Sud-yeh*
Pastries	**Fruit**

Kruh	Rulade
Krooh	*Roo-lah-deh*
Bread	**Rolls**

Toast	Maslo
Toast	*Mah-sloh*
Toast	**Butter**

Sol/poper   Sladkor
Sow/poh-per   *Slud-kohr*
Salt/pepper   **Sugar**

Specialitete
Spetseealeeteteh
Specialities

Lokalne specialiete
Loh-kul-neh spetsy-ahly-teh-teh
Local specialities

Malice   Vinska karta
Mah-lits-eh   *Veen-ska kar-tah*
Set menu   **Wine list**

Rdeča vina
Rdeh-chah veenah
Red wines

Bela vina   Roséji
Beh-lah veenah   *Roh-zeh-yee*
White wines   **Rosé wines**

Šumeča vina
Shoo-meh-chah veenah
Sparkling wines

Pivo
Peevoh
Beer

Pivo v steklenici/točeno pivo
Peevoh v steh-kleh-neetsee/toh-chen-oh peevoh
Bottled beer/draught (draft) beer

Brezalkoholne pijače
Breh-zahl-koh-holneh pee-yah-cheh
Non-alcoholic drinks

Mineralna voda
Mee-neh-rahl-nah voh-dah
Mineral water

Sadni sokovi
Sahd-nee soh-koh-vee
Fruit juices

Pomarančni sok
Poh-mah-runchnee sok
Orange juice

Limonada   Led
Lee-moh-nah-dah   *Leh-d*
Lemonade   **Ice**

Bela kava/črna kava/espresso
Beh-lah kah-vah/chr-nah kah-vah/espresso
White coffee/black coffee/espresso coffee

Čaj z mlekom/z limono
Chay z mleh-kom/z lee-moh-noh
Tea with milk/with lemon

Vroča čokolada
Vroh-chah choco-lah-dah
Chocolate (drink)

Mleko
Mleh-koh
Milk

Malice/Lahka kosila
Mah-leetse/La-h-kah koh-see-lah
Snacks/Light meals

Solate   Sendviči
Soh-lah-teh   *Sehn-dvee-chee*
Salads   **Sandwiches**

SLOVENIAN

S L O V E N I A N

Jajca
Yuy-tsah
Eggs

Klobasa
Kloh-bah-sah
Sausage

Kuhana jajca/jajca na
oko/umešana jajca
*Koo-hah-nah yuy-tsah/yuy-tsah nah
okoh/umeshahna yuy-tsah*
Boiled/fried/scrambled eggs

Typical Local Dishes

Potica
Poteetsa
**Traditional Slovenian cake
(with nuts, raisins, tarragon,
cinnamon etc.)**

Jota
Yota
A bean and sauerkraut stew

Ajdovi žganci
Aydovee zhgantsee
Buckwheat polenta

Kraški pršut
Krashkee prhshoot
**Prosciutto from the Karst
region**

Prekmurska gibanica
Prekmoorska geebaneetsa
**A pastry with layers of
fromage frais, poppy seeds,
apples, raisins and nuts**

Žlikrofi
Zhleekrofee
Slovene ravioli

Ričet
Reechet
**A pearl barley, smoked ham
and vegetable stew**

Štruklji
Shtrooklyee
**Stuffed steamed pastry
parcels**

GETTING AROUND

Public Transport

**Where is the (nearest) bus
stop/coach stop?**
Kje je (najbližja) postaja za
avtobus/mestni avtobus?
*Kyeh yeh (naybleezhya) postaya za
owtobooss/mestnee owtobooss?*

**When is the next/last bus
to...?**
Kdaj pelje naslednji/zadnji
avtobus do...?
*Gday pelyeh naslednyee/zadnyee
owtobooss do ...?*

**How much is the fare to the
city centre (downtown)/
railway (railroad) station/
airport?**
Koliko stane vožnja do središča
mesta/železniške postaje/
letališča?
*Koleeko staneh vozhnya do sre-
deeshcha messta/zhelezneeshkeh
postayeh/letaleeshcha?*

Will you tell me when to get off?
Me lahko opozorite, kdaj izstopim?
Meh lakhko opozoreeteh gday eestopeem?

Does this bus go to ...?
Ali ta avtobus pelje do ...?
Alee ta owtobooss pelyeh do ...?

Which number bus goes to ...?
Katera številka pelje do...?
Katera shteveelka pelyeh do ...?

May I have a single (one-way) /return (round-trip)/day ticket/book of tickets?
Enosmerno/povratno/dnevno vozovnico/blok vozovnic, prosim?
Enosmerno/povratno/dnevno vozohnitso/blok vozohnits prosseem?

I would like to go to ... How much will it cost?
Grem v ... Koliko stane vožnja?
Grem v ... Koleeko staneh vozhnya?

Please may I stop here?
Lahko ustavite, prosim?
Lakhko oostaveeteh prosseem?

I would like to order a taxi today/tomorrow at 2pm to go from ... to ...
Rad bi naročil taksi za danes/jutri ob dveh popoldne za vožnjo od ... do ...
Rad bee narocheel taksee za danes/yootree ob dvekh popohdne za vozhnyo od ... do ...

Entertainment

Can you recommend a good bar/nightclub?
Mi lahko priporočite dober bar/nočni klub?
Mee lakhko preeporocheeteh dober bar/nochnee kloob?

Do you know what is on at the cinema (playing at the movies)/theatre at the moment?
Mi lahko poveste, kaj trenutno igra v kinu/gledališču?
Mee lakhko povessteh kay trenoot-no eegra v keenoo/gledaleeshchoo?

I would like to book (purchase) ... tickets for the matinee/evening performance on Monday
Rad bi rezerviral(kupil) ... kart(o) za matinejo/večerno predstavo v ponedeljek
Rad bee rezerveeral (koopil) ... kart(o) za mateeneyo/vecherno predstavo v ponedelyek

What time does the film/ performance start?
Kdaj se prične film/predstava?
Gday seh preechneh feelm/ predstava?

S L O V E N I A N

Post

How much will it cost to send a letter/postcard/this package to Britain/ America/ Canada/Australia/ New Zealand?
Koliko stane, če pošljem tole pismo/razglednico/tale paket v Veliko Britanijo/Ameriko/ Kanado/Avstralijo/Novo Zelandijo?
Koleeko staneh che poshlyem toleh peesmo/razgledneetso/taleh paket oo Veleeko Breetaneeyo/ Amereeko/ Kanado/Owstraleeyo/Novo Zelandeeyo?

I would like one stamp/two stamps
Rad bi eno znamko/dve znamki
Rad bee eno znamko/dve znakee

I'd like ... stamps for postcards to send abroad, please
Rad bi ... znamk za razglednice za tujino, prosim
Rad bee ... znamk za razgl edneetseh za tooyeeno prosseem

Phones

I would like to make a telephone call/reverse the charges to (make a collect call to) ...
Rad bi telefoniral (na povratne stroške) v ...
Rad bee telefoneeral (na povratneh stroshkeh) v ...

Which coins do I need for the public telephone?
Kaj potrebujem za uporabo javnih telefonskih govorilnic?
Kay potrebooyem za ooporabo jowneekh telefonskeekh govoreelneets?

The line is engaged (busy)
Linija je zasedena
Leeneeya yeh zasedena

The number is ...
Telefonska številka je ...
Telefonska shteveelka yeh ...

Hello, this is ...
Dober dan (Dobro jutro/večer), tukaj je ...
Dober dan (Dobro yootro/vecher), tookay yeh ...

Please may I speak to ...?
Bi lahko govoril(a) z ... prosim?
Bee lahkho govoril(a) z ... prosseem?

He/she is not in at the moment. Please can you call back?
Trenutno ga/je ni tu. Lahko pokličete pozneje, prosim?
Trenootno ga/yeh nee too. Lahkho pokleecheteh pozneyeh prosseem?

SHOPPING

Shops

Knjigarna/Papirnica
Knyeegarna/Papeerneetsa
Bookshop/Stationery

Zlatar/Darila
Zlatar/Dareela
Jeweller/Gifts

Čevljar
Chewlyar
Shoes

Železnina
Zhelezneena
Hardware

Frizer
Freezer
Hairdresser

Pekarna
Pekarna
Baker

Supermarket
Soopermarket
Supermarket

Trgovina s fotografsko opremo
Trhgoveena s fotografsko opremo
Photo shop

Potovalna agencija
Potovalna agentseeya
Travel agent

Lekarna
Lekarna
Pharmacy

In the Shops

What time do the shops open/close?
Ob kateri uri se zaprejo odprejo/trgovine?
Ob kateree ooree seh zapreyo od-preh-yoh/trhgoveeneh?

Where is the nearest market?
Kje je najbližji trg?
Kyeh yeh naybleezhyee trhg?

Can you show me the one in the window/this one?
Mi lahko pokažete tistega v izložbi/tega?
Mee lahko pokazheteh teestega v eezlozhbee/tega?

Can I try this on?
Lahko tole pomerim?
Lahko toleh pomereem?

What size is this?
Katera številka je tole?
Katera shteveelka yeh toleh?

This is too large/too small/too expensive. Do you have any others?
Tole je preveliko/ premajhno/ predrago. Imate še kaj drugega?
Toleh yeh preveleeko/premaykhno/ predrago. Eemateh sheh kay droogega?

My size is ...
Nosim številko ...
Noseem shteveelko ...

S L O V E N I A N

Where is the changing room/children's/cosmetic/ladieswear/menswear/food department?
Kje so kabine za pomerjanje/otroški oddelek/oddelek s kozmetiko/ženski/moški oddelek/oddelek s hrano?
Kyeh so kabeeneh za pomeryanyeh/otroshkee oddelek s kozmeteeko/zhenskee/moshkee oddelek/oddelek s khrano?

I would like ... a quarter of a kilo/half a kilo/a kilo of bread/butter/ham/this fruit
Rad(a) bi ... četrt kilograma/pol kilograma/kilogram kruha/masla/šunke/tega sadja
Rad(a) bee ... chetrht keelograma/pol keelograma/keelogram krookha/massla/shoonkeh/tega sadya

How much is this?
Koliko stane tole?
Koleeko staneh toleh?

I'll take this one, thank you
Tega bi vzel(a), prosim
Tega bee oozel(a) prosseem

Do you have a carrier (shopping) bag?
Ali imate vrečko?
Ah-lee eemah-teh vrech-koh?

Do you have anything cheaper/larger/smaller/of better quality?
Imate kaj cenejšega/večjega/manjšega/kvalitetnejšega?
Eemateh kay tseneyshega/vechega/manshega/kvaleetetneyshega?

I would like a film/to develop this film for this camera
Rad(a) bi kupil(a) film za tale aparat/Rad(a) bi razvil(a) film
Rad(a) bee koopeel(a) feelm za taleh aparat/Rad(a) bee razveel(a) feelm

I would like some batteries, the same size as this old one
Rad(a) bi baterije, iste velikosti kot so tele stare
Rad(a) bee batereeyeh, eesteh veleekostee kot so teleh stareh

Would you mind wrapping this for me, please?
Mi lahko to zavijete, prosim?
Mee lahkho to zaveeyeteh prosseem?

Sorry, but you seem to have given me the wrong change
Oprostite, ampak niste mi prav vrnili drobiža
Oprossteeteh ampak neesteh mee prow vrhneeleh drobeezha

Car Hire (Rental)

I have ordered (rented) a car in the name of ...
Rezerviral(a) sem avto na ime ...
Rezerveeral(a) sem owto na eemeh ...

How much does it cost to hire (rent) a car for one day/two days/a week?
Koliko stane najem avtomobila za en dan/dva dni/en teden?
Koleeko staneh nayem owtomobeela za en dan/dva dnee/en teden?

Is the tank already full of petrol (gas)?
Je rezervoar napolnjen?
Yeh rezervoar napohnyen?

Is insurance and tax included? How much is the deposit?
Sta zavarovanje in davek vključena? Kolikšen polog moram plačati?
Sta zavarovanyeh een davek ooklyoochena? Koleekshen polog moram plachatee?

By what time must I return the car?
Do kdaj moram avto vrniti?
Do gday moram owto vrhneetee?

I would like a small/large/ family/sports car with a radio/cassette
Rad(a) bi manjši/večji/ družinski/športni avto z radiem/kasetophonon
Rad(a) bee manshee/vechee/ droozheenskee/shportnee owto z radeeyem/kassettophoonoom

Do you have a road map?
Imate avtokarto?
Eemateh owtokarto?

Parking

How long can I park here?
Kako dolgo lahko tu parkiram?
Kako dohgo lahkho too parkeeram?

Is there a car park near here?
Je tu v bližini kako parkirišče?
Yeh too v bleezheenee kako parkeereeshcheh?

At what time does this car park close?
Ob kateri uri se to parkirišče zapre?
Ob kateree ooree seh to parkeereeshcheh zapreh?

Signs and Notices

Enosmerna ulica
Enosmerna ooleetsa
One way

Vstop prepovedan
Oostop prepovedan
No entry

Parkiranje prepovedano
Parkeeranyeh prepovedano
No parking

Obvoz
Obvoz
Detour (Diversion)

Stop
Stop
Stop

Neprednostna cesta
Neprednosstna tsessta
Give way (Yield)

Spolzka cesta
Spohzka tsesta
Slippery road

Prepovedano prehitevanje
Prepovedano prekheetevanyeh
No overtaking

S
L
O
V
E
N
I
A
N

Pozor!
Pozor!
Danger!

At the Filling Station
(Na Črpalki)

**Unleaded (lead free)/
standard/premium/diesel**
Neosvinčeni/navadni/super/
dizel
*Neosveenchenee/navadnee/sooper/
deezel*

Fill the tank please
Polno, prosim
Pohno prosseem

Do you have a road map?
Imate avtokarto?
Eemateh owtokarto?

How much is the car wash?
Koliko stane pranje
avtomobila?
*Koleeko staneh pranyeh
owtomobeela?*

Breakdowns

I've had a breakdown at...
Imel(a) sem okvaro v ...
Eemel(a) sem okvaro v ...

**I am a member of the ...
[motoring organisation]**
Sem član (članica fem.) ...
Sem chlahn (chlahnitsa) ...

I am on the road from... to...
Sem na cesti med ... in ...
Sem na tsestee med ... een ...

**I can't move the car. Can you
send a tow-truck?**
Ne morem premakniti
avtomobila. Lahko pošljete
vlečno vozilo?
*Ne morem premakneetee
owtomobeela. Lakhko poshlyeteh
vlechno vozeelo?*

I have a flat tyre
Počila mi je guma
Pocheela mee yeh gooma

**The windscreen (windshield)
has smashed/cracked**
Vetrobran je razbit/počen
Vetrobran yeh razbeet/pochen

**There is something wrong
with the engine/brakes/
lights/steering/gearbox/
clutch/exhaust**
Nekaj je narobe z motorjem/
zavorami/lučmi/volanom/
menjalnikom/sklopko/izpuhom
*Nekay yeh narobeh z motoryem/
zavoramee/loochmee/volanom/meny
alneekom/sklopko/eespookhom*

It's overheating
Pregreva se
Pregreva seh

It won't start
Noče vžgati
Nocheh oozhgatee

Where can I get it repaired?
Kje ga (jo fem.) lahko
popravim?
Kyeh ga (yo) lakhko popraveem?

Can you take me there?
Me lahko tja odpeljete?
Meh lakhko tya odpelyeteh?

Will it take long to fix?
Bo popravilo trajalo dolgo?
Bo popraveelo trayalo dohgo?

How much will it cost?
Koliko bo stalo popravilo?
Koleeko bo stalo popraveelo?

Please can you pick me up/give me a lift?
Me lahko pridete iskat, prosim/Me lahko peljete, prosim?
Meh lakhko preedeteh eeskat prosseem/Me lakhko pelyeteh prosseem?

Accidents and Traffic Offences (Violations)

Can you help me? There has been an accident
Ali mi lahko pomagate? Prišlo je do nesreče
Ah-lee mee lah-h-koh poh-mah-ghah-teh? Pree-shloh yeh doh nes-reh-cheh

Please call the police/an ambulance
Prosim, pokličite policijo/rešilec
Proh-seem poh-klee-chee-teh poh-lee-tsee-yoh/reh-shee-lets

Is anyone hurt?
Je kdo poškodovan?
Yeh kdoh poh-shkoh-doh-vahn?

Sorry, I didn't see the sign
Oprostite, spregledal(a) sem znak
Oprossteeteh, spregledal(a) sem znak

Must I pay a fine? How much?
Ali moram plačati kazen? Koliko?
Alee moram plachatee kaz'n? Koleeko?

Pokažite dokumente
Pokazheeteh dokoomenteh
Show me your documents

HEALTH

Pharmacy (Lekarna)

Do you have anything for a stomach ache/headache/sore throat/toothache?
Imate kaj proti bolečinam v želodcu/glavobolu/bolečem u grlu/zobobolu?
Eemateh kay protee bolecheenam v zhelodsoo/glavoboloo/bolechem oo grhloo/zoboboloo?

I need something for diarrhoea/constipation/a cold/a cough/insect bites/ sunburn/travel (motion) sickness
Rad(a) bi nekaj proti diareji/zaprtosti/prehladu/ kašlju/pikom insektov/ opeklinam/morski bolezni
Rad(a) bee nekay protee deeyarey-ee/zaprhtostee/prekhladoo/kashly-oo/peekom insektoh/opekl eenam/morskee boleznee

How much/how many do I take?
Kako naj jemljem zdravila?
Kako nay yemlyem zdraveela?

363

S L O V E N I A N

I am taking anti-malaria tablets/these pills
Jemljem tablete proti malariji/te tablete
Yemlyem tableteh protee malareeyee/teh tableteh

How often do I take it/them?
Kako pogosto naj ga/jih jemljem?
Kako pogossto nay ga/yeekh yemlyem?

I am/he is/she is taking this medication
Jemljem/Jemlje tale zdravila
Yemlyem/yemlyeh taleh zdraveela

How much does it cost?
Koliko to stane?
Koleeko to staneh?

Can you recommend a good doctor/dentist?
Mi lahko priporočite dobrega zdravnika/zobozdravnika?
Mee lahko preeporocheeteh dobrega zdrowneeka/zobozdrowneeka?

Is it suitable for children?
Je to primerno za otroke?
Yeh to preemerno za otrokeh?

Doctor (Pri Zdravniku)

I have a pain here/in my arm/leg/chest/stomach
Boli me tule/roka/noga/prsni koš/trebuh
Bolee meh tooleh/roka/noga/prhsnee kosh/trebookh

Please call a doctor, this is an emergency!
Pokličite zdravnika, prosim, nujno je!
Pokleecheeteh zdrowneeka prosseem, nooyno yeh!

I would like to make an appointment to see the doctor
Rad(a) bi se naroči(a)l pri zdravniku
Rad(a) bee seh narocheel(a) pree zdrowneeku

I am diabetic/pregnant
Sem/diabetik(diabetičarka)/ noseča
Sem deeabeteek (deeabeteecharka)/nossecha

I need a prescription for ...
Potrebujem recept za ...
Potrebooyem retsept za ...

Can you give me something to ease the pain?
Mi lahko daste nekaj proti bolečinam?
Mee lahko dasste nekay protee bolecheenam?

I am/he is/she is/allergic to penicillin
Alergičen/Alergična sem na penicilin
Alergeechen/Alergeechna sem na peneetseeleen

Ali tole boli?
Alee toleh bolee?
Does this hurt?

Morate/Mora/Mora iti v
bolnišnico
*Morateh/mora/mora eetee oo
bolneeshneetso*
**You must/he must/she must
go to hospital**

Tablete jemljite enkrat/dvakrat/
trikrat dnevno
*Tableteh yemlyeeteh enkrat/dvakrat/
treekrat dnewno*
**Take these once/twice/three
times a day**

**I am/he is/she is taking this
medication**
Jemljem/Jemlje tale zdravila
Yemlyem/yemlyeh taleh zdraveela

I have medical insurance
Sem zdravstveno zavarovan(a)
Sem zdrowsstveno zavarovan(a)

**I have toothache/my filling
has come out**
Zob me boli/plomba mi je
padla ven
*Zob meh bolee/plomba mee yeh
padla v'n*

**I do/do not want to have an
injection first**
Želim najprej injekcijo/
Ne želim/injekcije
*Zheleem/nayprey eenyekseeyo/
Ne zheleem eenyekseeyeh*

Help!
Na pomoč!
Na pomoch!

Fire!
Gori!
Goree!

Stop!
Stop!
Stop!

**Call an ambulance/
a doctor/the police/
the fire brigade!**
Pokličite rešilca/zdravnika/
policijo/gasilce!
*Pokleecheeteh resheeltsa/
zdrowneeka/poleetseeyo/gaseeltse!*

**Please may I use a
telephone?**
Bi lahko od tod telefoniral(a)?
Bee lahko od tod telefoneeral(a)?

**I have had my traveller's
cheques/credit cards/
handbag/rucksack/luggage/
wallet/passport/mobile phone
stolen**
Moje potovalne čeke/Mojo
kreditno kartico/Mojo
torbico/Moj nahrbtnik/Mojo
prtljago/Mojo denarnico/potni
list/mobilni telefon so ukradli
*Moyeh potovalneh chekeh/Moyo
kredeetno karteetso/Moyo
torbeetso/Moy nakhrhbtneek/Moyo
prhtlyago/Moyo denarneetso/pot-nee
leest/moh-beel-nee teh-leh-fon
so ookradlee*

**S
L
O
V
E
N
I
A
N**

May I please have a copy of the report for my insurance claim?
Ali lahko, prosim, dobim kopijo poročila za zavarovalnico?
Ah-lee lah-h-koh, proh-seem, doh-beem koh-pee-yoh poh-roh-cheelah zah zah-vah-roh-vahl-neetsoh?

Can you help me? I have lost my daughter/son/my companion(s)
Mi lahko pomagate prosim? Izgubil(a) sem hčer/sina/ prijatelja/prijateljico (**fem.**)/ prijatelje (**pl.**)
Mee lahhko pomagateh prosseem? Eezgoobeel(a) sem khcher/seena/ preeyatelya/e/preeyatelyeeko/ preyatelyeh

Please go away/leave me alone
Prosim, pojdite stran/pustite me na miru
Prosseem poydeeteh stran/ poosteeteh meh na meeroo

I'm sorry
Oprostite
Oprossteeteh

I want to contact the British/American/Canadian/ Irish/Australian/New Zealand/South African Consulate
Rad(a) bi navezal(a) stike z Britansko/Ameriško/Kanadsko/ Avstralsko/Novozelandsko/Južn oafriško Ambasado
Rad(a) bee navezal(a) steekeh z Breetansko/Amereeshko/Kanadsko/ Owstralsko/Novozelandsko/ Yoozhnoafreeshko Ambassado

I'm ill/lost/injured
Bolan (Bolna) sem/Izgubil(a) sem se/Ranjen(a) sem
Bolan (Bohna) sem/Eazgoobeel(a) sem she/Ranyen(a) sem

He (she) is ill/lost/injured
Bolan (Bolna) je/Izgubil(a) se je/Ranjen(a) je
Bolan (Bohna) yeh/Eezgoobeel(a) seh yeh/Ranyen(a) yeh

They (we) are ill/lost/injured
Bolni so (smo)/Izgubili so (smo) se/Ranjeni so (smo)
Bohnee so (smo)/Eezgoobeelee so (smo) se/Ranyenee so (smo)

UKRAINIAN

INTRODUCTION

Ukrainian is the sole official state language. A member of the eastern Slav languages and similar to Russian, it was discouraged for centuries by Tsarist and Soviet authorities. It is still widely spoken in western and central Ukraine, although Russian is very widely spoken, and is the main language spoken in Kyiv (Kiev), Eastern Ukraine and Crimea. The present Government is using every opportunity to promote the revival of Ukrainian.

U
K
R
A
I
N
I
A
N

Addresses for Travel and Tourist Information

Canada: *Ukrainian Embassy*, 331 Metcalfe St, Ottawa, Ontario K2P 1S3. Tel: (613) 230 2961. Fax: (613) 230 2400.

UK: *Ukrainian Embassy*, Consular/Visa Section, 78 Kensington Park Rd, London W11 2PL. Tel: (020) 7243 8923. Fax: (020) 7727 3567.

USA: *Consulate General of Ukraine*, 240 East 49th St. New York, NY 10017. Tel: (212) 371 5690. Fax: (212) 371 5547.

Official tourism website: www.ukraine.org/tourism.html

Ukraine Facts

CAPITAL: Kyiv (Kiev)
CURRENCY: 1 Hryvnya = 100 kopiyok (singular: kopiyka).
OPENING HOURS: Banks: vary, but mostly Mon–Fri 0900–1200 and 1400–1630, Sat 0900–1100. Shops: mostly Mon–Sat 0800–1700. Museums: larger ones 1000–1800, many smaller ones 1000–1400; some close Mon.
TELEPHONES: To dial in, +380. Outgoing, 810 and the country code. Police, 02. Fire: 01, Ambulance 03.
PUBLIC HOLIDAYS: Jan 1; Jan 7–8; Mar 8; Apr 9–12; May 1–2; May 9; Jun 15–16; Aug 24; Nov 7–8.

Technical Language Hints

- Ukrainian is written with the Cyrillic alphabet.
- You may notice that Ukrainian shares some traits with Polish.

Alphabet and Pronunciation

	Name	Pronounced
А а	a	a as in father
Б б	be	b as in brother
В в	ve	v as in move
Г г	ge	g as in garden
Д д	de	d as in bid
Е е	e	a as in man
Ж ж	zhe	zh like s in pleasure
З з	ze	z as in zoo
І і	i	i as in milk
И и	yui	i as in with
Й й	yot	y as in yacht
К к	ka	k as in kit
Л л	el'	l as in milk
М м	em	m as in mother
Н н	en	n as in not
О о	aw	aw sound as in all
П п	pe	p as in put
Р р	er	r as in red
С с	es	s as in sister
Т т	te	t as in taxi
У у	u	short oo sound as in book
Ф ф	ef	f as in fill
Х х	ha	h as in house
Ц ц	tse	ts as in cats
Ч ч	cha	ch as in charm
Ш ш	sha	sh as in shoe
Щ щ	scha	sh but softer than Ш
Ь ь	m'yakiy znak	softens the previous consonant
Ї ї	iyi	yee as in yeast
Є є	ye	ye as in yesterday
Ю ю	yu	yoo as in you
Я я	ya	ya as in yard

Basic Words and Phrases

Yes
Так
Tak

No
Hі
Ni

Please
Будь ласка
Bud' laska

Thank you
Дякую
Dyakuyu

Hello
Здрастуйте/Привіт
Zdrastuite/Pryvit

Goodbye
До побачення
Do pobachenya

Excuse me
Перепрошую
Pareproshuii

Sorry
Вибачте
Vybachte

That's O.K.
Все гаразд
Vse garazd

Perhaps
Можливо
Mozhlivo

How
Як
Jak

When
Коли
Koly

Why
Чому
Chomu

What
Що
Scho

Who
Хто
Hto

UKRAINIAN

To
До, У
Do, U

From
З, Від
Z, Vid

Here
Тут
Tut

There
Там
Tam

I don't understand
Я не розумію
Ya ne pozumiyu

I don't speak Ukrainian
Я не розмовляю
по-українськи
Ya ne rozmovlyaiu po-ukrains'ky

Do you speak English?
Ви розмовляєте
по-ангійськи?
Vy rozmovlyaite po-anglyis'ky?

Can you please write it down?
Будь ласка, чи не могли б ви
записати це?
Bud' laska, chi ne mogly, b vy zapisaty tse?

Please can you speak more slowly?
Будь ласка, говоріть
повільніше
Bud' laska, govorit' povil'nishe

Greetings

**Good morning/
Good afternoon/
Good evening/Good night**
Доброго ранку/Добрий
день/Добрий вечір/На
добраніч
Dobroho ranku/Dobryi den'/Dobryi vechir/Na dobranich

Pleased to meet you
Приемно познайомитись
Pryiemno poznayomytys'

How are you?
Як справи?
Jak spravy?

**I am well, thank you.
And you?**
Дякую, добре. А у вас?
Dyakuyu dobre. A u vas?

My name is …
Мене звуть …
Mene zvitj …

**This is my friend/boyfriend/
girlfriend/husband/wife/
brother/sister**
Ц мій (моя) друг/хлопець/
дівчина/чоловік/жінка/брат/
сестра
Tse myi (moja) druh/hlopiets/ divchina/cholovik/zhinka/brat/sestra

Where are you travelling to?
Куди ви їдете?
Kudy vy yidete?

I am/we are going to...
Я/ми їдемо до …
Ya/my yidemo do...

How long are you travelling for?
Як довго ви подорожуєте?
Yak dovho vy podorozchuete?

Where do you come from?
Звідки ви?
Zvidky vy?

**I am/we are from …
Australia/Britain/
Canada/America**

Я/ми з ... Австралії/Британії/
Канади/Америки
Ya/My z...Avstraliyi/Britaniyi/
Kanady/Ameryky

We are on holiday
Ми у відпустці
My u vidpuststi

This is our first visit here
Ми тут вперше
My tut vpiershe

How old are you?
Скільки вам років?
Skil'ky vam rokiv?

I am ... years old
Мені ... років
Meni ... rokiv

**I am a business person/
doctor/journalist/manual
worker/administrator/
scientist/student/teacher**
Я бізнесмен/лікар/журналіст/
робітник фізичної праці/
адміністратор/вчений/
студент/викладач(вчитель)
*Ya bisnesmen/likar/zhurnalist/
robitnyk phizichnoi pratsi/
administrator/vchenyi/student/
vykladach*

**I am waiting for my husband/
wife/boyfriend/girlfriend**
Я чекаю на свого
чоловіка/свою жінку/свого
хлопця/свою дівчину
*Ya chekaiu na svoho cholovika/svoiu
zhinky/svoho hloptsya/svoiu divchinu*

**Would you like a cigarette/
may I have a cigarette?**
Чи не хочете ви закурити/
Чи ви не дасте мені цнгарку?

*Chy ne hochete vy zakurity/Chy vy
ne daste menie tsyharku?*

Do you mind if I smoke?
Ви не заперечуєте, я закрую?
Vy ne zaperechuete ya zakuriu?

Do you have a light?
Дозвольте прикурити?
Dozvol'te prykuryty?

Days

Monday
Понеділок
Ponedilok

Tuesday
Вівторок
Vivtorok

Wednesday
Середа
Sereda

Thursday
Четвер
Chetver

Friday
П'ятниця
P'yatnytsa

Saturday
Субота
Subota

Sunday
Неділя
Nedilya

Morning
Ранок
Ranok

Afternoon/Evening/Night
День/Вечір/Ніч
Den'/'Vechir/Nich

Yesterday
Вчора
Vchora

Today
Сьогодні
Syogodni

Tomorrow
Завтра
Zavtra

Numbers

Zero	**One**
Нуль	Один
Nul'	*Odyn*

Two	**Three**
Два	Три
Dva	*Try*

Four	**Five**
Чотири	П'ять
Chotyry	*P'yat'*

Six	**Seven**
Шість	Сім
Shyst'	*Sim*

Eight	**Nine**
Вісім	Дев'ять
Visim	*Devyat'*

Ten	**Eleven**
Десять	Одинадцять
Desyat'	*Odynatsyat'*

Twelve	**Thirteen**
Дванадцять	Тринадцять
Dvanatsyat'	*Trynatsyat'*

Fourteen	**Fifteen**
Чотирнадцять	П'ятнадцять
Chotyrnatsyat'	*P'yatnatsyat'*

Sixteen	**Seventeen**
Шістнадцять	Сімнадцять
Shistnatsyat'	*Simnatsyat'*

Eighteen	**Nineteen**
Вісімнадцять	Дев'ятнадцять
Visimnatsyat'	*Dev'yatnatsyat'*

Twenty	**Twenty-one**
Двадцять	Двадцять один
Dvatsyat'	*Dvatsyat'odyn*

Twenty-two	**Thirty**
Двадцять два	Тридцять
Dvatsyat' dva	*Trytsyat'*

Forty	**Fifty**
Сорок	П'ятдесят
Sorok	*P'yatdesyat*

Sixty	**Seventy**
Шістдесят	Сімдесят
Shistdesyat	*Simdesyat*

Eighty	**Ninety**
Вісімдесят	Дев'яносто
Visimdesyat	*Dev'yanosto*

One hundred	**Five hundred**
Сто	П'ятсот
Sto	*P'yatsot*

One thousand	**One million**
Тисяча	Мільйон
Tysyacha	*Mil'on*

Time

What time is it?
Котра година?
Kotra hodyna?

It is ...
Зараз ...
Zaraz ...

9.00
Дев'ять годин
Dev'yat' hodyn

9.05
Дев'ять годин п'ять хвилин
Dev'yat' hodyn pyat' hvylyn

9.15
Девять п'ятнадцять/Чверть
на десяту

Dev'yat' p'yatnatsat'/Chvert' na desyatu

9.20
Дев'ять годин двадцять хвилин
Dev'yat' hodyn dvatsyat' hvylyn

9.30
Пів на десяту
Piv na desyatu

9.35
Дев'ять тридцять п'ять
Dev'yat' trytsyat'' p'yat'

9.40
Без двадцяти хвилин десята
Bez dvatsyaty (hvylyn) desyata

9.45
Без п'ятнадцяти хвилин десята
Bez p'yatnatsyay (hvylyn) desyata

9.50
Без десяти хвилин десята
Bez desyaty (hvylyn) desyata

9.55
Без п'яти хвилин десята
Bez p'yaty (hvylyn) desyata

12.00/Midday/Midnight
Дванадцята година/Полудень/Північ
Dvanatsyata hodyna/Poludenya/Pivnich

Money

I would like to change these traveller's cheques/this currency
Я хотів би обміняти дорожні чеки/цю валюту

Ya hotiv by obminyaty dorojni checky/tsyu valiutu

How much commission do you charge? (What is the service charge?)
Скільки ви берете комісійних?
Skil'ky vy berete komisiynyh?

Can I obtain money with my Mastercard?
Чи можу я получити гроші з Мастеркард?
Chi mozhu ya poluchity hroshi z mastercard?

Where is the nearest ATM?
Де знаходиться найближчий банкомат?
De znakhoditsja najblizhchi banko-mat?

My name is … Some money has been wired to here for me to collect
Мене звуть … Для мене сюди був зроблений грошовий переказ
Mene zvitj … Dlya mene sjudi biv zrobleni groshovi perekaz

ARRIVING AND DEPARTING

Airport

Excuse me, where is the check-in desk for ... ?
Перепрошую, де відбувається реєстрація на ...?
Pereproshuyu de vitbuvaietsya reestratsiya na ...?

What is the boarding gate for my flight?
Через який вихід іде посадка на рейс?
Cherez yakyi vyhid ide posatka na reis?

What is the boarding time for my flight?
О котрій відбувається посадка на рейс?
O kotryi vitbudetsya posatka na reis?

How long is the delay likely to be?
Наскільки затримується рейс?
Na skil'ky zatrymuietsya reis?

Where is the duty-free shop?
Де знаходиться магазин безмитної торгівлі?
De znahodytsya magazyn bezmytnoi torhivli?

Which way is the luggage reclaim?
Як пройти до видачі багажу?
Yak proity do vydachi bahazhu?

I have lost my luggage. Please can you help?
Я загубив/загубила свій багаж. Ви не могли б мені допомогти?
Ya zahubyv/zahubyla sviy bahazh. Vy ne mohly b meni dopomohty?

I am flying to ...
Я лечу у ...
Ya lechu u ...

Where is the bus for the city centre (downtown)?
Звідки йде автобус до центру міста?
Zvidky yde aftobus do tsentra mista?

Trains and Boats

Where is the ticket office/information desk?
Де знаходиться квиткова каса/інформаційна служба?
De znahodytsya kytkova kasa/informatsiyna sluzhba?

Which platform does the train/speedboat/ferry to... depart from?
З якої платформи відправляється потяг/катер/паром до ...?
Z yakoi platformy vidpravlyaietsya potyah/kater/parom do...?

Where is platform ...?
Де знаходиться платформа ...?
De znahodytsya platforma...?

When is the next train/boat to ...?
Коли відправляється наступний потяг/корабель до ...?
Koly vidpravlyaietsya nastupnyi potyah/korabel' do ...?

374

Is there a later train/boat to...?
Чи є пізніше потяг/корабель до ...?
Chi ye piznishe potyah/korabel' do...?

Notices and Signs

Вагон-буфет/Вагон-ресторан
Vahon-bufet/Vahon-restoran
Buffet (Dining) car

Автобус
Avtobus
Bus

Питна/технічна вода
Pytna/tehnichna voda
Drinking/non-drinking water

Вхід
Fhid
Entrance

Вихід
Vyhid
Exit

Лікарня
Likarnya
Hospital

Інформаційна служба
Informatsiyna sluzhba
Information

Камера схову (зберігання)
Kamera shovu (zberihan'ya)
Left luggage (Baggage claim)

Автоматична камера схову
Aftomatychna kamera shovu
Luggage lockers

Пошта
Poshta
Post office

Платформа
Platforma
Platform

Залізничний вокзал
Zaliznychnyi vokzal
Railway station (Railroad)

Аеропорт
Aeroport
Airport

Відділення міліції
Vitdilen'ya militisiy
Police station

Порт
Port
Port

Ресторан
Restoran
Restaurant

Місце для паління/Не палити
Mistse dlya palinnya/Ne palyty
Smoking/non smoking

Телефон
Telephon
Telephone

Квиткова каса
Kvytkova kasa
Ticket office

U K R A I N I A N

Вікно реєстрації
Vikno reiestratsyi
Check-in desk

Розклад
Rosklad
Timetable (Schedule)

Туалети
Tualety
Toilets (Restrooms)

Жіночий/Чоловічий
Zhinochyi/Cholovichyi
Ladies/Gentlemen

Метро
Metro
Underground (Subway)

Зал очікування
Zal ochikuvan'ya
Waiting room

Buying a Ticket

**I would like a first-class/
second-class/third-class single
(one-way)/return (round-trip)
ticket to….**
Мені потрібен квиток
першого класу/другого
класу/третього класу в один
бік/зворотній до (у) …
*Menie potriben kvytok pershoho
klasu/druhoho klasu/tretioho klasu v
odyn bik/zvorotniy do (u)…*

**Is it an express (fast)
train/bus?**
Це швидкий потяг/автобус?
Tse shvydkyi potyah/aftobus?

**Is my rail pass valid on this
train/ferry/bus?**
Мій проїзний дійсний на
цьому потязі/паромі/
автобусі?
*Myi proiyizdnyi diysny na tsiomu
potyazi/paromi/aftobusi?*

**I would like an aisle/window
seat**
Я хотів(ла) б(и) місце біля
проходу/місце біля вікна
*Ya hotiv(la) b(y) mistse bilya pro-
chodu/mistse bilya vikna*

No smoking/smoking please
Не палити/Місце для паління
Ne palyty/Mistse dlya palinnya

We would like to sit together
Ми хотіли б сидіти разом
My hotily b sydity razom

**I would like to make a seat
reservation**
Я хотів(ла) б(и) замовити
місце
Ya hotiv(la) b(y) zamovyty mistse

**I would like to reserve a
couchette/sleeper for one
person/two people/my family**
Я хотів(ла) б(и) забронювати
місце/спальне місце для
однієї людини/двох
чоловік/моєї родини
*Ya hotiv(la) b(y) zabronuvaty
mistse/spal'ne mistse dlya odnieil
yudyny/dvoh cholovik/moyei rodynyi*

**I would like to reserve a
cabin**
Я хотів(ла) б(и) замовити
каюту
Ya hotiv(la) b(y) zamovyty kajutu

Timetables (Schedules)

Прибуття
Prybutya
Arrive

Стоянки (Зупинки)
Stoyanky (Zupynky)
Calls (Stops) at

Харчування
Harchuvan'ya
Catering service

Пересадка на
Peresatka na
Change at

Зв'язок/Через
Zv'yazok/Cherez
Connection/Via

Щоденно
Schodenno
Daily

Кожні сорок хвилин
Kozhni sorok hvylyn
Every 40 minutes

Перший клас
Pershyi klas
First class

Кожної години
Kozhnoi hodyny
Hourly

Бажано бронювати місця
Bazhano bronjuvaty mistsya
**Seat reservations are
recommended**

Другий клас
Druhyi klas
Second class

Оплачується додатково
Oplachuietsya dodatkovo
Supplement payable

Luggage

**How much will it cost to
send (ship) my luggage in
advance?**
Скільки коштуватиме
відправити (погрузити) мій
багаж заздалегідь?
*Skil'ky koshtuvatyme vidpravyty
(pohruzyty) miy bahazh
zazdalehyd?*

**Where is the left luggage
(baggage claim) office?**
Де знаходиться камера схову
(вимоги) багажу?
*De znahodytsya kamera skhovu
(vymogy) bahazhu?*

**What time do you
open/close?**
О котрій ви
відчиняєте/зачиняєте?
*O kotriy vy vidchynyaiete/
zachynyaiete?*

**Where are the luggage
trolleys (carts)?**
Де знаходяться візки для
багажу?
*De znahodyatsya visky dlya
bahazhu?*

Where are the lockers?
Де знаходяться автоматичні

377

UKRAINIAN

камери схову?
De znahodyatsia avtomatychni kamery shovu?

I have lost my locker key
Я загубив ключа від автоматичної камери схову
Ya zahubyv kl'ucha vid (avtomatychnoiy) kamery shovu

On Board

Is this seat free?
Це місце вільне?
Tse mistse vil'ne?

Excuse me, you are sitting in my reserved seat
Вибачте, ви сидите на моєму місці
Vybachte vy sydete na moiemu mistsi

Which station is this?
Яка це станція?
Yaka tse stantsya?

What time is this train/bus/ferry/flight due to arrive/depart?
О котрій має прибути/відправитись цей потяг/автобус/паром/рейс?
O kotryi mae prybuty/vidpravytys' tsei potyah/aftobus/parom/reis?

Travelling with Children

Do you have a high chair/babysitting service/cot?
Чи є у вас високий стілець/служба по догляду за дітьми/дитяче ліжечко?
Chy ye u vas vysokyi stilets'/sluzhba

po dohlyadu za dit'my/dytyache lizhechko?

Where is the nursery/playroom?
Де знаходиться кімната матері та дитини/кімната для ігор?
De znahodytsya kimnata materi ta dytyny/kimnata dlya ihor?

Where can I warm the baby's bottle?
Де можна підігріти дитячу пляшечку?
De mozhna pidihryty dytyachu plyashechku?

Customs and Passports

Будь ласка, пред'явіть паспорти
Bud' laska, priedyavit' pasporty
Passports please

I have nothing to declare
Мені нічого декларувати
Meni nichoho deklaruvaty

I have wine/spirits (alcohol)/tobacco to declare
Я хочу задекларувати вино/алкогольні напої/тютюнові вироби
Ya hochu zadeklaruvaty vyno/alkohol'ni napoi/tyutyunovi vyroby

I will be staying for ... days/weeks/months
Я буду перебувати ... днів/тижнів/місяців
Ya budu perebuvaty... dniv/tyzhniv/misyatsiv

SIGHTSEEING

Asking the Way

Excuse me, do you speak English?
Перепрошую, ви розмовляєте по-англійські?
Pereproshuju vy rozmovlyaiete po-angliyski?

Excuse me, can you help me please?
Перепрошую, ви не могли б мені допомогти?
Pereproshuju, vy ne mohly b meni dopomohty?

Where is the tourist information office?
Де знаходиться служба інформації для туристів?
De znahodytsya sluzhba informatsyi dlya turystiv?

Excuse me, is this the right way to...?
Вибачте, я правильно йду до ...?
Vybachte, ya pravyl'no yidu do...?

... the cathedral/the tourist information office/the castle/the old town
... собору/туристичної агенції/замку/старого міста
...soboru/turystychnoi ahentsiyi/zamku/staroho mista

Can you tell me the way to the railway (railroad) station/ bus station/taxi rank/city centre (downtown)/beach?
Як пройти до залізничного вокзалу/автовокзалу/стоянки таксі/центру міста/пляжу?
Jak proity do zalieznychnoho vokzalu/aftovokzalu/stoyanky taksi/tsentru mista/plyazhu?

Перший/другий поворот/ ліворуч/праворуч/прямо
Pershyi/druhyi povorot/livoruch/ pravoruch/pryamo
First/second left/right/ straight ahead

На розі/Біля світлофору
Na rozi/Bilya svitloforu
At the corner/At the traffic lights

Where is the nearest police station/post office?
Де знаходиться найближче відділення міліції/поштове відділення?
De znakhoditsya najblizhche viddilennya militsii/poshtove viddilennya?

Is it near/far?
Це близько/далеко?
Tse blyz'ko/daleko?

Do I need to take a taxi/catch a bus?
Мені треба взяти таксі/їхати автобусом?
Meni treba vzyaty taksi/yihaty aftobusom?

Do you have a map?
У вас є карта?
U vas ye karta?

Can you point to it on my map?
Ви можете показати, де це на карті?
Vy mozhete pokazaty, de tse na karti?

U K R A I N I A N

U K R A I N I A N

Thank you for your help
Дякую за допомогу
Dyakuju za dopomohu

How do I reach the motorway/main road?
Як виїхати на шосе/головну дорогу?
Jak vyiyhaty na shose/holovnu dorohu?

I think I have taken the wrong turning
Мені здається, я не там повернув
Meni zdaietsya, ya ne tam povernuv

I am looking for this address
Я шукаю цю адресу
Ya shukaju tsiu adresu

I am looking for the ... Hotel
Я шукаю готель ...
Ya shukaiu hotel'...

How far is it to ... from here?
Як далеко до ... звідси?
Jak daleko do ... zvidsy?

Їхати прямо ... кілометрів
Yihaty pryamo ... kilometriv
Carry straight on for ... kilometres

Наступний поворот праворуч/ліворуч
Nastupnyi povorot pravoruch/livoruch
Take the next turning on the right/left

Поверніть праворуч/ліворуч на наступному перехресті/світлофорі
Povernit' pravoruch/livoruch na nastupnomu perehresti/svitlofori

Turn right/left at the next crossroads/traffic lights

Ви ідете (йдете) не в тому напрямку
Vy yidete (ydete) ne v tomu napryamki
You are going in the wrong direction

Where is the cathedral/ church/museum/pharmacy?
Де знаходиться собор/ церква/музей/аптека?
De znahodyt'sya sobor/tserkva/ muzei/apteka?

How much is the admission/ entrance charge?
Скільки коштує вхід?
Skil'ki koshtue fhid?

Is there a discount for children/students/senior citizens?
Чи є знижка для дітей/ студентів/людей похилого віку?
Chi e znyzhka dlya ditei/studentiv/l'udei pohyloho viku?

What time does the next guided tour (in English) start?
Коли починається наступна екскурсія (англійською мовою)?
Koly pochynayetsya nastupna ekskursiya (anhliys'koi movoyu)?

One/two adults/children please
Будь ласка, один/два дорослих/дитячий
Bud' laska, odyn/dviyko doroslyh/ditei

May I take photographs here?
Тут можна фотографвати?
Tut mozhna fotohrafuvaty?

At the Tourist Office

Do you have a map of the town/area?
У вас є карта міста/району?
U vas ye karta mista/raionu?

Do you have a list of accommodation?
У вас є перелік житла?
U vas ye perelik zhitla?

Can I reserve accommodation?
Чи можу я зняти житло?
Chi mozhu ya znyaty zytlo?

ACCOMMODATION

Hotels

I have a reservation in the name of ...
У мене заброньовано номер на ім'я ...
U mene zabroniovano nomer na im'ya ...

I wrote to/faxed/telephoned you last month/last week
Я присилав вам листа/факс/ телефонував минулого місяця/минулого тижня
Ya prysylav vam lysta/fax/ telefonuvav mynuloho misyatsya/mynuloho tyzhnya

Do you have any rooms free?
У вас є вільні кімнати?
U vas ye vil'ni kimnaty?

I would like to reserve a single/double room with/ without a bath/shower
Я б хотів(ла) зняти одномісний/двомісний номер з ванною/душем/без ванноі/ душа
Ya b hotiv(la) zn'yaty odnomistnyi/ dvomistnyi nomer z vannoyu/ dushem/bez vannoi/dusha

I would like bed/breakfast/ (room) and full board
Мені потрібне місце/сніданок/(кімната) і повний пансіон
Meni potrybne mistse/snidanok/ (kimnata) i povnyi pansion

How much is it per night?
Скільки це коштує за добу?
Skil'ky tse koshtuie za dobu?

Is breakfast included?
Чи входить сніданок у вартість?
Chi vhodyt' snidanok u vartist'?

Do you have any cheaper rooms?
Чи є у вас дешевші кімнати?
Chi ye u vas deshevshi kimnaty?

I would like to see/take the room
Я б хотів(ла) подвитись/ зняти кімнату
Ya b hotiv(la) podyvytys'/znyaty kimnatu

I would like to stay for ... nights
Я б хотів зупинитись на ... діб
Ya b hotiv(la) zupynytys' na ... dib

U
K
R
A
I
N
I
A
N

The shower/light/tap/ hot water doesn't work
Душ/світло/кран/гаряча вода не працює
Dush/svitlo/kran/haryatcha voda ne pratsuie

At what time/Where is breakfast served?
О котрій/Куди(де) подають сніданок?
O kotriy/kudy(de) podaut' snidanok?

What time do I have to check out?
Коли мені треба виїхати?
Koly meni treba vyiyhaty?

Can I have the key to room number ...?
Я можу отримати ключ від кімнати номер ...?
Ya mozhu otrymaty kliuch vid kimnaty nomer...?

My room number is...
Номер моєї кімнати...
Nomer moyei kimnaty...

My room is not satisfactory/not clean enough/too noisy. Please can I change rooms?
Моя кімната/ліжко в поганому стані/брудна(е)/ надто гомінка. Я можу її поміняти?
Moya kimnata/lizhko v pohanomu stani/brudna(e)/nadto hominka. Ya mozhu iyi pominyaty

Where is the bathroom?
Де знаходиться ванна?
De znuhoditsya vanna?

Do you please have a safe for valuables?
Скажіть, будь ласка, у вас є сейф для коштовностей?
Skazhit', bud' laska, u vas ye seif dl'ya koshtovnostei?

Is there a laundry/do you wash clothes?
Чи є у вас пральня/ви перете одяг?
Chi ye u vas praln'ya/vy perete odyah?

I would like an air-conditioned room
Я хочу зняти кімнату з кондиціонером
Ya hochu znyaty kimnatu z conyitsionerom

Do you accept traveller's cheques/credit cards?
Ви приймаєте дорожні чеки/кредитні картки?
Vy pryimaete dorozhni cheki/credytni kartky?

May I have the bill please?
Я можу отримати рахунок?
Ya mozhu otrymaty rahunok?

Excuse me, I think there may be a mistake in this bill
Вибачте, мені здається, у рахунку помилка
Vybachte, meni zdaietsya u rahunku pomylka

Youth Hostels

How much is a dormitory bed per night?
Скільки коштує спальне місце у гуртожитку за добу?
Skilky koshtuie spal'ne mistse u hurtozhitku za dobu?

I am/am not an HI member
Я не є членом ейч-ай
Ja ne ye chlenom eich-ai

May I use my own sleeping bag?
Я можу користуватися власним спальним мішком?
Ya mohu korystuvatys' vlasnym spal'nym mishkom?

What time do you lock the doors at night?
О котрій ви зачиняєте двері ввечері?
O kotriy vy zachynyaiete dveri vvecheri?

Camping

May I camp for the night/two nights?
Я можу зупинитися на добу/дві доби?
Ya mozhu zupynytysya na dobu/dvi doby?

Where can I pitch my tent?
Де я можу розташувати намет?
De ya mozhu roztushuvaty namet?

How much does it cost for one night/week?
Скільки це коштуватиме за добу/тиждень?
Skil'ky tse koshtuvatyme za dobu/tyzhden'?

Where are the washing facilities?
Де знаходиться ванна (душ)?
De znahodytsya vanna (dush)?

Is there a restaurant/supermarket/swimming pool on site/nearby?
Тут є ресторан/супермаркет/басейн неподалік/поблизу?
Tut ye restoran/supermarket/basein nepodalik/poblyzu?

Do you have a safety deposit box?
У вас є камера схову?
U vas ye kamera shovu?

EATING AND DRINKING

Cafés and Bars

I would like a cup of/two cups of/another coffee/tea
Будь ласка, принесіть чашку/дві чашки/ще кави/чаю
Bud' laska, prynesit' chashku/dvi chashky/sche kavy/tchayu

With/without milk/sugar
З молоком/без молока/цукром(у)
Z molokom/bez moloka/tsukrom(u)

I would like a bottle/glass/two glasses of mineral water/red wine/white wine, please
Будь ласка, принесіть пляшку/стакан/два стакана мінеральної води/червоного

UKRAINIAN

вина/білого вина
Bud' laska, prynesit' pliashku/stakan/dva stackana mineral'noi vody/chervonoho vyna/biloho vyna

I would like a beer/two beers, please
Будь ласка, принесіть пиво/два пива
Bud' laska, prynesit' pyva/dva pyva

Please may I have some ice?
Будь ласка, принесіть льоду?
Bud' laska, prynesit' l'odu?

Do you have any matches/cigarettes/cigars?
У вас продаються сірники/цигарки/цигари?
U vas prodaiutsia sirnyky/tsyharky/tsyhary?

Restaurants

Can you recommend a good/cheap restaurant in this area?
Ви можете порекомендувати тут гарний/недорогий ресторан?
Vy mozhete porekomendovat' tut harnyi/nedorohyi restoran?

I would like a table for ... people
Я хочу замовити столик на ... чоловік
Ya hochu zamovyty stolyk na ... cholovik

Do you have a non-smoking area?
У вас є зала для тих, хто не курить?
U vas ye zal dlya tyh, hto ne kuryt'?

Waiter! Waitress!
Офіціант! Офіціантка!
Ofitsiant! Ofitsiantka!

Excuse me, please may we order?
Вибачте, ми можемо зробити замовлення?
Vybachte, my mozhemor zrobyty zamovlennya?

Do you have a set menu/ children's menu/wine list in English?
У вас є меню/список вин англійською?
U vas ye meniu/ditjache menyu/spysok vyn angliys'koi?

Do you have any vegetarian dishes?
Чи є в Вас вегетаріанські страви?
Chi e v Vas vegetarians'ki stravi?

Do you have any local specialities?
У вас є якісь місцеві страви?
U vas ye yakis' mistsevi stravy?

Are vegetables included?
Чи включено овочі?
Chi vkliucheno ovochi?

Could I have it well-cooked/ medium/rare please?
Можна підсмажити/добре/ з кров'ю?
Mozhna pidsmazhity/dobre/z krov'u?

What does this dish consist of?
З чого приготовлено цю страву?
Z choho pryhotovano tsiu stravu?

I am a vegetarian. Does this contain meat?

Я вегетаріанець. Чи є в цій страві м'ясо?

Ya vegetarianets'. Chi e v tsij stravi mjaso?

I do not eat nuts/dairy products/meat/fish

Я не їм горіхи/молочні продукти/м'ясо/рибу

Ya ne yim horihy/molochni produkty/myaso/rybu

Not (very) spicy please

Не (дуже) гострий(е), будь ласка

Ne (duzhe) hostryi(e) bud' laska

I would like the set menu please

Принесіть будь ласка меню

Prynesit' bud' laska meniu

We have not been served yet

Ми все ще чекаємо на обслуговування

Mi vse shche chekaemo na obslugovuvannya

Please bring a plate/knife/fork

Будь ласка принесіть тарілку/ніж/виделку

Bud' laska prinesit' tarilku/ nizh/videlku

Excuse me, this is not what I ordered

Вибачте, це не те, що я замовляв

Vybachte, tse ne te shcho ya zamovlyav

May I have some/more bread/water/coffee/tea?

Можна мені ще хліба/води/кави/чаю?

Mozhna meni shche hliba/vody/kavy/chayu?

May I have the bill please?

Я можу отримати рахунок?

Ya mozhu otrymaty rahunok?

Does this bill include service?

Вартість обслуговування входить до рахунку?

Vartist' obsluhovuvann'ya vhodyt' do rahunku?

Do you accept traveller's cheques/Mastercard/ US dollars?

Ви приймаєте дорожні чеки/Мастеркард/ американські долари?

Vy pryimaiete dorozhni cheky/ mastercard/americans'ki dolary?

Can I have a receipt please?

Будь ласка, ви можете дати чек (рахунок)?

Bud' laska, vy mozhete daty check (rachunok)?

Where is the toilet (restroom) please?

Де знаходиться туалет?

De znahodytsya tualet?

U
K
R
A
I
N
I
A
N

385

UKRAINIAN

On the Menu

Сніданок/Обід/Вечеря
Snidanok/Obid/Vecherya
Breakfast/Lunch/Dinner

Перші страви	Супи
Pershi stravy	*Supy*
First courses	**Soups**

Основні страви	Рибні
Osnovni stravy	страви
Main courses	*Rybni stravy*
	Fish dishes

М'ясні страви	Яловичина
M'yasni stravy	*Yalovichina*
Meat dishes	**Beef**

Біфштекс	Свинина
Bifshteks	*Svinina*
Steak	**Pork**

Телятина	Курча
Telyatina	*Kurcha*
Veal	**Chicken**

Ягня	Шинка
Yagnya	*Shinka*
Lamb	**Ham**

Вегетаріанські страви
Vehetarians'ki stravy
Vegetarian dishes

Овочі
Ovochi
Vegetables

Смажена картопля
Smazhena kartoplya
Chips (french fries)

Варена/тушована
картопля/пюре
*Varena/Tushovana
kartolya/Pjure*
**Boiled/sauté/mashed
potatoes**

Рис	Десерти
Ris	*Deserty*
Rice	**Desserts**

Морозиво	Торт
Morozivo	*Tort*
Ice cream	**Cakes**

Печиво	Фрукт
Pechivo	*Frukt*
Pastries	**Fruit**

Хліб	Булочка
Khlib	*Bulochka*
Bread	**Rolls**

Грінка	Масло
Grinka	*Maslo*
Toast	**Butter**

Сіль/перець	Цукор
Sil'/perets'	*Tsukor*
Salt/pepper	**Sugar**

Фірмові страви
Firmovi stravy
Specialities

Місцеві страви
Mistsevi stravy
Local specialities

Комплексне меню
Kompleksne menju
Set menu

Карта вин
Karta vin
Wine list

Червоні вина
Chervoni vina
Red wines

Білі вина
Bili vina
White wines

Рожеві вина
Rozhevi vina
Rosé wines

Ігристі вина
Igristi vina
Sparkling wines

Пиво
Pivo
Beer

Пиво у пляшках/Пиво з бочки
Pivo u pljashkah/Pivo z bochki
Bottled beer/draught (draft) beer

Безалкогольні напої
Bezalkogolni napoi
Non-alcoholic drinks

Мінеральна вода
Mineral'na voda
Mineral water

Фруктові соки
Fruktovi soku
Fruit juices

Помаранчевий сік
Pomaranchevi sik
Orange juice

Лимонад
Limonad
Lemonade

Лід
Lid
Ice

Кава з молоком/Чорна кава/Еспресо
Kava z molokom/Chorna kava/espreso
White coffee/black coffee/espresso coffee

Чай з молоком/з лимоном
Chaj z molokom/z limonom
Tea with milk/with lemon

Шоколад
Shokolad
Chocolate (drink)

Молоко
Moloko
Milk

Закуски/Легкі страви
Zakuski/Legki stravi
Snacks/Light meals

Салати
Salati
Salads

Бутерброди
Buterbrodi
Sandwiches

Яйця
Yajtsa
Eggs

Ковбаса
Kovbasa
Sausage

Варені/Смажені яйця/Омлет
Vareni/Smazheni yaitsa/Omlet
Boiled /fried/scrambled eggs

Typical Local Dishes

Борщ
Borsch
Borsch (beetroot soup with vegetables)

Вареники
Varenyky
Varenyki (dough filled with meat or cabbage, potatoes or fruit)

U
K
R
A
I
N
I
A
N

Голубці
Holubtsi
Holubtsy (rice with meat filling rolled into cabbage leaves fried in soured cream)

Копчене сало
Kopchene salo
Kopchene salo (smoked pork fat)

Горілка
Horilka
Horilka (strong alcoholic drink)

GETTING AROUND

Public Transport

Where is the bus stop/coach stop/nearest metro (subway) station?
Де знаходиться зупинка автобуса/міжміського автобуса/найближча станція метро?
De znahoditsya zupynka aftobusa/mizhmis'koho aftobusa/naiblyzhcha stantsia metro?

When is the next/last bus to ...?
Коли йде наступний/останній автобус до ...?
Koly ide nustupnyi/ostanniy aftobus do ...?

How much is the fare to the city centre (downtown)/railway (railroad) station/airport?

Скільки коштує доїхати до центру міста/залізничного вокзалу/аеропорту?
Skil'ky koshtuie doyihaty do tsentra mista/zaliznychnoho vokzalu/aeroportu?

Will you tell me when to get off?
Ви скажете коли мені виходити?
Vy skazhete koly meni vyhodyty?

Does this bus go to ...?
Цей автобус йде до ...?
Tsei aftobus yide do ...?

Which number bus goes to ...?
Який номер автобуса йде до ...?
Yakyi nomer aftobusu ide do ...?

May I have a single (one-way)/return (round-trip)/day ticket/book of tickets?
Я можу придбати квиток на одну поїздку/туди й назад (в обидва боки) проїзний на один день/квиткову книжку?
Ya mozhu prydbaty kvytok na odnu poyizdku/tudy i nazad (v obydva boky)/proizdnyi na odyn den'/kvytkovu knyzhku

Taxis (Таксі)

I would like to go to ... How much will it cost?
Я б хотів(ла) доїхати до ...
Скільки це коштує?
Ya b hotiv(la) doyihahty do ... Skil'ky tse koshtuie?

Please may I stop here?
Будь ласка, можете зупинити тут?
Bud' laska, mozhete zupynyty tut?

I would like to order a taxi today/tomorrow at 2pm to go from ... to ...
Я б хотів(ла) замовити таксі сьогодні/завтра о другій годині дня, щоб доїхати з ... до ...
Ya b hotiv(la) zamovyty taksi s'ohodni/zavtra o druhiy hodyni dn'ya shchob doiyhaty z ... do ...

Entertainment

Can you recommend a good bar/nightclub?
Ви можете порекомендувати хороший бар/нічний клуб?
Vy mozhete porecomenduvaty horoshiy bar/nichnyi club?

Do you know what is on at the cinema (playing at the movies)/theatre at the moment?
Ви не знаєте що зараз йде в кіно/театрі?
Vy ne znaiete shcho zaraz ide v kino/teatri?

I would like to book (purchase) ... tickets for the matinee/evening performance on Monday
Я б хотів замовити (купити) ... квитки на ранкову/вечірню виставу в понеділок
Ya b hotiv zamovyty (kupyty)... kvytky na rankovu/vechirniu vystavu v ponedilok

What time does the film/performance start?
О котрій починається фільм/вистава?
O kotriy pochynaietsia fil'm/vystava?

Post

How much will it cost to send a letter/postcard/this package to Britain/America/Canada/Australia/New Zealand?
Скільки коштує відправити листа/поштову листівку/цю посилку до Британії/Америки/Канади/Австралії/Нової Зеландії?
Skil'ky koshtuie vidpravyty lysta/poshtovu lystivku/tsiu posylku do Brytaniyi/Ameryky/Kanady/Avstraliyi/Novoi Zelandiyi

I would like one stamp/two stamps
Дайте, будь ласка, одну/дві марки
Daite, bud' laska, odnu/dvi marky

I'd like ... stamps for postcards to send abroad, please
Дайте, будь ласка ... міжнародних марок для поштових листівок
Daite, bud' laska ... mizhnarodnyh marok dlya poshtovyh lystivok

U K R A I N I A N

Phones

I would like to make a telephone call/reverse the charges to (make a collect call to) ...
Я б хотів(ла) подзвонити/за рахунок абонента, що викликається ...
Ya b hotiv(la) podzonyty/za rahunok abonenta, shcho vyklykaietsya ...

Which coins do I need for the telephone?
Які монети потрібні для телефону?
Yaki monety potribni dl'ya telefonu?

The line is engaged (busy)
Лінію зайнято
Liniyu zainyato

The number is ...
Номер ...
Nomer ...

Hello, this is ...
Здрастуйте, це ...
Zdrastuite, tse ...

Please may I speak to ...?
Перепрошую, я можу поговорити з ...?
Pereproshuyu, ya mozhu pohovority z ...?

He/she is not in at the moment. Please can you call back?
Його/її зараз нема. Будь ласка, передзвоніть пізніше?
Joho/jiyi zaraz nema. Bud' laska, peredzvonit' piznishe?

Shops

Книги/Канцтовари
Knyhi/Kanstovary
Bookshop/Stationery

Ювелірний/Подарунки
Juvelirnyi/Podarunky
Jeweller/Gifts

Взуття
Vzut'ya
Shoes

Господарчі товари
Hospodarchi tovary
Hardware

Перукарня
Perukarnya
Hairdresser

Булочна
Bulochna
Baker

Супермаркет
Supermarket
Supermarket

Фототовари
Fototovary
Photo shop

Туристичне Бюро
Turystychne Biuro
Travel agent

Аптека
Apteka
Pharmacy

In the Shops

What time do the shops open/close?
О котрій зачиняються відкриваються магазини?
O kotriy zachinyaietsya vidkrivayutjsa/mahaziny?

Where is the nearest market?
Де знаходиться найближчий ринок?
De znahoditsya naiblyzhchiy rynok?

Can you show me the one in the window/this one?
Ви можете показати мені оце що на вітрині/оце?
Vy mozhete pokazaty meni otse scho na vitryni/otse?

Can I try this on?
Я можу це приміряти?
Ya mozhu tse prymiryaty?

What size is this?
Який це розмір?
Yakiy tse rozmir?

This is too large/too small/too expensive. Do you have any others?
Це надто великого розміру/надто маленького розміру/надто дорого. У вас є інші?
Tse nadto velykoho rozmiru/nadto maleikoho rozmiru/nadto dorohu. U vas ye isnhi?

My size is...
Мій розмір ...
Miy rozmir...

Where is the changing room/children's/cosmetic/ladieswear/menswear/food department?
Де примірочна/дитячий/парфюмерний/жіночий/чоловічий/продовольчий відділ?
De prymirochna/dytyachyi/parfiumernyi/zhinochyi/cholovichyi/prodovolchyi viddil?

I would like ... a quarter of a kilo/half a kilo/a kilo of bread/butter/ham/this fruit
Дайте будь ласка ... двісті п'ятдесят грамів/півкілограму/кілограм хліба/масла/шинки/цих фруктів
Daite, bud' laska ... dvisti pyatdesyat hramiv/pivkilohramu/kilohram hliba/masla/shinki/tsyh fructiv

How much is this?
Скільки це коштує?
Skilki tse koshtuie?

I'll take this one, thank you
Я візьму це, спасибі
Ya viz'mu tse, spasybi

Do you have a carrier (shopping) bag?
Чи є в Вас візок для товарів?
Chi e v Vas vizok dlya tovariv?

Do you have anything cheaper/larger/smaller/of better quality?
У вас є щось дешевше/більше/менше/кращої якості?
U vas ye shchos' deshevshe/bil'she/menshe/kraschoi yakosti?

I would like a film/to develop this film for this camera
Я б хотів купити плівку/ проявити плівку з цього фотоапарату
Ya b hotiv(la) kupyty plivku/proyavyty plivku z tsioho fotoaparatu

I would like some batteries, the same size as this old one
Дайте, будь ласка батарейки такого ж розміру, як ось оця стара
Daite, bud' laska batareiky takoho zh rozmiru, jak os' otsya stara

Would you mind wrapping this for me, please?
Будь ласка, загорніть це для мене
Bud' laska, zahornyt' tse dlya mene

Sorry, but you seem to have given me the wrong change
Вибачте, але, здається, ви невірно дали мені здачу
Vybachte, ale, zdaetsya, vy navirno daly meni zdachu

MOTORING

Car Hire (Rental)

I have ordered (rented) a car in the name of ...
Я замовив (взяв напрокат) машину на ім'я ...
Ya zamovyv (vzyav na prokat) mashynu na im'ya ...

How much does it cost to hire (rent) a car for one day/two days/a week?
Скільки коштує найняти (взяти напокат) машину на
день/на два дні/на тиждень?
Skil'ky koshtuie nainyaty (vzyaty na prokat) mashynu na den'/na dva dni/na tyzhden'?

Is the tank already full of petrol (gas)?
Бак вже заповнений бензином?
Bak vzhe zapovnenyi benzinom?

Is insurance and tax included? How much is the deposit?
Чи включені страховка і податки? Який розмір застави?
Chi vklyutcheni strahofka i podatky? Yakyi rozmir zastavy?

By what time must I return the car?
До якого часу я повинен (повинна) повернути машину?
Do yakoho chasu ya (povynenna) povernuty mashinu?

I would like a small/large/family/sports car with a radio/cassette/
Я б хотів(ла) взяти невелику/велику/сімейну/ спортивну машину з радіо/магнітофоном
Ya b hotiv(la) vzyaty nevelyku/velyku/simeinu/sportyvnu mashynu z radio/mahnitofonom

Do you have a road map?
У вас є карта автомобільних шляхів?
U vas ye karta avtomobil'nyh shlyahif?

Parking

How long can I park here?
Як довго тут можна стояти?
Jak dovho tut mozhna stoyaty?

Is there a car park near here?
Чи є неподалік автостоянка?
Chy ye nepodalik avtostoyanka?

At what time does this car park close?
О котрій зачиняється ця стоянка?
O kotriy zachynyaietsya tsia stoianka?

Signs and Notices

Односторонній рух
Odnostoroniy ruh
One way

В'їзд заборонено
V'iyizd zaboroneno
No entry

Зупинка заборонена
Zupynka zaboronena
No parking

Об'їзд
Ob'iyizd
Detour (Diversion)

Стоп
Stop
Stop

Дай дорогу
Dai dorohu
Give way (Yield)

Ожеледиця
Ozheledytsia
Slippery road

Обгін заборонено
Obhin zaboroneno
No overtaking

Небезпека!
Nebezpeka!
Danger!

At the Filling Station
(На Автозаправці)

Unleaded (lead free)/ standard/premium/diesel
Неетілований/звичайний/ вищої якості/дизельне паливо
Neetilovanyi/zvychainyi/vyshchoi yakosti/dyzilne palivo

Fill the tank please
Будь ласка, наповніть бак
Bud' laska napovnit' bak

Do you have a road map?
У вас є карта автомобільних шляхів?
U vas ye karta avtomobil'nyh shlyahif?

How much is the car wash?
Скільки коштує помити машину?
Skil'ki koshtuie pomyty mashinu?

MOTORING

Breakdowns

I've had a breakdown at ...
У мене зламалася машина
на ...
U mene zlahmalasya mashyna na ...

**I am a member of the ...
[motoring organisation]**
Я є членом ...
Ya e chlenom ...

**I am on the road from ...
to ...**
Я знаходжуся на дорозі з ...
до ...
Ya znahozhus' na dorozie z ...do ...

**I can't move the car. Can you
send a tow-truck?**
Я не можу завести машину.
Ви можете приспати тягача?
*Ya ne mozhu zavesty mashynu.
Vy mozhete pryslaty tyahacha?*

I have a flat tyre
Я проколов шину
Ya prokolov shynu

**The windscreen (windshield)
has smashed/cracked**
Лобове скло
розбилося/тріснуло
Lobove sklo rozbylosya/trisnulo

**There is something wrong
with the engine/brakes/ lights/
steering/gearbox/clutch/
exhaust**
Щось трапилося з двигуном/
гальмами/фарами/кермовим
управлінням/коробкою
передач/зчепленням/
глушником
*Shchos' trapylosya z dvyhunom/
hal'mami/faramy/kermovym*

*upravlin'yam/korobkoiu
peredach/zcheplen'yam/hlushnikom*

It's overheating
Він перегрівається
Vin perehrivayet'sya

It won't start
Він не заводиться
Vin ne zavodyt'sya

Where can I get it repaired?
Де це можна полагодити?
De tse mozhna polahodyty?

Can you take me there?
Ви можете відбуксувати мене
туди?
*Vy mozhete vidbuksuvaty mene
tudy?*

Will it take long to fix?
Чи багато часу піде на
ремонт?
Chi bahato chasu pide na remont?

How much will it cost?
Скільки це коштуватиме?
Ski'lky tse koshtuvatyme?

**Please can you pick me
up/give me a lift?**
Підвезіть мене, будь ласка
Pidvezit' mene, bud' laska

Accidents and Traffic Offences (Violations)

Can you help me? There has been an accident
Ви не могли б мені допомогти? Там трапився нещасний випадок
Vi ne mogli b meni dopomogti? Tam trapivsya neschasnii vipadok

Please call the police/an ambulance
Будь ласка подзвоніть до міліції/швидкої допомоги
Bid' laska pozvonit' do militsii/shvid-koi dopomogi

Is anyone hurt?
Чи є хтось поранений?
Chi e khtos' poranenij?

I'm sorry, I didn't see the sign
Вибачте, я не побачив знака
Vybachte, ya ne pobachiv znaka

Must I pay a fine? How much?
Я повинен заплатити штраф? Скільки?
Ya povynen zaplatyty shtraf? Skil'ky?

Пред'явіть ваші документи
Pred'yavit' vashi dokumenty
Show me your documents

HEALTH

Pharmacy (Аптека)

Do you have anything for a stomach ache/headache/sore throat/toothache?
У вас є щось від болю в шлунку/головного болю/ангіни/зубного болю?
U vas ye shchos' vid boliu v shlunku/holovnoho boliu/anhiny/zubnoho boliu?

I need something for diarrhoea/constipation/a cold/a cough/insect bites/sunburn/travel (motion) sickness
Мені потрібно щось від проносу/запору/застуди/кашлю/укусів комах/сонячного опіку/захитування
Meni potribno shchos' vid pronosu/zaporu/zastudy/kashliu/uku siv komah/sonyachnoho opiku/zahytuvan'ya

How much/how many do I take?
Скільки треба приймати?
Skil'ky treba pryimaty?

I am taking anti-malaria tablets/these pills
Я приймаю таблетки проти малярії/ці капсули
Ya pryimaiu tabletky proty malyariy/tsi kapsuly

How often do I take it/them?
Як часто їх спід приймати?
Yak chasto iyh slid pryimaty?

I am/he is/she is taking this medication
Я/він/вона приймає ці ліки
Ya/vin/vona pryimaie tsi liky

How much does it cost?
Скільки це коштує?
Skil'ky tse koshtuie?

Can you recommend a good doctor/dentist?
Ви можете порекомендвати гарного лікаря/зубного лікаря?
Vy mozhete porekomendovaty harnoho likarya/zubnoho likarya?

Is it suitable for children?
Це підходить для дітей?
Tse pidhodyt' dlya ditei?

Doctor (Лікар)

I have a pain here/in my arm/leg/chest/stomach
У мене болить
тут/рука/нога/груди/живіт
U mene bolyt' tut/ruka/noha/hrudy/zhyvit

Please call a doctor, this is an emergency
Будь ласка, терміново викличте лікаря
Bud' laska, terminovo vyklychte likarya

I would like to make an appointment to see the doctor
Мені треба записатися на прийом до лікаря
Meni treba zapysatys' na pryiom do likarya

I am diabetic/pregnant
Я діабетик/вагітна
Ya diabetik/vahitna

I need a prescription for...
Мені треба рецепт для ...
Meni treba retsept dlya...

Can you give me something to ease the pain?
Ви можете дати мені щось болезаспокійливе?
Vy mozhete daty meni shchos' bolezaspokiylyve?

I am/he is/she is/allergic to penicillin
У мене/нього/неї алергія на пеніцилін
U mene/n'oho/neyi/alerhiya na penitsilin

Тут болить?
Tut bolyt'?
Does this hurt?

Ви повинні/він повинен/вона повинна звернутись до лікарні
Vy povynni/vin povynen/vona povynna zvernutys' do likarni
You must/he must/she must go to hospital

Приймайте це один/два/три рази на день
Pryimaite tse odyn/dva/try razy na den'
Take these once/twice/three times a day

I am/he is/she is taking this medication
Я/він/вона приймає ці ліки
Ya/vin/vona pryimaie tsi liky

UKRAINIAN

I have medical insurance
У мене є медична страховка
U mene ye medychna strahovka

Dentist (Зубний Лікар)

I have toothache/my filling has come out
У мене болить зуб/випала пломба
U mene bolyt' zup/vypala plomba

I do/do not want to have an injection first
Я хочу/не хочу щоб мені спочатку зробили укол
Ya hochu/ne hochu shchob meni spochutku zrobyly ukol

EMERGENCIES

Help!
Допоможіть!
Dopomozhit'!

Fire!
Пожежа!
Pozhezha!

Stop!
Стій!
Stiy!

Call an ambulance/a doctor/the police/the fire brigade!
Викличте швидку/лікаря/ міліцію/пожежних!
Vyklychte shvydku/likarya/ militsiyu/pozhezhnyh!

Please may I use a telephone?
Я можу від вас подзвонити?
Ya mozhu vid vas podzvonyty?

I have had my traveller's cheques/credit cards/ handbag/rucksack/luggage/ wallet/passport/mobile phone stolen
У мене вкрали дорожні чеки/кредитні картки/ сумочку/рюкзак/багаж/ гаманець/паспорт/мобільний телефон
U mene vkraly dorozhni cheki/kredytni kartky/sumochku/ riukzak/bahazh/hamanets'/ passport/mobil'ni telefon

May I please have a copy of the report for my insurance claim?
Чи можна мені отримати копію звіту для страхової заяви?
Chi mozhna meni otrimati kopiyu zviti dlja strakhovoi zajavi?

Can you help me, I have lost my daughter/son/my companion(s)?
Допоможіть, будь ласка, моя донька/мій син/мій товариш(і) загубився(лись)?
Dopomozhit', bud' laska, moja don'ka/miy syn/miy tovaryshch(y) zahubyvsya(lys')?

Please go away/Leave me alone!
Идіть звідси/Залиште мене у спокої!
Yidyt' zvidsy/Zalyshte mene u spokoiy!

UKRAINIAN

U K R A I N I A N

I'm sorry
Вибачте (мені дуже шкода)
Vybachte (meni duzhe shkoda)

I want to contact the British/American/Canadian/ Australian/New Zealand/ South African Consulate
Мені треба зв'язатись з Британським/Американським/ Канадським/Австралійським/ Новозеландським/ Південноафриканським Консульством
Meni treba zv'yazatys' z Britaniys'kym/Amerykans'kym/ Kanad'skym/Avstraliys'kym/ Novozelands'kym/ Pivdennoafrykans'kym Konsul'stvom

I'm/we're/he is/she is ill/lost/injured
Я/ми/він/вона/захворів(ли) (ла)/загубився(лися)(лася) постраждав(ли)(ла)
Ya/my/vin/vona/zahvoriv(le)(la)/ zahubyvsya(les')(las')/postrazhdav (le)(la)

They are ill/lost/injured
Вони/захворіли/загубилися/ постраждали
Vony/zahvorily/zahubylysya/ postrazhdaly

If you found this phrasebook useful, or even if you didn't, please help us to improve future editions by taking part in our reader survey. Every returned form will be acknowledged, and to show our appreciation we'll also give you £1 off your next purchase of any Thomas Cook guidebook. Please take a few minutes to complete and return this form to:

The Editor, Eastern European Phrasebook,
Thomas Cook Publishing, PO Box 227,
Units 15-16, Coningsby Road, Peterborough PE3 8SB, UK.

When and where did you buy this book? (Please give town/country and if possible name of retailer).

When was/is your trip and which countries did you/will you visit?

Did you/do you intend to buy any other guidebooks for your trip? Please specify:

What tempted you to buy this book? Please tick as many as appropriate:

❏ Price   ❏ Cover   ❏ Content   ❏ Size

Other (Please specify)

What do you think of:

The cover design?

The design and layout styles within the book?

The content?

Please rate the following features of the Eastern European Phrasebook for their value to you:
(Circle the 1 for "Little or no use", 2 for "useful", 3 for "very useful").

Language introduction sections	1	2	3
Alphabet and pronunciation guides	1	2	3
Phonetic spellings	1	2	3
Side indexing	1	2	3
Menu sections	1	2	3

Please use this space to indicate any additional phrases you would find useful.

Please use this space to tell us about any features that in your opinion could be changed, improved, or added in future editions of the book, or any other comments you would like to make about the book.

Your age category: ☐ Under 21 ☐ 21-30 ☐ 31-40 ☐ 41-50 ☐ 51 +

Mr/Mrs/Miss/Ms/Other

First name or initials:

Surname:

Your full address (please include postal or zip code):

Your daytime telephone number:

E-mail address: